Measuring Time with Artifacts

D1547693

Measuring Time with Artifacts

A History of Methods in American Archaeology

R. Lee Lyman and Michael J. O'Brien

UNIVERSITY OF NEBRASKA PRESS

LINCOLN AND LONDON

Set in Quadraat by
Kim Essman
Designed by R. W. Boeche.

Library of Congress
Cataloging-in-Publication
Data
Lyman, R. Lee.
Measuring time with artifacts : a history
of methods in American archaeology /
R. Lee Lyman and Michael J. O'Brien.
p. cm.
Includes bibliographical
references and index.
ISBN-13: 978-0-8032-2966-2
(hardcover : alk. paper)
ISBN-10: 0-8032-2966-6
(hardcover : alk. paper)
ISBN-13: 978-0-8032-8052-6
(pbk. : alk. paper)
ISBN-10: 0-8032-8052-1 (pbk. : alk. paper)
1. Archaeology—Research—United
States. 2. Archaeology—United
States—Methodology. 3. Time
measurements. 4. Chronometers—United
States—History. 5. Indians of North
America—Antiquities. I. O'Brien, Michael
J. (Michael John), 1950– . II. Title.
CC95.L96 2006
930.1072'073–dc22
2005026723

Contents

Figures and Table

Table

Preface

The history of archaeology has become something of a cottage industry. Books and articles on the subject are now published every year. They focus on one or more topics from a historical perspective. What was the origin of stratigraphic excavation? Who invented the seriation method? Was the direct historical approach used for something other than a chronological anchor? The reasons for attempting to answer these and a near plethora of similar questions are varied, as we discuss in Chapter 1. We do it for one simple reason. Figuring out how we as archaeologists know what we think we know about humankind's remote past has been the driving force behind our historical research. Although at times an arduous journey, it has always been an exciting and an intellectually rewarding one. If readers who examine the chapters that follow find an occasional exciting or rewarding nugget, or if they are stimulated to sift through a set of letters written by one of the major players named in those chapters, we will have attained at least one goal in producing this book. If there is an occasional "Ah-ha!" as one reads the book, then that means we attained yet another goal of illuminating for someone else how (or perhaps why) a particular analytical technique works the way that it does.

Versions of all but Chapters 1 and 10 of this volume originally appeared as articles in journals. Chapters 2 through 9 have been variously revised, edited, and updated for inclusion here, but we owe a considerable debt to those who commented on the original versions. Over the years, many people read and commented on the original manuscripts. Sometimes those referees signed their reviews, sometimes they did not. Whether or not they signed their review, those who took the time to read the manuscripts typically provided suggestions on how to improve the discussion. Often they demanded more accuracy, more complete analysis, and more efficient wording. In the process they made us better historians. Therefore, to all those listed below, we owe a heartfelt "Thank you!" for your insightful comments.

Chapter 2: C. Michael Barton, Geoffrey A. Clark, and E. J. O'Brien.

Chapter 3: Lawrence Straus, Reed Wadley, and four anonymous reviewers.

Chapter 4: John Darwent, Lynne Goldstein, E. J. O'Brien, Gordon R. Willey, Steve Wolverton, and two anonymous reviewers.

Chapter 5: Charlotte Beck, George T. Jones, Robert L. Leonard, and especially Judy Harpole. One portion of this paper was prepared at the request of James Truncer; another portion of it was prepared at the request of Todd VanPool and Marcel Harmon. Without their requests and encouragement, the final result would not have been produced.

Chapter 6: John H. House, Charlie H. McNutt, E. J. O'Brien, Greg Waselkov, an anonymous reviewer, and especially John Darwent.

Chapter 7: Jeremy Sabloff, James Skibo, Robert Whallon, and E. J. O'Brien.

Chapter 8: Christyann Darwent, Robert C. Dunnell, Don D. Fowler, Douglas R. Givens, Donald K. Grayson, George T. Jones, Robert D. Leonard, William A. Longacre, E. J. O'Brien, Jeremy A. Sabloff, Michael B. Schiffer, Steve Wolverton, and an anonymous reviewer.

Chapter 9: George Cowgill, E. J. O'Brien, Lynne Goldstein, three anonymous reviewers, and especially Steve Wolverton.

We thank Gary Dunham for his interest in this project. Copyediting by Robert Burchfield is appreciated. Comments from readers with different perspectives on historical events discussed here would also be appreciated.

Measuring Time with Artifacts

1. Introduction

As we enter the third millennium, American archaeologists are taking ever more frequent and penetrating looks at the history of their discipline (e.g., Browman and Williams 2002; Fowler and Wilcox 2003). This growing interest in the history of the discipline appears to be the result of several factors, one of which is that it is a phase (to borrow an archaeological term) of nearly every field of inquiry that its practitioners look back at their discipline's history (e.g., Hallowell 1965). Another reason is that knowledge of that history grants insights to why the discipline is where it is at present. History in this sense is something of a security blanket—we are what we are because of who our ancestors were—so this kind of history is often internalist (written by a practitioner of the discipline). Yet another reason for studying the history of a discipline might be to establish a niche within the discipline for oneself. Given that the population of professional archaeologists has grown considerably in the past five decades (Schiffer 1979), there are fewer and fewer ways for a novice to make a name for himself or herself. Being known as a historian or keeper of the archives of the discipline could be good for one's career.

There are, of course, other reasons to study the history of archaeology. To consider these, it is useful to note that extant histories can be loosely categorized as one of several different forms. For example, a history might provide a detailed outline of who dug which site when. This sort of history is exemplified by Fitting's (1973) edited book. That volume contains short chapters by regional experts outlining, literally, who dug where when. This kind of history may touch only briefly and occasionally on why someone dug a specific site by perhaps noting that a particular question needed an answer. Another kind of history has focused on the social, political, and personal context of the discipline (e.g., Givens 1992; Kehoe 1998; Kehoe and Emmerichs 1999; Lyon

1996; Patterson 1995; Snead 1996). These histories provide an ethnography or sociology of the discipline; they are sometimes written by nonpractitioners of the discipline, and when they are, the history is externalist. They provide interesting and even occasionally startling insights to the development of the discipline, but they have usually done so without examining the development of archaeological method and theory. Questions pertaining to why a particular technique or approach was invented, modified, or used by someone rather than a different technique or approach are seldom posed and less often answered in such studies. In contrast, a third kind of (typically internalist) history has tended to ignore much of the human context in which archaeology developed in favor of exploring the details of the development of various methods, occasionally delving into the typically implicit theory or model that underpinned a particular technique (e.g., Lyman et al. 1997b). Finally, some histories attempt to include all of the above-mentioned sorts of elements into the story (e.g., Christenson 1989; O'Brien and Lyman 1998; O'Brien et al. 2005; Trigger 1989). One of the best in this category is Willey and Sabloff's *History of American Archaeology*, which has gone through three editions (1974, 1980, 1993). *Measuring Time with Artifacts* reflects one of our preferences—that for the third kind of history, the one focusing on archaeological method and attendant theory.

Many of the histories focusing on the development of archaeological method and theory have taken as their subject the development of chronometric tools (Nash 2000; O'Brien and Lyman 1999b; Truncer 2003), at least in part because the construction of such tools was the focus of archaeologists for much of the first half of the twentieth century. In building chronometers and developing analytical techniques for measuring how old archaeological materials were and for monitoring culture change, archaeologists were contending with the fact that the archaeological record is a modern phenomenon. But archaeologists then wanted, and indeed still want, to know when particular materials constituting that record were created, used, and deposited. Knowing how the timing or age of artifact creation, use, or discard is determined— how do the chronometers work, why do they work the way that they do, and what are the units attending them—is therefore a necessary part of being an archaeologist.

We find any goal for studying the historiography of our discipline sufficient justification for historical studies. But what is of most interest to us, and we would argue what is necessary to doing archaeology, is to consider the underpinning ontological (theoretical model of how some portion of the world works) and epistemological (methods to analyze subject phenomena) bases of chronometers and related analytical tools. The chapters in this volume explore these bases at some length, delving into the history and development of select archaeological chronometers. The book, however, includes much more than just history. A number of concepts must be explored in order to understand the chronometers and their attendant units and why they were thought by archaeologists to measure time. For example, the difference between specific historical analogy and general comparative analogy is described in Chapter 7, where the chronometer under consideration is the familiar direct historical approach. The differences and similarities, if any, among frequency seriation, time-series analysis, and marker types or historical index types are discussed in various chapters, as is the important concept known as "overlapping" (Ford 1938b). The concept of overlapping is critically important because it reveals the underpinning (and typically implicit) view of culture change as an evolutionary process minimally involving cultural transmission and inheritance, or what during the first half of the twentieth century was referred to commonsensically as persistence (Rouse 1939) or tradition (Willey 1945). The manner in which the historical development of cultural and artifact lineages—literally, lines of heritable continuity signified by temporally sequent artifacts of similar types—came to be analyzed, summarized, and presented to the discipline reveals much about what at the time were relatively implicit and poorly developed notions of culture history.

We have explored aspects of the early twentieth-century history of American archaeology in several places (Lyman et al. 1997b; O'Brien 1996). These publications include journals, where typically longer versions of Chapters 2–9 originally appeared. For purposes of this volume, we have updated, corrected, and edited those original pieces. Editing generally involved deletion of discussions not central to the history of a chronometer or its attendant units. As well, some redundancies between chapters were omitted, but some remain so that each chapter can stand more or less on its own, with perhaps a bit of skimming of another chapter or two. The original manuscripts were written over the span of seven years, and essays written later often cited those written earlier. Here we have not cited the original publication unless absolutely necessary; rather, we cite the chapter in which the version printed here appears.

There are a number of reasons to bring these essays together under one cover, not least of which is that as a set they outline what we take to be central and critical episodes in the history of American archaeology during the first half of the twentieth century. These episodes were in many ways independent of one another, yet they were also interrelated by their common focus on the age of archaeological materials. That common focus dictated how archaeology was accomplished between about 1910 and 1950 and thus highlights many of the reasons why we know what we think we know about the human past. There are other important episodes in the history of American archaeology, but the ones we consider here concern the development of artifact-based chronometers, where a chronometer is a technique for telling time. In the case of archaeology, the chronometers were actually tools for assessing how old one artifact was relative to another. To fully appreciate how these chronometers work and why they work the way that they do, we need to understand the basic ontology to which many archaeologists subscribed, if only implicitly. Ontology is the branch of philosophy that concerns the nature of entities in the world. Chemical elements are one kind of unit that are stable and that behave or respond to stimuli in predictable ways; biological species are a different kind of unit that are seldom stable but instead change more or less continuously in unpredictable ways. We consider the models and theories that explain these different kinds of entities to be variations in ontology.

Given that the nature of the units used by various chronometers to measure time vary, these units, too, must be understood. Modern wristwatches use seconds, minutes, and hours to measure time, and many of them also use days of the week, day in the month, and even the solar year to measure time's passage. Some archaeological chronometers use unique measurement units such as particular artifact types that were made and used during limited time periods, or what are sometimes referred to as marker types or index types. Other archaeological chronometers utilize frequencies of various artifact types as the units of measurement, whereas still others use geological units of deposition as unit boundaries within which artifact types distinct from those in other depositional units are used as temporal units. Keeping the different sorts of temporal units used by archaeologists separate, and understanding their nature, is critically important to understanding how individual chronometers work.

Once the various sorts of chronometric units used are clear, then we can turn to the actual chronometer itself. Is the wristwatch a digital or analog chronometer? Both use the same measurement units, but they present age or time in different ways. Similarly, not all archaeological chronometers measure time in the same way, though all of the chronometers we discuss are typically described as ones that measure time on an ordinal scale—event A signified by phenomenon A' is older (or younger) than event B signified by phenomenon B', but we cannot say how much older (or younger); the temporal distance between events cannot be measured in standard temporal units such as hours or years. Deciding on which kinds of units to use is an epistemological issue. Epistemology is the branch of philosophy that deals with the nature of knowledge about the world; how the knowledge is generated makes epistemology both theoretical and methodological. We use the term to highlight the latter but emphasize that method is but method if its application and the knowledge it supposedly generates are not guided by an ontology or theory concerning how the portion of the world under study works.

One thing that has gone largely unremarked in much of the literature is that time can be measured discontinuously or continuously (O'Brien and Lyman 1999c). In this volume we explore this and other aspects of archaeological research from the historical perspective of how and why chronometers and units were designed the way they were. The remainder of this chapter briefly outlines the volume's contents and then turns to a consideration of why we think this sort of history is important. In anticipation of potential criticism for the histories we have written, we conclude this chapter with some comments about why we have studied the history of American archaeology the way that we have.

Ontology

In the early twentieth century A. V. Kidder, Nels Nelson, and others named in the various chapters of this volume subscribed to some notion of cultural development or evolution. This notion was often implicit and typically weakly developed in a conceptual and theoretical sense. Yet there was a common thread running through these notions. At least some of the variation in the artifacts comprising the archaeological record was thought by archaeologists to reflect cultural *change* and thus the passage of time (Lyman et al. 1997b). We emphasize the word "change" because it not only denotes the passage of time but also implies some sort of connection or continuity between earlier and later archaeological manifestations above and beyond mere difference in the relative age or positions in time of those phenomena. "Development" can be a synonym for change because it, too, implies some kind of connection between earlier and later phenomena, perhaps an ancestor-descendant affinity (phylogenetic relationship), although it can also denote ontogeny or the transition from newborn to infant to juvenile to adult to senility. Phylogeny and ontogeny are different biological and physiological processes, so using a synonym that could denote either of them is ill-advised. Ontogeny involves change of an individual as that individual grows and matures; phylogeny involves change in a population of individuals affected by change in the membership (the kinds of members included, the frequencies of different kinds of members, or both) of that population. Evolution was not a popular concept among American anthropologists and archaeologists between about 1900 and 1950, so, not surprisingly, "development" was the word many archaeologists working in the early twentieth century used when they discussed the history of the culture(s) they were studying. The history of the ontological basis of archaeological chronometry involved the basic notion of evolution as change over time; an overview of that history is provided in Chapter 2, and several critical nuances of it are described in detail in Chapter 7.

What came to be known after the 1960s as the culture history paradigm or approach constituted the first body of methods and interpretive principles used by American archaeologists of the twentieth century to derive meaning from the archaeological record (Binford 1968a, 1968c; Deetz 1970; Dunnell 1978, 1986b; Gorenstein 1977; Lyman et al. 1997b; Willey and Sabloff 1993). Although often described as merely history and simply descriptive by many archaeologists first entering the discipline in the 1960s and 1970s (Lyman and O'Brien 2004b), culture historians were in fact concerned with much more than "constructing 'time-space grids,' " as one of those later observers described it (Flannery 1967:119). The founders of the paradigm saw as their initial—but certainly neither the only nor final—goal the establishment of a chronology of archaeological phenomena. Although they did build large "time-space grids," they also wanted to do more, and indeed they often (but admittedly not always) did more.

Gordon Willey (1953a:361), for example, observed in a statement on the then state of the art that the "two major objectives of modern archaeology [are] (1) processual understanding and (2) skeletal chronology and [geographic] distribution." In making this distinction, he was seeking to underscore the important point that "even the barest sort of chronological-distributional study of artifact forms is necessarily linked with implicit theory involving cultural process" (Willey 1953a:361). The word "process" implies that the desired (processual) understanding involved something that took place over time rather than at a point in time. Archaeologists have virtually since the beginnings of the discipline sought to determine why particular cultures developed the way that they did over time; to answer the "why" question, they have called upon "cultural processes" such as diffusion, innovation, adaptive change, and the like. Identifying the pertinent cultural process(es) for a particular set of archaeological data, one of Willey's two objectives, involved various analytical steps. The first step was to assign ages to the phenomena so that one could be sure that some span of time (rather than a point in time) was involved. Further, because a cause necessarily precedes an effect, knowing the correct temporal sequence of phenomena will avoid the conflation of an effect with a cause and thus help with the identification of the pertinent process.

Willey's wording, particularly that "theory" was "implicit," was, in our view, more accurate than he probably imagined, as is made clear in many of the following chapters. But regardless of this, how were the two objectives to be reached? Our specific focus in this volume concerns how the necessarily first (given the requisite distinction of cause and effect) chronological objective was reached. In Willey's and his predecessors' view, these "objectives are approached by the study and manipulation of three basic factors: form, space, and time" (Willey 1953a:361). Distributions of artifact forms across space and through time comprise the basic data of archaeology. Those distributions rendered as data could be analyzed in various ways depending on the methods chosen, and they could also be interpreted in various ways depending on available explanatory models, notions, and theories. Lest the cart be put before the horse, what constituted the data that were to be explained? What were the artifact forms whose distributions were to be studied? What kinds of analytical units were necessary to do what archaeologists wanted to do? Subsequent chapters seek to answer these and related questions from a historical perspective that documents the development of various chronometric methods (and their attendant units) invented by culture historians. Given the focus of early culture historians on the temporal dimension and de-emphasis of the spatial (geographic) dimension, we follow suit. Little about how to study and explain spatial variation will be found in these chapters, which is not to say that this dimension was ignored by culture historians, because it decidedly was not (e.g., Kroeber 1931a). Rather, their initial focus was on chronological matters because time was invisible, or more correctly the ages of artifacts (when were they made and used) were initially unknown and had to be determined analytically. Only after this was done could questions of culture process be addressed.

Epistemology: Measurement Units and Chronometers

American archaeologists were sometimes accused of being obsessed with artifacts and artifact typology (e.g., Kluckhohn 1960). But virtually all of the chronometers they developed had as their measurement units some kind(s) of categories of artifacts. We therefore suggest that their alleged obsession was driven by the desire to build units—typically termed types or styles after about 1920—that measured temporal and, hopefully, cultural differences (Lyman et al. 1997b). That archaeologists trained in North America in the first half of the twentieth century would attempt to carve up what might be more or less continuous variation in artifact form into analytically useful units, particularly ones that were useful in answering questions of history, reflects the training of those archaeologists. During the first half of the twentieth century (and still today), most North American archaeologists were trained in a university-based department of anthropology. Therefore, any use of artifacts as the basis of chronometric units had to contend with the fact that artifacts were viewed by most anthropologists as "material culture" and as "cultural traits" (e.g., Bennett 1954), the analytical unit of choice for ethnographers between about 1890 and 1940 (Chapter 3). Cultural traits could be tracked over time and geographic space, and so could artifact types. We show in Chapter 3 that cultural traits were implicitly conceived of as units of culture transmission and argue that this is why many of them worked well in the ethnological approach known as "historical ethnology" (e.g., Radin 1933). For similar reasons, when artifact types were conceived of as units equivalent to cultural traits, they were useful for tracking ethnic relationships using the direct historical approach (Chapter 7).

But not just any old artifact types worked equally well as the units attending an archaeological chronometer. Instead, only particular sorts of types would work, and the types that worked depended in part on the chronometer. Part of the problem was that various kinds of types measured time and space differently. As we show in Chapters 4 and 6, some types were found to have wide distributions in space and minimal distribution across time, whereas other types had narrow distributions across space but were found to span considerable durations of time. The former sorts of units were eventually called "horizon styles" and the latter "traditions" (e.g., Willey 1945), but before these kinds of differences were recognized, various individuals had to grapple with designing units to measure the dimension of interest. Kroeber (Chapter 5) struggled with exactly this problem during his career, in the process both inventing frequency seriation and developing a technique to measure cycles of culture change in the hopes that the latter would substantiate his beliefs regarding patterns and causes of culture change (that humans simply rode along on the flowing cultural stream, the current of which tended to move in a circle, thought Kroeber). Until the differences in each effort were pointed out in the original version of Chapter 5 (Lyman and Harpole 2002), many who commented on Kroeber's analyses conflated both the units and the analytical techniques he used. Kroeber's efforts highlight the importance of the relationship between kind of units and kind of chronometer. His efforts also underscore what can be done with diachronic data (data that span relatively long periods of time) once the ages of the various phenomena are known.

Probably the first chronometer used by anthropologists and archaeologists was the direct historical approach; it was briefly described but not labeled as such by Edward B. Tylor in the 1880s. Despite (or perhaps because of) the fact that the precise protocol of this important method was never described in detail, it actually had three distinct analytical functions. We touch on the ontology that underpinned its use as a chronometer in Chapter 4 and describe the approach's protocol in some detail in Chapter 7, where we show that the approach served as a chronometer, as a way to identify the ethnicity of human groups that had deposited sets of artifacts, and as a source of direct historical analogs for interpreting artifacts. Regardless of the analytical function attending a particular application, the units that the direct historical approach used could be cultural traits, artifact types, or a combination of both. The critically important concept of overlapping that informs frequency seriation originated in the direct historical approach (Chapters 5 and 9).

Artifact types equivalent to horizon styles are sometimes referred to as marker types or perhaps index fossils. Culture historian James Ford is remembered in standard histories of American archaeology as someone who popularized seriation as an artifact-based chronometer (Willey and Sabloff 1993). However, Ford actually never really used seriation, particularly frequency seriation, instead opting to use one of two other chronometers. As we show in Chapter 7, early in his career Ford used marker types to sort collections into one of several temporal periods and cultures. The artifact types he designed for this effort work well as marker types; they work less well as units that can be used to perform a frequency seriation and to thereby order collections of artifacts in a hypothetical temporal sequence. Poor frequency-seriation results occur because most of the types Ford designed as marker types have properties of marker types with respect to the magnitude of time and space contained whereas only a few of them have properties of seriable types.

Perhaps the second oldest chronometer used by archaeologists involves the geological principle of superposition—that strata deposited first will be on the bottom of a column of strata whereas strata deposited last will be on the top of the column. Translated into archaeological usage, this principle reads something like "artifacts in the bottom stratum are older than artifacts in the top stratum" and is operationalized via the several techniques of stratigraphic excavation. Although the principle of superposition concerns the temporal order of deposition rather than the age of the deposited particles (whether sediments or artifacts), the archaeological translation of it for chronological purposes is a reasonable hypothesis, though as with all hypotheses, it requires testing with independent data (O'Brien and Lyman 1999c; Rowe 1961). One of the most explored historical topics in American archaeology concerns the origins of stratigraphic excavation in North America. A critically important part of that history that is not considered by many historians is the role of artifact units in facilitating its adoption by archaeologists. As we argue in Chapter 8, it seems to us that since at least the 1870s, archaeologists were well aware of superposition as a potential chronometric principle. What they had to do was shift from thinking of general artifact categories as cultural traits to focusing on variants of each of those traits to perceive change in artifacts from the bottom to the top of a stratified column of sediments.

Once it was determined that chronologies of artifacts could be worked out, the final task was to present analytical results in such a manner that other archaeologists and anthropologists could ascertain what had been determined. Cultural chronology based on artifacts could work only if the artifacts had changed; the units of change were made up of some kind of differences between artifacts, whether in their kinds, in the frequencies of representation of kinds, or both. This was conceived of as a manifestation of cultural change—artifacts were material culture and physical manifestations of cultural traits—so to show not only chronological results but also that culture had changed required innovative means of presenting the critical data demonstrating that change had indeed occurred. Those data were originally presented as tables of artifact frequencies or illustrations of strata with artifacts drawn in the stratum from which they were recovered. Eventually, several kinds of graphs were used to illustrate shifts in frequencies of artifacts, though sometimes these graphs depicted the archaeologist's beliefs about change rather than actual data. As we show in Chapter 9, differences between graphs of suspected change and graphs of empirical data showing change were seldom explicitly identified in the literature, though there are visual clues that allow one to distinguish them.

Why Study the History of Archaeological Chronometry?

One might ask why archaeologists working in the early twenty-first century should be concerned with chronometers invented in the nineteenth and early twentieth centuries, especially given the current widespread use in archaeology (and paleontology) of radiometric dating techniques. Are the early chronometers merely curious historical footnotes to the overall history of archaeologists' efforts to measure time and thus of interest only to the pedant? As we show in Chapter 5, Kroeber presented one of the first time-series analyses of cultural data when he tracked changes in women's evening fashions over time. This is precisely the sort of analysis archaeologists attempted to perform and illustrate with their various graphing techniques (Chapter 9). The distinction between using artifacts to measure time (building and using artifact-based chronometers) and using the known age of artifacts to track culture change (time-series analysis) is blurred in many of the original pieces of literature that we cite in later chapters. Kroeber's time-series work with women's fashions is an exception, but even it has been confused with chronometry in recent literature. That is one obvious reason to study the history of archaeological chronometry—to avoid confusion.

Given the important and ubiquitous role that the various radiometric dating techniques play in modern archaeology, it is little wonder that today's students might view earlier efforts to establish chronological ordering as relatively imprecise and unworthy of in-depth study. We have several responses.

First, the large body of literature that grew out of the efforts of archaeologists working during the first half of the twentieth century reveals that they developed numerous clever methods to determine the ages of archaeological phenomena, often with considerable precision, if only on an ordinal scale. These methods were not replaced by radiometric dating; rather, they supplemented, and continue to supplement, these new chronometers. This is so for two reasons. First, the old chronometers utilize artifact-based units and thus constitute what is sometimes referred to as direct dating of the target event, such as the deposition of an artifact assemblage, rather than indirect dating of some stratigraphically associated event, such as the death of a plant, the charred remnants of which are submitted to a radiocarbon laboratory. Second, some of the old artifact-based chronometers measure time as a continuous variable rather than as a set of internally homogeneous periods separated by a moment in time during which all change occurs (e.g., Plog 1974). Discussions of radiometric chronometers with which we are familiar typically do not acknowledge this difference in how the variable time can be measured.

Another response to those who suggest that the history of early archaeological chronometry is unnecessary or unworthy of attention aligns with David Meltzer's (1989:12) comment that "the best way to understand why we do what we do is to unfold the beliefs that have structured, and continue to structure, our work." Perhaps the best exemplar of how our work is structured by our beliefs is to note that virtually all archaeologists would agree that the ideal is to excavate a site stratigraphically. Why this should be the ideal is not always explicit in introductory textbooks. If it is explicit, it may be incomplete. Or sometimes when it is explicit, the underpinning principle of superposition is stated incorrectly as "older artifacts are on the bottom, young artifacts on top of a stratified column of sediment" rather than the correct form that it concerns chronological order of deposition rather than the age of the deposited materials. To make the underpinning principle explicit and to describe it correctly requires knowledge of the history of the principle.

Yet another reason to study the history of early chronometers is reflected by Bohannan and Glazer's (1988:xv) comment that ignorance of a discipline's past can result in "unnecessary originality," whereas knowledge of that past can "give one a great many good ideas." Understanding the early development of chronometers in archaeology, especially with respect to the kinds of units used, reveals the nature of measuring the passage of time, how time itself is viewed, and the implications of those issues for how and why American archaeologists have explained culture change the way that they have. Such an understanding helps those interested in studying the evolutionary development of cultures as revealed by the archaeological record. Those with such interests must first determine the historical lineages of artifacts and then explain why lineages look the way that they do (O'Brien and Lyman 2000; O'Hara 1988). These two interests are merely another way of stating the "two major objectives of modern archaeology" that Willey (1953a) mentioned—chronology and processual understanding of that chronology. The determination of historical lineages of artifacts is precisely what American culture historians of the first half of this century were constantly engaged in doing (Lyman et al. 1997b), although the lineages they produced were largely by-products of efforts aimed at bringing chronological control to the archaeological record. We can refer to those chronologies as lineages because, as is shown in various of the chapters that follow, the underpinning assumption of most chronometers was that their included artifact and cultural units were phylogenetic affines.

A final reason to study early artifact-based chronometers is that archaeologists working in the early twenty-first century do make use of those chronometers. Therefore, they should know something not only about the history of those chronometers but also about how they work epistemologically and their underlying ontology. If archaeologists do not know these things, then those same archaeologists may find themselves in the intellectually and/or politically awkward position of having to explain such things as why the direct historical approach assists in the identification of the ethnicity of someone who died several hundred or even a thousand or more years ago. This is a critically important concern, as we hint in Chapter 7, with respect to the Native American Graves Protection and Repatriation Act (Public Law 101–601, 25 U.S.C. 3001 et seq.). That law asserts that the ethnicity of unmarked graves must be determined so that the human remains contained in them can be turned over to the biological and cultural descendants of the interred individual. If there are conflicting claims about the ethnicity of the dead individual by potential descendants of varied ethnicity, then the archaeologist(s) making the determination of ethnicity on the basis of the direct historical approach should be able to explain how that approach works so that all involved parties understand how a determination was made. Whether they agree philosophically with that determination is another matter.

Why We Study the History of
American Archaeology the Way That We Do

There are of course other reasons to study the history of archaeology. Our interest in the history of American archaeology has as yet unreported beginnings, and thus the intentions of our work are sometimes misinterpreted. For example, various individuals who have commented on our historical research imply that we have done that research out of presentist interests (e.g., Snead 1998; Trigger 1998). By "presentist interests" we mean that we are accused of writing history in a manner meant to legitimate our own theoretical preferences by showing that they mirror our intellectual predecessors'. Nothing could be further from the truth. To demonstrate this, in this section we outline the history of our research on the history of American archaeology.

Lyman long had an interest in the history of what is generally referred to as the culture history approach, particularly as it played out in Washington State, though he did not begin to explore that history until recently (e.g., Lyman 2000). He was also interested in how culture historians generally knew what they thought they knew. Lyman had been trained in a rather traditional (1960s) fashion. He learned the basic methods of culture history, and he read Willey and Phillips's (1958) *Method and Theory in American Archaeology* and Trigger's (1968) *Beyond History: The Methods of Prehistory* in the late 1960s and early 1970s. Although informative, the lectures and texts did not really answer critical ontological and epistemological questions, particularly when held against various interpretive statements made by those attempting to explain the cultural history of the northwestern United States. Those questions remained, if increasingly subconsciously, between 1974 and 1994. Over that twenty-year period, Lyman did zooarchaeological research, focusing on taphonomy. By the end of the period, he had come to a turning point when he finished a book on vertebrate taphonomy (Lyman 1994). At about the same time O'Brien asked him to read a manuscript of what would become a book entitled *Paradigms of the Past*, the goal of which was to tell the historical story of archaeological research in Missouri. Reading that draft quickly brought a question that had been tugging at the back of Lyman's mind to the surface: How does the culture history approach to archaeology work?

The next research project was obvious to Lyman—write a book about the history of archaeological research in the northwestern United States. It quickly became apparent, however, that little innovative work with respect to method and theory had been done there, given that archaeological research in the Northwest did not really begin in earnest until after World War II, by which time the culture history approach was fully developed. The book that needed to be written seemed, therefore, to be one on the development of the culture history approach, focusing on its epistemology and ontology. After several months of research, Lyman asked O'Brien to assist in writing the book. Later, Lyman brought Robert Dunnell into the project, the net result of which was The Rise and Fall of Culture History (Lyman et al. 1997b) and a collection of reprinted classic papers exemplifying the method and theory of culture history (Lyman et al. 1997a). Books on James Ford (O'Brien and Lyman 1998, 1999b) and on the methods and techniques of relative dating (O'Brien and Lyman 1999c) followed. Along the way, we continued to explore aspects of the history of American archaeology, sometimes with the assistance of an interested student. The result was a series of essays, several of which are reprinted here in edited and updated form.

On the one hand, a few commentators liked the Darwinian perspective we brought to our historical analysis of the culture history paradigm (e.g., Dancey 1998; Emerson 1998). Some critics, on the other hand, argued that such things as our adoption of a Darwinian perspective provided a "narrow treatment" of topics and resulted in books that were "difficult to use" (Longacre 1998:795). As noted earlier, our narrow focus was also said to result in "presentist" history (Snead 1998:266; Trigger 1998:365). Presentist history is written for the sake of the present—to show intended progress and improvement from the past to the present, to glorify the present, and to justify it (Stocking 1965). We did not intend to produce any of the indicated (seemingly negative) characteristics. Lyman did not intend to adopt the Darwinian perspective from which to view the history of the culture history approach; he had not even considered it in previous research. Rather, he was simply trying to figure out how culture history as an approach to the archaeological record worked. The more we read, the more it became apparent that what we were studying was decidedly not, to borrow from yet another review of our work, "the caricatures portrayed in the critiques by Walter Taylor (1948) and Lewis Binford (1972)" (Custer 2001:406). Something else was indicated by our research. That something else is simply this: The interpretive and explanatory intentions and conventions of culture historians themselves ultimately led us to take a Darwinian perspective in our historical studies because it was precisely that sort of perspective that guided what they themselves were doing (Chapter 2). There never should be any confusion about this because, as we originally said, culture historians "came rather close to developing an evolutionary (in a Darwinian sense) archaeology" (Lyman et al. 1997b:11).

Those who accuse us of a presentist agenda may misunderstand either the nuances of presentism or the nuances of doing historical research or both. As philosopher David Hull (1979) makes clear, it is impossible to do history without some degree of presentism, though he also makes clear that presentism can indeed produce bad history in the sense of being used to legitimate some aspect of the present. Recognition of this possibility should assist in avoiding the writing of bad history. But presentism inevitably creeps into history for several unavoidable reasons. First, to think that a historian is completely ignorant of the present—the culture (including academic training) in which he or she was raised—is absurd. Second, if one must (assuming one can) ignore his or her own modern sociocultural context, then what terms and concepts are to be used to study and hopefully understand the past? If the terms and concepts of the past are to be understood, then interpretation of that past is required, as well as a great deal of knowledge about that past (where the culture into which scholars were enculturated was different than that of today). And third, history is usually done not just for the historian but for others interested in history; what terms and concepts are to be used by the historian to communicate that history? If one cannot use a common (modern) cultural context from which to interpret the past, then consumers of history must be trained in the terms and concepts of the past to avoid presentist history. The remainder of Hull's discussion is far too detailed for summation here. Suffice to say that Hull (1979:4, 5) argues that "knowledge of present-day language, logic, and science is necessary not only for investigating the past but also for communicating the results of these investigations to the historian's contemporaries" and that the historian "must use the theories, methods, and data available to him in reconstructing the past or use nothing at all." We agree with Hull and attempt to avoid bad history and presentist history, but we also use modern concepts and terms to interpret, discuss, and make sense of our intellectual predecessors.

Reference to various processes of biological evolution were often used by culture historians as metaphors for cultural processes during the early twentieth century (e.g., Kidder 1915; Kidder and Kidder 1917; Nelson 1919b). Some of these uses were by individuals with professional training in biology or paleontology (e.g., Colton 1939; Colton and Hargrave 1937; Hargrave 1932; McKern 1939), but even those who were not so trained used the terms (e.g., Ford 1938a, 1938b; Gladwin and Gladwin 1930, 1934; Kroeber 1931b). Regardless of their training, they all took as the goal of their research the solution of "the problems of cultural evolution" (Kidder 1932:8). As a result, many of them used biological terms such as a "genetic" relationship when speaking of the affinities of artifacts (e.g., Colton and Hargrave 1937; Ford 1938b; Kidder 1936b; Rouse 1955; Willey 1953a; Wissler 1916c). How could a historian interested in how the culture history approach worked—which necessarily means considering what it was intended to accomplish—not adopt a modern Darwinian conception of evolution when discussing the research efforts of culture historians?

We did not, as some might think, start with Robert Dunnell's favored evolutionary paradigm, nor did he insist that we adopt it after we asked him to work with us on *The Rise and Fall of Culture History*. Rather, what we found fascinating was the typically implicit Darwinian aspects of the vague notions of cultural development—by which they meant evolution—held by many culture historians of the 1920s, 1930s and 1940s. We perceived, contrary to Longacre's (1998) or Kehoe's (2000) claim, minimal evidence of Lewis Henry Morgan's and Edward B. Tylor's cultural evolution in what we read. That perception led us to explore the differences between the two kinds of evolution and why Darwinism was ultimately replaced with Leslie White's and Julian Steward's versions of cultural evolution by archaeologists working in the 1940s and 1950s (Chapter 2). We were led to explore this issue again, but from a rather different perspective, when we turned to studying the epistemology of the direct historical approach (Chapter 7), a multifunctional analytical method we had basically ignored in *The Rise and Fall of Culture History*. Again, there was no hidden presentist agenda when we undertook that study; we were led to our analytical perspective and conclusions by the discussions in the literature that we read during our research.

There were different and more direct, yet still nonpresentist, reasons to write other chapters in this volume. David Browman and Douglas Givens (1996), for example, published an interesting study on the history of stratigraphic excavation in the Americas. We found that study provocative for several

reasons, not the least of which was its bold assertion that stratigraphic excavation had originated in North America in the second decade of the twentieth century with the work of Nels Nelson, Manuel Gamio, and A. V. Kidder because they sought to revolutionize the discipline of archaeology. Based on what we had read in 1995 and 1996 when preparing *The Rise and Fall of Culture History*, we believed otherwise. The net result was a version of what is included here as Chapter 8. A historical footnote about this paper is that it was submitted to *American Anthropologist*—the journal where Browman and Givens's study had appeared—in early 1997. Twelve months later, the editors told us that they had been unable to find anyone to review the manuscript. We were dumbfounded, particularly given that within six months another journal provided four favorable reviews and a notice that our manuscript had been accepted for publication. Browman (2002b, 2003) subsequently continued his study of the history of American stratigraphic excavation and has discovered some important things about that history, details of which we have used to update our discussion in Chapter 8.

In our view, Browman's later research on the origins of stratigraphic excavation in North America overturns some of the conclusions he reached in the middle 1990s. We agree with many of his newer conclusions but disagree on others. That is part of the excitement of history—it is research with differing viewpoints and interpretations, and in studying history we learn much while we try to figure out why we disagree. Who is correct is perhaps less important than the fact that we learn. But as well, Browman's later research compared to his earlier research underscores an important point about the chapters here. They were written over a span of about seven years; during that period, we learned much. If we had to write the first of the chapters over again (or the last for that matter), some things would be different. The chapters themselves, though updated for inclusion in this volume, reflect the history of our research on the history of archaeology. We hope that the nuanced differences of various points made in several chapters will overwhelm what otherwise might be perceived as redundancy.

When we wrote *The Rise and Fall of Culture History*, we noted that virtually all American archaeologists working between about 1900 and 1950 had been trained in departments of anthropology and thus were aware of what was then current ethnological theory. The basic analytical unit of ethnology at the time was a cultural trait, a unit that we pointed out served historical ethnology;

that service was, however, vague because the nature of the unit itself was rather vague (Lyman et al. 1997b:18–20). We were uncomfortable with our superficial treatment but at the time did not explore that particular unit further for fear of losing sight of the main task of *Rise and Fall*. Later, we came back to examine this seemingly basic unit in detail, writing what is here reproduced in edited form as Chapter 3. In preparing that manuscript, we found that our initial impressions were correct. The cultural trait was an ambiguous analytical unit because it could vary in scale from a design motif on a ceramic vessel to a ritual complex such as the Ghost Dance. We were surprised to find that a cultural trait was a unit of cultural transmission, but this property of the unit was not well developed nor was it discussed in a larger theory or model of cultural heredity, perhaps because the subject of cultural transmission was viewed by many anthropologists and archaeologists working between about 1900 and 1960 as commonsensical (Lyman 2001). The awkward properties of the cultural trait unit and its lack of theoretical context resulted in its abandonment in the 1960s and 1970s, yet as we noted earlier, it served as a sort of post hoc warrant for treating artifact types as units of transmission. Artifacts were, after all, conceived of as empirical manifestations of cultural traits.

Longacre (1998:795) has lamented that we did not explore the roots of the Midwestern Taxonomic System in *Rise and Fall*. That is true. What we did explore, though not in excessive detail, was the roots of the Midwestern Taxonomic Method, noting that it was often mislabeled as a system (Lyman et al. 1997b:160–166). We subsequently devoted a year to researching the history of the method, finding that its originator—Will C. McKern—had minored in paleontology in college. He had developed the Midwestern Taxonomic Method out of a desire for a classification system modeled on the Linnaean taxonomic system in the hope that the cultural taxonomy would eventually, perhaps, reveal phylogenetic affinities between its included cultural units, just as the Linnaean system had (Lyman and O'Brien 2003). This revelation confirmed, in our view, that we had chosen a good platform from which to study the history of the American culture history approach when we chose Darwinian evolution. An earlier, similar analysis we did of Gordon Willey and Philip Phillips's (1958) treatise on cultural historical method and cultural evolution in the New World had also indicated that we had chosen a legitimate platform (Lyman and O'Brien 2001). Something of a presentist agenda may have crept into our writing by about the year 2000, but it was, we think, secondary to our seeking to understand the history of our profession.

To assist in understanding the culture history approach to archaeological research, we turned to the discipline that had pioneered the use of Darwinian evolutionary theory to explain a prehistoric record. That meant reading paleontological literature, something Lyman had been exposed to during his postgraduate work on zooarchaeology. What we found was intriguing. For example, as we document in Chapter 4, geologist Charles Lyell had worked out a faunal chronometer that shared features with the direct historical approach and also with occurrence seriation. This was despite the fact that at the time—in the 1830s—Lyell did not believe that biological evolution had occurred but instead thought that species were static units; when one went extinct, another was created by divine intervention. Our examination of Lyell's faunal chronometer helped clarify the different nature of units, such as an archaeologist's horizon styles and traditions and the fact that those varying natures depended on how the units were created by the archaeologist. Given these observations, with the help of two students, we explored the influences that differences in archaeological units had on the success of different chronometers for measuring time (Chapters 5 and 6).

We have never had a hidden presentist agenda in mind when exploring the history of the culture history approach to archaeological research. In the histories we have written, we have tried to show how the culture history approach worked, why it worked the way that it did, and why it failed when it did. To do justice to these topics, we had to be interested in the nuances of the approach's ontology and epistemology. To understand these aspects of the approach, we had to consider what the goals of the approach were, and they simply were to determine and to explain the developmental or evolutionary history of cultural lineages. Culture historians succeeded quite remarkably at attaining the first goal but had some trouble with the second goal, as the processual archaeologists of the 1960s did not hesitate to point out (e.g., Binford 1968a, 1968c; Flannery 1967). For the history of archaeology, this meant that the culture history approach, for the first time, had a competitor in the form of processual archaeology. Some commentators imply that we argued in *The Rise and Fall of Culture History* that the culture history approach was no longer pursued after the middle 1960s (e.g., Longacre 1998). That is not what we suggested.

The methods of culture history were hardly discussed in *American Antiquity* after the late 1960s, though some of its results continued to be presented there. Further, as far as we can determine, no textbook devoted to the protocols of culture history was published after Trigger's (1968) *Beyond History: The Methods of Prehistory*. Instead, virtually every textbook afterward included discussion of how to study culture processes in the archaeological record. A prime example is Irving Rouse's (1972) *Introduction to Prehistory: A Systematic Approach*. Rouse (e.g., 1939) was a culture historian (some might say an archetypical one). His 1972 textbook contained discussions of traditional culture history processes such as migration, but it also devoted space to Walter W. Taylor's (1948) conjunctive approach and to settlement pattern studies, two topics claimed by many processualists. In his textbook Rouse also described some intriguing models of cultural evolution that are more Darwinian than anything presented by Leslie White or Julian Steward. Yet it was precisely these sorts of observations on the shifting contents of textbooks and journal contents that led us to conclude that the culture history approach had fallen from favor in the discipline. We never said it went extinct, nor did we say that the approach was not used by anyone ever again. This is another reason to study the history of the culture history approach. Because it is still used by many practicing archaeologists, the more we know about how it works—including its strengths and weaknesses—the better the archaeology that is done using it will be.

Why Artifact-Based Chronometry?

If we really thought that the culture history paradigm had died in the 1960s, we would not have written a textbook on many of the chronometric methods culture historians invented (O'Brien and Lyman 1999c). We wrote that book because many practitioners of paradigms other than culture history seemed unaware of those artifact-based chronometers, how they worked, and how to implement them given the plethora of radiometric chronometers available in the 1980s and 1990s. The clear majority of the artifact-based chronometers, as we document in various chapters that follow, rested on a vague notion typically referred to as historical continuity in the literature of the early twentieth century. That term is actually more correctly glossed as heritable continuity because it rests on the process of cultural transmission (e.g., Boyd and Richerson 1985).

Transmission, whether of genetic material between organisms or cultural ideas between humans, is what creates what biologists call lineages and archaeologists refer to as traditions. This simple historical process makes the paleontological and archaeological records historical and creates a particular kind of affinity between at least some temporally sequent phenomena that is more than mere chronological propinquity, a point we made near the beginning of this chapter. Because the paleontological and archaeological records are historical, they require, perhaps as an initial step as Willey (1953a) argued, chronometric analysis, by which we mean their constituent elements must be placed in time relative to one another. Then one can determine analytically the kind of affinities between artifacts (or fossils) as a step toward determination of the processual relationships between them. Although this involves writing the history of the artifact lineages, it is also arguably scientific given that it is guided (if typically only implicitly) by an explanatory theory (Lyman and O'Brien 2004b).

The theory is, of course, some form of evolutionary theory, of which there are several, as we discuss in Chapters 2 and 7. We prefer the one known as Darwinism because it, in a modern form adapted to the archaeological record, provides much of what culture history lacked (Lyman et al. 1997b). The modern form of Darwinism as it was written in the 1940s involved living organisms; for that reason, it was difficult to apply to the paleontological record. As we document at some length elsewhere (O'Brien and Lyman 2000, 2003), Darwinian evolutionary theory had to be rewritten and adapted to the fossil record. Part of that rewriting involved the model of evolution known as punctuated equilibrium in the 1970s. This rewriting concerned the difference between what is known as microevolution and macroevolution. The former was what the 1940s neo-Darwinian synthesis concerned, and it generally means change in the gene pool of a population over time. Today, macroevolution concerns change from one taxon (species, genus, or higher) to another. The artifact-based chronometers archaeologists invented can be conceived of as involving macroevolution for the simple reason that they do not concern whatever the cultural equivalent of a gene is (Chapter 3) but rather what are probably equivalent to bundles of genes manifest as attribute combinations archaeologists tend to refer to as artifact types.

Recall that Darwin (1859) described evolution as "descent with modification." Today we could refer to the descent process as involving transmission and the modification process as involving genetic mutation or cultural innovation and also involving sorting of variants such that fidelity of replication is less than perfect. It is, of course, the uniqueness of phenomena that makes them time sensitive. January 13, 1951, is a unique date; organisms born on that day and artifacts made on that day are of a unique age relative to other phenomena that were born or made on a different day. How is heritable continuity found among phenomena that undergo descent with modification?

Darwin (1859) was explicit about the fact that determination of phylogenetic affinities between organisms depended on how those organisms were classified. "We have no written pedigrees; we have to make out community of descent by resemblances of any kind. Therefore we choose those characters which, as far as we can judge, are the least likely to have been modified in relation to the conditions of life to which each species has recently been exposed" (Darwin 1859:425). The importance of characters or attributes used in a classification the goal of which is to represent evolutionary pedigree "depends on [the characters'] greater constancy throughout large groups of species; and this constancy depends on such organs having generally been subjected to less change in the adaptation of the species to their conditions of life" (Darwin 1859:417). In Darwin's (1859:427) view, then, "analogical or adaptive characters, although of the utmost importance for the welfare of the being, are almost valueless to the systematist" who is interested in revealing descent and phylogenetic affinity.

Darwin's theory of descent with modification provided a logical causal explanation as to why there should also be both some formal differences and some formal similarities between organisms. Some differences were the result of adaptive change; some similarities were the result of transmission from a common ancestor: "By unity of type is meant that fundamental agreement in structure, which we see in organic beings of the same class, and which is quite independent of their habits of life. On my theory, unity of type is explained by unity of descent" (Darwin 1859:206). But "propinquity of descent—the only known cause of similarity of organic beings—is the bond, hidden as it is by various degrees of modification, which is partially revealed to us by our classification" (Darwin 1859:413–414). Pedigrees are only partially and imperfectly revealed because of modification driven by various sorting processes, such as natural selection and drift during descent. Thus Darwin (1859:417) emphasized that one should consider "an aggregate of characters."

Darwin's reasoning was sound. To determine descent, formal variation in characters manifest as diverse character states must be documented, and those that track heritable continuity and phylogenetic descent must be chosen for analysis over those that track the influence of natural selection. Failure to do this results in the confusion of similarity caused by common ancestry with that caused by the processes of parallelism and convergence. Parallelism results from the development of similar adaptive designs among closely related phenomena; convergence results from the development of similar adaptive designs among remotely related phenomena (Eldredge 1989). As Kroeber (1931b) pointed out early in the history of the culture history approach, one should be distinguishing homologous characters from analogous characters. Homologous characters result from shared ancestry and analogous characters from parallelism or convergence. There are actually two kinds of homologous characters—those that are primitive (ancestral) and those that are derived. The former have been formally static, and the latter have been modified as a result of an evolutionary process, such as natural selection or some vagary of transmission.

We highlight Darwin's suggested approach to classification in the service of determining phylogenetic affinities for two reasons. First, it will be obvious after reading the following chapters that the classification of artifacts underpins artifact-based chronometers. Change rendered as shifting combinations of the attributes of artifacts or changing frequencies of types of artifacts, with some combinations and types occurring in several contiguous time periods, is explained as heritable continuity, though it was usually described as historical continuity in the pre-1960 archaeology literature. Second, despite its critical importance, artifact classification is in fact where culture historians got into trouble. As Binford (1968a) pointed out, culture historical classifications did not distinguish between the two kinds of similarities, despite Kroeber's (1931b) earlier insistence that they should, given that they were directed toward historical sorts of analyses and conclusions. Some of the trouble probably could have been avoided if culture historians had followed Kroeber's advice or perhaps if they had paid more attention to how paleobiologists went about figuring out the evolutionary history and phylogenetic relationships of organisms (O'Brien and Lyman 2000).

Mimicking of paleontological methods was indeed attempted, if implicitly, in the context of the Midwestern Taxonomic Method (Lyman and O'Brien 2003), but that effort failed in part because it was aimed at too large and inclusive a scale—a culture—rather than at the classification of discrete objects called artifacts. A focus on artifacts would have avoided much of the criticism that the evolution of cultural phenomena is reticulate whereas the evolution of organisms is cladogenetic (Steward 1944), though it is likely that even that shift to a finer scale would not have saved the method (Lyman and O'Brien 2003). This is so because after the middle 1940s, culture historians in general abhorred any implication that the evolution of culture occurred in a Darwinian-like manner (Chapter 2). This is exemplified by Willey and Phillips's (1958:30) argument that horizons and traditions were merely "integrative" units that denoted "some form of historical contact," but the "contact" they denoted did not signify "phylogeny." Willey's (1953a:368) suggestion that "principles of continuity and change are expressed in the degrees of trait likeness and unlikeness which are the mechanisms of establishing genetic lines binding the assemblages together" thus was metaphorical with respect to cultural transmission and (phylo)"genetic lines" connecting assemblages. Of course there was in fact nothing metaphorical at all about the process that bound artifact assemblages together; it was, simply, cultural transmission.

Phillips and Willey (1953:628) indicated that a tradition was "a major large-scale space-time cultural continuity, defined with reference to persistent configurations in single technologies or total (archeological) culture, occupying a relatively long interval of time and a quantitatively variable but environmentally significant space." This is more a description of the spatio-temporal distribution of some archaeological manifestation than a definition. In particular, it does not specify any mechanism for the persistence of a cultural phenomenon. Several years later Thompson (1956:38) identified that mechanism when he defined a tradition as "a socially transmitted form unit (or a series of systematically related form units) which persists in time" and noted that the "socially transmitted" part of the definition "place[s] emphasis where it seems to belong." Thus Thompson's definition not only indicated the spatio-temporal distribution of a tradition, it also indicated why a tradition would have that distribution. Willey and Phillips (1958) did not pick up on this key addition to the definition, and this failure, along with other evidence that there was no strong effort to develop a theory of cultural transmission (Lyman 2001), suggests to us that culture historians were not interested in explicitly considering the evolution of cultures from a Darwinian perspective. That precisely this sort of evolution underpinned many of cultural historians' chronometers is, we think, one of the great ironies of the history of archaeology.

Histories as Secondary Sources

Whatever reason(s) one chooses for studying the history of a scholarly discipline, one must be prepared to unlearn various things. This is so because any written history is actually at best a secondary source, typically based on literature written closer in time and context to the event(s) of interest, perhaps even by a participant in the event. Thus the best way to learn about the history of a discipline is to read the primary literature, that written by the participants. That literature does not have to be published; it can be correspondence stored in some musty, dusty archive. For a number of reasons, however, it is not always possible for everyone to read the primary literature. A history such as this one, therefore, written by those who have read the primary literature, is a reasonable starting point. Much, though certainly not all, of the original literature pertinent to this volume is found in a collection of what one commentator referred to as "ancient writings" that we compiled some years ago (Lyman et al. 1997a). That would be a good place to pursue various of the historical topics we discuss in the chapters that follow.

The chapters focus on artifact-based chronometers that American archaeologists developed and used during the period from about 1880 until about 1950. The lesson or two to be learned from reading each chapter should be clear in each of those chapters. What we hope to provide by the structure of the presentation is a feel for how any scientific discipline works. To begin, one must have a notion, a model, a theory about how that portion of the world under investigation works—an ontology. Then one must have an epistemology that guides which observations are made and how they are made. Observations are categorized and sorted into types or classes and comprise data. The structure of those classes is (or should be) dictated by the ontology and the problem one seeks to solve. In the case of culture historians, the problem to be solved was how to measure time in a modern archaeological record. The classes of observations (artifacts) that they designed depended on the chronometer in use, just as the ontology was supposed to indicate. Culture historians muddled along because of imperfect ontologies, epistemologies, and units and imperfect correspondences between them. Yet they managed to write much about what we know of humankind's prehistory. We find the stories about how they did this to be intriguing. We hope you do, too.

I. Ontology

In Chapter 1, we noted that ontology is the branch of philosophy that concerns the nature of entities in the world and pointed out that we consider the models and theories that explain these different kinds of entities to be variations in ontology. We explore such differences in ontology in Chapter 2, where we outline the history of evolutionary thinking as manifest among American anthropologists and archaeologists between about 1900 and 1960. We argue that although early in the twentieth century the basic evolutionary view was somewhat (if implicitly) Darwinian, arguments by Boas, Kroeber, Steward, and others who were major figures in the discipline caused a shift away from Darwinian evolution to the form of cultural evolution outlined by Lewis Henry Morgan, Edward B. Tylor, and others during the nineteenth century and popularized in the middle of the twentieth century by Leslie A. White and Julian H. Steward. Arguments to abandon Darwinism were simple. First, biological species did not hybridize, but cultures did. Second, biological (Darwinian) evolution was diversifying (or cladogenetic, to use the modern term), whereas cultural evolution was reticulate; cultures not only diversified, they hybridized. Third, biological evolution could only occur between generations, whereas cultural evolution could take place within a generation; the latter was so much faster than the former that the key mechanism of biological evolution identified by Darwin as natural selection could not possibly have influenced the evolutionary development of a culture.

In Chapter 2 and elsewhere (e.g., O'Brien and Lyman 2000, 2003) we suggest that the arguments against adapting, not just adopting, a Darwinian form of evolution to the study of cultural phenomena are misguided. One reason for this is that the equation of a culture with a species is unwarranted; what distinguishes a species is its supposed inability to hybridize with another species, but what distinguishes one culture from another is unclear in the literature produced early in the twentieth century, and this is still a problem today (Palmer et al. 1997 and references therein). Another reason we find arguments not to utilize Darwinian evolutionary theory to assist in explaining the archaeological record, one that is not explored in Chapter 2, concerns the mechanism of cultural inheritance, now typically referred to as "cultural transmission" (Boyd and Richerson 1985). This evolutionary mechanism results in the process of hereditary continuity, a critically important aspect of most artifact-based chronometers, yet it was hardly mentioned in the archaeological literature of the time (Lyman 2001). Nor is cultural transmission given detailed consideration in most renderings of the cultural evolution popular among many archaeologists today (e.g., Spencer 1997). Interestingly, it was Leslie White—arguably a cultural anthropologist who had significant influence on the emergence of processual archaeology (O'Brien et al. 2005)—who perhaps did more to clarify and explicate the cultural transmission process than any other cultural anthropologist. This is something we did not appreciate sufficiently in 1996 when Chapter 2 was written. White (1947a:693) indicated that because culture was "dependent on the use of symbols, . . . its elements are readily transmitted [and thus] culture becomes a continuum; it flows down through the ages from one generation to another and laterally from one people to another." Cultural transmission—and its attendant processes of innovation, integration, and the like—constituted what White (1948:586) termed the "culture process," defined by him as "a stream of [culture] elements that are continually interacting with one another, forming new combinations and syntheses, eliminating some elements from the stream, and incorporating new ones." White's culture elements would later be called "symbolates" (White 1959a), units of cultural transmission equivalent to the cultural traits of historical ethnologists (Chapter 3).

According to White (1948:586), the culture process "has its own principles and its own laws of change and development," and he insisted that "culture as culture can only be explained in terms of culture, i.e., culturologically." As we point out in Chapter 2, White (1943:339) rather arrogantly proclaimed that the "culturologist knows more about cultural evolution than the biologist, even today, knows about biological evolution." Thus there was no need to consult with a Darwinist about possible principles and laws of change and evolutionary development. Rather, it seems that White would have argued that the consultation should be the other way around; biologists should be consulting culturologists. Whether White was correct or not, the history of the ontology of evolution within anthropology and how that ontology changed during the early twentieth century had a significant influence on how archaeologists went about building chronometers and the units that attended them. It is important to have a firm grasp of the basics of that ontology so as to understand why it was thought that the chronometers worked the way that they did.

In Chapter 2 we describe two evolutionary ontologies that American archaeologists variously used (often implicitly) to help explain the archaeological record. We bring the story up to the early 1960s, when what is generally referred to as "processual archaeology" emerged (O'Brien et al. 2005). We focus particularly in Chapter 2 on two sets of differences: that between the evolution of Charles Darwin and that of Herbert Spencer, and that between A. L. Kroeber's conception of history and evolution and the conceptions of Leslie White. Spencer and White subscribed to a version of evolution referred to in biology as orthogenesis. We reserve detailed discussion of orthogenesis for Chapter 7, where the nuances of that version serve to highlight the ontology underpinning the direct historical approach.

2. The Concept of Evolution in Early Twentieth-Century American Archaeology

Culture historians had as one of their goals the writing of the evolutionary histories of cultural lineages (Lyman et al. 1997b). They implicitly used various models or theories of evolution founded on distinct ontologies to assist their writing. Given that different models of evolution—how it works and why it works the way that it does—serve as the (typically implicit) explanatory basis of archaeological research focused on building archaeological chronometers based on artifacts and also as the basis of writing the developmental histories of cultural lineages, it is critical to consider the history of evolutionary approaches in American archaeology. Two models—Darwinian evolution and cultural evolution—played major roles in American archaeology during the twentieth century. In this chapter we do two things. First, we outline how the two evolutionary models differ in biology and in anthropology. Second, we document how and why the cultural model made its way into archaeology during the 1950s and replaced the Darwinian model. American archaeologists early in the twentieth century made efforts to incorporate elements of Darwinian evolution in their work, but that version of evolution fell from favor in the 1940s. More or less simultaneously, archaeologists began to shift their attention from building and using artifact-based chronometers to more anthropologically oriented pursuits. The temporal correlation of these two events suggests a causal linkage between them. We explore aspects of that linkage here and focus on one such aspect in Chapter 7.

Culture History: The Backbone of the Discipline

Documenting and interpreting culture change—usually referred to as "cultural development" by archaeologists early in the twentieth century—were the central themes of American archaeology beginning with the birth of the culture history paradigm in the second decade of the twentieth century (Lyman et al. 1997a, 1997b). As Wissler (1917b:100) remarked in what can be taken as the birth announcement of that paradigm, American archaeology not only now had some important questions to answer, but it also, for the first time, had a way to produce answers:

> [H]ow long has man been in America, whence did he come, and what has been his history since his arrival? . . . [T]he archaeologist finds in the ground the story of man and his achievements. The new, or the real archaeology is the study of these traces and the formulation of the story they tell. . . . [The archaeologist] must actually dissect section after section of our old Mother Earth for the empirical data upon which to base his answers. It is not merely the findings of things that counts; it is the conditions and interassociations that really tell the story.

This had been the goal of archaeology since the beginning of the twentieth century. As Boas (1904:521–522) remarked, "the sequence of types of culture as determined by the artifacts of each period [is among] the fundamental problems with which archaeology is concerned. The results obtained have the most immediate bearing upon the general question of the evolution of culture, since the ideal aim of archaeology practically coincides with this general problem, the solution of which would be contained in a knowledge of the chronological development of culture." Establishing the sequence involved the use of artifact-based chronometers; Wissler was speaking particularly about stratigraphic excavation when he mentioned dissecting "section after section of our old Mother Earth." Other techniques for addressing the issues raised by Wissler and Boas—the latter having recognized that "in the study of American archaeology we are compelled to apply methods somewhat different from those used in the archaeology of the Old World" (Boas 1902:1)—involved studying the fluctuation of frequencies of artifact types through time, with the passage of time initially confirmed and later established by the stratigraphically superposed positions of the artifacts themselves (Chapter 8).

That the goals of culture history never varied for the next several decades is clear from the remarks of one of the parents of the paradigm, A. V. Kidder:

> Archaeologists, noting that modern biology has mounted above the plane of pure taxonomy [that is, classification], have attempted to

follow that science into the more alluring fields of philosophic interpretation, forgetting that the conclusions of the biologist are based
on the sound foundation of scientifically marshalled facts gathered
during the past century by an army of painstaking observers. This
groundwork we utterly fail to possess. Nor will it be easy for us to
lay, because the products of human hands, being unregulated by the
more rigid genetic laws which control the development of animals and
plants, are infinitely variable. But that is no reason for evading the
attempt. It has got eventually to be done, and the sooner we roll up
our sleeves and begin comparative studies of axes and arrowheads and
bone tools, make classifications, prepare accurate descriptions, draw
distribution maps and, in general, persuade ourselves to do a vast deal
of painstaking, unspectacular work, the sooner shall we be in position
to approach the problems of cultural evolution, the solving of which
is, I take it, our ultimate goal [Kidder 1932:8].

Kidder's remarks outline the goals of the culture history paradigm and
indicate how culture historians conceived of the phenomena they were studying. Cultures evolved; a historically documented culture had a developmental
heritage or lineage, and it was the job of the culture historian to describe
that lineage and to determine why it had the form that it did. Kidder correctly
indicated that archaeology lacked both the basic data and a theory consisting
of cultural processes parallel to the biological ones of genetic inheritance
and natural selection to help explain a culture's lineage in evolutionary terms.
Despite the fact that Wissler (1916c) had earlier noted that cultural phenomena
had "genetic[-like] relations," Kidder, like his contemporaries (Lyman 2001),
never really discussed the theoretical role of what today would be referred
to as cultural transmission (this process creates lineages), choosing instead
to focus on another issue that underlies Darwinian evolutionary theory—the
documentation of variation. Compiling the data and building the theory would
take some work, Kidder suspected, and in the long run, only the former has
today been met with any sort of empirically verifiable success. Chronologies
of artifact types and larger units variously termed cultures, phases, complexes,
and the like have been constructed, tested, refined, and empirically verified and
are now available for many areas of the Americas. Darwinian explanations of
those sequences are, however, lacking. Instead, another kind of evolutionary

explanation is available for many sequences (see the various chapters and references in Maschner [1996] and references in Spencer [1997]). To understand why this is so, we must begin with a consideration of the differences between the two kinds of evolutionary explanations.

The Ontologies of Evolution

In biology (better known as "natural history" at the time), Charles Darwin's (1859) version of evolution was not the first or the only version available in the nineteenth century. For example, Jean Baptiste de Lamarck had a version, and at one time or another it was as popular with segments of the scientific community as Darwin's came to be. But in the end, Darwin's version took hold. Relative to biology, our concern here is only with Darwinian evolution. There also was a theory of evolution that concerned nonbiological phenomena, including such things as human society and technology. This was the version of evolution that Herbert Spencer was selling in the mid-nineteenth century; it is quite different than Darwin's version (Alland 1972, 1974; Carneiro 1972, 1973; Dunnell 1980; Freeman 1974; Mayr 1982; Rindos 1985). Throughout this chapter, we use the term "cultural evolution," or "Spencerian evolution," to denote the kind of evolution espoused by Spencer and his intellectual descendants, including such luminaries as Lewis Henry Morgan and Edward B. Tylor during the nineteenth century and Leslie White, Julian Steward, Marshall Sahlins, Elman Service, Morton Fried, and Robert Carneiro during the twentieth century.

To denote the kind of evolution introduced by Darwin, we use the term "biological evolution," or "Darwinism." Darwinism was not some monolithic theory that swept through biological science in the 1860s and set it on an unwavering course (Mayr 1982, 1991). Just as with its biological subjects, Darwinian theory evolved. Darwinian evolution of the 1980s was not the same theory that it was in the 1880s or that it was in the 1930s. Understanding both the evolutionary history and the ontological underpinnings of Darwinian evolutionary theory is key to understanding why American archaeology ultimately rejected it and adopted cultural evolution in the 1950s.

We use the unmodified term "evolution" to denote change, regardless of the mechanism, process, or form. As indicated above, culture historians since the second decade of the twentieth century were interested in documenting, studying, and explaining cultural change. Theirs was a historical science, in many ways similar to that of paleobiologists, whose business it is to document and explain the phylogenetic histories of organisms. But whereas paleobiologists were able to erect an explanatory theory of biological change after the synthesis of genetics and natural selection took place in the late 1930s and early 1940s (Mayr 1982), archaeologists of that period followed a different path and adopted a different approach to explaining their subject matter. The most significant difference between paleobiology and American archaeology resides in the fact that by adopting different theories of evolution, the two fields adopted different ontologies. Biologists in the early twentieth century subscribed to an essentialist ontology, and it was not until the mid-1950s that they began to replace it with Darwin's materialist ontology (Gould 1986; Mayr 1982). Anthropologists and archaeologists of the early twentieth century tended to subscribe to a notion of evolution that was in many respects materialistic, but they replaced that notion with an essentialist one in the 1950s. What, then, are these two ontologies?

Essentialism presumes the existence of discoverable, discrete kinds of things. Things are of the same kind because they share essential properties—their "essences"—and these essential properties dictate whether a specimen is of kind A or kind B. Essential properties define an ideal, or archetype, "to which actual objects [are] imperfect approximations" (Lewontin 1974:5). This view renders nonessential variation between specimens as simply "annoying distraction" (Lewontin 1974:5). An advantage of the essentialist ontology is that prediction is possible because the kinds or types are real and thus are always and everywhere of the same sort; they will therefore always interact in the same manner, and the same result will be produced by their interaction. Laws, in a philosophical sense, can be written because the interactions of particular kinds of things will always be the same. The things, as well as the interactions between things, will always, regardless of their positions in time and space, be the same because the essential properties of the things themselves never change. Specimens grouped within natural, essentialist kinds always, by definition, share essential properties. Ahistorical sciences such as chemistry employ an essentialist ontology, since what they are measuring is difference as opposed to change (Hull 1965; Mayr 1959; Sober 1980).

It is impossible to measure change under essentialism. Only the difference between various kinds, or types, can be measured. For this reason, essentialism is referred to as "typological thinking" (Mayr 1959). As Mayr (1959:2) notes,

"Since there is no gradation between types, gradual evolution is basically a logical impossibility for the typologist. Evolution [change], if it occurs at all, has to proceed in steps or jumps." Change is transformational. The only way that things with essences can evolve is by dropping one essence and adopting another in a sort of Midas-touch process. Thus a specimen of kind A is kind A in this time and place, but in another time and place it somehow has transformed into kind B. The difference in time between A and B contributes to the perception that what has transpired is change. As Mayr (1982:38–39) states in regard to biological speciation, "Genuine change, according to essentialism, is possible only through the saltational origin of new essences [species]." Change is neither gradual nor continuous; it is jerky and saltational. In fact, the word "change" denotes some sort of connection between A and B (see below), but that connection is obscure (if simply nonexistent) when it is sought between essentialist types.

Materialism holds that phenomena cannot exist as bounded, discrete entities because they are always becoming something else. With reference to organisms, Mayr (1959:2) pointed out that "all [things] are composed of unique features and can be described collectively only in statistical terms. Individuals . . . form populations of which we can determine an arithmetic mean and the statistics of variation. Averages are merely statistical abstractions, only the individuals of which the populations are composed have reality." Further, "For the [essentialist-thinking] typologist, the type is real and the variation an illusion, while for the [materialist-thinking] populationist the type (average) is an abstraction and only the variation is real" (Mayr 1959:2). As a direct result of its materialist metaphysic, a historical science can monitor change in phenomena. Here change is in the makeup of the population of individuals. Species, metapopulations (collections of demes), and demes (local populations) evolve (change) because their membership shifts continuously over time as a result of mutations and various sorting mechanisms, such as drift and natural selection. The resulting variation between and among individual specimens "is the cornerstone of [Darwinian evolutionary] theory" (Lewontin 1974:5). Hence Kidder's focus on documenting the variation of form among artifacts was aligned with Darwinism, though it is unclear if Kidder actually realized this. No one else seems to have realized it either, though as we observe in later chapters, with such chronometers as frequency seriation and percentage stratigraphy what archaeologists were doing was documenting change in membership of populations over time. Constructing units to document variation is, therefore, critical.

Classification Units

To study variation, we construct a set of units that allows properties or attributes of phenomena to be measured. Archaeology is a spawning ground for units, many of which—type, group, class, period, phase, and so on—are rarely defined explicitly. We use the term "measurement" to denote the assignment of a symbol—letter, number, word—to an observation made on a phenomenon according to a set of rules. The rule set includes specification of a scale (e.g., Stevens 1946) and the relation between the symbols and the scale. Observation and recording of attributes on specimens comprise measurement. But which attributes should we observe and record?

The analyst selects attributes that are, according to some theory, relevant to a problem, and those attributes and their combinations result in the sorting of specimens into internally homogeneous, externally heterogeneous piles. Importantly, specimens that share attributes—those that end up together in one of the analyst's piles—do not have an essence (Mayr 1987). They have been grouped together not because of some inherent, shared quality but rather because they hold in common some attributes selected by the analyst. Theory is the final arbiter of which attributes out of the almost infinite number that could be selected are actually chosen by the analyst. Theory also specifies the kinds of units to be measured. We might decide, based on theory, that the color of a stone tool is not related to its function, whereas the angle of the working edge is; thus if we are interested in functional variation in stone tools, we choose as our attributes edge angles, traces of use wear (edge damage), and other attributes that theoretically are causally related to the property of analytical interest.

Because we decide on the attributes to be recorded, the resulting units— variously termed in archaeology types or classes—are ideational; they are not real in the sense that they can be seen or picked up and held. An edge angle— itself an ideational unit with different empirical manifestations—is measured, using a goniometer, in other ideational units known as degrees. Ideational units are tools used to measure or characterize real objects. An inch and a centimeter are used to measure length; a gram and an ounce are used to measure weight. Inches, centimeters, grams, and ounces do not exist empirically; they are units used as analytical tools to measure attributes of empirical units. A pencil is an empirical unit that can be placed in a set of things that are all six inches long, but only if the attribute distinguishing the set specifies that the things within it must be six inches long to be included. Our theory tells us what length is and how to measure it and how it differs from width, color, and so on.

An empirical unit is a thing that has a real existence; it is phenomenological. We use the term "type" for units of unspecified kind; they may be ideational, or they may be phenomenological. This is not always the meaning given to "type" by culture historians. We use the term "classification" in a general sense to denote the construction or modification of units of whatever kind (see Dunnell 1971, 1986b; Lyman and O'Brien 2002; O'Brien and Lyman 2002 for additional discussion).

What Is Change?

Under the materialist view, things are continually in the process of becoming something else—not in a saltational sense but in the sense of slow, gradual change. Populations of phenomena change continuously over time as some members die or leave and others are recruited (are born or immigrate). Depending on the scale of measurement we use, that change may be difficult or relatively easy to detect and monitor. Change is measured as alterations in the frequencies of analytical kinds, or ideational units. The classic model of the evolution of the modern horse (*Equus caballus*) from *Eohippus* to *Miohippus* to *Merychippus* and finally to *Equus* (Simpson 1967) is a heuristic device that simplifies the phylogeny of equids into terms that allow discussion and description. In such a phylogeny, different types of equid are given a (taxonomic) name and arranged against a time scale. Variation in the populations of horses that existed at different times and places is masked by such a procedure, but Darwinian paleobiologists recognize this and use the names of various populations—each of a different ideational form—merely to discuss equid evolution. A realistic materialist phylogeny would include frequencies of those different forms plotted against time and space, with—and this is crucial—indications of the particular variant forms and specimens that represented particular taxa (e.g., Simpson 1951; Vrba 1980). The arbitrary character of the taxa—the units of measurement—would be clear in such an illustration (Figure 2.1).

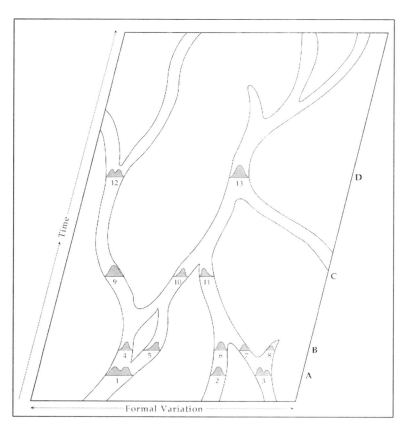

Figure 2.1. The braided (reticulate) continuum of Darwinian/materialist evolutionary change. Each shaded curve represents the frequency distribution of formal variants at a particular point in time. At time A, lineages 1 and 3 are diverging. At time B, lineage 1 has diverged into two (4 and 5), lineages 6 and 7 are converging, and lineage 8 is nearing extinction. At time C, lineages 10 and 11 are converging, hence the skewed frequency distributions of formal variants. At time D, lineage 12 is diverging. If each plotted frequency distribution represents an artifact assemblage or component (or set of fossils) and these distributions comprise the total known archaeological (fossil) record for an area, the analytical problem of culture history (paleobiology) is to determine their evolutionary relationships, such as are indicated by the variously flowing, diverging, and converging lineages.

If two things are similar but also somewhat different in form and also different in age, do they indicate that change has somehow taken place? From a modern Darwinian viewpoint, they represent change (in frequencies of alleles manifest in individuals within the population) only if they are phylogenetically related, in which case the similarity of form and difference in age signify inheritance and thus continuity—an ancestor-descendant lineage. How does one demonstrate that two phenomena are parts of a lineage? One way modern paleobiologists do this is by identifying homologous traits, or attributes, of the two phenomena. If the two phenomena share one or more such traits, they are by definition phyletically related.

Identifying homologous traits is a significant analytical hurdle (e.g., Fisher 1994; Forey 1990; Smith 1994; Szalay and Bock 1991) because a trait that is shared by two phenomena may be analogous—the result of convergence. How are analogous and homologous traits to be distinguished? Kroeber (1931b:151) suggested that "where similarities are specific and structural and not merely superficial . . . has long been the accepted method in evolutionary and systematic biology" for distinguishing analogous and homologous traits. He was correct, for this was, and is, precisely how biologists distinguish the two (see references in Lyman 2001). The wings of eagles and those of crows are structurally as well as superficially similar; this is homologous similarity. The wings of eagles and those of bats are superficially, but not structurally, similar; this is analogous similarity. The issue of distinguishing analogous and homologous traits was rarely mentioned by culture historians, which contributed to the paradigm's fall from favor in the second half of the twentieth century (Lyman et al. 1997b). But what is of most interest here is why culture historians abandoned a materialist conception of evolution in favor of an essentialist conception. Among other things, by adopting the latter, the ability to distinguish the two kinds of similarity became unimportant.

Evolution in the Early Twentieth Century

Many archaeologists believe that "cultural evolution was generally anathema as late as the 1950s" but that it was revived by the end of that decade (Willey and Sabloff 1993:220; for an alternative view, see Trigger 1989:295). To be sure, cultural evolution—in the sense we have defined it here—did enjoy only minimal status within American archaeology between about 1900 and the middle 1950s, faring only slightly better in anthropology as a whole (Carneiro 2003). Willey and Sabloff's (1993:306) contention that cultural evolution was dead during the first half of the century apparently was based in part on the fact that Haag (1959) listed "only a limited number of evolutionary efforts in the field." Haag's article, however, was not intended to be an extensive review of the evolutionary-archaeological literature, nor was it written to adequately sample that literature. Willey's (1960) review contained many more references, but most of them were to works that were published in the 1950s and represented recent syntheses that Willey, following an earlier effort (Willey and Phillips 1958), was using to discuss the overall evolutionary trajectory of American cultural lineages.

It is easy to demonstrate that the general notion of evolution—cultural or otherwise—played a major role in the growth and development of the culture history paradigm in American archaeology. Given the goal of that paradigm, how could it not have? Use of the general notion of evolution(ary change over time) was often covert and seldom explicit, but it was present nonetheless (South 1955). Archaeology, after all, had one thing that cultural anthropology did not—access to an extensive temporal record, and everyone knew that evolution takes place over time. Once it was clear that measurable temporal difference existed in the archaeological record of the Americas, evolution of some kind was an obvious if not always explicit or well-developed explanation of that difference: "Cultural or artifact lineages developed or evolved." The kind of evolution used by archaeologists in the first several decades of the twentieth century was at least conceptually of the Darwinian, or materialist, sort. In the 1940s and 1950s an essentialist cultural evolution usurped the role previously played by materialist evolution. How and why did this replacement happen?

Evolution in Cultural Anthropology

Received wisdom holds that Boas killed any notion of cultural evolution at the end of the nineteenth century—an erroneous assumption attributable in large part to the grumblings of White (1943, 1945a, 1945b, 1947b, 1959a, 1959b) but also to the reading of the death notice by others (e.g., Lesser 1952). However, Boas and some other leading figures in anthropology at the time did not reject outright the basic notion of evolution (Sanderson 1990), a point White (e.g., 1947b) occasionally acknowledged. In reality, Boas (1896b:904) was concerned with the fact that the model of cultural evolution resulted in a comparative anthropology founded on the interpretive "assumption that the same [cultural] features must always have developed from the same causes, [leading] to the conclusion that there is one grand system according to which mankind has developed everywhere; that all the occurring variations are no more than minor details in this grand uniform evolution" (see also Boas 1904:519). Given that the key assumption—essentialist change was the only kind that had occurred—was demonstrably wrong, Boas (1896b:907) pre-

ferred the "historical method" and what he believed was its ability to discover
the processes that resulted in the particularistic development of different cultures. The historical method was more in line with the materialist metaphysic
and would ultimately reveal—inductively, in Boas's (1896b, 1904) view—laws
concerning how cultures evolved rather than assume them, as did the comparative method.

It was clear to Boas that each culture's heritage—its developmental
lineage—was unique. He noted that in the second half of the nineteenth
century, the "regularity in the processes of [Spencerian] evolution became the
center of attraction [to Morgan and Tylor and others] even before the processes
of [cultural] evolution had been observed and understood" (Boas 1904:516).
Thus, in Boas's view, as more data accumulated, Spencerian evolutionary
theory came to be less and less tenable. As a result, Boas (1904:522) indicated
that instead of "a simple [universally applicable] line of evolution there appear
a multiplicity of converging and diverging lines [or cultural lineages] which it
is difficult to bring under one system." Bidney (1946:297n2) pointed out that
"Boas never rejected the concept of cultural evolution but merely the notion of
uniform laws of cultural development and the a priori assumption that cultural
development was always from a hypothetical simplicity to one of complexity."
In addition, Naroll (1961:391) observed that "the reason Boas rejected 19th
century [Spencerian] evolutionism was neither theoretical [n]or conceptual,
but methodological. . . . Boas always maintained that the study of cultural
evolution was a major task of cultural anthropology, but Boas was bitterly
opposed to confusing speculation with scientific generalization." Thus Boas
rejected the interpretive assumption of Spencerian cultural evolution, and in
so doing he rejected its essentialist metaphysic. He retained the materialist
notions of evolution as history and variation as critical to the study of evolution. The classification units he and his colleagues used to track evolutionary
lineages—cultural traits—were less than ideal, but that is getting ahead of the
story, so we reserve discussion of those units for Chapter 3.

Some of Boas's intellectual progeny followed his lead and made some astute observations that would greatly influence archaeological thinking. Kroeber (1923a:3) used the term "tradition" to label the processes of cultural transmission and heredity, thus distinguishing them from the biological "force" of
genetic heredity. Both biological evolution and cultural development involved
transmission (as Boas 1904 had indicated), but because transmission within

the latter could be between individuals who were not "blood descendants," the concept of biological evolution—genetic transmission and change—was "ambiguous" in a cultural setting (Kroeber 1923a:7). Thus Kroeber paralleled Darwin's view. Darwin (1859) avoided the term "evolution"—it was used by Spencer to label his social philosophy—and instead used "descent with modification." Morgan and Tylor had used the term "evolution" precisely in the Spencerian sense, and Kroeber (and Boas) rejected that sense of the term, not the basic notion of evolution as change through time or descent with modification.

Kroeber not only rejected cultural evolution, he rejected Darwinism as a potential contributor to culture theory as well. Regarding the latter, cultural lineages were not the result of genetic transmission. As a result, in Kroeber's (1923a:8) view, "the designation of anthropology as 'the child of Darwin' is most misleading. Darwin's essential achievement was that he imagined . . . a mechanism [natural selection] through which organic evolution appeared to be taking place. . . . [As a result, a] pure Darwinian anthropology would be largely misapplied biology." Apparently, cultures were not subject to natural selection. What had "greatly influenced anthropology," according to Kroeber (1923a:8), "has not been Darwinism, but the vague idea of evolution. . . . It has been common practice in social anthropology to 'explain' any part of human civilization by arranging its several forms in an evolutionary sequence from lowest to highest and allowing each successive stage to flow spontaneously from the preceding—in other words, without specific cause." This had been Boas's (1896b, 1904) point, too. Kroeber saw this Spencerian, essentialist notion as nonsense. As Bidney (1946:295) argued, the "stages of cultural development are but abstractions, useful to the student of culture, but not ultimately intelligible or explanatory of the dynamics of culture." (We discuss the archaeological conception a cultural stage in Chapter 7.) To Kroeber (1923a:5), the development of a cultural lineage was historical, and historians "deal with the concrete, with the unique; for in a degree every historical event has something unparalleled about it. . . . [Historians] do not lay down exact laws." This did not mean that cultures do not evolve; it only meant that the Spencerian universal model of essentialist cultural evolution was incorrect. Was there an alternative?

For Kroeber (1917a), culture was like a stream—it had a flow. It was heritable not in any genetic sense but rather was transmitted via learning (see also Boas 1904). Kroeber's notion of culture change was well expressed by his student Nels Nelson (1932:103), who wrote of "implements or mechanical inventions, i.e., material culture phenomena, as parts of a unique unfolding process which has much in common with that other process observed in the world of nature and generally called organic evolution." The evolution of culture was not only continuous, it also was gradual: A "study of the history of mechanization reveals few if any absolutely original contrivances that were not essentially the results of gradual transformation or combination of older inventions; that in reality spurts, mutants or leaps are as rare among artificial (intellectual) phenomena as among natural phenomena" (Nelson 1932:122). There was a "mechanical culture stream" (Nelson 1932:109).

Kroeber "added time depth to the essentially synchronic ethnology of Boas" (Steward 1962:203) and believed that the evolution of a cultural lineage involved a braided stream—what a Darwinist today would label a reticulate pattern of intersecting and diverging lineages—created by such processes as diffusion, trade, and migration as well as enculturation from a parental to a descendant generation. That this idea came from Boas is clear:

> There is one fundamental difference between biological and cultural data which makes it impossible to transfer the methods of the one science to the other. Animal forms develop in divergent directions, and an intermingling of species that have once become distinct is negligible in the whole developmental history. It is otherwise in the domain of culture. Human thoughts, institutions, activities spread from one social unit to another. As soon as two groups come into close contact their cultural traits will be disseminated from the one to the other [Boas 1932:609].

Kroeber "constantly saw changes in styles as flows and continua, pulses, culminations and diminutions, convergences and divergences, divisions, blends and cross-currents by which cultures develop and mutually influence one another" (Steward 1962:206). He did not, however, attempt to determine causes of culture change, no doubt because his mentor (Boas) had indicated that the reticulate evolution of cultures "puts the most serious obstacles in the way of discovering the inner dynamic conditions of change. Before morphological comparison [read "evolutionary synthesis"; see Boas 1896b] can be attempted, the extraneous elements due to cultural diffusion must be eliminated" (Boas 1932:609). Probably as a result, Nelson (1932:122) wrote that "final explanations of [culture change], as well as of the driving force and the ultimate goal of culture, may be left to the philosophers."

Genetic transmission was omitted from consideration of cultural development by Kroeber and his students for two reasons: Cultural ideas or traits (Chapter 3) were not genetically transmitted, and the transmission and inheritance of ideas could be up as well as down between generations and also within a generation. This prompted Kroeber (1923a) to avoid adopting the biological version of evolution then current—a version that, after 1900, was dominated by genetics and its attendant mechanisms, such as transmission, mutation, inheritance, and speciation. Natural selection and phenotypic variation were relegated to the back room; these two critical concepts would only assume their proper place in biological theory with the synthesis of the late 1930s and early 1940s (Mayr 1982). There was another reason not to transfer Darwinian evolution as an explanatory theory to culture—the evolution of culture was reticulate, whereas the evolution of biological organisms was only diversifying or branching. This was made clear by Kroeber (1948) when he illustrated the differences between the evolution of organisms and the evolution of cultures (Figure 2.2).

Kroeber (1931b:149) had written that while a "culture complex is 'polyphyletic' [and] a [biological] genus is, almost by definition, monophyletic. . . . the analogy does at least refer to the fact that culture elements [traits] like species represent the smallest units of material which the historical anthropologist and biologist respectively have to deal with." The stumbling block was the implicit equation of a culture with an essentialist biological concept. Today a biological species (a genus being comprised of one or more species) is a population that is reproductively isolated from other such populations; in 1930 the concept was more strongly founded in the essentialist ontology than in materialism (Mayr 1982). Kroeber chose the wrong biological unit—species—to equate with cultures. Further, early in the twentieth century a culture had become a reified, essentialist unit, a view now seen as erroneous (Palmer et al. 1997).

Evolution in Archaeology

In the 1930s cultural anthropologists found a Darwinian model (and ontology) of evolution to be inapplicable to cultures for various reasons. Yet a

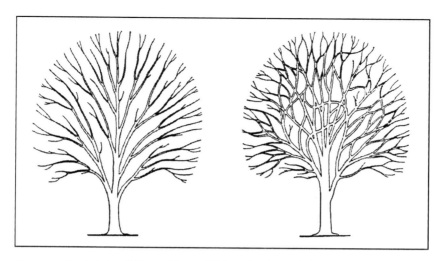

Figure 2.2. Kroeber's (1948:Figure 18) tree of biological evolution (left) and tree of cultural evolution (right). Note the simple branching structure of the former and the reticulate (branching and intersecting) nature of the latter.

Darwinian sort of evolution played a major role within culture history virtually since its birth as a viable paradigm in American archaeology. For example, when commenting on Uhle's (1907) stratigraphic excavations at the Emeryville Shellmound in San Francisco Bay, Kroeber (1909:16) noted that most artifact types were found throughout the stratigraphic sequence and that although there was "some gradual elaboration and refinement of technical process . . . it was change of degree only" (see Chapter 8 for more details). Historians have tended to focus on the last phrase and have argued that Kroeber's vision of culture change was of the essentialist kind (Rowe 1962a). Although this is correct, Kroeber clearly was aware of the fact that what he was looking at involved change of the materialist sort, though he could not have recognized that his conception of culture change involved a particular ontology. He measured just such materialist change a few years later when he invented frequency seriation (Kroeber 1916a, 1916b; Chapters 4 and 5).

Two of Kroeber's students mimicked this materialist method of measuring the passage of time. Nelson's (1916) excavations in the Southwest and his use of percentage stratigraphy to show the waxing and waning of a pottery style's popularity were decidedly materialistic (Chapters 8 and 9). Nelson's data consisted of the frequencies of ideational units termed "types" and showed continuous and gradual change through time given the differential overlap of types across multiple strata. He had excavated precisely because he wanted to establish the chronological continuity—not just the relative temporal positions—of his pottery types; without using the term, he sought "overlapping" types, which in turn imply heritable continuity or what would within a few decades be referred to as historical continuity. Leslie Spier (1917a, 1917b) also used percentage stratigraphy and frequency seriation of ideational units to measure culture change in the Southwest (Chapter 8). Although Nelson and Spier tended to avoid using the terms of Darwinian evolution in discussing what they documented, others were not so shy.

Kidder discussed different styles of pottery in terms of ancestor-descendent relationships. For example, one pottery type might "father" another (Kidder 1915:453), and in wording similar to that of Nelson, a pottery type might become "extinct" (Kidder and Kidder 1917:348). Kidder's types were of a kind that, hopefully, reflected the passage of time as well as evolutionary or phyletic relations, as is clearly implied in his 1917 paper on sequences, or "series" (Kidder 1917), of ceramic designs (Figure 2.3). Kidder (Kidder and Kidder 1917:349) stated that "one's general impression is that [the types] are all successive phases of [particular pottery traits], and that each one of them developed [read "evolved"] from its predecessor." Kidder's word "phase" is a commonsense English designation for a portion of a continuum. To measure time, Kidder erected types that were both "more or less arbitrarily delimited chronological subdivisions of material" (Kidder 1936b:xxix) and "chronologically seriable" (Kidder 1936a:625). Kidder's types were ideational units constructed to measure time: Conceptually, variation was continuous—things were in the continuous process of becoming, and thus types had to be of the ideational sort to allow the measurement of change; change in the frequencies of types or variants reflected the passage of time. This was, simply, the materialist ontology.

Numerous individuals (e.g., Dutton 1938; Ford 1935a; Hawley 1934; Kniffen 1938; Martin 1936; Olson 1930; Reiter 1938a; Schmidt 1928; Strong 1925; Vaillant 1935) over the next two decades mimicked the methods and techniques of Kroeber, Nelson, Spier, and Kidder. Without explicitly recognizing it, they were using the materialist ontology and ideational units to document culture lineages. But they all also talked about sections of the materialistically measured cultural continuum—sections that were variously labeled cultures,

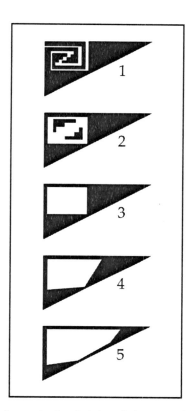

Figure 2.3. Kidder's (1917) example of a phyletic evolutionary "series" of southwestern ceramic design elements. Element 1 is earliest, or oldest; element 5 is latest, or youngest.

complexes, periods, phases, and the like—as if they were real, phenomenological units (e.g., Kidder 1924, 1927). Such discussions represented what has been termed the materialist paradox (Dunnell 1995). If cultures evolved, how could such units be real? Even Kroeber (1916a, 1916b), who recognized that his periods were arbitrary chunks of the continuum, treated his cultural units as if they were real, as did everyone else. What were a few randomly selected frames of a reel of film—or arbitrarily chosen (they were accidents of sampling) one-foot sections of a mile-long cultural stream—conceptually came to have essentialist realities.

Kroeber (1925b:296) encountered the materialist paradox head-on when he indicated that he was interested in the documentation that archaeology could provide on "the development of culture" in California. By that time it was clear to Kroeber (1925b:927) and other culture historians that "the correct [excavation] procedure [was] to follow lines of deposition in instituting comparisons; but this is not practical, stratification being confined to limited areas and often wholly imperceptible" (Chapter 8). After examining the shifting frequencies of various artifact types across selected vertical columns of sediment, Kroeber (1925b:926, 930) concluded that geographic subdivisions, or provinces, of the California culture area "were determined a long time ago and have ever since maintained themselves with relatively little change"; that "the basis of culture remained identical during the whole of the shell-mound period"; and that in California, "civilization, such as it was, remained immutable in all fundamentals." That his artifact types were variously functional or descriptive and not historical went unnoticed. As our discussion in Chapter 5 shows, Kroeber was in other contexts well aware of the influence of type or unit construction on whether the linear flight of time's arrow could be measured; why he failed to recognize this with respect to California archaeology is unclear. It may be because he had slipped away from a materialist ontology toward an essentialist one.

Kroeber (1925b:931) indicated, first, that types "must, of course, be interpreted as periods"; second, differences in types represented differences in culture; and third, cultures differed because the human groups that bore the cultures and made the artifacts differed. Kroeber's types of artifacts and types of cultures were in some sense real or essentialist units. Spier (1917a, 1917b, 1918a, 1919) had interpreted his pottery data from the Southwest in just such terms, as had others (e.g., Kidder 1924, 1927; Schmidt 1928; Vaillant 1935). With respect to his own work, Kidder recognized the materialist paradox:

> The division of the Glaze ware of Pecos into six chronologically sequent types is a very convenient and, superficially, satisfactory arrangement. For some time I was very proud of it, so much so, in fact, that I came to think and write about the types as if they were definite and describable entities. They are, of course, nothing of the sort, being merely useful cross-sections of a constantly changing cultural trait. Most types, in reality, grew one from the other by stages well-nigh imperceptible. My groupings therefore amount to a selection of six recognizable nodes of individuality; and a forcing into association with the most strongly marked or "peak" material of many actually older and younger transitional specimens. . . . This pottery did not stand still; through some

three centuries it underwent a slow, usually subtle, but never ceasing metamorphosis [Kidder 1936b:xx].

This is the materialist paradox—the conceived materialistic "slow, usually subtle, but never ceasing metamorphosis" of artifact forms through time was monitored using typological, essentialist, "recognizable nodes of individuality." Despite this realization, the equation of types of artifacts with particular cultures became an interpretive algorithm for culture history. Such an equation represented the first step toward adoption of essentialism and would eventually lead to the rejection of materialist evolution. The conceived reality of the sections of the temporal continuum was reinforced by the eventual conception of the artifacts within a stratum as representative of a discrete cultural occupation (e.g., Fowke 1922; Thompson 1956; Wissler 1917a). We return to the history of that conception in Chapter 8.

Darwinism's Last Hurrah

The basic notion of Darwinian evolution informed the interpretations of early culture historians, but they hardly considered cultural transmission other than to note the reticulate evolution of culture. Kroeber managed early in the 1930s to identify one of the significant aspects of biological evolution that should have been employed by culture historians. He pointed out that the "fundamentally different evidential value of homologous and analogous similarities for determination of historical relationship, that is, genuine systematic or genetic relationship, has long been an axiom in biological science. The distinction has been much less clearly made in anthropology, and rarely explicitly, but holds with equal force" (Kroeber 1931b:151). Kroeber went on to imply that a "true homology" denoted "genetic unity," and he argued that

> there are cases in which it is not a simple matter to decide whether the totality of traits points to a true [homologous] relationship or to secondary [analogous, functional] convergence. . . . Yet few biologists would doubt that sufficiently intensive analysis of structure will ultimately solve such problems of descent. . . . There seems no reason why on the whole the same cautious optimism should not prevail in the field of culture; why homologies should not be positively distinguishable from analogies when analysis of the whole of the phenomena in question has become truly intensive [Kroeber 1931b:151, 152–153].

Kroeber's remarks were largely ignored, leading him to lament a decade later that anthropology was still "backward" with regard to distinguishing between analogous and homologous similarities (Kroeber 1943:108). Instead of implementing Kroeber's suggestions, archaeologists adopted the more easily conceived and implemented dictum that "typological similarity is [an] indicator of cultural relatedness" (Willey 1953a:363). This notion is found in the morphological species concept of early twentieth-century biologists who still adhered to the essentialist ontology: Morphologically similar species were members of the same genus and thus were phylogenetically related (Mayr 1969, 1982). In both archaeology and biology, the notion puts the cart before the horse. As Simpson (1961b:69) pointed out, "individuals do not belong in the same taxon because they are similar, but they are similar because they belong to the same taxon." Archaeologists noted similarities between artifact types, assemblages of artifacts, and the like, but those similarities might not be of the homologous sort requisite to determining phylogenetic relations and writing phylogenetic histories. Many archaeologists adopted Willey's axiom. As we show later, the few objections raised led to the rejection of any archaeological utility of Darwinian evolution.

Ceramic and Cultural Phylogenetics

Shortly after Kroeber's (1931b) paper was published, a Darwinian manifestation within American archaeology prompted several commentators to reiterate Kroeber's reasons for rejecting Darwinism as a viable theoretical model for the explanation of culture change. Harold Gladwin, working in the Southwest, created not only a binomial system of pottery classification explicitly modeled on the biological genus and species concepts (Gladwin and Gladwin 1930), but he also created a hierarchical structure for organizing archaeological units variously termed roots, stems, branches, and phases (Gladwin and Gladwin 1934). These units were meant specifically to assist in the working out of "a comprehensive scheme by which relationships and relative chronology could be expressed" (Gladwin and Gladwin 1934:8–9). In a few short years, Gladwin (1936) abandoned the scheme. His statement to that effect is revealing:

> My original suggestion . . . of using a generic [read "genus"] and a specific [read "species"] name for pottery types implied a biological analogy which I now think was a mistake. The idea is being carried

too far along biological or zoological lines, and men do not realize the profound differences which exist between zoological species and the things which have been made by men and women.

Zoological species do not cross and intergrade; evolution is so slow as to be hardly distinguishable. The evolution of culture . . . was stepped up to almost incredible speed, and on every side we find evidence of merging and cross-influences [Gladwin 1936:158].

The individuals who were carrying the idea too far included Harold Colton, a professional biologist by training who left a professorship of biology to pursue archaeological interests. Along with Lyndon Hargrave, Colton published a major statement on the phylogenetic implications of pottery types. A *type* was "a group of pottery vessels which are alike in every important characteristic except (possibly) form," and a *series* was "a group of pottery types within a single ware in which each type bears a genetic relation to each other" (Colton and Hargrave 1937:2–3). Thus Colton and Hargrave's series was identical to Kidder's (1915, 1917). Colton and Hargrave carried the biological analogy further than their predecessors and distinguished derived, collateral, and ancestral types and graphed the relations among them (Figure 2.4). Although Colton's knowledge of Darwinian evolution underpinned their scheme, the key to it was in the supposition that related forms were related because they were similar (see Lyman and O'Brien 2003 for more detailed discussion). As we pointed out above, it should be the other way around. Colton and Hargrave offered no argument—nor did anyone else at the time—that the similarities described were of the homologous sort.

Kidder's (1915, 1917) simpler phyletic scheme (Figure 2.3) denoted some of the same sorts of relations between types, but his contemporaries did not heap criticism on him the way they did on Colton and Hargrave. Ford (1940:265) noted that Colton and Hargrave had ignored the problem of selecting "a class of features [attributes] which will best reflect cultural influences [e.g., transmission via contact or heredity], and which in their various forms will be mutually exclusive, to serve as guides in the process" of determining ancestor-descendent relations. Ford was speaking of homologous similarity. Colton and Hargrave (1937:2–3, 5) indicated that genetic relations among types were "obvious" and "clearly revealed" and that "definite evolutionary characters were recognized," but they provided no list of them, nor did they

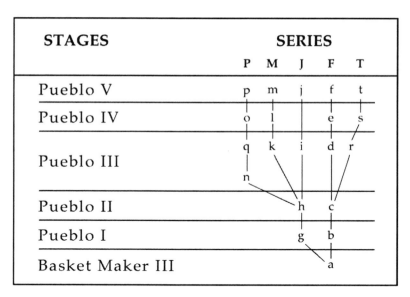

STAGES	SERIES				
	P	M	J	F	T
Pueblo V	p	m	j	f	t
Pueblo IV	o	l		e	s
Pueblo III	q	k	i	d	r
	n				
Pueblo II			h	c	
Pueblo I			g	b	
Basket Maker III				a	

Figure 2.4. Colton and Hargrave's (1937:Figure 1) model of the phylogenetic evolution of pottery. Each uppercase letter represents a ceramic "series" in the sense of Kidder (1917; see Figure 2.3); each lowercase letter represents a type; phylogenetic relationships of types are indicated by the vertical lines connecting lowercase letters. Colton and Hargrave's figure caption reads, in part, "type c is collateral to types d and r, derivative [descended] from type b, and ancestral to types f and t . . . types q and n are both ancestral to type o, but collateral to each other, and derivative from types h, g, and a."

provide guidance as to how such characters were to be analytically identified. They apparently were unaware of Kroeber's (1931b) guidance in this regard. Not surprisingly, then, Reiter (1938a:490) noted that he "was unable to find a single instance of proof" of the genetic relations of Colton and Hargrave's pottery types.

Reiter (1938b:490) also noted that Colton and Hargrave's pottery typology tended to ignore variation, and he insisted that "variation tendencies cannot be overlooked if genetic or chronologic emphasis is strong." Reiter's comments underscored that a materialist conception of change was requisite to what Colton and Hargrave were attempting. But Colton and Hargrave's types were not ideational units that could be used to measure variation. The types were empirical, as evidenced by Colton and Hargrave's (1937:30–31) suggestions that the members of a type "will not [always] fit the [type] description perfectly" and that "there are sherds that are intermediate between types."

Colton and Hargrave's classification scheme was hierarchical, but that structure was void of explanatory content. Colton (1939) later employed the terms then becoming popular within the Midwestern Taxonomic Method (Chapter 7), a method explicitly void of explanatory content (McKern 1934, 1937a, 1939) but the hierarchical structure of which (incorrectly) implied to many a sort of phylogenetic tree (Lyman and O'Brien 2003). Colton's (1939) phylogenetic interpretations were, not surprisingly, criticized. Reed (1940:190) remarked that Colton's "genetic and temporal approach seems more desirable in a region such as this where chronology is relatively well-known." Chronological control is indeed a requisite of determining a phylogenetic history, but it is only one of several requirements. Reed's failure to note that Colton had not established that the typological similarities he discussed were of the homologous sort was, however, typical.

Steward rejected Colton's analytical procedure and results for the same reason that Kroeber had earlier rejected Darwinian evolution—it was nonapplicable to cultural phenomena:

> It is apparent from the cultural relationships shown in this scheme that strict adherence to a method drawn from biology inevitably fails to take into account the distinctively cultural and unbiological fact of blends and crosses between essentially unlike types. . . . It is true that cultural streams often tend to be distinct, but they are never entirely unmixed and often approach a complete blend. A taxonomic scheme cannot indicate this fact without becoming mainly a list of exceptions. It must pigeon-hole. . . . [T]he method employed inevitably distorts true cultural relationships [Steward 1941:367].

Steward could not accept a taxonomic structure for any classification of cultural phenomena because such a structure implied the same thing to him that the Linnaean taxonomy tended to imply to some biologists—branching evolution (Lyman and O'Brien 2003). This is clear in Steward's (1942, 1944) discussion of the Midwestern Taxonomic Method. Steward (1942:339) offered the typical criticism of that method when he noted that it produced a "set of timeless and spaceless categories." In response, McKern (1942) protested that he had merely set those dimensions aside for the moment in favor of the formal dimension and had explicitly not discarded the time-space dimensions.

Steward's (1944:99) rebuttal entailed two elements and is where the heart of the matter resides. He could not conceive of how taxonomic or hierarchical classification, which for him denoted branching evolution (even though there is no necessary relationship between the two but rather only a fortuitous coincidence of architecture), could be forced onto cultural phenomena that not only diverged through time but that also converged to create reticulate evolutionary descent. Steward's implicit equation of species and cultures—both conceived as essentialist units—is clear. Second, Steward could find no utility in the method because it lacked any reference to theory; although an astute observation, it had minimal impact on archaeological thought. The most damaging criticism of what had begun as Kidder's (1917) phyletic series of ceramic designs and what eventually grew into Colton and Hargrave's (1937) collateral and descendent types resided elsewhere.

Pots Do Not Breed

Brew (1946:46) argued that classifications are arbitrary constructs of the analyst—"no typological system is actually inherent in the material"—and that a classification should fit the purpose of the investigation. He recognized the interplay of theory and unit construction and argued that we should change our classifications "as our needs change and as our knowledge develops" (Brew 1946:64). His conception of cultural change was the same as Kroeber's: "We are dealing with a constant stream of cultural development, not evolutionary in the genetic sense, but still a continuum of human activity" (Brew 1946:63). In holding to such a materialist conception of culture change, Brew (1946:65) argued, we "must ever be on guard against that peculiar paradox of anthropology which permits men to 'trace' a 'complex' of, let us say, physical type, pottery type, and religion over 10,000 miles of terrain and down through 10,000 years of history while in the same breath, or in the next lecture, the same men vigorously defend the theory of continuous change." The paradox emanates "from the belief that the manufactured groups [types] are realistic entities and the lack of realization that they are completely artificial. . . . Implicit in [the belief] is a faith . . . in the existence of a 'true' or 'correct' classification for all object, cultures, etc., which completely ignores the fact that they are all part of a continuous stream of cultural events" (Brew 1946:48).

Brew, like Kidder before him, had described the materialist paradox. But Brew (1946:53) also made a unique observation when he pointed out that the evolutionary implications of the Gladwin-Colton scheme were unacceptable because "phylogenetic relationships do not exist between inanimate objects" such as potsherds. This statement was repeated by Beals et al. (1945:87), who saw Brew's manuscript before it was published. Ironically, they mimicked Kidder's (Figure 2.3) technique of constructing ceramic series, as did others (e.g., Wheat et al. 1958). Brew's discussion drove the final nail into the coffin containing the Gladwin-Colton scheme; no one after that time discussed ceramic series in such flagrantly Darwinian terms. That this was the singular impact of his arguments probably resulted because Brew could offer no clearly articulated alternative. For example, he stated that the "only defense there can be for a classification of [artifacts] based upon phylogenetic theory is that the individual objects were made and used by man" (Brew 1946:55), but he failed to make the conceptual leap to "replicative success" (Leonard and Jones 1987)—one cornerstone of a Darwinian archaeology—for two reasons.

First, to Brew, as to Kroeber and others before him, evolution involved only the processes of genetic transmission and genetic change. There was only a weak correlation between an organism and the "artifacts" that that organism might produce, such as birds and eggshells or mollusks and mollusk shells, and no connection at all between people and their artifacts (Brew 1946:55–56). Since artifacts were not genotypic phenomena, they were not subject to evolutionary forces. That it is the phenotype—of which behaviors are an expression, and artifacts are manifestations of behaviors—that undergoes selection escaped Brew's—and biologists'—attention for a number of years (Leonard and Jones 1987; Mayr 1982). Second, Brew quoted a single biologist—a geneticist—who argued that a phylogenetic history did not explain organisms; hence to Brew (1946:56), it could not explain artifacts. Of course a phylogenetic history is not an explanation, but such a construct is a requirement of using Darwinian evolutionary theory to explain the diversity of forms of organisms and their distributions in time and space (Szalay and Bock 1991).

Brew's (1946) and Steward's (1941, 1942, 1944) criticisms of any suggestion that the evolution of cultures might have some similarities to Darwinian evolution precluded any such notions from being stated explicitly. Archaeologists still used Kidder's (1917) phyletic-seriation technique (e.g., Beals et al. 1945; Wheat et al. 1958), but they were not explicit about the underpinning Darwinian mechanisms or any Darwinian implications of the results.

Rather than retooling materialist evolution into something that was applicable to archaeological phenomena and that aligned with their materialistic conceptions of culture change, just as paleobiologists had done to make it applicable to the fossil record (fossil bones, like pots, do not interbreed), culture historians did something else. They adopted both Willey's (1953a:363) axiom that "typological similarity is [an] indicator of cultural relatedness" and a reborn version of Spencerian cultural evolution. There were problems with both, but the adoption was not a long and painful one because there was no effective competition; the only potential competitor had been eliminated, and the winner was therefore chosen by default.

Typological Similarity and Homologous Similarity

Willey (1953a) disliked the Gladwin-Colton scheme, and he and Philip Phillips explicitly stated that the archaeological "use of the organic evolutionary model is, we believe, specious" (Phillips and Willey 1953:631). Their basic operative unit was a phase—an archaeological manifestation of a culture that had some ethnographic reality. They suggested that the use of traditions and horizon styles would reflect the braided stream of the evolution of cultures and allow one to correlate phases. As Irving Rouse noted, a metaphor could be drawn between the use of horizons and traditions as integrative devices for archaeological materials distributed across an area and a rectangular piece of cloth, the side edges representing the geographical limits of the area, and the top and bottom edges representing the temporal limits: "The warp threads of the cloth consist of a series of regional traditions running from the bottom towards the top of the cloth, while the weft is composed of a number of horizon styles which extend from one side of the cloth towards the other. The cloth is decorated with a series of irregularly arranged rectangles, each representing a single culture [read "phase"], and these are so colored that they appear to form a series of horizontal bands" (Rouse 1954:222).

But Rouse (1955) was concerned that Willey's dictum that typological similarity denoted cultural relatedness was too simplistic. Rouse wanted to determine the phylogenetic relations among phases rather than merely to track the distributions of a few artifact classes, as the horizon and tradition units did. To illustrate this, he distinguished three ways to correlate phases. First, one might use a Midwestern Taxonomic Method–like procedure to group phases that shared traits. Why the traits were shared was a separate issue. Second, one

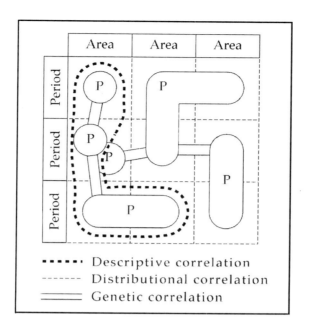

Figure 2.5. Rouse's (1955:Figure 4) model of the results of comparing phases (P) to show their relative contiguity in form, time, and space. Phases that were formally similar as well as contiguous in time and space were likely to have "genetic" relationships.

could note similarities in the time-space distributions of phases. Identical or adjacent distributions of two or more phases "establish contemporaneity and contiguity, or lack thereof, and nothing else" (Rouse 1955:717). To argue that contemporaneous phases were phylogenetically related "because they share a given horizon style . . . is on the genetic rather than the distributional level of interpretation, for it requires an assumption that the style has diffused from one phase to the others with little or no time lag" (Rouse 1955:718). Third, one might trace the "genetic" relations among phases by establishing that the phases had been in "contact" temporally and spatially by using horizons and traditions that comprised homologous types (Rouse 1955:719). One needed to distinguish between analogous and homologous similarity, the linchpin to this kind of comparison, to ensure the relations were "genetic." The modeled result of such analyses is shown in Figure 2.5.

Willey and Phillips (1958:31) responded to Rouse (1955) by arguing that his "genetic" relations could only "be revealed and expressed by means of integrative concepts that are culturally determined." The phrase "culturally determined" was critical. Horizons and horizon styles by definition reflected cultural transmission or diffusion over space. A tradition was "a (primarily) temporal continuity represented by persistent configurations in single technologies or other systems of related forms" that operated at Rouse's (1955) "genetic level of interpretation" (Willey and Phillips 1958:38) and reflected transmission or heredity across time. Thus Willey and Phillips's conception of cultural development was well captured by the flowing braided-stream metaphor. Each trickle was a tradition that to varying degrees met and mixed with other trickles as denoted by horizons and horizon styles. Such a conception presumed that the typological similarities denoted by horizons and traditions were of the homologous sort.

For Willey and Phillips, horizons and traditions provided the empirical warrants for discussing the historical development of cultures. They were "integrative" units that denoted "some form of historical contact" rather than "implications of phylogeny" (Willey and Phillips 1958:30). Culture history demanded "culturally determined" integrative concepts such as horizons and traditions, not phylogenetic ones (Willey and Phillips 1958:30–31). Willey's (1953a:368) suggestion that "principles of continuity and change are expressed in the degrees of trait likeness and unlikeness which are the mechanisms of establishing the genetic lines binding the assemblages together" thus was purely metaphorical. But cultural or historical "relatedness," when couched in a temporal framework aimed at studying the developmental lineages of cultures, such as that envisioned by Willey and Phillips, cannot fail to be phylogenetic in the sense of being based on (cultural) transmission, and (genetic) transmission was certainly central to Darwinian evolutionary theory in the 1950s (Mayr 1982).

The generally discipline-wide abhorrence of anything Darwinian resulted in the contradiction internal to the Willey and Phillips scheme going unrecognized. Further, Kroeber's (1931b, 1943) earlier critical point regarding the importance of the distinction between analogous and homologous similarity, despite repetition by Rouse (1955), was overlooked. It was, we suspect, overlooked at least in part because there was an alternative version of evolution that did not require this critical distinction, rendering it pointless to consider; that version did not entail genetic transmission, rendering further consideration of the mechanisms of heritability and thus consideration of continuity unnecessary; and that version did not consider whether evolution was merely branching or reticulate, rendering this problem unworthy of further discussion. That version of evolution was Spencerian, or cultural, and it had been lurking within anthropology since the early 1940s, precisely when Brew, Steward, and others were refuting the applicability of Darwinism to cultural phenomena.

The Rebirth of Cultural Evolution

The 1940s witnessed the rebirth of cultural evolution within anthropology (Carneiro 2003; Sanderson 1990), initially at the hands of White (1943, 1945a, 1945b, 1949:363–393) and later with contributions by Steward (1949, 1951, 1953). Not surprisingly, Kroeber was not impressed, and he and White exchanged broadsides into the late 1950s (Kroeber 1946, 1960; White 1945a, 1945b, 1947b, 1959a, 1959b). Several aspects of their exchange are significant in the present context. These do not entail White's famous dictum (later adopted by the processual archaeologists of the 1960s) that culture is humankind's extrasomatic means of adaptation. Similarly, they do not entail the statement (also adopted by processualists) by White (1959b:30) that in his view, history is ideographic and evolution nomothetic (Lyman and O'Brien 2004b). Rather, the important points are that Kroeber's view of culture change was more in line with the materialist ontology, whereas White's was strongly essentialist. Detecting this difference is difficult because of the manner in which the two antagonists distinguished between history and evolution.

Although both conceived of cultural change as involving transmission and heritability and referred to it metaphorically as a flowing stream or continuum, White (1945b) and Kroeber (1935a, 1946) viewed history and evolution very differently. White (1938) viewed specific events as varying formally—structurally and/or functionally—with each event occupying a particular position in the time-space continuum (White 1938). Kroeber (1946) apparently agreed. How these three dimensions—to borrow Spaulding's (1960) term—of form, space, and time were analytically interrelated is how White distinguished between history and evolution: "Events are related to each other spatially, and we may deal with [them] in terms of spatial, or formal, relationships, ignoring the aspect *time*" (White 1938:375). White (1945b:222) later termed this the "formal (functional) process, which presents phenomena in their non-temporal, structural, and functional aspects." Formal-functional aspects of events could be "repetitive," by which White (1945b:229) meant different events as phenomena could have "generic likenesses." In our terms, events could be classified according to a set of ideational units or classes, and thus while each event as a phenomenon occupied a unique time-space position, events in a class shared certain features. A class of event could occur in more than one time-space location.

In White's (1945b:222) view, history concerned "non-repetitive" events: "History is that way of sciencing in which events are dealt with in terms of their temporal relationships alone. Each event is unique. The one thing that history never does is repeat itself" (White 1938:374); the "temporal process [history] is a selective arrangement of events according to the principle *time*" (White 1938:376); the historic process is the one "in which specific and severally unique events take place in a purely temporal context" (White 1938:380). White (1945b:222) later referred to the historic process as the "temporal process, being a chronological sequence of unique events, the study of which is history." In our terms, history concerns a set of empirical units—labeled events by White—arranged in a temporal sequence, each event in a particular spatial position. Because events were empirical, they had locations in the time-space continuum.

Evolution, in White's view, was distinct from history: "The temporal-spatial process is an evolutionary, or developmental process. . . . Evolution is temporal-alteration-of-forms" (White 1938:377). The "historic process [dimension] is merely temporal, the evolutionary process is formal as well: it is a *temporal-sequence-of-forms*" (White 1938:379). The evolutionary process involves "new forms grow[ing] out of preceding forms" (White 1938:380). White (1945b:222) later described this as the "temporal-formal process, which presents phenomena as a temporal sequence of forms, the interpretation of which is evolutionism." Evolution was not a "chronological sequence of particular and unique events [this was history], but [rather] a general process of chronological change, a temporal-sequence-of-forms, with the growth of one form out of an earlier, into a later, form" (White 1945b:224). Thus evolution was different than history: "[T]he historic process and the evolutionist process are alike in that both involve temporal sequences. They differ, however, in that the historic process deals with events determined by specific time and space coördinates, in short with *unique* events [empirical units], whereas the evolutionist process is concerned with *classes* of events [ideational units] independent of specific time and place" (White 1945b:230).

Kroeber (1946) could not understand White's distinction between history and evolution. His confusion no doubt arose from several sources, one being that White (1945b:222) indicated both that evolution was "non-repetitive," suggesting that evolutionary events were unique empirical units rather than ideational classes and that evolution concerned "*classes* of events" (our ideational units) (White 1945b:230, 238). Perhaps White merely misspoke here, because it is relatively straightforward to see in the bulk of his discussions that in the formal dimension events were ideational units, in the historical (temporal) dimension events were empirical units, and in the evolutionist view events were ideational. For example, in more than one place White (1945b:239) indicated that historians were interested in "the unique event at a specific time and place," whereas evolutionists were interested in "a class of events."

To Kroeber (1946), history and evolution were one and the same—a point accepted by most biologists today (see discussion and references in Lyman and O'Brien 2004b). In fact, the difference between Kroeber and White was their respective ontology. Kroeber (1946:9) observed that apparently "what White means by evolution is a fixed, necessary, inherent, and predetermined process. . . . White's evolution thus seems to be an unfolding of immanences." By the last we suspect Kroeber meant essentialist units. These kinds of units, and their inevitable "unfolding," were sources of disagreement between Kroeber and White. What White was speaking of is known in biology as the theory of orthogenesis (see Chapter 7 for additional discussion of this theory), a point that was made by at least one anthropologist and an evolutionary biologist at the time White was writing. Birdsell (1957:399) noted that White was a "modern advocate of the orthogenetic evolution of culture." In the hands of Spencer, Morgan, and Tylor, the orthogenetic evolution of cultures was a "single inflexible and limited theory of culture change [that had] left scars on 20th century anthropology. . . . [An] unreasonable amount of time and energy had been spent [by White and Steward] on beating [this] dead and specialized theory of evolution" (Birdsell 1957:399). Why was Birdsell so concerned?

Dobzhansky (1957:382–383), in a companion article to Birdsell's, noted that orthogenetic evolution consisted of

> "unfolding or manifestation of pre-existing rudiments"; there is in it nothing accidental or creative [no mutation], for evolution "proceeds

in accordance with laws," through a predetermined sequence of stages or phases. . . . Theories of orthogenesis represent evolution as unfolding of pre-existing but latent forms [Kroeber's immanences]. . . . [An] idea popular among believers in orthogenesis is that the evolution of most phyletic lines tends towards evolutionary senility and extinction. If we were to accept this idea then all we can hope to do for our descendants is to postpone the inevitable.

When discussing his view of evolution, White repeatedly said that "new forms grow out of preceding forms" (1938:380, 1945b:224, 1947b:175), that the evolutionary process was lawlike (1949, 1959b), and that the sequence of stages was inevitable in the sense that all societies would eventually represent civilizations, whether they all were at one time chiefdoms or not (1947b, 1959b).

It is not difficult to perceive orthogenesis in White's (1943) seminal discussion of his view of cultural evolution. Essentialism is even easier to see in his discussion of evolutionary stages. "For those who recognize that one form grows out of another, the concept of stages will be found useful as a descriptive, interpretative, and evaluative device. . . . [Stages] serve to mark off steps in development. . . . Stages are merely the succession of significant forms in the developmental process" (White 1947b:179). White never stated what made a stage "significant," but no doubt it was the fact that ontologically it was a real, essentialist category. Steward's (1955:89) "cultural core" and "cultural type" were also essentialist units. Every anthropologist recognized a hunter-gatherer economy or tribal-level social organization or the like; these sorts of anthropological phenomena must therefore be real (recall Morgan and Tylor's "savagery-barbarism-civilization" categories). When they occurred in particular combinations—and they seemed to covary in nonrandom fashion—they comprised a certain evolutionary stage (a point later shown to be fallacious by Leonard and Jones 1987; see also Rambo 1991). This was an essentialistic view. Kroeber and other Boasians could not fathom what White was talking about because they held a more materialistic view, even though they seldom recognized that the materialist paradox consistently tended to thwart their explanatory efforts.

The cultural evolutionary process was another matter of some concern. Despite White's (1943:339) disclaimer that he was not saying that "man deliberately set about to improve his culture," close reading of what he says indicates that he strongly believed all organisms, including humans, had an "urge" to improve and that this was the "motive force as well as the means of cultural evolution." White (1943:339) thus proclaimed that the "culturologist knows more about cultural evolution than the biologist, even today, knows about biological evolution."

White (1947b:177) also regularly indicated that he and other cultural evolutionists "did not identify evolution with progress [and that they] did not believe progress was inevitable." But by default, cultural evolution was synonymous with progress: "[B]y and large, in the history of human culture, progress and evolution *have gone hand in hand*" (White 1943:339). The key evolutionary mechanism—urge or necessity as a motive force—demanded no reference to a source of variation, to natural selection, or to the shape of lineages— all of which are of critical interest in Darwinian evolution. In White's view, every human invented new tools as necessary, which were always better than the preceding tools because they allowed the procurement or exploitation of additional energy. White (1947b:187) wrote:

> The best single index [of progress] by which all cultures can be measured, is *amount of energy harnessed per capita per year*. This is the common denominator of all cultures. . . . Culture advances as the amount of energy harnessed per capita increases. The criterion for the evaluation of cultures is thus an objective one. The measurements can be expressed in mathematical terms. The goal—security and survival—is likewise objective; it is the one that all species, man included, live by. Thus we are able to speak of cultural progress objectively and in a manner which enriches our understanding of the culture history of mankind tremendously. And finally, we can evaluate cultures and arrange them in a series from lower to higher. This follows, of course, from the establishment of a scientifically valid criterion of value and means of measurement.

What gave White's evolution its distinctive saltational form was his belief that change could occur in only two ways. Either improve the efficiency of old tools or invent new tools. Evolution via the former was limited, however, such as is exemplified in White's (1943:343) statement that the "extent to which man may harness natural forces [energy] in animal husbandry is limited" and his later statement that "some progress can of course be made by increasing the efficiency of the technological means of putting energy to work, but there is a limit to the extent of cultural advance on this basis" (White 1959b:369). This is another expression of orthogenetic evolution.

Technological revolutions were important and resulted in "tremendous" changes, "extremely rapid" progress, and "great cultural advances" (White 1945b:342, 344). Such breakthroughs gave cultural evolution its jerky, discontinuous appearance. The other sort of change—improvement of the efficiency of existing tools—produced "no fundamental difference" (White 1945b:344). To Kroeber, the evolution of a cultural lineage was continuous and slow, like a gradually ascending ramp (Figure 2.6); to White, cultural evolution was not a ramp but a staircase, perhaps with each step at a slight incline to reflect the fact that existing technology was constantly being improved, but the risers were most significant because they represented the technological (or economic) breakthroughs and the fundamental differences between what came to be referred to as stages (see Chapter 7 for additional discussion of the kind of unit a cultural stage was thought to be).

Archaeologists opted for White's version, with its cultural stasis punctuated by relatively abrupt change, because it showed that cultural change was discontinuous, thereby fitting the discontinuous nature of change evidenced by stratigraphically superposed artifact assemblages (Lyman et al. 1997b; Chapter 8). This in turn fit well with White's (1947b:175) notion that, as a cultural evolutionist, an archaeologist "would begin, naturally, with the present, with what we have before us. Then we would arrange other forms in the series in accordance with their likeness or dissimilarity to the present form. . . . Stratigraphy is often involved here."

Cultural Anthropology and Evolution in the 1950s

In 1953 Steward reiterated the usual objections to the application of Darwinian evolution to cultural phenomena:

> [C]ultural evolution is an extension of biological evolution only in a chronological sense. The nature of evolutionary schemes and of the developmental processes differs profoundly in biology and culture. In biological evolution it is assumed that all forms are genetically related and that their development is essentially divergent [branching]. . . . In cultural evolution, on the other hand, it is assumed that patterns

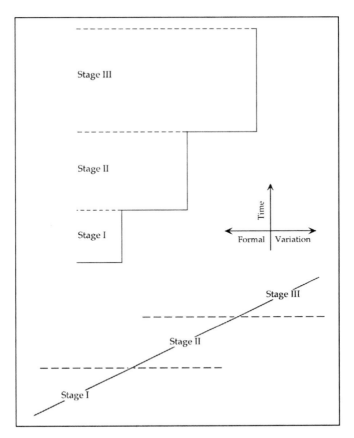

Figure 2.6. A model of essentialist cultural evolution (upper) and a model of materialist Darwinian cultural evolution (lower). In the latter, the term "stage" is metaphorical, and stage boundaries are arbitrarily assigned by the analyst. Time passes from bottom to top, and formal variation changes along the horizontal axis in both; change in the essentialist model is restricted to the boundaries between stages denoted by the dashed lines.

are genetically unrelated and yet pass through parallel and historically independent sequences [Steward 1953:313].

Steward (1953:315) went on to suggest that the use of cultural evolution as an explanatory model demanded two "vitally important assumptions. First, it [assumes] that genuine parallels of form and function develop in historically independent sequences or cultural traditions. Second, it explains those parallels by independent operation of identical causality in each case." Cultural evolution was concerned with generalities of processes and change—

with cross-cultural regularities or laws—and was therefore scientific (Steward 1953; White 1945b, 1959b). These aspects of cultural evolution no doubt are what made it so attractive to the processual archaeologists of the 1960s and 1970s (Lyman and O'Brien 2004b). Culture historians had adopted it a decade earlier (Krieger 1953a, 1953b; South 1955; Spaulding 1955; Willey and Phillips 1955, 1958) because it was the only available alternative. The Darwinian model had been discarded as a result of its conceived inapplicability to cultural phenomena.

The second "assumption" of cultural evolution—that causality was identical in case after case and did not involve natural selection—was part of the orthogenetic version of evolution. Steward (1953, 1955, 1956) advocated multilinear evolution as distinct from what he characterized as the unilinear evolution of White, but there really was little significant difference, as White repeatedly (1945b, 1959a, 1959b) indicated (see also Sanderson 1990). Steward, we suspect, never had White's distinction of history and evolution clear in his mind, just as Kroeber had not. But Steward, like White, saw "order" (Steward 1956:73) in cultural evolution; this was typically glossed as "progress"—a notion that several individuals have argued is inappropriate in the biological and cultural realms (Dunnell 1988; Mayr 1982, 1991).

Such notions were reinforced by some biologists writing in the mid-twentieth century. For example, Huxley (1956) implied that because cultural evolution was superorganic and involved the psycho-social realm, it could be directed by human intent. Simpson (1949:344–345, 1961a) agreed. Huxley also reinforced White's views that (1) "every biological improvement appears eventually to reach a limit," such that coincident with the time the first culture-bearing hominids appeared, "biological evolution on this planet had reached the limit of its advance" (Huxley 1956:6)—this is orthogenesis (Chapter 7); (2) "evolution includes advance, or improvement in organization" (Huxley 1956:5)—this is progressionism; and (3) in cultural evolution, just as in biological evolution, "major advance proceeds by large steps, each marked by the spread of the successful new type of organization" (Huxley 1956:10)—this is essentialism. Evolution was saltational and consisted of one dominant type or group being "replaced" by another "related but improved type" (Huxley 1956:6).

Kroeber (1960:15) agreed with how Huxley (1956) distinguished between biological and cultural evolution. Huxley (1956:3) indicated that he did "not believe that any purely biological concepts and principles can be immediately applied or directly transferred to anthropology"—a notion that was strong in Kroeber's (and Boas's and Steward's) thinking from the start. Kroeber also appreciated that Huxley made several other observations that were in line with his own thinking:

- "The evolutionary approach in anthropology has been bedeviled by false starts and false premises—notably the erroneous idea that biological evolution could be represented by a single straight line of inevitable progress, [and this created] an evolutionary strait-jacket for culture" (Huxley 1956:15).
- Culture was not only that which was transmitted, it was also the mechanism of transmission and thus of reproduction (Huxley 1956:9).
- "Evolution still works in man, but overwhelmingly as a cultural, not a biological process. . . . [C]ultural (psycho-social) evolution shows the same main features as biological evolution." Cultures advance, progress, diverge, and stabilize, but the mechanisms of change are different, and cultures tend to converge, whereas biological evolution involves only divergence (Huxley 1956:23–24).

Huxley's ideas were expressed before explicit recognition within biology of the distinction between the materialist and essentialist ontologies. Recognition of essentialism in biology came initially in the 1950s and was subsequently discussed at length (e.g., Hull 1965; Mayr 1959, 1972, 1982; Simpson 1961b; Sober 1980). The distinction was made explicit in archaeology and anthropology in 1982 (Dunnell 1982). What happened in American archaeology in the 1950s?

Archaeology and Evolution in the 1950s

That culture historians adopted cultural evolution as an explanatory framework in the 1950s is evidenced by papers such as Krieger's (1953b), in which four adaptational stages are described. The abhorrence of anything evolutionary prompted Willey and Phillips (1958:67) to label Krieger's (1953b) set of stages and a similar one proposed a few years earlier by Steward (1949) as "historical-developmental schemes." They proposed their own developmental scheme in what would become—with the later substitution of PaleoIndian for Lithic—a well-known set of terms for five stages: Lithic, Archaic, Formative,

Classic, and Postclassic (see Lyman and O'Brien 2001 for additional discussion). They noted that their scheme had been derived "from an inspection of archaeological sequences throughout the hemisphere," and in an extremely important statement they concluded that the stages were "abstractions which *describe* culture change through time in native America. The stages are not formulations which *explain* culture change" (Willey and Phillips 1958:200).

With respect to Willey and Phillips's scheme, Swanson (1959:121) observed that "no theory has been developed. What is *assumed* is an evolutionary theory about the nature of culture, though Willey and Phillips are shy about admitting this. Moreover, no history has been written." The parallels between Willey and Phillips's scheme and White's notions of cultural evolution are clear from both the assumed (orthogenetic) theory and the lack of history, in White's sense of the term, inherent in Willey and Phillips's scheme. Another parallel is found in the fact that Willey and Phillips characterize their developmental scheme of stages as descriptive rather than explanatory; recall that Bidney (1946) characterized White's scheme as lacking explanatory power. White no doubt would counter with the claim that his model included explanatory capabilities because it included the capture of more energy or more efficient energy capture as a critical process. Bidney may have been worried that White was unclear if energy capture was the cause or the effect of change; casting human intent as the catalyst—as White does—renders this point irrelevant. Alternatively, Bidney's concern may have been that an intended or planned change in energy capture might be construed as the proximate cause of cultural change; if so, this left the ultimate cause unidentified. In Darwinism, ultimate causes "are causes that have a history and that have been incorporated into the system through many thousands of generations of natural selection" (Mayr 1961:1053).

White's students took up his banner. Sahlins and Service (1960) sought to clarify, solidify, and expand various issues. Of most concern here is their distinction of general and specific evolution. The former was defined as "passage from less to greater energy transformation, lower to higher levels of integration, and less to greater all-around adaptability. Specific evolution is the phylogenetic, ramifying, historic passage of culture along its many lines, the adaptive modification of particular cultures" (Sahlins 1960:38). Given his admission that the five developmental stages he had proposed earlier with Phillips were not explanatory, it is not surprising that Willey (1961:442) found general evolution to be of little use because "its processes are obscure"; it was descriptive rather than explanatory, so explicit incorporation of particular evolutionary processes was unnecessary. Specific evolution was useful, however, because it combined "history plus explanation of process—the story of how a given culture, or culture continuum, changed through time by the processes of its adaptations to natural and superorganic environments" (Willey 1961:442). Continuing, Willey (1961:443) noted that "until the processes of this general evolution are better understood, particularly as these pertain to the way in which the many streams of specific evolution feed into the main one, I cannot appreciate the difference between a general universal evolution of culture and a general universal culture history."

Cultural Evolution or Biological Evolution?

Shortly after archaeologists had abandoned a materialist ontology and its attendant model of evolution, Haag (1959:104) perceptively observed that

> the usual reason for the rejection [by anthropologists and archaeologists] of the biological model [of evolution] is either, a) that genetic mutations create "new materials" whereas human mutations (inventions) do not; or b) that man can control and direct his evolution whereas animal mutations are random. . . . Once the understanding of the nature of culture is gained, there is no longer any confusion between the genetic process in [biology] and the culture process in man.

Haag hit the nail squarely on the head as far as most anthropologists and archaeologists were concerned; there really were two kinds of evolution—one biological and one cultural—and a different theory was needed for each. Haag's views of what cultural evolution entailed were no different than those of his contemporaries: a decidedly Spencerian and Whitean approach, complete with orthogenetic notions of progress, human intent, essentialist stages, and the like, and lacking any appeal to a materialistic conception of variation.

That Spencerian and Darwinian evolution are dissimilar is clear. American archaeologists and cultural anthropologists of the early twentieth century appear to have recognized at least some of the differences between the two: cultural evolution was reticulate, whereas biological evolution was only branching; cultural evolution did not involve the transmission of genes, whereas biological evolution did; and people were not subject to the forces of natural selection because they intentionally directed the evolution of their cultures, whereas biological evolution depended on the natural selection of random mutations. Spencerian evolution avoided these problems, but it lacked a developed conception of cultural transmission that could be readily adapted to the metaphor of culture change as a gradually, continuously flowing braided stream. This is evident by the fact that the analytical unit of choice of early twentieth-century anthropologists—culture traits (Chapter 3)—were units of cultural transmission, yet minimal theory of that kind of transmission was constructed. Further, traits were viewed largely from the essentialist ontology; typological thinking was rampant. We turn in the next chapter to a detailed consideration of culture traits. The poor conceptualization of these units exemplifies the weakly developed nature of a theory of cultural transmission during the time when most artifact-based chronometers were being developed by archaeologists.

II. The Epistemology of Measurement Units

As we noted in Chapter 1, epistemology is the branch of philosophy that concerns knowledge claims, particularly how methodology is driven by theory. But we also noted that ontology influences beliefs about the kinds of units that are thought to attend various methods. Cultural anthropology during the time when the culture history approach to the archaeological record was popular—approximately 1915 to 1950—focused largely on units termed cultural traits or cultural elements. In Chapter 3 we show that these units were in fact often treated as if they were units of cultural transmission very much like genes are the units of biological transmission. The spatial and temporal distributions of cultural traits could be tracked and mapped and had to be if one was to write the history of a culture, which was little more than a particular set of traits with a particular set of spatial and temporal coordinates. Because archaeologists (and anthropologists in general) working between 1915 and 1950 conceived of artifacts as "material culture," and because cultural traits could be kinds of artifacts, it was easy to interpret artifact types in exactly the same way as cultural traits. Artifact types were treated like empirical manifestations of the units of cultural transmission; their spatial and temporal distributions could be mapped. The vague and poorly understood equation between an artifact type and, say, a cultural ideal or norm—what Binford (1965) would later refer to as "normative theory"—elicited little comment other than the implicit recognition that artifact types, if designed correctly, behaved (had spatio-temporal distributions) as if they were accurate reflections of norms (Lyman and O'Brien 2004a).

The struggle to develop artifact-based chronometers that consistently and validly measured time (and, by implication, cultural transmission) involved a major effort directed toward unit construction on the part of culture historians. Sometimes the units seemed to be found over long durations of time; other times the units seemed to occupy short periods. Add to this a similar range of variation in how they were distributed over space, and it is no wonder that culture historians often stumbled as they grappled with measuring formal variation in artifacts in such a way as to create units that reflected the passage of time. To help illustrate this, and to underscore how ontology can influence results, Chapter 4 presents an integrative model of the three dimensions of (more or less continuous) variation in form, space, and time identified by Willey (1953a; see Chapter 1). The model shows how that variation might be carved up into units that are analytically useful to archaeological chronometers and why some units might not be so useful. The model is compared to an early one used in a paleontological chronometer designed by Charles Lyell, sometimes given the title of "father of modern geology" (e.g., Camardi 1999). One of the startling things that emerges in this chapter is that even though Lyell did not believe in evolution when he designed the chronometer—at the time, he thought species were fixed entities—his chronometer depended on a form of overlapping identical to that underpinning the direct historical approach, introduced in Chapter 4 and discussed in detail in Chapter 7, and frequency seriation, introduced in Chapter 4 and discussed in detail in Chapter 5, where it is contrasted with time-series analysis.

Overlapping is critical to many, but not all (Chapter 6), artifact-based chronometers. Although never explicitly defined in the literature on archaeological chronometry, we argue in Chapter 4 that it was knowledge of the principle of overlapping that ultimately drove Nels Nelson to excavate stratigraphically in 1915. That principle holds that cultural traits and artifact types that are shared across—overlap—multiple aggregates of traits and types arranged in a temporal sequence are shared because they (or at least the concept[s] behind them) were culturally transmitted. Overlapping thus denotes heritable continuity affected by cultural transmission. Importantly, it also allows one to measure time as a continuous variable—one that has an infinite number of values that fall between any two values. A discontinuous variable is sometimes referred to as a discrete variable; it is one that has no additional value between any two values. As will become clear in the chapters that follow, it is rather easy to carve up a continuous variable (such as time) such that it appears discontinuous if one uses units that are of sufficiently coarse resolution. Chronometers we describe in Chapters 4 and 5 measure time as a continuous variable; the chronometric unit we describe in Chapter 6 tends to measure time as a discontinuous variable (as does stratigraphic excavation, described in Chapter 8). We include Chapters 4, 5, and 6 in this section on the epistemology of measurement units because they focus mostly on the units that result in whether time is measured continuously or discontinuously rather than on the chronometer.

In Chapter 5 we continue to explore how units influence artifact-based chronometers. In that chapter we show that A. L. Kroeber used two rather different kinds of units in his analyses of culture change. When he invented frequency seriation, he was interested in a chronometer that measured time as nonrepetitive or linear. Time units had to be distinctive, just like the year AD 1000 is distinct from AD 1001, and both of these are distinct from AD 1002 and from AD 2000, and so on. But when Kroeber sought evidence that cultural change was somehow cyclical (perhaps not unlike a spiral staircase, always progressing [upward] but never really moving [laterally]), he used time units that were repetitive, like January, February, March, and so on. Such units would cycle back through and not be distinguishable from previous Januarys, Februarys, and so on. In carefully choosing his units, Kroeber was clever, perhaps without realizing it and certainly without explicitly admitting it, because the units he chose did precisely what they were supposed to do. Where Kroeber initially erred with his notion that culture change was perpetual but cyclical was in failing to realize that unit choice influenced results, and thus he had not really tested his notion of cyclical change. He eventually abandoned this notion.

Chapter 6 concludes the theme of units influencing chronometry by describing how culture historian James Ford built types that occupied brief spans of time yet had large spatial distributions, or what are readily categorized as marker types for the brief time spans they signify. These were rather the opposite of the units Kroeber and Ford used in frequency seriation and percentage stratigraphy (Chapters 8 and 9), respectively. In Chapter 6 the integrative model of form-space-time introduced in Chapter 4 is modified and expanded to include units that model Ford's marker types. In light of that modeling, it is not surprising that when these units are used in a frequency seriation, many of them do not work as well as units like those in Kroeber's seminal frequency seriation. This result corroborates the linkages between ontology, units, and epistemology.

3. Cultural Traits as Units of Analysis in Early Twentieth-Century Anthropology

As indicated in Chapter 2, the focus of culture-historical study was on the evolutionary development of cultures, so heritable continuity between cultures had to at least be assumed if not demonstrated. This demanded a unit of heritability or transmission analogous to biology's gene. During the first half of the twentieth century, "cultural trait" and the synonymous "cultural element" were commonly used as labels for units of cultural transmission (and hence were analogous to genes), but neither the process of transmission nor the "thing" being transmitted was discussed within the context of a theory of cultural transmission. Most anthropologists provided commonsensical remarks about the unit and used it to determine something about the "development of American Indian cultures and tribal groups" (Bennett 1944:162).

Modern researchers have proposed names for units of cultural transmission—"meme" (Aunger 1999, 2000, 2002; Blackmore 1999, 2000; Dawkins 1976) and "culturgen" (Lumsden and Wilson 1981) being two of the better-known terms—but there is little consensus today as to what the units entail (Benzon 2002; Williams 2002). Many of the modern difficulties involved in understanding the nature of the units and their role in cultural transmission have their roots in late nineteenth- and early twentieth-century anthropology. In this chapter we focus on cultural traits as units of cultural transmission. We begin by distinguishing between two kinds of analytical units, the conflation of which has long made it difficult to operationalize the concept of cultural trait. We next summarize what was said about cultural transmission prior to about 1940 and then turn our attention to various statements made by ethnologists about cultural traits. Our coverage is limited primarily to the late nineteenth century and the first two-thirds of the twentieth century. This allows us to examine the work of Edward B. Tylor, Franz Boas, and A. L. Kroeber, all of whom had profound intellectual impacts on how cultural traits were conceived of, formulated, and used.

Kinds of Analytical Units

As we indicated in Chapter 2, if our interest is in the historical development of cultures, then our explanatory theory should include consideration of cultural transmission, and the theory's analytical units should comprise units of transmission. To help us understand how early anthropologists thought about cultural traits as culturally transmitted entities, we need to elaborate a distinction between two kinds of units that we made in Chapter 2. Empirical units are things that can be seen and held, such as a fossil tooth or a ceramic jar. Empirical units have properties, and we use ideational units to measure them. Ideational units such as centimeters do not exist in any empirical sense, but they do exist in a conceptual sense. As such, they are useful for measuring properties of empirical units (Dunnell 1971; Lyman and O'Brien 2002; O'Brien and Lyman 2002). Those properties or characters can exist at any scale. The character "width" is a property that can be measured with ideational units termed centimeters. A jar with a 0.8-cm-wide lip is an empirical unit, and so is a 1.5-cm-wide fossil tooth. Ideational units can be descriptional, used merely to characterize a thing, or they can be theoretical, created for specific analytical purposes.

Ideational units can be derived either intensionally or extensionally. An intensional definition comprises the necessary and sufficient conditions for membership in a unit; it explicitly lists the definitive character states that a phenomenon must display to be identified as a member of the unit. The phenomenon will exhibit states of other characters, but those are nondefinitional (descriptive) and hence are ignored. The definitive character states of theoretical units are drawn from theory. We may specify three classes of rim angle for ceramic jars—1–30 degrees, 31–60 degrees, and 61–90 degrees— based on a theory of vessel function that indicates some angles are necessary for some functions, whereas other angles are necessary for other functions. We may never find specimens with rim angles of 31–60 degrees, but the fact that something might not exist has no bearing on unit construction.

As opposed to an intensional definition, which is imposed on empirical specimens, an extensional definition is derived by enumerating select character states shared by a unit's members. The definitive criteria are literally an extension of observed character states of specimens in a group. The definition of a group is written after the group is created, and thus the definitive criteria are seldom theoretically informed in an explicit manner. Because the unit definitions depend on the specimens examined, three problems result (Lyman and O'Brien 2002; O'Brien and Lyman 2002). First, the distinction between definitive character states and descriptive ones is seldom explicit. Second, the fact that a set of phenomena can be sorted into piles and a definition of an average specimen in each pile can be written reinforces the notion that the piles are somehow real rather than analytical products. Third, there is no guarantee that the resulting units will be of the same scale. Some may be defined by one character, others by two characters, others by three, and so on. As a result, some units will be general and inclusive, whereas others will be specific and exclusive (Lyman and O'Brien 2002, 2003). All three problems are found in early discussions of cultural traits.

Cultural Transmission

A major research focus at the end of the nineteenth century and for the first several decades of the twentieth century was "historical ethnology" (Goldenweiser 1925; Radin 1933). Research cast in this mold had as its goal the reconstruction of the historical development of particular cultures. Cultural transmission played a critical role in the history of each culture and was discussed in commonsensical terms. During the first half of the twentieth century, culture was viewed as being largely a mental phenomenon (Boas 1891; Kluckhohn and Kelly 1945; Tylor 1871), and the transmission of culture was viewed as involving the movement of ideas from person to person (Bruner 1956; Spaulding 1955). This view has several important implications that are exemplified by a sample of the literature of the first half of the twentieth century. First, language is critical to efficient and accurate cultural transmission (Bidney 1944). Second, what is transmitted is a cultural trait, whether in the form of an idea or an object (Barnett 1940, 1942; Boas 1904, 1924; Driver 1973; Kluckhohn and Kelly 1945; Kroeber 1940; Linton 1936; Malinowski 1931; Murdock 1940; Wissler 1923). Third, culture is not inherited like genes; rather, culture is "acquired," typically by learning but also by "borrowing" and "mimicking" (Bruner 1956; Kroeber 1923a; Murdock 1932, 1940; Redfield et al. 1936; Tylor 1871; Willey 1929; Wissler 1916d, 1917a, 1923). Fourth, cultural transmission can take several paths, all of which can lead to similarities among cultures (Boas 1909, 1924; Steward 1929). Fifth, cultural transmission can be from genetic ancestor to genetic descendant, but it can also be between genetically unrelated individuals (Kroeber 1923a; Murdock 1932). Sixth, cultural transmission results in the accumulation of culture. This accumulation is never ending. Whereas the number of genes an organism has is finite—despite the number of transmission events (generations) leading up to its production—there is no such limit on the number of ideas that an individual human can have (Kroeber 1923a; Murdock 1932).

Early Views on Cultural Traits

In his introduction to Stanislaw Klimek's (1935) statistical analysis of cultural traits, Kroeber (1935b:1) remarked that "culture elements or traits . . . have long been in ethnological employ without criticism on methodological grounds, so far as I know." He pointed out that Wissler (1916b, 1917a, 1927, 1928; see also Kroeber 1931a) had used them to formulate culture areas, which Kroeber also had recently done (Driver 1962). To Wissler, a culture was characterized by the "enumeration of its observable traits," and a cultural trait was "a unit in the tribal culture" that included artifacts, "mannerisms," and "concepts" (Wissler 1923:50).

Otis Mason (1886, 1890, 1895, 1896) had discussed similarities and differences in what he variously termed "arts" or "inventions" across different geographic areas that approximated what would become Wissler's cultural areas. For Mason (1895:101), "arts" included "words, industries, social structures, customs, folk-tales, beliefs and divinities." Inventions included "useful and decorative arts, language, literatures, social fabrics, laws, customs, fashions, creeds and cults" (Mason 1890:3). For Mason (1896:639), arts were cultural traits: "By arts of life are meant all those activities which are performed by means of that large body of objects usually called apparatus, implements, tools, utensils, machines, or mechanical powers, in the utilization of force derived from the human body, from animals, and from natural agencies, such as gravity, wind, fire, steam, electricity, and the like." An art, then, was something cultural that could comprise an "activity," an idea ("social structure"), or what today we would consider an artifact. Archaeologist William Henry Holmes (1903) used the term "arts" in the same way Mason had. For both, an "art" was a generic, somewhat inclusive trait.

Like most of their contemporaries, Wissler and Mason defined cultural traits extensionally on the basis of observed behaviors and artifacts. Given that cultural traits had long been used by ethnologists, we suspect that Mason and Wissler did not find it necessary to devote much effort to discussing their epistemological basis. A major part of that basis is found in the writings of Tylor and Boas, who in the late nineteenth and early twentieth centuries laid major portions of the foundation for the use of cultural traits as analytical units.

Edward B. Tylor

Edward B. Tylor (1871) typically used the terms "institutions" and "customs" for what later would be termed cultural traits. This is illustrated by his concept of "survivals," defined as "processes, customs, opinions, and so forth which have been carried on by force of habit into a new state of society different from that in which they had their original home, and they thus remain as proofs and examples of an older condition of culture out of which a new has been evolved" (Tylor 1871:16; see also Lowie 1918). Tylor's (1889:246) interest in what he termed "adhesions," or customs that "accompany" one another, also reflected his use of cultural traits.

Tylor did not define what kind of unit a survival or an adhesion was, although in practice they seem to have been empirical manifestations of behaviors. This is reflected in two ways in *Primitive Culture*. First, Tylor (1871:7) instructed the analyst to "dissect" civilization "into its details, and to classify these in their proper groups" for comparison. The details could include weapons such as spears, clubs, bows and arrows; textile arts such as matting and netting; myths on various topics such as eclipses and place names; and ritual practices such as sacrifices to spirits. Definitions of categories of cultural traits were derived extensionally from observable phenomena, whether artifacts or behaviors. Second, cultural traits were empirical because they were like "species of plants and animals" (Tylor 1871:8), paralleling the views of contemporary naturalists that species were real entities waiting to be discovered (Mayr 1969). "To the ethnographer," Tylor (1871:8) continued,

> the bow and arrow is a species, the habit of flattening children's skulls is a species, the practice of reckoning numbers by tens is a species. The geographical distribution of these things, and their transmission from region to region, have to be studied as the naturalist studies

the geography of his botanical and zoological species. . . . Just as the catalogue of all the species of plant and animals of a district represents its Flora and Fauna, so the list of all the items of the general life of a people represents that whole which we call its culture.

Franz Boas

Franz Boas (1904:517, 519) used the terms "elements" and "traits of culture" in much the same way that Wissler would. He also discussed "the theory of [the] independent origin" of elements and "their transmission from one part of the world to another" (Boas 1904:519). In an early study of folklore, Boas (1896a) applied his training in geography to study the distributions of cultural traits "for purposes of historical interpretation" (Lowie 1956:1003). Boas (1896a:3–4), in fact, provided the interpretive algorithm for such studies when he wrote, "the nearer the people, the greater the number of common elements; the farther apart, the less the number"; and "similarity between two tales . . . is more likely to be due to dissemination [diffusion] than to independent origin." He was concerned about the psychological basis of culture and believed that empirical culture phenomena were the products of ideas.

Boas (1891) had earlier described how to contend with the fact that in the Americas, one had to study present-day (spoken) folklore in the absence of written history. Boas added his own twist to Tylor's comparative method when he defined the analytical unit of the method, terming it an "element" and noting that "a single element may consist of a number of incidents which are very closely connected and still form one idea" (Boas 1891:14). Here "incidents" are the empirical specimens that are manifestations of ideas, and the latter are ideational units termed "elements." This distinction between elements as ideas and their empirical manifestations as myths or tales was not made in Boas's (1896a) later study. In subsequent studies of variation in decorative motifs, Boas (1903, 1908) extended the concept—without explicit mention of the term "element"—to material items such as moccasins, parfleches, baskets, and needle cases. That similarity in the form of geographically or temporally separated artifacts, particularly the "style" of their decoration, was evidence of social transmission was made clear when Boas (1909:536) remarked that a continuous distribution of formally similar artifacts "suggests very strongly that a line of migration or of cultural contact may have extended" over the area in question. This became an interpretive algorithm not only of anthropology in general but of Americanist archaeology in particular (Lyman et al. 1997b). What went largely unremarked was that the unit of transmission was actually an idea or a concept that had empirical manifestation as a form of artifact or of one or more character states thereof. This point was made by the architects of another school of thought.

German Diffusionism

Parallel to Wissler's age-area model of cultural history was a developing body of diffusion theory in Germany known as *Kulturkreislehre* (e.g., Graebner 1905, 1911). Its goal involved "explaining the totality of culture history in time and space through the identification and spread of trait complexes, groups of culture elements that are empirically found in association with each other. The theory [rested on] the hypothesis that cultural history can be traced back to a number of distinct cultural centers as opposed to one single locus of origin [and that] these centers spread through trait complexes, not individual traits" (Golbeck 1980:230). Boas (1911) correctly pointed out that there was a permanence to the units employed by the diffusionists in their identification of *Kulturkreise*, or "culture circles." A "fundamental" tenet of the theory was "that a given cultural element, or a complex of traits, can retain its identity while being passed from one people to another over the principal parts of the earth's inhabited surface" (Herskovits 1945:147). Fritz Graebner (1905) referred to such static traits as "type fossils." This was not a part of the Boasian view, which held that diffused traits typically were modified in order to be integrated into the recipient culture (Boas 1911). Not surprisingly, then, given the diffusionist view of static traits, Boas (1930:104) noted that diffusionist theory minimized the "possibility of the independent origin of similar ideas." We approve of Boas's use of the word "idea" because this was exactly how the diffusionists viewed the traits they used—as ideas—but they were often at very general and rather inclusive scales.

In an insightful study of the *Kulturkreise* school and its attendant methods, Clyde Kluckhohn (1936) made three points that are of interest here. First, he noted that most ethnologists failed to understand that for the diffusionists, traits were rather general ideas, not specific empirical units. Second, the definitions of cultural traits were "inevitably somewhat subjective." Third, the creation of units—what he referred to as "atomization"—often "does real violence to the cultural phenomena in question" (Kluckhohn 1936:170).

Kluckhohn's points concern matters of classification and scale. Ralph Linton (1936:400) echoed the concern for classification when he remarked, "definitions and classifications are among the most valuable tools for the research worker, and anthropology is still sadly lacking in both." Similarly, Homer Barnett (1940:21) observed, "too often we deal in catchwords and arbitrary categories which are useless as tools and of uncertain value for purposes of classification." Although the significance of classification was recognized, few attempted to deal with it.

A. L. Kroeber and Culture-Element Distributions

A. L. Kroeber was one of the few anthropologists to grapple with problems of classification and scale of cultural traits, but prior to so doing his interest was solely in studying their distributions (Kroeber 1904, 1908, 1917b, 1923b). An example of how he did this is shown in Figure 3.1, taken directly from one of his publications (Kroeber 1923b). He provided no caption, but in the associated text he indicated that the "idea of this diagram is to suggest geographical relations by horizontal arrangement, temporal relations by vertical disposition" (Kroeber 1923b:128). Kroeber (1923b:128) noted that the "genetic assumption which underlies the arrangement of elements in the diagram is that, other things equal, widely distributed traits are likely to be ancient; locally limited ones, of more recent origin," a necessary assumption of the age-area notion (Kroeber 1931a). Kroeber (1923b:128) bemoaned the fact that graphs such as Figure 3.1 included but "a fraction of those [cultural traits] that might have been chosen." Perhaps in part for this reason, Kroeber and his students and collaborators undertook statistical analyses of successively longer lists of traits with the intention of formalizing and making more objective the analytical protocol of historical ethnology (Bennett 1944).

Statistical Analyses

In 1926 three of Kroeber's students (Clements, Schenck, and Brown 1926) proposed a technique for strengthening and systematizing the study of distributions of cultural traits. They applied chi-square analysis to 282 traits distributed across several Pacific islands. Those islands that shared many traits were thought to have "affiliations" with one another. Wilson Wallis (1928:95) expressed concern over the method and "the weight to be attached to common traits which have similar specific forms in two or more groups" and suggested that whether a trait was "generic" or "specific" would influence efforts to

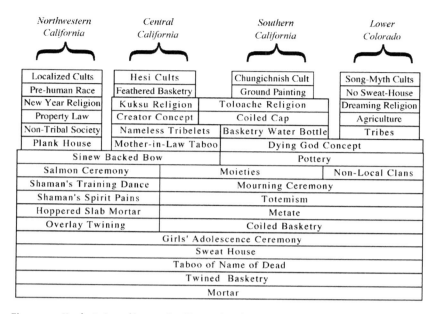

Northwestern California	Central California	Southern California	Lower Colorado
Localized Cults	Hesi Cults	Chungichnish Cult	Song-Myth Cults
Pre-human Race	Feathered Basketry	Ground Painting	No Sweat-House
New Year Religion	Kuksu Religion	Toloache Religion	Dreaming Religion
Property Law	Creator Concept	Coiled Cap	Agriculture
Non-Tribal Society	Nameless Tribelets	Basketry Water Bottle	Tribes
Plank House	Mother-in-Law Taboo	Dying God Concept	
Sinew Backed Bow		Pottery	
Salmon Ceremony	Moieties		Non-Local Clans
Shaman's Training Dance	Mourning Ceremony		
Shaman's Spirit Pains	Totemism		
Hoppered Slab Mortar	Metate		
Overlay Twining	Coiled Basketry		
Girls' Adolescence Ceremony			
Sweat House			
Taboo of Name of Dead			
Twined Basketry			
Mortar			

Figure 3.1. Kroeber's (1923b) example of how cultural traits can be plotted in time and space to detect historical development of culture areas. Each rectangle contains a cultural trait. Geographic space varies along the horizontal axis, and Kroeber suggested that time passes along the vertical axis.

detect diffusion. Here Wallis was calling attention to the scale of a trait. A generic trait is one that is general and inclusive (recall W. H. Holmes's use of the term "art" as a sort of generic trait); a specific trait is exclusive and particular. Wallis (1928) believed that a generic trait, whether technologically complex or not, was likely to have a wide geographic distribution precisely because it was generalized and inclusive. He also believed that technologically complex traits were likely to be invented only once, and thus their distribution was a result of diffusion.

Forrest Clements (1928:302) replied that a "generic trait" tends to be "composed of simpler traits" and hence "is a complex trait which in turn may be part of a still larger trait complex. Thus it will be seen that unless we are dealing with the simplest units, the question of what is or is not generic is quite relative. The use of generic traits as such, then, is not to be recommended, and in the statistical method it is essential for all traits to be reduced to their simplest elements. That is to say, the sample must consist of *specific* traits only." He then noted that the "more complex the generic trait, the greater will be the number of its specific elements" (Clements 1928:303). These statements beg several questions. First, what is a trait complex? Wissler (1923:52) had earlier implied that a trait complex comprises a number of functionally interrelated traits that are meant to achieve a particular end. Several years later Melville Herskovits (1926:231) suggested that a "culture complex" is made up of a set of cultural traits that merely "go together," which sounds a bit like Tylor's (1889) "adhesions." Herskovits (1945:149) was later explicit about this when he said that complexes are "conglomerates of traits related only in the mind of the student, not in the thinking and behavior of the peoples in whose cultures they are found." Robert Lowie (1920:13) used the term "linked traits" to approximate Tylor's adhesions. In contrast, Edward Sapir (1916:29) indicated that a trait complex is an "assemblage of specific elements [or traits that are] functionally unified, as a rule," a definition preferred by Kroeber (1931b:149). Sapir (1916:52) also noted that "the greater the specialization of function, the more neatly are the parts of a complex apt to be bound together."

It is not surprising that the unit variously termed trait complex or cultural complex would not have a universal meaning, given that the basic unit of cultural trait did not. The confusion was exacerbated by the common perception that cultures were made up of "congeries of disconnected traits, associated only by reason of a series of historic accidents, the elements being functionally unrelated" (Spier 1931a:455). This view is epitomized by Lowie's (1920:441) characterization of a culture as a "planless hodge-podge, that thing of shreds and patches."

Another question begged by Clements's remarks is, what is the finest, least-inclusive scale at which traits can be defined? As Kluckhohn (1939:347) observed, the "degree to which a 'generic trait' is broken down cannot be fully standardized." Driver and Kroeber had addressed this concern when they posed a question and then gave their answer:

> Are our elements or factors, the culture traits, independent of one another? While we are not prepared to answer this question categorically, we believe that culture traits are in the main if not in absolutely all cases independent. Within the limits of ordinary logic or common sense. Essential parts of a trait cannot of course be counted as separate traits: the stern of a canoe, the string of a bow, etc. Even the bow and arrow is a single trait until there is question of an arrow-less bow. Then we have

two traits, the pellet bow and arrow bow. Similarly, while the sinew backing of a bow cannot occur by itself, we legitimately distinguish self-bows and sinew-backed bows; and so, single-curved and recurved bows, radically and tangentially feathered arrows, canoes with blunt, round, or sharp sterns, etc. [Driver and Kroeber 1932:213].

Here Driver and Kroeber were defining the concept of a cultural trait as a minimal functional unit, at least in terms of artifacts. It is unclear what a minimal functional unit of social organization might be. A few pages later they lapsed back into the standard definition of cultural traits as "the smallest units recognizable or definable" (Driver and Kroeber 1932:216).

Kroeber (1908) had earlier used a biological metaphor when discussing the validity of the three culture areas of California mentioned in Figure 3.1. He noted that when compared with one another, the three areas

contrast strongly. But the moment each of these three is considered alone, culturally well-defined groups of tribes are evident within it. This does not weaken the value of the recognition of culture-areas. The genus breaks up when we consider species. Even the species seems no longer a unit when attention is allowed to be given to races. But the differences between genera become insignificant when the family and the order are in view. Neither the order nor the species, the race nor the genus, is, therefore, unimportant or unreliable. A biology recognizing only species is a scientific impossibility; but a biology dealing with nothing lower than genera would be equally impossible. The culture area, broad or minute, has its value, and in fact is indispensable, as a means to an historical understanding of its components; but it has value only so long as its relativity is recognized [Kroeber 1908:286].

Kroeber did not use this biological metaphor when speaking of the scale of cultural traits, perhaps because a minimum functional unit of culture—what he and Driver later proposed—was not so empirically obvious as a species of organism. Cultures, Kroeber (1917b:399) wrote, "are like organisms, which incorporate countless pieces of other organic material not by mechanical aggregation but by assimilation, thus attaining or retaining their own proper entity and organic form. The analysis of culture into its elements, and the tracing back to these individual units, must be the first task of the ethnologist as of the historian." This metaphor was obviously not as well developed as the one used earlier for culture areas, though it may have eventually fed into the notion expressed by Driver and Kroeber (1932) of a minimum functional unit. An individual organism, not its various parts, is the minimum functional unit that can stand alone. One can study pelage color, tail length, reproductive behaviors, and the like among organisms, but those characters are not stand-alone, independently functioning units.

The analytical unit known as a cultural trait was a commonsensical one that required minimal theoretical discussion. Since the 1870s traits had been used to record rapidly disappearing cultural information on American Indians and to write cultural histories in terms of independent invention, diffusion, and affiliation (Driver 1962)—uses that did not demand any explicit theoretical warrant; historical ethnology simply assumed cultural transmission of cultural traits. Thus similar traits suggested a genetic-like relationship between the possessors of the traits. The attitude seems to have been that the units worked analytically, so there was little need to worry about what they actually were or the actual mechanisms of transmission. Nevertheless, there was some discussion of how to operationalize the concept in ethnological settings, where the goal was to record cultural data for purposes of comparative analyses. Salvage ethnography might not require much rigidity in data-recording units, but analytical studies focusing on the similarities of trait lists clearly demanded that the traits be similar from list to list. This is probably what prompted Kroeber to consider the concept of cultural trait more explicitly.

Culture Elements

In his introduction to the first published "Culture Element Distribution" study, Kroeber (1935b:1) remarked that "the question of first importance is whether the elements operated with are justifiable units." Kroeber indicated that to answer that question affirmatively, three conditions had to be satisfied: "First, the elements must be sharply definable. Second, they must be derived empirically, not logically. And third, they must be accepted for use without bias or selection" (Kroeber 1935b:1). The condition of definability was meant to ensure that elements could be differentiated: "[I]t is the equivalent of measurability in other types of material" (Kroeber 1935b:1). The condition of empirical derivation meant that the unit definitions should be extensionally derived from specimens, whether observed artifacts or behaviors, or from informants' testimonies. Kroeber (1935b:2) feared that if elements were defined intensionally (our term), data would be "encountered which do not fit unambiguously into the concepts." Here he failed to keep a description distinct from a definition. The third condition, "nonselection of data, is of course axiomatic in any statistical approach, and should be equally so in any nonstatistical one" (Kroeber 1935b:1). This condition signifies that the elements chosen should be a probabilistic sample of all possible ones.

Initially, Kroeber (1923b) used negative elements (ones that did not exist in a culture) when he listed "No Sweat-Houses" for the Lower Colorado area of California (Figure 3.1). A decade later Kroeber (1935b:2) argued that "negative elements" were not to be included in analysis. Both positions, but particularly the latter, indicate that cultural traits were to be defined extensionally. When arguing against the use of negative traits, Kroeber (1935b:3) noted that this "is really an extension of the principle that procedure must be wholly empirical, never merely logical." Otherwise, culture elements could be "of different cultural weight, 'size,' or importance" (Kroeber 1935b:3). Klimek's (1935) statistical efforts with lists of culture elements had forced Kroeber (1935b:11) and his students to generate "data of greater precision." No longer could an ethnologist simply generate a list of cultural traits; the units had to meet the three conditions Kroeber outlined. No such conditions had been described previously.

Kroeber (1936:101) later defined "culture elements" as the "minimal definable elements of culture." The following year he remarked that an element list "is a plastic thing, which is constructed in larval form from knowledge of a specific ethnography" (Kroeber 1937:1). This statement also suggests that definitions of elements were derived extensionally. Support for this suggestion is found in the fact that each element was thought to be "reliable" when multiple informants independently agreed when asked if an element existed in their culture (Driver 1938:212). (Despite the multiple informant property, many anthropologists were skeptical that cultural elements had emic qualities.) John Bennett (1944:177) pointed out a few years later that many cultural traits were "non-comparable entities," and his discussion makes clear that this was a result of their definitions having been derived extensionally. Such derivation virtually ensured that there was no consistency among units in scale or definition, particularly when different analysts compiled the lists.

Other Efforts and Comments

Few anthropologists of the time would have disagreed with Kroeber's (1937:1) point that culture elements provided "data far more satisfactory for comparative purposes than the customary monographic studies with their large areal gaps, dissimilarities of interest and approach, and poverty of negative statements." Nor would many have disagreed that one goal of anthropology was to answer questions of culture history. Quibbles over the reliability of culture-element data were, however, exacerbated by the fact that no consensus existed on exactly what a cultural trait was in a theoretical sense. We illustrate this by considering the remarks of several individuals who commented on the concept of cultural trait at the same time that Kroeber was developing his culture-element distribution surveys and proposing criteria for cultural traits.

Ralph Linton

Ralph Linton's idea of what cultural traits entail was markedly different than those of many early twentieth-century anthropologists. To him, cultural traits are "arbitrary divisions" (Linton 1936:394). He may have used "arbitrary" to indicate that the traits are not some kind of natural units waiting to be discovered, but in our view he was searching for natural (emiclike) units rather than arbitrary (eticlike) ones. Linton was skeptical about the value that anthropologists routinely attributed to cultural traits. In particular, he noted that "differentiating" among traits "masked the actual interrelations of culture elements and made it extremely difficult for the reader to see them in their proper settings" (Linton 1936:396). Linton argued that a cultural trait has an empirical form, a function, and a meaning within its particular cultural context. Trait lists effectively divorce the traits from their cultural contexts, causing them to lose various of their emic qualities, such as function and very often meaning.

Linton indicated that because traits vary in scale, they can be classified hierarchically (Figure 3.2). He defined traits as "the individual acts and objects which constitute the overt expression of a culture" (Linton 1936:397). But traits "can be analyzed into a number of still smaller [less-inclusive] units" called "items" (Linton 1936:397). For example, to Linton (1936:397), a "bow is a culture trait, yet a comparative study of bows from several different cultures will reveal differences in the sort of wood used, the part of the tree from which the wood is taken, the shape, size, and finish of the completed object, the

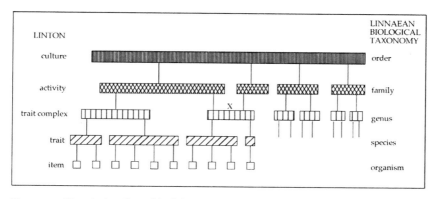

Figure 3.2. Linton's (1936) model of the scale, classification, and interrelationships of cultural traits to one another and to a culture. The structure approximates what is known as an aggregative hierarchy such as the Linnaean biological taxonomy, but it is not a perfect example of such because specimens in categories at lower levels can contribute to multiple units at higher levels of inclusiveness. For example, the trait complex labeled X contributes to two activities; this is not allowed in the Linnaean taxonomy.

method of attaching the string, and the material used for the string. As far as a particular culture is concerned, the bow is a trait; the various details of wood, form, and string are items within a trait."

Traits can be cumulative to form what Linton termed a "trait complex." He adopted the view that traits forming a complex have to be functionally interrelated, and thus "every trait is intimately associated with some other trait or traits to form a larger functional unit commonly known as a *trait complex*. The traits within such a complex are all more or less interrelated and interdependent from the point of view of both function and use" (Linton 1936:397). Linton suggested that multiple trait complexes can be "combined to form a still larger functional unit [termed] an *activity*. Lastly, the sum total of these activities constitutes the complete overt expression of the culture" (Linton 1936:397) (Figure 3.2).

Linton acknowledged two potential problems with his suggested classification scheme. First, the number of levels of inclusiveness can be "expanded almost indefinitely" (Linton 1936:398). He blamed this problem on the subjective judgment of the classifier and the complexity of the phenomena being classified. Linton did not comprehend that taxonomic classification can avoid these problems (Lyman and O'Brien 2002, 2003). That the complexity of the phenomena can create classification problems signifies that the definitions of his items, traits, complexes, and activities were extensionally derived. There was no specification of the scale of an item, nor did he specify the scales of traits, complexes, and activities. He did indicate that the smallest unit pertinent to functional studies is a trait complex because this seemed to be the perception of an "average member of any society" (Linton 1936:403).

The second potential problem with Linton's classification scheme is that traits can occur in more than one complex. In a perfect aggregative hierarchy, such as that represented by the units of the Linnaean biological taxonomy, groups of individuals make up species, groups of species make up genera, groups of genera make up families, and so on. Importantly, each organism is a member of only one species, each species is a member of only one genus, and so on (Valentine and May 1996). Not so in Linton's taxonomy of cultural units (Figure 3.2). Thus "the bow, in addition to its use with the arrow, might be used as part of a fire-making or drilling complex" (Linton 1936:399). Here Linton failed to keep a trait's form distinct from its function.

Ruth Benedict

Ruth Benedict (1932) proposed a unit similar to Linton's complex. She worried that the study of cultural traits "detached from their [cultural] contexts" could not lead to a robust understanding of a culture as an "organic and functioning whole" (Benedict 1932:1). She therefore argued that one should study "configurations of culture," characterized as a set of traits integrated "into consistent patterns in accordance with certain inner necessities that have developed within the group" (Benedict 1932:2). The scale of a configuration was more inclusive than a single trait or a minimal functional unit because it concerned the functional interrelations of traits.

Homer Barnett

Homer Barnett (1940) echoed Linton (1936) and argued that a cultural trait had a form, a function, and a meaning within its cultural context. It was the "behavior" of traits resulting from their transmission from one culture to another that was of interest to Barnett. Did the traits retain their original function but not their meaning, for example? Barnett (1940:42) believed that "the process of diffusion and integration of functionally equivalent complexes parallel very closely, if they are not identical with, those characterizing invention and acceptance within a single cultural framework." In terms of cultural development, it made little difference if a cultural trait originated within the culture under study or if the trait originated elsewhere and diffused into the culture under study. Barnett's point was that a trait could be transmitted and retain its form, function, and meaning, or it could be transmitted and not retain any one, two, or perhaps all three of these qualities. Later, Barnett (1953) did not use the term "trait" but instead used "idea" when discussing diffusion, adhesions, and complexes. He wrote that adhesions were "persistent linkages between idea-sets as they diffuse across ethnic boundaries. Artifacts of this sort are called complexes because the analyst finds them to be made up of more than one component" (Barnett 1953:356).

George Murdock

George Murdock (1932:204) noted that anthropologists defined cultural traits as "group habits or customs," whereas sociologists "almost universally speak of them as 'folkways.'" He perceived a "general agreement" that "the constituent elements of culture, the proper data of the science of culture, are group habits. Only the terms employed are at variance" (Murdock 1932:204). He argued that the term "cultural trait" was troublesome because it included not only group habits such as forms of salutation, burial practices, and religious concepts but also "material objects or artifacts, which are not group habits, indeed not habits at all but facts of a totally different order" (Murdock 1932:205). Murdock (1932:205) maintained that artifacts are "outgrowths of habits" (here Murdock's thinking parallels Bidney's [1944] definition of culture as acquired through "habituation"), and although artifacts themselves might be transmitted via trade, knowledge of how to make them is what in fact allows them to become habits. Murdock favored the term "folkway" over cultural trait because the former term signified not the artifacts but the social setting of the artifacts. Adopting "folkway" to signify "group habits" would, Murdock (1932:205) reasoned, provide analytical units that were "objective behavioristic facts susceptible to repeated verification—an absolute prerequisite for a scientific study." The criterion of replicability via observation indicates that Murdock derived his definitions of folkways extensionally. Repeated observations by the anthropologist was an attempt to get at the ideas underlying the observed behaviors.

Sociological Perspectives

Sociologist M. W. Willey (1929:207) defined cultural traits as "habits carried in the individual nervous systems" and stated that it was these "which constitute the elements of culture." He thought that because traits were so "multitudinous," it was impossible to enumerate them. To overcome this problem, he suggested that traits "in association may more readily be studied" and designated a "grouping of traits [as] a culture complex" (Willey 1929:207). A complex was more than a group of traits; it constituted an integration of associated habits much like Benedict's (1932) configurations of culture.

Sociologist Thomas McCormick was interested in quantitative analyses of cultural elements, including their frequencies of occurrence rather than just their presence in a culture. Unlike most anthropologists, though, McCormick (1939:464) was explicit about the fact that cultural elements "in any particular study may be whatever we regard as 'elementary' for our purposes and level of interest." For him, cultural elements were eticlike, and the scale of an element was an analytical decision. What McCormick referred to as the "idea" of a particular behavior might be the same across multiple cultures, but it might have a unique empirical expression within each culture as a result of environmental differences. McCormick made clear that the reducibility of a cultural element into smaller, less inclusive units that could be recombined into other elements indicated that many elements were in fact compound units of some sort. He was after "natural units" in the eyes of both the informant(s) and the investigator, particularly in the sense that the elements were not reducible to their component parts without destroying the integrity or function of the element (McCormick 1939:464), thus echoing Driver and Kroeber's (1932) culture element as a minimal functional unit. Anthropologists did not adopt McCormick's view that cultural traits were units constructed for some analytical purpose.

Archaeological Views

W. C. McKern (1934, 1939; McKern et al. 1933) used the term "cultural trait" in his formulation of the Midwestern Taxonomic Method of classifying archaeological cultures. The term was used to denote artifact units of various scales. McKern never defined cultural trait, but the manner in which he and other archaeologists used the term indicates that traits were artifact types (Lyman and O'Brien 2003). Types were used in the direct historical approach (McKern

1934; Steward 1942; Wedel 1938), which involved comparing lists of traits compiled from both ethnographies and the archaeological record (Chapter 7). Likewise, seriation (Chapters 4 and 5) and percentage stratigraphy (Chapters 8 and 9) rested on the equation of artifact types with cultural traits.

Walter Taylor (1948) made explicit what previously had been implicit among American archaeologists. As might be expected from a student of Kluckhohn's, Taylor (1948:98) believed that "culture is a mental construct, having to do with the contents of minds and not with material objects or observable behavior." A cultural trait is an idea and as such can "be either shared [identical from individual to individual] or idiosyncratic" (Taylor 1948:96). Cultural heritage is a result of cultural transmission over time. Because cultural traits are ideational, they have to be "inferred from the objectifications, from behavior or the results of behavior," such as artifacts (Taylor 1948:100).

Cultural Traits into the 1950s, 1960s, and 1970s

To early twentieth-century anthropologists, cultural traits were ideas at various scales of inclusiveness and levels of complexity that were transmitted over space and through time. If those traits could be identified, they could then be used as analytical units. But there were numerous problems in so doing. Lowie (1917:85), for example, remarked that survivals may show "an *organic* relation between [traits] that have become separated and treated as distinct by the descriptive ethnologist. In such cases, one trait is the determinant of the other, possibly as the actually preceding cause, possibly as part of the same phenomenon." The first part of that statement is clearly focused on historical questions with the explicit addition of historical cause, and the last part is a reference to the fact that "cultural traits may be functionally related" (Lowie 1917:88). Paul Radin (1933:53, 140) was referring to both the problem of scale and the problem of definition when he argued that traits had the character of "fictitious definiteness"—a problem manifest in attempts to determine if a trait in one culture was the same trait in another culture. This is a typical problem with extensionally derived units: The definitive criteria are idiosyncratic because they depend on the specimens examined and also on the individual analyst deriving the definition. When Radin noted that the concept of cultural trait resulted in features of cultures being divorced from their sociocultural and human contexts, he was suggesting that traits could not be used for anything but historical ethnology.

Bronislaw Malinowski (1931:624) maintained that the method of identifying traits was the "weakest point" in any analysis of such units. Further, he emphasized that the form of a trait did not necessarily reflect its function and that "it is the diversity of function not the identity of form that is relevant to the student of culture" (Malinowski 1931:625). He later reiterated this view by arguing that the only legitimate way to define a trait was "by placing it within its relevant and real institutional setting" (Malinowski 1960:54). Failure to agree on "what is the definite isolate in the concrete cultural reality [would preclude] any science of civilization" (Malinowski 1960:39). Because of such comments by Malinowski, Radin, Benedict, Willey, and Murdock, many anthropologists by the early 1940s believed that an irreducible minimal unit of culture was a "methodological impossibility" because "modern functional theory shows the interdependence of cultural phenomena at all levels" (Bennett 1944:178). As a result, Bennett (1944:178–179), for example, concluded that a cultural trait was "an abstraction having no value other than the immediate one placed upon it by the user. . . . At what level must traits be abstracted to serve the [analytical] problem in view?" This was one of only two clear statements—McCormick's (1939) being the other—explicitly acknowledging that cultural traits were analytical units. That they should be contingent on their cultural contexts meant that they should be defined extensionally.

Murdock (1945) continued to use the concept of a cultural trait and perceptively noted that cultural traits did not have universal distributions because their empirical expressions varied from instance to instance. If geographically separated traits appeared to be identical, it was because of "similarities in classification, not in content. [This is because cultural traits] represent categories of historically and behaviorally diverse elements which nevertheless have so much in common that competent observers feel compelled to classify them together" (Murdock 1945:125). He also noted that traits that were perceived to be shared cross-culturally were so perceived as a function of their scale, generality, and inclusiveness. These points regarding the classification and scale of cultural traits were precisely the right ones to make. They had in fact been made earlier by Kroeber but with little apparent effect. Murdock, however, seemed to pay them little heed in later analyses (e.g., Murdock 1949) and hardly mentioned them at all in still later programmatic statements (e.g., Murdock 1957a, 1957b). He did admit that there were no doubt "errors" in his classification of cultural traits, but these were variously the result of "the arbitrariness inherent in any system of classification [and] faulty judgment in the categorization of data" (Murdock 1957b:687). Rather than perfect the classification, Murdock worked to enlarge the sample of cultures in his database. This prompted A. J. F. Köbben (1967) to highlight inconsistencies in the definitions and scales of cultural traits. These fundamental problems permeated virtually the entire history of the concept of cultural trait.

Similar weaknesses attended efforts such as Linton's (1936) regarding trait complex, activity, and culture to account for variation in the scale of cultural traits. The scale of such units was unclear ideationally, so it was unclear empirically as well. Herskovits's (1945:158) suggestion that cultures are made up of traits that "merge into larger divisions called complexes" that in turn merge into "culture patterns" did not help matters. Nor did Opler's (1959) substitution of the term "component" for cultural trait and "assemblage" for trait complex. Opler (1959:955) at least defined his new terms explicitly: A behavioral event is "an associated body of ideas, symbols, artifacts, and behavior[s]" termed "components," and an "assemblage" is "the total group of components which are activated by the event and are considered appropriate in coping with or referring to [the event]." These are, however, commonsensical definitions that did not concern a unit of cultural transmission.

There was also discussion about how to make the social or ethnic units from which individual trait lists were generated somehow comparable (Naroll 1964), but few mentioned how to define the traits themselves. Driver (1965:329) observed that the concept of a cultural trait "is much more difficult to objectify and establish than the ethnic unit." He noted that Opler's (1959) proposed taxonomy of components and assemblages "introduced some order in the continuum from small to larger and larger cultural units, but they are insufficient to account for the indefinitely large number of subject units in the indefinitely numerous hierarchies of classes within classes of cultural phenomena" (Driver 1965:329). More than a decade later McNett (1979:52) again highlighted the classification problem when he noted that one may be forced to use a "proxy measure" when "coding" cultural traits for purposes of cross-cultural study. Davis (1983:60) did not view this as a problem, observing that disciplines other than anthropology "have made little effort to specify a priori the kind or kinds of entities that diffuse."

Units of Cultural Transmission

Historical ethnologists who grappled with the concept of cultural trait had the right idea in monitoring cultural transmission. Although they failed to develop a solid concept of a unit of transmission, their discussions reveal some of the properties of such a unit that some anthropologists thought were important and other properties that other anthropologists thought were fatal to any analytical utility such units might have. These early workers typically defined cultural traits extensionally, probably in an effort to make their units have emic properties, but that protocol resulted in a host of difficulties, one centering on the scale of a trait and another being the comparability of traits recorded for different cultures. Even ignoring these problems, it seems that no majority of anthropologists actually thought cultural traits had emic qualities. About the time these issues were being identified as potentially fatal to the unit known as a cultural trait, historical ethnology fell from disciplinary favor, and the cultural context, function, and meaning of sets of traits termed complexes, patterns, and configurations became important. These larger units, which encompassed multiple cultural traits, had the same epistemological problems that the smaller units had. Recognition that all of these units were potentially useful analytically demanded an explicit theory of cultural transmission, something that only became available in the 1980s (e.g., Boyd and Richerson 1985; Cavalli-Sforza and Feldman 1981).

Although they struggled, early anthropologists provided a conceptual basis, if somewhat muddled, for studying culture as a phenomenon that was transmitted from person to person and thus was, in a sense, inherited. This in turn provided the basis for artifact-based chronometers such as seriation that were designed by archaeologists and that were typically said to be based on "historical continuity." As we show in the next two chapters, the concept of historical continuity is better expressed as the notion of heritable continuity, regardless of the nature of the unit of transmission. In archaeology, an artifact type was treated as more or less equivalent to a cultural trait. But successful use of artifact-based chronometers meant that the units attending those chronometers had to have certain properties, whether or not they were really cultural traits, however one conceived of those units.

4. Chronometers and Units in Early Archaeology and Paleontology

Archaeologists and paleobiologists share a number of goals, and practitioners in both disciplines would agree that two of these are to determine and to explain the evolutionary history of humans and nonhuman organisms through study of the archaeological and paleontological records. Given that one must be able to determine analytically the ages of different portions of these prehistoric records, it is not surprising that there is overlap in the methods that the two disciplines bring to bear on the problem of how to measure the passage of time. Both disciplines use Nicolaus Steno's principle of superposition, and both realize that superposition might allow one to determine the chronological order of the deposition of strata but not necessarily the relative ages of particles or sediments comprising the strata (Harper 1980; Rowe 1961; Chapter 8). Further, both disciplines employ a form of chronostratigraphic correlation based on distinctive fossils and/or artifacts found within particular strata. This method is termed biostratigraphy in both geology—the discipline in which it was first developed (Rudwick 1996)—and paleontology (e.g., Eldredge and Gould 1977) and typological cross-dating, or just cross-dating, in archaeology (e.g., Patterson 1963).

Archaeologists, geologists, and paleontologists have long used similar though not identical chronometers. The similarities suggest similar logic underlies each, but a critical difference resides in the kinds of units by which the chronometers are operationalized. Here we do not explore the historical nuances of interdisciplinary borrowing and cross-pollination—a topic that has been covered elsewhere in detail (e.g., Grayson 1983; Sackett 1981; Van Riper 1993). Rather, our interest is in the chronometers themselves and, particularly, the units they use to measure time. We first describe the geological chronometer and then turn to two chronometers developed by American archaeologists. We explain the reasoning behind the chronometers and highlight the epistemological and ontological similarities and differences between them. Understanding the reasoning behind the chronometers clarifies the nature of the units used to measure time with a particular chronometer.

A Chronometer for Geology and Paleontology

The analytical principles and tools for interpreting earth history were developed at the end of the eighteenth and the beginning of the nineteenth centuries (Rudwick 1996), such that by 1830 geologists were attempting to build an understanding of earth history based on stratigraphic analysis. Their "attention was focused on the discovery of the correct order of succession of formations [and] 'characteristic fossils' were being used with increasing confidence as the most reliable (though not the only) criterion for the correlation of formations in different regions" (Rudwick 1978:226). Geologists of the early nineteenth century were struggling to establish what are today's biostratigraphic methods, and in the process they were worrying about what was meant by similarities and differences among the fossil faunas represented in different geological formations (Hancock 1977; Mallory 1970; Rudwick 1978). The source of concern resided in the various forms of what can loosely be labeled notions of the history of life (Mayr 1982). These notions had to be sorted through and a particular one adopted if taxonomically similar yet geographically separate fossil faunas were to serve geological inquiry in any analytically useful way.

Late in the 1820s Charles Lyell sought to develop a method that could be used to arrange geological strata in proper chronological order. Lyell's chronometer, in effect a paleontological clock, had as its centerpiece the notion that the proportion of extant molluscan species in a fossil fauna could serve as an indication of that fauna's relative age. Significant portions of his discussion are found in Chapters 4 and 5 of volume III of his *Principles of Geology*. In those chapters Lyell (1833) reasoned that the number of extant species relative to the number of extinct species would decrease as one moved back in time. In Lyell's (1833:59) words, there was an "increase of existing species, and gradual disappearance of the extinct, as we trace the series of formations from the older to the newer." This was a "radically original" idea for questions of geochronology, for as Rudwick (1990:xl) documents, Lyell was "not concerned merely to identify strata by a few specially characteristic fossils, as most of his contemporaries were doing. He [was] attempting instead to set up a roughly *quantitative* geological chronometer, which [would] indicate not merely the relative order of strata but also their absolute ages, although only approximately and not in years." Lyell's faunal chronometer would produce a clock much like Petrie's (1899) "sequence dates," but whereas Petrie suspected his clock kept time on an ordinal scale, Lyell could hope for an interval-scale chronometer because in his view the biota of the world changed "continuously and uniformly" (Rudwick 1990:xli).

Fully in line with anti-Lamarckian notions regarding the histories of species current at the time (Mayr 1982; Rudwick 1978, 1990), Lyell's faunal chronometer depended on the stability of species and their abrupt appearance in and disappearance from the fossil record. Lyell viewed species as entities that had an initial appearance at one point in time, a period of occurrence, and a point in time when they became extinct. Thus for Lyell and many of his contemporaries, each species was a discrete entity; it had a distinct life span, it occupied one more or less distinct portion of the temporal continuum, and it did not (and could not) evolve into a new species over time. They were essentialist units. Species were not the arbitrary chunks of a materialist continuum manifest as an evolutionarily continuous lineage as proposed by Darwin (1859) a quarter century later.

Lyell conceived of species as appearing and disappearing in "piecemeal" fashion (Rudwick 1978:233), although he provided no mechanism for their appearance other than to refer to them vaguely as the results of "intermediate causes" (Lyell 1881:467). Faunal turnover would be reflected in the fossil record by particular combinations of taxa occupying particular portions of the temporal continuum. In Lyell's view and in that of many of his contemporaries, each suddenly appearing new species would, given sufficient time, eventually become extinct. The identification of strata containing members of the same species "not only enables us to refer to the same era, distinct rocks widely separated from each other in the horizontal plane, but also others which may be considerably distant in the vertical series" (Lyell 1833:41). In Lyell's view, species could occur in more than one formation, and formations could be temporally ordered based on the particular combinations of species

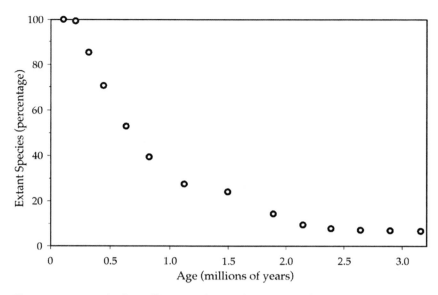

Figure 4.1. *An example of a Lyellian curve showing the percentage of extant mammalian species found in Europe during the Plio-Pleistocene (after Stanley 1979:Figure 5–8a).*

they contained. Lyell was not using one or a few index fossils as the basis of an ordering of formations; rather, he was using large suites of species. This was a decidedly different approach than Lyell's contemporaries such as William Smith, Georges Cuvier, and Alexandre Brongniart were using in their stratigraphic-correlation work (Rudwick 1996).

Despite the fact that several workers developed faunal chronometers similar to Lyell's, Rudwick (1978:241) suggests that they all failed to become a part of paleontology's analytical tool kit because of difficulties involved in identifying individual fossils as representing particular species. As Lyell (1833:49) noted, "the systematic arrangement of strata, so far as it rests on organic remains, must depend essentially on the accurate determination of species." For Lyell's fossil clock to work, fossil species A had always and everywhere to be identified consistently and to be readily distinguished from fossil species B, C, and D. Otherwise, the fluctuating relative frequencies of extant and extinct species would be a function of how fossils were identified taxonomically rather than a function of their actual occurrence in time.

Once Darwin's (1859) views on biological evolution and on species as unstable entities that changed continuously were introduced, Lyell's chronometer was perceived as unworkable. But more than 100 years later, species were again conceived of as being more or less stable, and Lyell's chronometer, like the phoenix, reappeared. Lyell's faunal chronometer today is graphed in what is termed "Lyellian curve" form (Stanley 1979:113). As exemplified in Figure 4.1, such graphs indicate the proportion of extant species or higher level taxa in fossil faunas, or what is termed the "Lyellian percentage" (Stanley et al. 1980). Beginning with a modern fauna containing only extant species, fossil faunas are sorted such that the proportion of extant taxa progressively decreases from sample to sample; that the curve identified by the plotted points in fact measures time must be confirmed with independent data derived from such methods as stratigraphic observation or radiometric dating (Stanley et al. 1980). Given an absolute-dating technique, Lyellian curves show the rate of extinction of prehistoric taxa through time and the rate of origination of extant taxa (Stanley et al. 1980).

There is a potentially fatal problem with constructing a Lyellian curve and thus with using it as a chronostratigraphic tool and interpreting the curve in terms of evolutionary processes. Lyell had hoped that his chronometer would eventually produce a universal chronostratigraphic device that could be applied worldwide, thereby allowing all strata to be correlated into one grand sequence of earth history. The problem, we now know, is that geographically separate populations of a taxon will not all be extirpated at the same time; spatially limited samples of fossils may thus produce inaccurate dates for the extinction of that taxon. In formal terms, homotaxial succession—similarity or identity in the stratigraphic order of taxa from one locality to the next (Harper 1980)— does not necessarily equal chronological order. As Stanley et al. (1980:422) note, "to be strictly valid, the Lyellian approach to biostratigraphy requires that the entire world has been characterized by a particular temporal pattern of extinction." This problem and the similar one of dating the first appearance of a taxon are well captured by the model of a taxon's spatio-temporal distribution shown in Figure 4.2. If the total real spatio-temporal range of a taxon is unknown, as is the case when only the left half of the distribution in Figure 4.2 is known, then the times of appearance and extinction of a taxon will influence the shape of the Lyellian curve based on such data. Archaeologists faced this same problem, and it plagued one of the chronometers they developed. Another chronometer was unaffected because it incorporated units that had a decidedly different distribution than that shown in Figure 4.2.

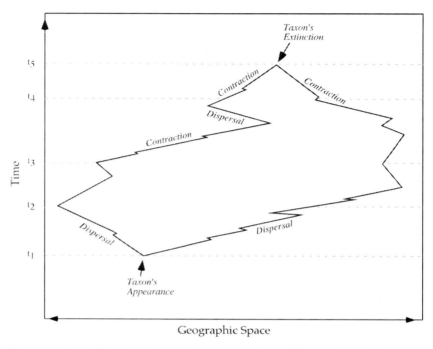

Figure 4.2. A model of the spatio-temporal distribution of a biological taxon (after Pearson 1998:Figure 5.4). Note that the spatial distribution of the taxon differs from time to time and that the temporal duration of the taxon varies from spatial location to spatial location.

American Archaeology's Early Chronometers

Archaeologists trained in the United States originally had little interest in time, largely because most of them generally believed that the time depth of human occupation of the Americas was shallow (Meltzer 1983, 1985). Nonetheless, by the end of the nineteenth century two chronometers were available. One, superposition and stratigraphic excavation (Lyman et al. 1997b; O'Brien and Lyman 1999c), is considered in detail in Chapter 8. The second chronometer, implemented through the direct historical approach, is of interest, as is a third chronometer, frequency seriation, which was developed during the second decade of the twentieth century. The last two chronometers overlap considerably in technique and underpinning logic, and thus in how they are implemented, but they differ markedly in the units they employ and that allow their implementation. We discuss each in turn before comparing them with Lyell's faunal chronometer.

Willey and Sabloff (1993:126) indicate that the method known as the direct historical approach "is almost as old as archaeology." We agree. Cyrus Thomas (1894) used it to help resolve the mound-builder controversy in the late nineteenth century (Chapter 7). A. V. Kidder (1916) explicitly stated that one of the reasons he chose Pecos Pueblo, New Mexico, for excavation was that it had been occupied into the historical period, which allowed him to track time from the present back into the past. How does the approach work? Edward B. Tylor (1881:10) wrote simply, "It is a good old rule to work from the known to the unknown." As we show in Chapter 7, few additional details were provided in later years, although numerous culture historians used the method (e.g., Collins 1932a; Stirling 1932; Strong 1935; Wedel 1938).

In the only detailed programmatic statement on the direct historical approach of which we are aware, Steward (1942:337) remarked that it "involves the elementary logic of working from the known to the unknown. First, sites of the historic period are located. . . . Second, the cultural complexes of the [historic-period] sites are determined. Third, sequences are carried backward in time to protohistoric and prehistoric periods and cultures." The approach would allow one to "carry sequences backward beyond the point where the traits of the known, historic peoples faded out" (Steward 1942:338). Unfortunately, these few statements, along with the remainder of Steward's paper, did not specify what a "cultural complex" was, what a "sequence" was, or how the latter was to be "carried backward in time," whether beyond "historic peoples" or not. Apparently, given how the direct historical approach was implemented by those cited by Steward (1942), a cultural complex comprised a set of cultural traits more or less unique to a particular culture (e.g., Wedel 1938). Knowing that individual traits occurred in different complexes allowed one to trace those cultural traits backward through time across successively preceding cultural complexes. Steward (1942) did not make explicit that one was tracking "sequences" back through time using the principle of overlapping—the same principle that guided Lyell's thinking.

In the first use of the term "overlapping" of which we are aware, Kidder (1924:45) noted that one can construct sequences "by the principle of overlapping," but he did not tell us what the term signified. Stirling (1929), Willey (1936), and Ford (1938a, 1938b) used the term, but none defined it.

Culture Traits or Artifact Types

Trait Lists	1	2	3	4	5	6	7	8	9	10	11	12
G	+	+	+	+	+	+	+	+	+			
F	+	+	+	+	+	+	+		+			
E	+	+	+	+	+	+			+	+		
D		+	+	+	+	+			+	+	+	
C		+	+	+	+					+	+	+
B			+	+	+					+	+	+
A			+	+						+	+	+

Figure 4.3. Diagram illustrating the principle of overlapping. Numbers 1–12 are cultural traits or artifact types used to order trait lists A–G, which could be derived from ethnographies or artifact assemblages. Plus marks indicate a trait is present; blanks indicate a trait is absent. Overlap, manifest as traits or types shared by lists, is a form of linkage that allows creation of a sequence of lists. Overlap implies transmission from one list to an adjacent one; the protocol for ordering the rows is therefore that each trait or type should have a single, continuous distribution. Time could be running in either direction through the sequence (from bottom to top or from top to bottom); additional information is needed to assess directionality. Compare with Figure 7.1, which has a chronological anchor in the historic period and thus indicates directionality.

Spier (1931b) provided an early clue as to what is meant by the term when he discussed Kroeber's (1916a, 1916b) seminal frequency seriation. Kroeber noted that "the wares of the historic ruins overlapped with those of the [protohistoric period]; the latter, with the [ruins of the prehistoric period]" (Spier 1931b:281). The principle of overlapping, then, concerns the occurrence of a cultural trait or artifact type in multiple cultural complexes or in artifact assemblages potentially of different age, and it is these shared, or overlapping, traits or types that serve as the basis for placing those complexes or assemblages adjacent to one another in an ordering thought to comprise a sequence (Figure 4.3). Overlapping is a form of "linkage" between archaeological phenomena (Ford 1938a:262; Strong 1935:68).

There are two significant aspects to the principle of overlapping, and both are found in Nelson's (1916:163) statement that when he excavated Pueblo

San Cristobal, New Mexico, he was explicitly seeking data indicating that one type of pottery "gradually replac[ed]" another rather than seeking mere "time relations" of the types; he already knew the latter on the basis of the stratigraphic contexts of the types (Chapter 8). Nelson (1916) excavated the way he did, and plotted ceramic type frequencies the way he did, because only in these ways could the gradual replacement of one or more types by one or more others—the overlapping of types across multiple assemblages— be found. Each type would appear, persist for a while, and finally disappear, but the various types would do so in piecemeal fashion. The principle of overlapping is therefore critical to the direct historical approach precisely because, as Nelson (1916:163) noted, an overlapping trait—one shared by multiple assemblages or complexes—"connects" them (Figure 4.3).

The two significant aspects of the principle of overlapping are that it helps ensure that time's passage is being measured and it does so because it implies a particular kind of continuity. With respect to the first, the implicit assumption allowing application of the direct historical approach is that prehistoric materials more similar to historically documented materials—the more traits they share—are the more recent; prehistoric materials that are less similar to historically documented materials date to more remote times. This is much like the use of modern taxa to construct a Lyellian curve, and it is what allows sequences to be built. With respect to the second aspect, the connections of cultural complexes denoted by overlapping traits—traits shared by complexes adjacent to one another in an ordering—have a particular but implicit meaning that not only warrants the temporal inference but provides an explanation for that inference. The principle of overlapping assumes a direct phylogenetic connection—a genetic-like continuity founded on transmission—between culture complexes that share traits (Lipo et al. 1997; O'Brien and Lyman 1999c, 2000). Although implicit, this is why traits overlap from complex to complex and why the complexes are viewed as being linked (Lyman 2001). It was exactly such a connection that was explicitly sought by Nelson and referred to by Kidder, Spier, Ford, Willey, and others. The direct historical approach thus demands the study of homologous similarity, a point largely unrecognized (Chapter 2) as the approach saw increased use during the first half of the twentieth century (Chapter 7).

Rather than explore and develop the theoretical implications of the principle of overlapping, culture historians discussed the value of the direct historical approach in strictly chronological terms. The approach was preferred by many early American archaeologists because it offered "a fixed datum point to which sequences may be tied" (Steward 1942:337). It provided a chronological anchor in the historical period to which archaeological materials of otherwise unknown relative age could be linked. Without a chronological anchor, sequences might be established, but they would have the unsavory characteristic of floating in time and perhaps have no indication of which way time was flowing through them. They would thus be of minimal utility in determining the developmental pathways of historically documented cultures. As Steward (1944:100) indicated, the direct historical approach "starts with the ready-made history contained in written documents. . . . [T]he historic period is an excellent starting point for prehistoric sequences, especially where archaeological complexes now remain unfixed in time for want of stratigraphy or other reference points." Perhaps more important, "material from [historic- and protohistoric-period] sites will show which [pottery-decoration] complex was the most recent and will determine which end of the chain of complexes constructed by overlapping is the latest. Without this tie-up it would be as logical for one end of the chronology to be recent as for the other" (Ford 1938a:263).

Given their focus on writing the histories of various cultural lineages, the direct historical approach was an obvious choice for archaeologists because it allowed them to trace those lineages from the present into the past. That the term "sequence" was used by Steward (1942, 1944) and others rather than the term "lineage" underscores the point we made in Chapter 2—archaeologists in the first half of the twentieth century were not thinking about cultural change in evolutionary (phylogenetic) ways but primarily in terms of chronology. Overlapping was required only because it showed linkages between sets of material, not because it denoted heritable continuity. It is clear, however, that the latter is what warranted the inference of time's passage. Failure to explore the underpinning notion of heritable continuity between analytical units may have been exacerbated by the focus of anthropology in general on culture traits or culture elements (Chapter 3). These were the units mentioned by archaeologists who used the direct historical approach (e.g., Steward 1929; Strong 1935), and we consider them further in a subsequent section of this chapter.

Frequency Seriation

In 1915 Kroeber (1916a, 1916b) invented the archaeological chronometer that came to be known as frequency seriation (Lyman et al. 1997b; Chapters 5 and 9). Standard dictionary definitions of "seriation" generally read, "arrangement in a series." But archaeologists believe that the series represents the ticking of a clock. Thus we particularly like the late John Rowe's (1961:326) definition of seriation as "the arrangement of archaeological materials in a presumed chronological order on the basis of some logical principle other than superposition." The logical principle is similarity; those things that are similar are put close together in the order whereas those things that are dissimilar are placed far apart (Cowgill 1972). We elaborate further on how similarity is measured in Chapter 5; here it suffices to note that Kroeber measured similarity on the basis of frequencies of artifact types. What is critically important here is the logic that underpinned Kroeber's invention, a logic that is summarized in one word—overlap.

Kroeber noted, based on repeated observations in a geographically limited area, that corrugated pottery was regularly associated with dilapidated, non-historically documented ruins and that it was seldom found associated with less dilapidated, historically documented ruins. He then reasoned that this type of pottery would occur with greatest frequency among the oldest ruins and over time would decrease in frequency relative to other types until it no longer occurred. Successively younger ruins would have progressively lower relative abundances of that ancient type associated with them and would have progressively greater frequencies of types used by historic Zuni people. On this basis, Kroeber ordered 15 sites in what he suspected might be a chronological sequence, placing Zuni Pueblo as the sixteenth and most recent site in the series (Chapter 5). Zuni was historically documented as having been occupied for much of the last several hundred years and had produced no specimens of the ancient pottery type (Kroeber 1916a, 1916b). Kroeber did not make explicit the fact that the principle of overlapping allowed him to order the sites and to infer that time's continuity was being measured by the ordering or that the underpinning warrant for the use of the principle of overlapping comprised heritable continuity created by cultural transmission.

Simultaneous with Kroeber's work, Nelson (1916) plotted the absolute frequency of each of several artifact types against their vertical-recovery provenience in a column of sediment in order to measure the passage of time (Chapter 8). One year later Spier (1917a, 1917b) and Kidder (Kidder and Kidder 1917) plotted the relative frequencies of each of several types of pottery from geographically limited areas against their superposed recovery positions to confirm what Kroeber and Nelson had found—relative frequencies of the pottery types fluctuated unimodally through time. This meant that types, if defined in particular ways on the basis of geographically limited samples, could be used in what came to be known as frequency seriation and percentage stratigraphy, and these two techniques could be used as chronometers. Within a few decades, however, percentage stratigraphy assumed center stage, and frequency seriation was relegated to a minor role in American archaeology (O'Brien and Lyman 1999c; Chapter 8). Important points in the present context concern Kroeber's reasoning and the units he and his contemporaries used.

First, just as with a paleontologist's Lyellian curve, the proof that an ordering of artifact assemblages produced by frequency seriation represents the passage of time must come from data independent of the seriation (Rowe 1961), a point Kroeber (1916b:20–21) recognized: "The final proof is in the spade. . . . [Otherwise,] in the present chaos of knowledge who can say which of these differences [in frequencies of sherd types] are due to age and which to locality and environment?" Second, in direct contrast to Lyell, Kroeber used a suspected ancient type as the basis for his ordering. Thus what might be termed a reverse Lyellian curve results when Kroeber's most ancient type— the one that served as the major basis for his frequency seriation of sites—is plotted (Figure 4.4). We call this a reverse Lyellian curve because the plot is based on the proportion of an ancient type rather than of a modern type, and thus the slope of the line defined by the plotted points is the reverse of that in a Lyellian curve (Figure 4.1). One of the two sites ("Kyakki W" [some site names are abbreviated for sake of simplicity]) that were exceptions to the principle of ordering—regular decrease in the relative abundance of the ancient type—was incorporated by Kroeber into his ordering on the basis of the relative abundance of another type suspected to be ancient and which met the ordering principle; the other site ("Kolliwa") was incorporated on the basis of the relative abundance of one apparently recent type that also met the ordering principle (Chapter 5).

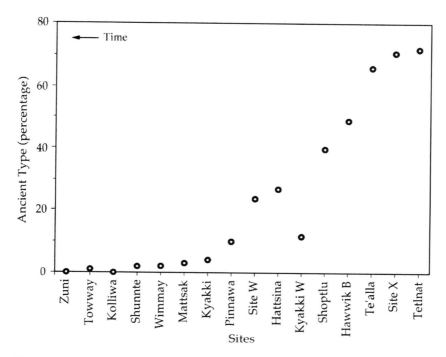

Figure 4.4. A reverse Lyellian curve for Kroeber's (1916a, 1916b) ceramic data from sites near Zuni Pueblo (some site names are abbreviated).

As with both Lyell's faunal chronometer and the direct historical approach, overlapping was critical to Kroeber's production of a successful frequency seriation and Kidder's and Nelson's production of successful percentage-stratigraphy graphs—ones with types that, once collections were ordered, displayed unimodal-frequency distributions. But the most critical point here is that Kroeber, Nelson, Kidder, and Spier were not plotting frequencies of cultural traits; they were instead plotting frequencies of variants of a trait (Chapter 8). This is what allowed them to measure time. Overlapping was common to both frequency seriation and the direct historical approach, and it implied heritable continuity in both, although this implication was basically ignored. There was a shift in the scale of units used to operationalize the chronometer of frequency seriation from the more inclusive scale of cultural trait often used by the direct historical approach—a scale consonant with Lyell's use of species—to that of trait variant. The units used by these archaeological chronometers, then, require further consideration.

Units

Kroeber, Nelson, Kidder and Spier viewed their pottery types as analytical tools rather than as somehow "real" entities. One indication of this is that these units quickly became known as styles rather than as cultural traits; we are aware of only one reference to seriated units by the latter term (Wissler 1916a), and it occurred just as the terminology was changing. The units plotted in Figure 4.4 are what are today known as styles or, more often, "historical types" (e.g., Krieger 1944; Rouse 1939). They are "ideational," specifically "theoretical," units; as we noted in Chapters 2 and 3, this means that they are units of measurement. Recall that such units are not empirically real but rather are conceptual units, what we call classes, that comprise particular combinations of properties, or attributes; at least some of those combinations will be displayed by real specimens.

Recall that, for Lyell, species were fixed, immutable units. They were also real in the sense that one could go out into the world and observe them; Lyell's notion of uniformitarianism demanded that fossil species be real. Darwin showed that the notion that species were immutable was incorrect, though the empirical reality of species lives in the modern biological-species concept, which defines a species as a group of one or more populations comprising individuals that actually or potentially interbreed and that are reproductively isolated from other such groups (Mayr 1969, 1982). Many modern paleobiologists (e.g., Eldredge and Gould 1972; Eldredge and Novacek 1985; Gould and Eldredge 1993; Vrba 1980) prefer the biological-species concept precisely because it has this biological meaning and therefore entails particular implications for biological evolution. Others (e.g., Fox 1986; Gingerich 1985; Rose and Bown 1986; Trueman 1979), realizing the problems involved in identifying interbreeding populations of organisms among inanimate fossils, employ the notion of chronospecies, which are more or less arbitrary chunks of the evolutionary, that is, morphological, continuum.

When drawing a Lyellian curve founded on units such as biological species, one must keep in mind the model of a species's spatio-temporal distribution shown in Figure 4.2. In drawing a Lyellian curve, a species's distribution is effectively converted to a rectangle. This conversion brings with it two problems that are graphically depicted in Figure 4.5. First, the real distribution may be much more complex than the relatively simple one

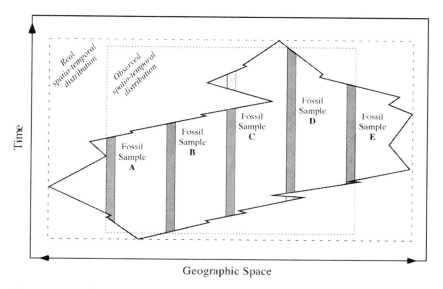

Figure 4.5. A model of what happens when the real spatio-temporal distribution of a biological taxon is converted into a unit that can be plotted in a Lyellian curve.

displayed in the figure; the more complex the real distribution, the greater the number of samples necessary to approximate that distribution accurately. Even the simple real distribution shown in Figure 4.5 will be poorly approximated if only samples A, C, and E in the figure are available. Second, the more complex the real distribution or the less adequate the available samples, the greater the discrepancy between the perceived and real distributions.

Kroeber, Nelson, Kidder, and Spier escaped these problems in archaeology by constructing ideational units of a particular kind—analytical units that allowed them to measure time while simultaneously controlling the spatial dimension. Given the view that artifact form varies more or less continuously both over time and across space, they built analytical units to have limited spatio-temporal distributions. To illustrate this, consider Figure 4.6. In this figure artifact form varies continuously along both axes, but there is no absolute scale on either axis. Each polygon represents an ideational unit used during analysis to measure variation; shaded areas represent formal variation not measured by those units. Each column of polygons (A–C) denotes a set of analytical units comprising a typology. In column A analytical units overlap through time but include spatial variation as well; thus both change over time and variation over space are included. In column B analytical units overlap

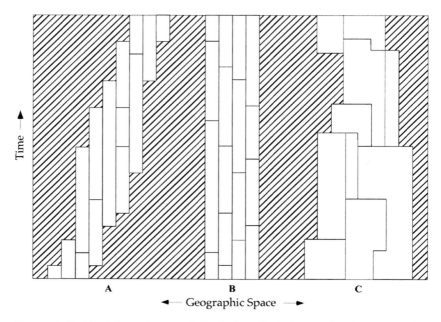

Figure 4.6. Models of the spatio-temporal distribution of units (polygons) used to measure time (morphology varies continuously along both axes). Artifact form varies continuously along both axes, but there is no absolute scale on either axis. Each rectangle represents a unit used during analysis to measure variation; shaded areas represent formal variation not measured by those units. Each column of rectangles (A–C) denotes a set of units comprising a typology: A, analytical units include relatively small geographic areas and overlapping time spans, but analytical units vary in location over time (compare with Figure 9.7); B, analytical units overlap through time but do not shift geographic location over time, thus only change over time is included; and C, analytical units overlap through time but include varying amounts of spatial variation. See Figure 6.2 for an additional model.

through time but do not include much spatial variation in form; thus only time is measured. In column C variation in time and space varies from unit to unit, and although units measure time and thus change, they also measure a great deal of spatial variation in form.

The types constructed by Kroeber, Nelson, Kidder, and Spier approximated the rectangles shown in Figure 4.6, column B. That is, they monitored the passage of time rather than difference in geographic location. This kind of analytical unit comprises what came to be known as a historical type, or style, and it had to be built by trial and error (Rouse 1939)—a point rarely acknowledged explicitly. Given such a mode of construction, the utility of a type for measuring the passage of time had to be tested—a significant point made explicit by Krieger (1944) when he indicated that archaeologically useful types must pass the historical-significance test. The test implications were that a useful historical type had to have a distribution similar to one of those shown in Figure 4.6, column B. Types that had distributions such as those in Figure 4.6, columns A and C, could be used, but they were less satisfactory in that they measured variation in space as well as variation in time. If the constructed types did not pass the historical-significance test, they were discarded, and new types were erected. This trial-and-error, classify—test—reclassify process continues to this day as archaeologists attempt to construct analytical units that allow them to measure the passage of time reliably and validly.

Species and artifact types might display distributions such as those signified by the rectangles in Figure 4.6, column B, but this is unknown when the units are first constructed. The historical-significance text determines whether the constructed units have such distributions. Species units often have spatio-temporal distributions such as that shown in Figure 4.2 and thus are potentially less reliable and valid measures of time. The complete spatial distribution of a species must be known in order to account for the taxon's varied spatial distribution over time and so that the time of that taxon's appearance and extinction can be determined accurately. This is not the case with the analytical units used by early archaeologists; they built their units to have limited spatio-temporal distributions such that they were useful for measuring time. The closer those units approximated the units depicted in Figure 4.6, column B, the more closely and precisely they measured the passage of time.

In contrast to the styles used in frequency seriation, units used by those who applied the direct historical approach were often cultural traits (Chapter 3). These units were much like Lyell's species in that they were frequently treated analytically as empirical, real entities. Although they were generally inclusive units, cultural traits could vary tremendously in scale—from a religious ceremony such as the Ghost Dance to a design motif on a ceramic vessel. They might change over time as a result of various processes (e.g., Barnett 1953 and references therein). Culture traits often had distributions such as that modeled in Figures 4.2, 4.5, and 4.6 (columns A and C), and this resulted in no end of debate over what their historical significance might comprise (e.g., Steward 1929). Further, they did not consistently measure the passage of time. This weakness was exacerbated by the failure to develop a robust theory of cultural transmission that incorporated units like cultural traits as units of transmission. It would take a shift to historically sensitive variants of those traits—to what came to be known as styles, or historical types—before time could consistently be measured (Chapter 8).

Overlapping

As chronometers, Lyellian curves, the direct historical approach, and frequency seriation share a number of properties. Each begins with a chronological anchor in the present, and each traces time backward by tracking changes in the frequencies of units based on the principle of overlapping. On the one hand, in archaeology this principle serves as a warrant not only for the purely temporal sequence of archaeological manifestations but also for the inference that the sequence comprises a cultural lineage—a line of heritable continuity—or what came to be known as a tradition. A (cultural) tradition is usually defined as "a (primarily) temporal continuity represented by persistent configurations in single technologies or other systems of related forms" (Willey and Phillips 1958:37) or as "a socially transmitted cultural form which persists in time" (Thompson 1956:39). The latter in particular underscores that a tradition is a lineage (Lipo et al. 1997; O'Brien and Lyman 1999c; Chapters 5, 7, and 9), and it emphasizes the warrant required by the direct historical approach and frequency seriation as chronometers.

Lyell's chronometer, on the other hand, required no such warrant. Lyell believed in the absolute stability of species and did not accept either the Lamarckian notion of transmutation or any of the other versions of biological evolution then being discussed. It was the piecemeal appearance and disappearance of taxa over time and their fixed, nonevolving nature that allowed Lyell to construct his chronometer. The fact that taxa evolve dissuaded geologists and paleobiologists from using Lyellian curves for over a century. Only in the last two or three decades have these curves been resurrected as useful analytical devices, and that resurrection came at the hands of those who view species as evolutionarily stable entities (e.g., Stanley 1979; Stanley et al. 1980) as opposed to constantly changing configurations.

Other parallels in dating techniques used by paleontologists and archaeologists are pertinent here. Archaeologists today use frequency seriation as a relative dating technique when absolute dating techniques cannot be used (e.g., Allen 1996; Johnson and Nelson 1990; Love 1993; Rafferty 1994), and they use theoretical units to build their seriations. Paleontologists continue to use species as the unit of choice when they do biostratigraphic analyses and have expanded their tool kit to include what archaeologists term interdigitation (Chapter 9) and they term "slotting" (e.g., Gordon and Reyment 1979). Paleobiologists rarely have used frequency seriation (exceptions are Brower and Burroughs 1982; McKee et al. 1995), probably because they would employ species as the units seriated and are well aware of the problems in so doing (Figures 4.2 and 4.5). Paleobiologists (e.g., Gould et al. 1987) who derogate frequency seriation do not understand the ontological differences between units imposed through the use of the biological-species concept and the theoretical units upon which frequency seriation depends (O'Brien and Lyman 1999c, 2000).

The difference between the units paleobiologists use to construct Lyellian curves and archaeologists use in the direct historical approach and the theoretical units used in frequency seriation is important. The model in Figures 4.2 and 4.5 comprises the spatio-temporal distribution of an empirical unit termed a biological species (Pearson 1998), and it applies equally well as a characterization of the distribution of many cultural traits. Such a unit has significant analytical constraints, the most important one in terms of measuring time being that its total spatio-temporal distribution must be known for a chronometer to be reliable and valid. Conversely, the kinds of units required by frequency seriation must be theoretical units that have spatio-temporally limited distributions like those in Figure 4.6, column B. Recognition of this point could result in paleobiologists using such units in frequency seriations and interdigitation, or slotting, to create faunal chronologies of much greater resolution than are currently available. Similarly, recognition could result in archaeologists becoming more interested in exploring the implications of overlapping units as they pertain to heritability, transmission mechanisms, and rates of transmission.

Previous discussions of the direct historical approach have been vague with respect to the principle of overlapping and its analytical and interpretive significance. Steward (1942) did not mention the principle in his discussion; those who used the term "overlapping" typically did not even indicate what the term meant analytically—the occurrence of a cultural trait in more than one cultural complex—let alone why its occurrence should allow the construction of a cultural sequence. Our impression is that everyone knew what it meant for analysis and that everyone also knew at least implicitly why cultural chronologies built using the direct historical approach comprised cultural lineages. The approach was commonly used in American archaeology between about 1910 and 1940, precisely when stratigraphic excavation, percentage stratigraphy, and frequency seriation were gaining popularity in the discipline (Lyman et al. 1997b), prompting Steward's (1942) post hoc programmatic statement. The theoretical model that underpinned all these methods—evolutionary descent with modification of cultural complexes—escaped comment because the mechanism ensuring hereditary continuity—cultural transmission—was understood as a given (Lyman 2001).

Chronology and Units

If one goal of a discipline is to write the history of its subject phenomena, then a means of measuring time must be developed. If another goal is to explain in historical terms why modern subject phenomena such as organisms and cultures have the appearance they do, then sequences alone are insufficient. Those sequences must somehow be linked to the modern phenomena through the creation of lineages. Lyell's paleontological clock, the direct historical approach, and frequency seriation as implemented by Kroeber accomplished both goals by using the principle of overlapping. Yet the units used—species, cultural traits, and historical types, respectively—were ontologically distinct. Lyell saw no evolutionary connections between species; for him, they were nonchanging, essentialist units. Overlapping held only temporal significance for Lyell's chronometer and no implication of heritable continuity other than within each taxon included. Anthropologists and archaeologists, however, appear to have conceived of just such connections between cultural traits, but because such units often had spatio-temporal distributions like those of biological species, they were not always useful for measuring time. Kroeber, Nelson, Kidder, and Spier implicitly viewed evolutionary connections between artifacts, but they also constructed units—types, or styles—that had spatio-temporally restricted distributions. Types allowed them to measure the passage of time, but they did not explore the underpinning phylogenetic implication of overlapping.

Lyell's chronometer could not be used when species were thought of as evolutionarily unstable entities, but when they were again viewed as stable units, his chronometer was resurrected. Archaeologists continued to use the direct historical approach after stratigraphic excavation became common-place and frequency seriation was invented (Chapter 7). Part of its contin-ued use resided in an analytical shift from units comprising cultural traits to ones comprising artifact styles. Frequency seriation (and percentage stratig-raphy) was successful because its analytical units were theoretical and built specifically to measure time. Failure to explore the theoretical implications of overlapping—the principle common to all three chronometers—resulted from a commonsense understanding of culture change, a focus on measuring time's passage alone, and a failure to recognize variation in the epistemology and ontology that underpin historical research. One of the most often cited studies of historical research and cultural change undertaken during the first half of the twentieth century is Kroeber's monitoring of change in women's clothing. A few years before he published the first part of that two-part study, he invented and applied frequency seriation. In neither case, however, was he particularly explicit about underpinning models of cultural change. Nor was he particularly clear about the nature of the units he used to accomplish both analyses. Yet close study of both of his analyses reveals some very significant properties of the units he built and the chronometers in which he used them. It is those topics that we turn to next.

5. A. L. Kroeber and the Measurement of Time's Arrow and Time's Cycle

Because he was steeped in Boasian historical particularism, A. L. Kroeber was interested in culture change and thus also in the age of cultural phenomena. Our focus in this chapter involves explication of the distinction between two of the analytical techniques Kroeber used to measure time's passage and cultural change. We explore the underpinning assumptions of each and by example illustrate how the measurement units Kroeber used influenced his analytical results. One analytical technique is frequency seriation (introduced in Chapter 4); the other analytical technique is time-series analysis (e.g., Chatfield 1975). Kroeber invented frequency seriation specifically to measure time's passage; he used time-series analysis to monitor cultural cycles. The measurement units Kroeber used for each analytical technique are different, and the analytical protocols of each technique are equally distinct. These epistemological differences have not previously been explored, which is perhaps why the results of the two techniques have sometimes been said to monitor the same thing. Understanding the differences underscores a central point of this book: the units used to measure time are causally linked to particular chronometers. Here we show that Kroeber seems to have been very aware of this linkage. Prior to discussing these matters, however, several things need to be made clear.

Prefatory Remarks

We use Gould's (1987) metaphors of "time's arrow" and "time's cycle" to denote the fact that although time is linear, it can be measured as either a non-recurrent linear phenomenon or as a recurrent, cyclical phenomenon. Whether one measures time's arrow or time's cycle depends on the measurement units used, such as the month of January measuring time's cycle every solar year, whereas the solar year AD 2001 measures time's arrow since the birth of Christ. Because of this possibility, we disagree with McGee and Warms's (2000:142n2) assessment of Kroeber as believing that time's cycle would be found in "all manner of cultural phenomena." Instead, we suspect that Kroeber realized from the start that time's cycle would only be perceivable in selected cultural phenomena if they were measured or classified in particular ways. We agree, however, with McGee and Warms's (2000:142n3) assessment of Kroeber's use of time-series analysis as being underpinned by an "evolutionary perspective" because the artifacts he used in that analysis comprise an evolutionary lineage.

A time-series analysis involves arranging phenomena in a temporal sequence based on the respective ages of the phenomena and subsequent study of changes in the phenomena across the ordering (Braun 1985; Chatfield 1975). Seriation is "a descriptive analytical technique, the purpose of which is to arrange comparable units in a single dimension (that is, along a line) such that the position of each unit reflects its similarity to other units" (Marquardt 1978:258). As Rowe (1961:326) put it, the "logical order on which the seriation is based is found in the combination of features of style or inventory which characterize the units, rather than in the external relationships of the units themselves," where "external relationships" include age. Archaeological seriation typically is done for purposes of measuring time's arrow (O'Brien and Lyman 1999c; Chapters 4 and 6). The important point to remember is that time-series analysis has a different analytical goal than seriation. For the former, time is known, and changes in phenomena are monitored over time; for the latter, a measure of historical or linear time is the goal, and phenomena are ordered so as to (hopefully) reflect time's passage.

A chronometer is a means of measuring the linear flight of time's arrow. Gould (1987:157) notes that "a chronometer of history has one, and only one, rigid requirement—something must be found that changes in a recognizable and irreversible way through time, so that each historical moment bears a distinctive signature." Early Americanist culture historians developed precisely such chronometers. Each was used successfully only when Gould's "rigid requirement" was met. If the thing(s) monitored recurred, then the chronometer was faulty because it rendered time not as the linear flight of an arrow but rather as a set of reversals, recurrences, and cycles. Time measured in the latter fashion is of no use to geologists, paleontologists, and archaeologists who are interested in the temporally linear history of things such as biological descent with modification and cultural change. Most archaeologists are aware of the recurrence problem when they seek to build, or use, a chronometer. A familiar example is found in the conversion of radiocarbon ages to calendar years; when converted, some radiocarbon ages give more than one calendar age.

Time-series analysis is not a chronometer in the sense indicated in the preceding paragraph. Seriation, as defined above, is often used by archaeologists as a chronometer. The distinction between time-series analysis and seriation is, however, sometimes ignored and the two methods conflated. For example, despite their own characterizations of their work as "seriation," Old World prehistorians performed time-series analyses when they plotted frequencies of types of stone tools against their ages as determined stratigraphically and interpreted the variation in those frequencies (Collins 1965; Mellars 1965). We call what they did percentage stratigraphy (Lyman et al. 1997b). Time-series analysis can be used to develop new chronometers, to discover additional chronometric units, or to refine existing chronometric units so as to have them reflect shorter temporal increments. Binford (1962b), for example, calculated a simple linear regression formula that expressed the relation between pipe-stem hole diameter and the age of the pipe. Harrington (1954) had originally documented the relation between hole diameter and age and had used 30-year increments to group pipes of known age into sets that comprised adequate samples for determining if hole diameter in fact decreased consistently over time. Harrington found such consistency—there were no reversals toward holes of larger diameter—and concluded that hole diameter was a good chronometer because there were no cycles or recurrences of particular diameters over time. Binford (1962b) desired a more precise way to estimate the absolute age of individual assemblages of pipes, and his regression formula provided a way to calculate a "mean date" for such assemblages.

Plog and Hantman (1986, 1990) followed Binford's (1962b) lead and regressed the age of southwestern ceramic types against the individual attributes comprising the types in an effort to develop chronological units of finer temporal resolution than were provided by the types. (Types are particular attribute combinations.) Braun (1985) regressed the thickness of ceramic vessel walls against time to study changes in that variable. There is a potential problem with this kind of use of time-series analysis (O'Brien and Lyman 1999c:135–

136). The regression equation comprises an empirical generalization derived from the specimens studied. Whether or not it applies to other specimens of the same type is a separate issue, although various data indicate it may not (e.g., Deetz and Dethlefsen 1965). Archaeologists, geologists, and paleontologists measure time indirectly with formal variation in artifacts, strata, and fossils, respectively, and that formal variation can occur in time differentially across geographic space, as should be clear from our discussion in Chapter 4. Therefore, chronometers and the units they comprise must constantly be tested to ensure that they are in fact chronometric such that not only does "each historical moment bear a distinctive signature" (Gould 1987:157) but also that the signature is equally historically distinctive irrespective of where in geographic space it is used as a chronometer. Once the ages of specimens have been determined with a chronometer, then time-series analysis is possible.

Although frequency seriation has been discussed by numerous individuals (see references in O'Brien and Lyman 1999c for an introduction), the three basic requirements of the technique are not always spelled out. We phrase them here in the typical sense of ordering assemblages of spatio-temporally associated artifacts (discrete objects owing one or more of their attributes to human activity). First, assemblages must represent relatively brief intervals of time; the duration of their formation—the time between the deposition of the first specimen to the time of the deposition of the last specimen— must be short. This requirement ensures that time's passage is measured rather than the durations of formation of assemblages (Dunnell 1970, 2000), but it begs the question of how short the duration of the formation of an assemblage must be. We return to this question later and here simply note that evolutionary theory (von Vaupel Klein 1994) and computer modeling (Lipo et al. 1997; Neiman 1995) suggest that a single generation—such as the modern market economy's fiscal year—is too short of a temporal unit for producing frequency-distribution curves that fluctuate smoothly and unimodally.

Second, the seriated assemblages must derive from the same cultural tradition, where a cultural tradition is a lineage resulting from transmission. The seriated assemblages must all derive from the same line of heritable continuity. The third requirement rests on the fact that transmission has both a temporal and a spatial aspect and demands that the seriated assemblages all come from the same local area. This requirement limits spatial variation in order to measure time; if one is interested in measuring transmission across space, then time must be limited (Dunnell 1970, 1981; Lipo 2001a, 2001b; Lipo et al. 1997; O'Brien and Lyman 1999c).

The frequency-seriation model holds that historical types will occur during only one span of time and will have unimodal (relative) frequency distributions over time (Dunnell 1970). Originally said to result from the "popularity" of types (see discussion in Lyman et al. 1997b), this is not an explanation of what has been observed but is rather an empirical generalization that simply restates what has been observed (Dunnell 2000; Teltser 1995). It is now clear that so-called historical types produce unimodal frequency distributions when seriated because the transmission processes that result in their persistence over time are stochastic. As Lowe and Lowe (1982:540) note, "styles are stochastic systems, neither entirely random nor deterministic, but instead a mixture of structure and chaos." The vagaries of transmission and replication result in the battleship-shaped or unimodal frequency distributions of seriable historical types (if the durations of the seriated assemblages are correct), a fact confirmed in computer simulations performed by archaeologists (e.g., Lipo et al. 1997; Neiman 1995) and paleontologists (e.g., Raup and Gould 1974; Raup et al. 1973). Seriable types that are successfully arranged via frequency seriation "are likely to have relatively neutral adaptive value in a culture" (Hole and Shaw 1967:86). The types must be functionally equivalent relative to one another so that they reflect only the vagaries of transmission.

Dunnell (2000:549) pointed out that when ordering assemblages via frequency seriation, the analyst could "insist on an exact match with the unimodal [frequency distribution] model before regarding the order as chronological, a *deterministic* solution; alternatively, one could accept the 'best fit' to the unimodal model as chronological, a *probabilistic* solution." He notes that deterministic solutions may seldom be found but does not elaborate on why this should be so. We suspect one important factor contributing to the regular failure to find deterministic solutions concerns the durations of the seriated assemblages, and we return to this issue later.

Frequency seriation is a chronometer that uses variation in the frequencies of formal artifact types to measure time as a nonrecurrent linear phenomenon; time-series analysis is meant to monitor and measure change, whether linear or cyclical, in artifacts already arrayed against the linear flight of time's arrow.

Kroeber knew the difference between the two analytical techniques and the role that units of artifact classification played in each even though he did not refer to what he did as frequency seriation or as time-series analysis.

Kroeber and Frequency Seriation

During the summer of 1915, Kroeber volunteered to help American Museum of Natural History personnel with their research in the Southwest (Wissler 1915). While walking across the countryside around Zuni Pueblo, Kroeber collected pottery sherds from the surfaces of more than a dozen sites. He noticed that some collections tended to be dominated by "red, black, and patterned potsherds," whereas other collections were dominated by "white" sherds that are "nearly always pale buff, pinkish, or light gray" (Kroeber 1916b:8). He concluded that there "could be no doubt that here, within a half hour's radius of the largest inhabited pueblo [Zuni], were prehistoric remains of two types and two periods, as distinct as oil and water" (Kroeber 1916b:9). Two lines of evidence suggested that he was dealing with temporal differences in the variants of pottery he found. First, historical data indicated that "several of the ruins were inhabited in Spanish times" (Kroeber 1916a:43), whereas other ruins were said by his informants to have been inhabited "long ago" (Kroeber 1916b:9). Second, Kroeber observed that historic "ruins normally include standing walls, and loose rock abounds. [Prehistoric] sites are low or flat, without walls or rock, [probably] due to the decay of age, or to the carrying away of the broken rock to serve as material in the nearby constructions of later ages" (Kroeber 1916a:43). Based on these two lines of evidence, Kroeber (1916b:9–10) concluded that white ware was "wholly prehistoric," whereas black and red ware "is the more recent [belonging] in part to the time of early American history."

Kroeber (1916b) presented the absolute frequencies of 10 types of sherds he collected from what he took to be historic sites in one table and the absolute frequencies of those 10 types of sherds from what seemed to be prehistoric sites in a second table. In a third table, he presented the relative or proportional frequencies of each of the 10 types from all sites he had visited, including Zuni Pueblo. His fourth table is critically important because in that table Kroeber lumped his 10 types into three more general types and presented the relative frequencies of the types from each site. A graph of the relative frequencies of those three general types across the ordering of sites he ultimately presents as

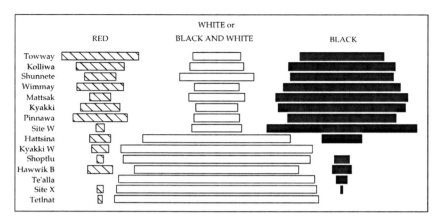

Figure 5.1. Centered-bar graph of relative frequencies of 3 of Kroeber's original 10 pottery types arranged in his final hypothesized chronological order (some site names are abbreviated). Note that the frequency distributions of none of the types approximates a unimodal curve. Compare with Figure 5.2.

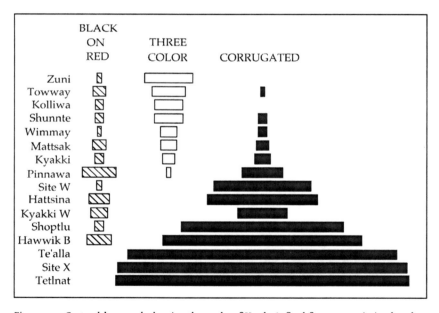

Figure 5.2. Centered-bar graph showing the results of Kroeber's final frequency seriation based on the relative frequencies of corrugated ware and Three Color (some site names are abbreviated). Only one—black on red—of several other types is included for comparison to show that the two types on which Kroeber based his final seriation fluctuate unimodally, with two exceptions. See the text for discussion of the exceptional Towway and Kyakki W assemblages.

a tentative chronology does not comprise a deterministic frequency seriation; none of the three general types displays anything approximating a unimodal frequency distribution (Figure 5.1). Our efforts to sort these collections on the basis of these three types have thus far failed to more closely approximate a deterministic solution.

Faced with such a problem, and recalling the innovative and noncomputer-aided nature of what Kroeber did, he seems to have taken the only possible, yet remarkably simple, route to a nearly perfect deterministic solution. Kroeber's original 10 types included both black corrugated ware and white corrugated ware, but those color differences seemed of no chronological significance. However, corrugated ware in general seemed to be relatively old, so Kroeber lumped the two colors into the general type corrugated ware. The collections of pottery from individual sites were arranged so that the relative abundance of corrugated ware decreased monotonically, with two exceptions, as indicated in his fifth table of data. Those data are graphed in Figure 5.2. The basis for this arrangement was Kroeber's (1916b:15) impression that corrugated ware, given its rare association with modern pottery types and its regular association with decayed ruins, gradually decreased in relative frequency as time passed; this allowed him to arrange "the sites in order accordingly" and would in 1916 come to be known as the "popularity principle," originally stated, but not named as such, by Nels Nelson (1916).

Kroeber reported that one of the two exceptions in his ordering—Kyakk W—comprised a nonrepresentative sample; only 25 sherds had been collected from this site, so Kroeber was likely correct that this sample was not representative of the site. The other exception—Towway—was placed in the order on the basis of one of Kroeber's original 10 types, what he called "Three Color." The relative abundance of Three Color increased monotonically once it appeared in the sequence and was most abundant in the modern Zuni assemblage. Here Kroeber was anticipating the observation made 50 years later that historical types may be missing from collections dating to the initial and the final periods of a type's duration (Dunnell 1970). He thus used a second type to finalize the ordering of the collections. Other types were simply appended to the arrangement, and thus their frequencies tend to fluctuate without pattern. We graphed only one of these other types—black on red—in Figure 5.2, as Kroeber did not present the relevant data in a fashion conducive to graphing all types. Kroeber suggested at least some of the fluctuation in these other types could be attributed to sampling error.

There are three important aspects of what Kroeber did. First, his lumping of types indicates that he conceived of those units as things created by the analyst as opposed to things to be discovered. If properly constructed, types were units that allowed measurement of the flight of time's arrow. The nineteenth-century phyletic seriations (Lyman et al. 1997b) of British gold coins by John Evans (1850, 1875), the phyletic seriation of Egyptian pottery by W. M. F. Petrie (1899), and other such efforts (e.g., Pitt-Rivers 1870, 1875a, 1875b; Uhle 1903) also measured that flight, but they played no role in Kroeber's invention of frequency seriation (see also Trigger 1989:200–202). That this is so is clearly reflected in two ways. First, Kroeber used ideational units to categorize his sherds; such units are required by frequency seriation but not by phyletic seriation. The presence or absence of empirical units is typical of phyletic seriation. Kroeber used relative frequencies of empirical specimens categorized as one of two ideational units—corrugated ware and Three Color—to seriate his collections. Second, Kroeber assessed the similarity of collections in a unique way—by measuring and comparing the relative frequencies of multiple types. Phyletic seriation simply measures the similarities of specimens, not the similarities of frequencies of specimens within categories.

The second important aspect of Kroeber's work at Zuni is that there was no explicit theoretical warrant for inferring that his seriated collections measured the passage of time, although it seems to us that he had in mind some notion of cultural change. Heritable continuity affected by cultural transmission, if reflected in pottery, would reflect (and allow the measurement of) the linear passage of time. Kroeber knew that artifacts could (and often did) change formally over time (how they might change was what was unclear), plus he had observed the association of different pottery types with ruins inferred to be of different ages. He was very aware of the hypothetical nature of the inference and noted, "I have not turned a spadeful of earth in the Zuni country" (Kroeber 1916b:14) and that the "final proof [of his hypothesized chronology] is in the spade" (Kroeber 1916b:20). The latter statement shows that Kroeber believed that stratigraphically superposed collections would provide the empirical proof that his ordering of collections was in fact chronological. Leslie Spier (1917a, 1917b) collected that proof in 1916 (Chapter 8).

The third important aspect of Kroeber's seminal frequency seriation resides in his (1916a:44) observation that the seriated assemblages "shade[d] into one another," and there was "no gap or marked break between" the prehistoric and historic periods. The prehistoric and historic periods might have been "as distinct as oil and water" (Kroeber 1916b:9) when distinguished on the basis of the degree of deterioration of associated ruins, but these were not the cultural phenomena used in the seriation. Kroeber (1916b:15) indicated that the prehistoric and historic periods "can normally be distinguished without the least uncertainty, and the separateness of the two is fundamental," but—and this is significant—his frequency seriation of pottery indicated the two periods "do not represent two different migrations, nationalities, or waves of culture, but rather a steady and continuous development on the soil." This was the clearest expression to that point in the history of American archaeology of the belief that time could be measured archaeologically as a continuous linear (noncyclical) dimension because the way in which artifacts were categorized suggested ethnic and thus heritable continuity. Although we suspect it was based on the same implicit reasoning that underpinned the direct historical approach (Chapters 4 and 7), this point was missed completely over the next twenty years as American archaeologists came to adopt stratigraphic excavation as the preferred method of building chronologies of cultures (Chapter 8).

Thirty-five years after Kroeber seriated his Zuni potsherds, he remarked that his effort was of "historical interest as regards method" for two reasons (Kroeber 1952:230). First, his work took place simultaneously with what he called the first "stirrings" of "confidence that time differences could be ascertained" in the archaeological record of the Americas (Kroeber 1952:230). Second, he had not had time to excavate and thus could not use the stratification of sediments as a chronometer, and thus he was forced to make what he now called "stylistic seriations" that he hypothesized comprised a "temporal sequence" (Kroeber 1952:230). We add to Kroeber's two historical reasons why his work is significant the fact that it rested implicitly on the patently evolutionary notion of heritable continuity among artifacts affected by cultural transmission. Frequency seriation provides a means to measure the continuous linear flight of time's arrow because it measures the continuous evolution of artifact lineages.

Kroeber (1916a, 1916b) did not use the term "frequency seriation" to describe what he did, nor did he use the term "seriation" until 36 years later (Kroeber 1952). Spier (1917a) used the latter term in reference not only to Kroeber's (1916a, 1916b) work but also to the very different work of Kidder (1917). Spier could use the term correctly to refer to both of those efforts because although Kroeber and Kidder followed distinctly different analytical protocols (Lyman et al. 1997b), both men were ordering artifacts based on the similarities of those artifacts. Seriation as an analytical method employed by archaeologists today comprises three different techniques, each of which involves the process of placing phenomena in an order or series based on a specific measure of similarity based in turn on a generic principle of arrangement (Dunnell 1970; O'Brien and Lyman 1999c; Rouse 1967; Rowe 1961). The generic principle involves formal similarity; the more similar two phenomena are formally—in terms of their attributes—the closer together they are placed in the arrangement.

Three specific measures of similarity have been used by archaeologists, only one of which comprises frequency seriation. First, similarity can be assessed by noting which attributes of discrete objects are shared. Kidder (1917; see Figure 2.3) followed the protocol of phyletic seriation when he mimicked what Petrie (1899) and others before him had done. Second, similarity can be assessed by noting which types are shared by multiple assemblages of artifacts; this is known as occurrence seriation (Dunnell 1970), a technique invented in 1963 (Dempsey and Baumhoff 1963) but with striking similarities to the direct historical approach (overlapping, artifact type or cultural trait presence/absence). The third technique for assessing similarity is the one Kroeber designed.

When Kroeber (1916a, 1916b) invented frequency seriation, he did two important things above and beyond using the generic ordering procedure of seriation. First, he assessed similarity in a new way—he noted the relative frequency of a kind of artifact in each of multiple collections of artifacts and then ordered those collections based on the similarities of the relative frequencies of that kind of artifact. This made his analytical protocol not only innovative but also distinct from that of Kidder and others who had used a protocol like Kidder's in the nineteenth century. Second, like those archaeologists who preceded him in using seriation as an ordering technique, Kroeber inferred that the resulting order was chronological. That it indeed measured the passage of time was, however, a hypothesis that Kroeber recognized as demanding a test.

Kroeber (1909:5) had earlier noted not only that a stratigraphically ordered set of artifacts described by Uhle (1907) was in fact chronological but also that Uhle's ordering showed little more than "passing change in fashion." Such "stylistic pulsations," as Wissler (1916d:195–196) and Spier (1918b:201) referred to them, would shortly come to occupy some of Kroeber's analytical energy. Importantly, Kroeber's (1916a, 1916b) discussion makes it clear that he was trying to measure the linear flight of time's arrow by monitoring changes in the relative frequencies of various kinds of artifacts. After several unsuccessful attempts to order his collections based on the relative frequencies of particular types, Kroeber succeeded in defining two types that displayed unimodal frequency distributions over what seemed to be the passage of time based on the condition of the ruins with which the sherds were associated. The significance of this point regarding the influence of artifact typology on analytical results cannot be overemphasized.

To produce a frequency seriation of types the frequencies of which fluctuate unimodally and thus theoretically measure the flight of time's arrow, the types, or analytical units, must be defined in particular ways. This is what Kroeber (1916a, 1916b) grappled with and what makes his work of significantly more importance than mere historical interest. The types used in a frequency seriation must comprise what came to be termed styles or historical types; their frequencies must comprise, in Gould's (1987) words, historically distinctive signatures. The relatively smooth unimodal frequency distributions of the types Kroeber ultimately defined (Figure 5.2) suggested to him that he was measuring not only time's passage but also "a steady and continuous development" of an artifact lineage (Kroeber 1916b:15). Frequency seriation worked as a chronometer because it measured heritable continuity (Lipo 2001a, 2001b; Lipo et al. 1997; Neiman 1995; Teltser 1995).

A Different Kind of Analysis

Shortly after his work at Zuni Pueblo, Kroeber used, if implicitly, the heritable-continuity notion, but he employed an entirely different kind of analytical unit and a different analytical protocol than he had used in his seminal frequency seriation. The unit Kroeber used a few years after his work with pottery sherds was similar, but not identical to, the sort of unit originally used by

Kidder (1917). In his famous study of changes in women's fashions, Kroeber (1919:235) sought to formulate a law concerning the "growths and declines [of] normally recurring events." He reasoned that a "generic [lawlike] principle" regarding the "rhythmic inevitability" of change in cultural phenomena could be found only with "verifiable measurements" that, when plotted against time, would display "a polygon of frequency or normal curve such as the statistical sciences employ" (Kroeber 1919:236, 237). But here Kroeber was not searching for the unimodal curve given by a type's frequency in a frequency seriation; instead, each curve he now sought would be multimodal and thus reflect cycles. Further, the curves or lines would here monitor changes in the observed averages of "measurements" of phenomena—each average representing a particular year—rather than the frequencies of various kinds of measurements such as types of sherds. Finally, the measurements and the lines they defined were to be arrayed against time's arrow, making Kroeber's study of women's fashions a time-series analysis. This was significantly different than what he had done with southwestern pottery a few years earlier. When he invented frequency seriation, the desired inference was the linear flight of time's arrow; when he measured women's fashions, Kroeber knew the flight of time's arrow and wished to infer patterns of cultural change, specifically cycles of cultural change rendered as multimodal curves.

For his study of women's fashions, Kroeber (1919:238–239) reasoned that the measurements would have to be taken not from "utilitarian pieces [because these] do not modify freely"; instead, they must come from artifacts that do not "vary in purpose" and are "purely stylistic." Therefore, to search for the rhythmic pulses, Kroeber (1919:239) chose "women's full evening toilette [because it] has served the same definite occasions for more than a century." The function of women's evening clothing had not changed over time, but its style had, and thus "styles" of cultural phenomena, because they were adaptively neutral, were the unit of choice for measuring cultural patterns manifest as recurrent phenomena. With respect to using averages of dimensions of women's evening wear, such as dress lengths, Kroeber correctly chose units that were functionally equivalent and reflected the vagaries of cultural transmission. Those units showed what he wanted them to show— cycles in cultural phenomena—and thus they are decidedly inappropriate to frequency seriation or any seriation technique meant to measure the linear flight of time's arrow. Such units make poor chronometric units because they fail to meet the rigid requirement of comprising a historically distinct signature (see below).

Kroeber (1919) measured eight variables on about 10 illustrations per year as shown in the pages of various magazines published between 1844 and 1919 inclusively. He collaborated with Jane Richardson 20 years later, increasing the temporal range included in his sample (Richardson and Kroeber 1940; see also Kroeber 1948:331–336; Kroeber 1957). Kroeber (1919) and Richardson and Kroeber (1940) plotted the annual average of each measured variable against time to produce a line that fluctuated as time passed; the shapes of the various lines were interpreted to reflect the process and pattern of stylistic change in women's fashion. Although Kroeber knew that he was monitoring heritable continuity, he assumed that he was using adaptively neutral units to do so. Lowe and Lowe's (1982) reanalysis of Richardson and Kroeber's data suggest his assumption was correct. With respect to how he dealt with those units analytically, however, Kroeber did not follow the procedure of frequency seriation.

Kroeber did not classify fashions as to type, nor did he plot the frequencies of those types against time. For his frequency seriation of southwestern pottery sherds, Kroeber used conceptual units known as types. For his study of women's evening wear, Kroeber used units expressed as averages of dress length and other dimensions. The latter analysis revealed cycles, or repetitions, in the occurrence of the average of individual dimensions of women's fashions. These averages cannot be used as chronometers because various averages recur at different points in time. For example, average dress length per decade both rises and falls but only so far in either direction. Reversals in dress length create cycles, such as in Figure 5.3, where it is shown that, based on Richardson and Kroeber's (1940) data, between 1710 and 1930 dress length (measured from the woman's mouth to the bottom of the hem) was 95 percent of a woman's height (measured from the woman's mouth to the bottom of her foot) five different times.

In both the case of southwestern pottery and the case of women's evening wear, Kroeber's results were dependent on the measurement units he chose. In both cases the units reflected heritable continuity and the vagaries of cultural transmission. Some investigators have failed to note this aspect of Kroeber's work and have attempted to explain observed periodicity in various phenomena by calling upon social forces, economics, and other cultural factors as the

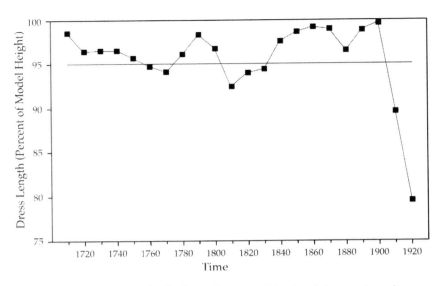

Figure 5.3. Grand average per decade of annual averages of dress length in women's evening wear (based on data in Richardson and Kroeber 1940). The closer the broken-stick line is to 100 percent, the longer the dress length. Note that if dress length is 95 percent of the height of the model (measured from the mouth of the model to the bottom of her foot), this category of dress length would not serve chronometric purposes because it occurs five times during the temporal period included in the graph.

causes of those cycles (e.g., Robinson 1975, 1976; Weeden 1977). Although such factors may in fact be causal, the linkages seem to us to be weak, just as they seemed to Kroeber (1952, 1957). We find stronger linkages and greater explanatory power elsewhere. In other studies at least some of the units displaying recurrences over time are not adaptively neutral (e.g., Braun 1985; Rands 1961) but are instead functional (Dunnell 1978), thus their cycles or periodicity are predictable from Darwinian evolutionary theory and a knowledge of the selective environment. We are not sure that the dimensions of women's evening dress measured by Kroeber are functional attributes, but further consideration of this issue is beyond our scope here.

Some later investigators interested in aspects of fashion history mimicked the analytical protocol Kroeber had used to study women's dresses (e.g., Robinson 1975, 1976; Weeden 1977). One analyst interested in the history of women's hats, however, stated that she was mimicking Kroeber's protocol of frequency seriation. Although there is nothing inherently wrong with the protocol followed, that analysis underscores how easily researchers might confuse frequency seriation as a chronometer with time-series analysis as a technique for studying cultural lineages. That some have misunderstood Kroeber's (1919) work is exemplified by misstatements of what he actually did and how it relates to frequency seriation.

Women's Bonnets

Inspired by Richardson and Kroeber's (1940) study of temporal changes in women's dresses, Sarah Turnbaugh (1979) undertook a study of the history of women's headgear. Rather than mimic Kroeber's (1919) protocol for the analysis of fashion, Turnbaugh used what she called the "seriational technique," characterized by her as "a new method for measuring . . . the incessant nature of stylistic change in fashion" (Turnbaugh 1979:241, 242,). Her analytical protocol comprises two steps. The first is "content analysis [which] involves the controlled observation and systematic counting of the frequency of occurrence of symbols or traits" (Turnbaugh 1979:242). The data source comprised "the total population of illustrations" of bonnets deemed fashionable between 1831 and 1895 and illustrated in *Godey's Lady's Book and Magazine* (Turnbaugh 1979:243), a monthly magazine published between 1830 and 1898 (Finley 1931). Turnbaugh (1979:243, 244) identified "four major categories" of bonnets (pamela, capote, bibi, and crownless bonnet) comprising 21 "distinct varieties"; these were her analytical units. For each year between 1831 and 1895 inclusively, she tallied the absolute frequency of illustrations of each of the 21 varieties, plus three additional categories labeled "hats," "caps," and "other/nothing."

The second step of Turnbaugh's analytical protocol involves what she called a "variant of seriation"; she (incorrectly) defines seriation as "the chronological ordering of the frequency and life span of a specific trait, or an object" and also states (incorrectly) that the seriation method "necessarily assumes that the popularity of any object is transient and may be measured." She continues: "After data have been collected by using content analysis, fashion counting, or other appropriate counting methods, seriation may be used to order the data for temporal analysis and interpretation" (Turnbaugh 1979:243). Recall that seriation in general has as its goal the ordering of phenomena based on some principle of similarity and that it is only inferentially a chronometer. Turnbaugh already knew the chronological order of the bonnets given the publication dates of the magazine issues, and she simply plotted the frequencies of illustration of each variety of bonnet against the year when those illustrations appeared. The direction of flight of time's arrow was already known, and the frequencies of kinds of headgear were plotted against that flight. Turnbaugh's analysis, like Kroeber's concerning dress lengths, is a time-series analysis rather than a seriation, although it is not unusual to find archaeologists labeling as seriation virtually any technique for plotting frequencies of artifacts against time (e.g., Deetz and Dethlefsen 1965; see also Chapter 9).

Turnbaugh's (1979:243) statement that seriation was an archaeological invention "developed as an analytical tool for the study of prehistoric cultural change" is a mischaracterization of history. All three seriation techniques were developed as chronometers that rest on the assumption that material culture changes over time. Turnbaugh (1979:243) is correct that frequency seriation "creates a type of bar graph" but is incorrect that the "frequency of occurrence is plotted against a time line to produce a 'battleship curve.'" Recall that time is inferred from the ordering resulting from the frequency seriation and that the ordering seeks to mimic a unimodal curve; in time-series analysis the phenomena are plotted against time and may not produce a battleship-shaped curve. Indeed, it is the shape of the resulting curve that is of analytical interest.

Turnbaugh (1979) presented data for the years 1830–1898 in the form of a centered-bar graph (Figure 5.4), but she did not provide counts of observations. We used the scale she published to extract counts from her graph and note that only counts for "hats" exist for 1830, only counts for "hats" and "other/nothing" exist for 1896 and 1897, and no illustrations were published in 1898. Turnbaugh (1979:243) characterized her bar graph as showing the "stylistic evolution of American [women's] headgear." If we adopt the probabilistic solution of frequency seriation, then some but not all of Turnbaugh's 21 varieties of bonnets approximate battleship-shaped curves. In Figure 5.4 and our analyses, we eliminated her "hat," "cap," and "other/nothing" headgear categories—A, B, and C, respectively. These types would be of little utility in a chronometer seeking an ordering within the time period 1831 to 1895 because they span the entire period.

Turnbaugh (1979:243) cites archaeological references to seriation (e.g., Dunnell 1970), but she does not cite Kroeber's (1916a, 1916b) seminal effort or Spier's (1917a, 1917b) follow-up study. That she in fact did not perform a frequency seriation in the sense Kroeber intended when he invented the technique is clear from the facts that in Turnbaugh's case, time's direction

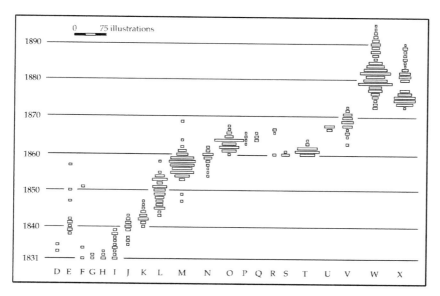

Figure 5.4. Turnbaugh's original graph of the absolute frequencies of illustrations of 21 varieties of women's headgear (D–X) published between 1831 and 1895, inclusively (after Turnbaugh 1979). Each variety is denoted by a capital letter. Turnbaugh's categories "Hat," "Cap," and "Other/Nothing" are not included.

was known and served as the basis for the ordering, absolute frequencies rather than relative frequencies of varieties of women's headgear per year were plotted, and absolute frequencies of illustrations rather than relative frequencies of the artifacts themselves were used (Figure 5.4). One could argue that illustrations of artifacts are themselves artifacts that might serve as the units in a frequency seriation or as the units in a time-series analysis. To use the ordering of illustrations of artifacts as a basis for determining the age of an artifact itself rather than an illustration of it, however, requires the assumption that there is a direct correlation between how often a style is illustrated and how many individual artifacts of that style were manufactured. That this assumption is perhaps at least partially met by Turnbaugh's sample is suggested by the fact that she was able to correctly date three of four bonnet specimens of known age using her temporal ordering of illustrations, and the fourth bonnet was dated within 10 years of its true age (Turnbaugh 1979:246–247). This test was successful because Turnbaugh (1979:247) established what she variously termed the "date range" or "seriational date" of each bonnet variety based on her time-series analysis (Figure 5.4). Her test also suggests that the varieties of bonnet she used in her analysis may at least approximately comprise historical types in the sense Kroeber intended when he was dealing with southwestern pottery sherds.

Questions remain, however. Are the bonnet varieties seriable—are they good chronometers—in Kroeber's original sense? Because the temporal order of the bonnets is already known, we rephrase this question: Do the relative frequencies of bonnet varieties approximate unimodal curves when plotted against time? Is a year a good temporal unit in the sense that it does not influence the shape of the frequency distribution? What should be the duration of the temporal units represented by seriated assemblages? Recall that the frequency-seriation technique requires that the assemblages be of short duration, but we wonder, how short? For example, in their classic studies of New England gravestones, Deetz and Dethlefsen (1965, 1967, 1971; Dethlefsen and Deetz 1966) used a time-series approach and chose (for unspecified reasons) to plot relative frequencies of styles of gravestones per decade; the resulting frequency distributions are good approximations of smooth, unimodal curves. Similarly, for unspecified reasons Turnbaugh plotted the data she compiled by year despite the fact that the magazine that served as the source of her data was published monthly and would have thus allowed finer-scale time-series analysis. Consideration of these various issues via reanalysis of Turnbaugh's data reveals some of the significant nuances of the frequency-seriation technique.

Reanalysis of Bonnet Frequencies

Few of the bonnet varieties in Turnbaugh's graph display the battleship-shaped frequency-distribution curves of a deterministic solution (Figure 5.4). Considering those varieties with more than two annual samples, only varieties H, K, P, and Q comprise deterministic solutions. Because we believe that it is indisputable that heritable continuity is intrinsic to the data graphed, there are two probable reasons why the majority of the variety-specific curves are not unimodal. First, the frequencies are absolute rather than relative. Second, each annual sample of bonnet illustrations is plotted. Simulations (Lipo et al. 1997; Neiman 1995) and theory (Teltser 1995; von Vaupel Klein 1994) suggest that approximately battleship-shaped frequency distributions will be produced but that their edges will be jagged to greater or lesser degrees when either of these conditions hold in a frequency seriation (assuming that the jaggedness is not

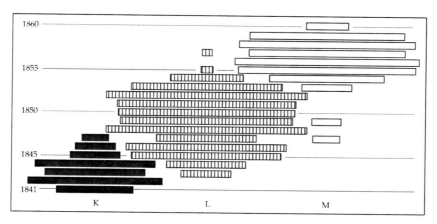

Figure 5.5. A portion of the data from Figure 5.4 plotted as relative frequencies. Note the lack of unimodal frequency distributions for each of the three varieties (K, L, M) of bonnet.

a result of sampling). To determine which of these conditions is influencing Turnbaugh's graph, we calculated the relative frequencies of each of the 21 varieties and generated a centered-bar graph of those frequencies plotted against time. Virtually none of the resulting curves is unimodal, as is illustrated in Figure 5.5, which shows a portion of the graph of relative frequencies of bonnet illustrations. This suggests either that the analytical units do not comprise good historical types in the sense of their being useful in the context of deterministic frequency seriation and/or that the annual durations of the assemblages of illustrations are inappropriate.

Recalling that in his seminal frequency seriation Kroeber (1916a, 1916b) treated his units as analytical constructs and that he lumped various types with red color into a general class he termed "Any Red" because the former, more discriminating types did not produce unimodal frequency distributions whereas the latter, more general type did, we followed suit and simplified Turnbaugh's 21 varieties of bonnets. Turnbaugh (1979:244) noted that the 21 varieties actually comprised "four major bonnet types: the pamela [D–F in Figure 5.4], the capote [G–J], the bibi [K–T], and the crownless bonnet [U–X]" (Figure 5.6). Because frequency seriation is based on relative frequencies of types and thus is subject to the problems of closed arrays (each row must sum to 100 percent), more than two types are necessary when one performs a frequency seriation, a fact recognized by Spier (1917a). McNutt (1973, 2001) incorrectly discounts the validity of frequency seriation as a chronometer because he fails to grasp the implications of this point, arguing that because

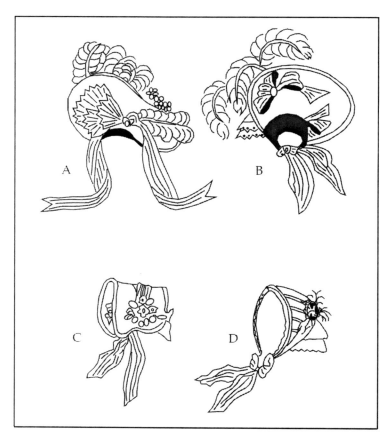

Figure 5.6. Four "types" of women's bonnets (after Turnbaugh 1979). A, pamela; B, capote; C, bibi; D, crownless bonnet.

problems arise when only two types are used, those same problems afflict cases when more than two types are used.

Turnbaugh's four "types" comprise a sufficient number for our purposes. We determined the relative frequencies of these four types and plotted them against each year. To simplify the graph, we plotted only one row of bars for multiple contiguous years every time the relative frequencies for all types were identical over contiguous years. The resulting graph is shown in Figure 5.7. The frequency distributions of each type fluctuate greatly, but they appear to fluctuate less than in Figure 5.4, where each year is plotted individually. This reduced fluctuation in abundance suggests that the four basic types may serve as good historical types—display smooth unimodal frequency distributions—

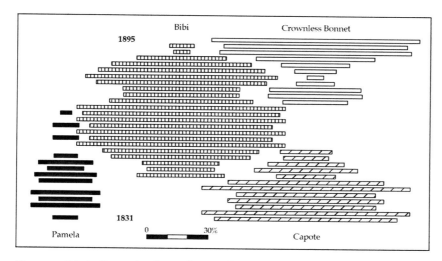

Figure 5.7. *Relative frequencies of types of women's bonnets between 1831 and 1895. Adjacent years with identical frequencies of all types are plotted only once. For example, the bar denoting 1895 actually comprises 1870–1895.*

if they were not plotted by year but rather by temporal units, each of which includes multiple years.

It is necessary here to briefly consider two terms that will be of use in the following discussion. The familiar term "generation" is typically defined as the average time between the births of parents and the births of their offspring, calculated over multiple parents and multiple offspring (Art 1993). A perhaps less familiar term is "cohort," which is defined as the group of animals born during the same time span, typically but not always a year, such that the group comprises individuals of the same age (Art 1993). Despite the fact that many (but not all) animals reproduce continuously during a solar year, both concepts are useful. The concept of a generation is useful for monitoring the history of the age of parents at reproduction and the like, and the concept of a cohort is useful for studying various demographic and mortality patterns of populations (Caughley 1977). These two concepts are also useful for thinking about the duration of the formation of an artifact assemblage. Like animals, artifacts may be produced more or less continuously throughout a year, thus rendering clear distinction of one generation or one cohort from the next difficult. The important point here is that simulations of biological reproduction and artifact replication tend to construe each temporally distinct sample of organisms or artifacts as a cohort that is parental to the temporally subsequent offspring cohort (e.g., von Vaupel Klein 1994; Neiman 1995). This has the effect of making each row of bars in a bar graph of frequencies (such as in Figures 5.2 and 5.5) equivalent to a generation in duration.

Many kinds of modern artifacts tend to have generations that are one year in duration given that the market economy rests on a fiscal year. Such artifacts include dress fashions, automobiles, and some computer hardware and software. Other artifacts have longer generations; still others have shorter generations. We do not know the duration in years of a generation of prehistoric pottery, but a generation of nineteenth-century bonnets probably approximated a year given the market economy of the time. The point to recognize is that the computer simulations performed to date suggest that, however long its duration might be for a particular category of artifact, a single generation seems to be an inappropriate duration for assemblages (cohorts) that one wishes to use in a frequency seriation. Assemblages representing longer durations comprising multiple generations would remove the jagged edges such as are apparent in Figure 5.5.

Because the temporal span of Turnbaugh's sample of illustrations is 65 years, we initially chose to divide that span of time by 6 to derive 10 assemblages of six-years duration each and a final, eleventh assemblage spanning five years. We calculated the relative frequencies of each of the four types for those multiyear temporal units and plotted them against time. The result is more than gratifying (Figure 5.8), and because of this we did not perform any other permutations of lumping multiple years. With one small exception, each type displays a deterministic solution—a nonjagged-edged, unimodal frequency distribution. The single exception in Figure 5.8 is the Pamela type, which decreases from a relative frequency of 19 percent in 1837–1842 to 2 percent in 1843–1848 and then increases to 3.5 percent in 1849–1854. This change occurs at the end of the life span (if you will) of this type, and thus it was rarely and discontinuously illustrated (Figure 5.4). It is at precisely such times, when a type rarely occurs, that not only a violation of the continuity of a historical type is permissible if not expected, but so, too, is it permissible (and expected) for a type's frequency not to decrease (or increase) monotonically shortly after it first appears or shortly before it disappears (Dunnell 1970). These are precisely the times when a type will be rare, and thus its frequencies in a collection will be subject to sampling error. This is in part why the previously mentioned deterministic model of frequency seriation may seldom be met.

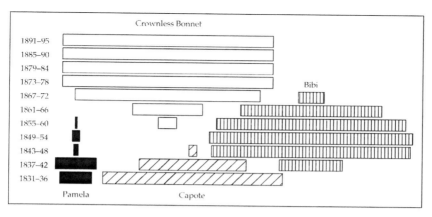

Figure 5.8. *Relative frequencies of four types of women's bonnets for six-year increments over time. The last bar comprises only five years (1891–1895).*

We adopt the deterministic model of frequency seriation. Given the preceding consideration of sampling error, we believe the fluctuation in the relative frequency of the Pamela type to be insignificant for chronometric purposes. The four general types of women's headgear comprise good historical types in the sense that their relative frequencies form the expected battleship-shaped frequency distributions over time if, and this is an important if, they are not plotted on a year-by-year—what we take to be a generation-by-generation—basis. When plotted on such a (here, annual) basis, the types do not form the unimodal frequency distributions demanded by the deterministic model, and thus their chronological utility is compromised. This returns us, then, to the questions: What is a generation in the archaeological record? What comprises a generation in terms of the artifacts we might try to seriate? Perhaps a generation is a set of artifacts comprising a so-called occupation, but we doubt this because the life span of an artifact varies based on numerous variables, such as what it is made of, its use-life history, and its potential for being recycled for the same or a different function. In our view, the issue of assemblage duration requires additional consideration, a point made previously in a different context for somewhat different reasons (Dunnell 1995; see also Lipo 2001a).

Seriation Is a Chronometric Method

Seriation is the process of ordering phenomena based on the generic principle of similarity of the phenomena; the most similar phenomena are placed close together in the ordering, the least similar are placed far apart. The ordering process has as its goal the production of the best, most consistent order possible. When used in archaeology, seriation has the second goal of building chronologies of phenomena, usually artifact types. Kroeber (1916a, 1916b) sought both goals when he invented and first used frequency seriation. When the method was adopted by European (and many American) archaeologists, both of these goals were met by use of the stratigraphic provenience of the artifacts. Thus the order of the artifacts through time was known, and the seminal European efforts to order artifacts chronologically (Collins 1965; Mellars 1965) more closely approximate Turnbaugh's time-series analysis than Kroeber's frequency seriation. As with Turnbaugh's analysis, there is nothing inherently wrong with such research; the results show the history of the frequencies of the artifact classes graphed (Chapter 9). But they are not frequency seriations in the original sense of Kroeber; rather, they literally comprise percentage stratigraphy, a particular form of time-series analysis.

The importance of classification to frequency seriation was implied by Kroeber's (1916b) invention of the technique, and it has been noted by more recent workers (e.g., Dunnell 1970; Lipo et al. 1997; Teltser 1995). Here we have underscored the important point that each assemblage must also comprise more than the archaeological equivalent of a single generation, whatever that might be. This, too, is a classification issue—it specifically addresses how assemblages are to be bounded—and it helps explain why the deterministic model may seldom be met—assemblages seriated are of inappropriate duration (have incorrect boundaries).

Kroeber was clever. When he invented frequency seriation, he gave archaeologists an analytical technique for measuring the flight of time's arrow and the evolution of artifact lineages that depended on particular kinds of measurement units. When he turned a few years later to a search for laws of cultural development, he employed time-series analysis, a different analytical technique that depended on different measurement units that allowed him to monitor time's cycle. Each analytical technique and each kind of unit was meant to attain a particular analytical goal. Keeping the distinction between those two techniques and two kinds of units clear is mandatory to successful archaeological research precisely because they comprise different sorts of analytical tools. Frequency seriation is a chronometer that uses change in the frequencies of formal artifact types to measure time as a nonrecurrent linear phenomenon; time-series analysis is meant to measure change, whether linear or cyclical, in artifacts already arrayed against time. The critical analytical step resides in the units chosen, and Kroeber recognized this. For his frequency seriations, he designed types that occupied small geographic areas and occurred over time periods of some duration (column B in Figure 4.6). These were types that had distributions like what are known as traditions. What about types that have distributions like horizons (occupy large geographic space and brief time periods)? We take up that sort of artifact type in the next chapter.

6. Time, Space, and Marker Types in James Ford's 1936 Chronology for the Lower Mississippi Valley

In 1936 James A. Ford used a series of pottery types to order 103 sites that he and Moreau Chambers had surface collected in the late 1920s and early 1930s while employed by the Mississippi Department of Archives and History. Received wisdom has it that Ford used frequency seriation to create the chronological ordering (e.g., Trigger 1989:200–202; Watson 1990:43). Probably because of the famous "thumbs-and-paper-clips" diagram that Ford (1962) later used to illustrate one way to perform frequency seriation, that technique has forever been linked to his name. But Ford never used frequency seriation in any of his work (O'Brien and Lyman 1998, 1999b), despite his own claims to the contrary (Ford 1962). Only in the most general sense did Ford "seriate" his and Chambers's pottery collections in 1936. In this chapter we show that Ford did not do what Kroeber had done when the latter invented frequency seriation (Chapter 5). What Ford did was nonetheless significant.

With respect to frequency seriation, as we noted in Chapter 5, similarity is measured by consideration of the relative frequencies of artifact types (Dunnell 1970; O'Brien and Lyman 1999c). Collections are arranged such that those with similar frequencies of shared types are close together in the arrangement in such an order that the frequency distribution of each type defines a unimodal curve (Chapters 5 and 9). Seriation in general as practiced by archaeologists has two tasks: ordering artifact collections based on their similarities and determining whether the ordering measures the passage of time (Cowgill 1968). The first task might entail, for example, creating a series of types and computing their relative frequencies per collection, and the second task might entail examining the stratigraphic positions of the frequencies of types created (Lyman et al. 1997b).

In contrast to frequency seriation as we have just described it, in our view Ford's 1936 effort is well characterized as "artifact (bio)stratigraphy for purposes of cross dating" (O'Brien and Lyman 1999c:209). Ford in fact "determined the most abundant marker type in each collection, then noted which decoration complex was most frequently represented by the marker types, and finally placed each collection in its appropriate decoration complex" (O'Brien and Lyman 1999c:209). These three steps comprise one way a biostratigrapher uses index fossils to correlate strata and assign them to geological periods (Chapter 4). It is only in this biostratigraphic sense that Ford's 1936 effort resulted in an "arrangement in a series" and thus that Ford performed a "seriation."

Ford's 1936 analysis is significant in that it produced the first archaeological chronology for the lower Mississippi Valley—a chronology that Ford would revise over the next several years as a result of the large Works Progress Administration project he directed in Louisiana (O'Brien and Lyman 1998, 1999b). In this chapter we examine in detail how Ford produced his chronology of 1936, particularly the rationale that dictated his choice of analytical units (artifact types) with which to measure the passage of time across a complex cultural landscape. The kinds of units he used—generally referred to as historical types—were not unique in American archaeology; one version had appeared in the Southwest during the second decade of the twentieth century. Ford employed a different version, and he used his units in a manner different from the way Kroeber, Spier, and Nelson used other units in the Southwest. Ford's pottery types were designed to be index fossils or horizon styles, and thus they encompass large spatial areas but have relatively brief temporal spans. That is how they differed from the units in the Southwest (Chapter 4).

Time, Culture Change, and Units

Throughout the twentieth century archaeologists have employed a multitude of units to keep track of time (Dunnell 1986b; Lyman et al. 1997a, 1997b; O'Brien and Lyman 1999c), with the choice of unit depending in large part on how time is viewed analytically. One perspective views time as a seamless continuum; any units used to subdivide it are nonreal in an empirical sense but certainly real in a theoretical sense. A second perspective, although it also views time as a continuum, holds that it is possible to segment time by identifying natural disjunctions, thus imparting a degree of reality to the divisions. How one conceives of culture change influences how one measures the passage of time (Chapters 2 and 5). Is change more like a series of stair steps, with natural breaks, or is it more like a ramp, with no natural breaks in the continuum (Figure 2.6)? Different units measure time, and therefore culture change, differently.

The units Ford used in his ordering were similar but, as we show, not identical to those used by Kroeber, Nelson, Kidder, and Spier in the Southwest almost 20 years previously, though Ford had little or no knowledge of what his forebears had done (O'Brien and Lyman 1998, 1999b). All five men used historical types—analytical units that marked time's passage. But Ford's historical types were of a kind different from those of his predecessors, and because of this, the manner in which Ford used these units to carve time and culture change into segments differed significantly from what had been done in the Southwest. Ford's views on culture change and how to measure it shifted continuously (O'Brien and Lyman 1998). One element present from the start, however, was that the entity called culture metaphorically flows along in unbroken fashion, always changing, always becoming something else. The Ford of the 1940s and early 1950s was adamant that although the cultural flow could be segmented for analytical purposes, those segments were in no sense real (e.g., Ford 1951). The Ford of the mid-1930s, however, was much less adamant and in fact attached considerable reality to the segments into which he subdivided culture's flow. This accounts in part for why he used what he called "marker types" in the first place and how he used them in 1936.

Ford's Use of Marker Types

The 103 ceramic assemblages used in Ford's analysis were from sites located in an area "roughly three hundred miles from east to west and two hundred miles from north to south, that lies in the northern part of the state of Louisiana and in central and southern Mississippi. This area extends across the wide alluvial valley of the Mississippi River and includes the hill country on either side" (Ford 1936a:26). Many of the sites were located along the various rivers. For the most part, Ford's sample was drawn from village sites, and when compiling his data he specifically ignored assemblages from burial sites, stating that "burial collections are subject to selection, peculiar mortuary styles, and possible lag due to ceremonial conservatism" (Ford 1936a:9). He concluded that assemblages from village sites were not susceptible to these problems, primarily because he believed that domestic wares found on such sites were more likely not to have stylistic constraints imposed on them. Village sites also offered an advantage because many were plowed and thus had good surface exposure, and as Ford (1936a:8) noted, "no midden deposits have been found in the local area that lacked decorated potsherds."

Collection procedures entailed gathering as many decorated sherds as possible from the surfaces of village sites. As land conditions changed from season to season, many sites were revisited and additional sherds collected. When collecting the material, Ford and Chambers carefully examined the spatial distribution of sherd types in a "number of sites" (Ford 1936a:11) to determine whether there was spatial segregation of pottery styles. Although Ford expected some clustering of sherd types, no such occurrence was observed, which he attributed to long-term plowing of the sites. Only sherds that "promised to yield information concerning vessel decoration, shape, tempering material, or appendages" were collected (Ford 1936a:11). To ensure that assemblages from his sites were randomly collected, Ford calculated an average variation in type frequencies for multiple collections at 13 localities. Most of the average variation in type frequencies was below 5.0 percent, with a maximum of 7.3 percent.

To build a chronology of ceramic art in the region, Ford (1936a:12) believed it was necessary to "evaluate correctly the relative popularity of different decoration types." In his view this procedure was important for three reasons:

1. It may be expected that two sites occupied through the same period of time, under the sway of the same school of ceramic art, will yield nearly identical decorations in about the same proportions.

2. The assumption is usually possible that, while decorations characteristic of a school of art will form a major proportion of the material at their native sites, on contemporaneous sites of different modes to which they might have been traded or were the results of imitation, they will be in the minority.

3. Provided the factor of population [size] had remained nearly constant, a village inhabited through two style periods could be expected to show a majority of the material characteristic of the period in which it existed . . . longer [Ford 1936a:12].

The Classification System

To observe patterns associated with these assumptions Ford needed a classification system that was able to track change in pottery decoration over time. The system he devised was an experiment, and he used it only once. His concern was to develop a system that could both measure the flow of time accurately and be replicated by anyone. His 1936 system met both demands (O'Brien and Lyman 1998). This contrasted with one of his earlier attempts—a system based on a mixture of pottery attributes such as decoration type, temper, paste, thickness, hardness, and vessel shape—that failed to "detect significant correlations" (Ford 1936a:18). The types did not measure the passage of time. In moving to a system in which the types were built primarily around stylistic dimensions, Ford minimized the effects of functional characteristics, which are susceptible to recurrence through time (Dunnell 1978; O'Brien and Lyman 1999c).

Ford's (1936a:19–22) system was based on three dimensions of variation in the sense of a paradigmatic classification (Dunnell 1971; Lyman and O'Brien 2002, 2003). Of the three, two dimensions—motif and element—were used in the creation of each class. As Ford (1936a:19) explained, "Motif is the plan of the decoration: scroll, parallel features, herringbone, etc. Elements are the means used to express the motif, i.e., incised lines, rows of punctat[ion]s, rouletting, etc." The third dimension, which he labeled "adaptation and arrangement of motifs," was used inconsistently. For each dimension, Ford listed a series of different attributes, which in the case of motif were characteristics such as chains of triangles, scrolling, and bands of elements. Each attribute received a unique numeric code, and types were created by stringing together specific attributes in the order of motif, element, and (if used) adaptation. As an example, one of his types was designated 61;24;7. By definition, every specimen that he placed in that type had to have the following characteristics:

> 61. Motif—Arranged parallel to the vessel lip;
>
> 24. Element—Overhanging lines, [i]ncised with a flat, pointed instrument, held at such an angle that the tops of the lines are deeply incised, while the bottoms rise flush with the surface of the vessel wall; and
>
> 7. Arrangement—Elements placed over three-eight[h]s of an inch apart [Ford 1936a:20, 22].

The only aspects of the system that kept it from being a true paradigmatic classification were that some of the attributes were not mutually exclusive within each dimension and some of the definitions contained "and/or" statements.

Using this classification system, Ford (1936a) identified 84 pottery types. Although the system was successful in that it measured variation, its success was probably its downfall. Ford likely abandoned the system after its publication because he "came to the conclusion that the system was far too detailed even for his own purposes" (O'Brien and Lyman 1998:86). The amount of variation it measured was unwieldy and unnecessary—over 20,000 types were possible—and as a result Ford turned to a limited number of marker types to order his sites.

Marker Types and Decoration Complexes

Ford's marker types—some of which he created based on his excavation of Peck Village in Louisiana (Ford 1935a) and on his firsthand knowledge of the pottery from excavations at Marksville in Louisiana (Setzler 1933a, 1933b) and at Deasonville in Mississippi (Collins 1932b)—included those types that were found in larger proportions at sites and hence were "more likely to be found in small site collections" (Ford 1936a:26). Ford designated 19 of the 84 pottery types as marker types, each of which was placed into one of seven "decoration complexes," which he defined as "a group of pottery decorations characteristic of an area at a definite period of time" (Ford 1936a:74). A marker type, therefore, was quite similar to a horizon style, and a decoration complex was similar to a horizon, concepts that were formally defined about a decade later by Kroeber (1944) and Willey (1945). For Ford, one or more marker types were the definitive criteria for each decoration complex. Each decoration complex was placed in one of three periods (Figure 6.1). Complexes included in Period III were determined by the presence of pottery types found in sites known to have been inhabited by one of the four historic-period groups in the region— the Caddo, Choctaw, Natchez, and Tunica. The order of the three prehistoric complexes—Marksville, Deasonville, and Coles Creek—was determined by superposition of marker types at excavated sites, especially Peck Village.

The manner in which Ford presented his complexes (see also Ford 1935b) indicates that the Marksville complex was ancestral to the later complexes. Following Marksville (Period I) there was a division into two complexes: Dea-

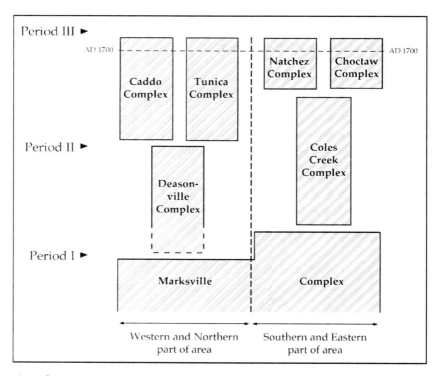

Figure 6.1. Diagram produced by Ford showing the chronological positioning of seven ceramic decoration complexes from northeastern Louisiana and southwestern Mississippi (after Ford 1935c). Period designations are temporal boundaries.

sonville in the northern and western parts of the region and Coles Creek in the southern and eastern parts (Period II). Each of these complexes in turn was viewed as being ancestral to other (in this case, historic period) decoration complexes: Deasonville was ancestral to Caddo and Tunica, and Coles Creek was ancestral to Choctaw and Natchez. But this ancestor-descendant relationship was, in Ford's view, illusory; for example, Coles Creek was ancestral to Choctaw and Natchez only in a temporal sense, not in any sense of heritable continuity between the two, either genetic or cultural. Ford (1935a:10) was clear on this: "Although the Caddo had occupied the territory where they were first described longer than had the Natchez, both cultures at comparatively recent times had displaced others which had entirely different pottery designs and which very likely represented an entirely different people." We show below that it is likely that this was because the marker types he used were not designed to display overlapping, a signature of heritable continuity (Chapters 4 and 5).

Although Ford stated that it was important to determine the relative abundance of marker types in an assemblage to ascertain its chronological position, he did not use this reasoning to order his sites. Rather, sites were correlated and grouped within a decoration complex on the basis of their most abundantly represented marker type(s); no attempt was made to order them within a complex. Indeed, Ford (1936a:10) stated explicitly, "In this study the desired results are not the ages of individual sites, but the relative ages of the different schools of ceramic art," or what he termed "decoration complexes." His failure to order site-specific assemblages within each complex underpins our view that he did not at that time use frequency seriation. Ford was interested in isolating large chunks of time—his decoration complexes—and not in ordering the sites except at the coarse scale of period. Importantly, always in the background was the equivalence of decoration complexes with ethnic groups, be they ethnohistorically known groups or prehistoric groups. In Ford's mind there was little or no heritable continuity between chronologically adjacent complexes. Rather, one complex had replaced another.

Ford's Interpretations

Several of the 103 sites Ford examined, especially those that had been occupied during the historic period, contained sherds of only one decoration complex, but many of them in the southern part of the region contained sherds of both the Marksville and Coles Creek complexes, and many of those along the Yazoo and Big Black rivers in western Mississippi contained sherds of both the Marksville and Deasonville complexes. Ford illustrated this overlap in his master sequence for the region (Figure 6.1, Periods I–II). A few sites that were known locations of the historic-period Caddo and Tunica contained rare Coles Creek–complex sherds, but no Choctaw or Natchez sites contained Coles Creek sherds, nor did any historic-period sites contain Deasonville-complex sherds. This pattern led Ford to suspect that the Coles Creek complex might have been in part contemporaneous with the Caddo and Tunica complexes and that it outlasted the Deasonville complex, as shown in Figure 6.1 (Periods II–III):

> In searching for connections between the historic and prehistoric horizons, it will be noted that the sites of the Tunica and Caddo have a conspicuous amount of types that are characteristic of the Coles Creek complex. Also several of the Coles Creek sites show small amounts of

Caddo and Tunica marker types. As typical Coles Creek sites are not found in the region of either of the two historic complexes, it is easily possible that at one time Coles Creek may have existed in its geographical area [temporally] alongside the Caddo and Tunica. The evidence of interinfluence points to this condition. Neither the Choctaw nor the Natchez complex shows any relation to the Coles Creek or any other of the prehistoric complexes. Evidently the Tunica and Caddo were established in their regions before the Choctaw or the Natchez appeared in the area.

None of the historic complexes show any direct relation to Deasonville. Although at one time it was contemporaneous with Coles Creek, it seems to have disappeared before the advent of either of the two earlier historic complexes, Caddo and Tunica. Tunica took over part of the area that Deasonville had occupied [Ford 1936a:254].

Ford realized that "mixing" of sherds of different decoration complexes could result from several factors. Earlier he had commented that there is "system to this mixing of complexes. It can usually be attributed to one or two causes. Mixture often results from trade or borrowing of ideas having occurred between neighboring, contemporaneous complex areas [e.g., the presence of Deasonville sherds on sites containing primarily Coles Creek sherds], so that foreign designs become incorporated in the village refuse dumps" (Ford 1935c:34–35). Reoccupation—occupation after a preceding abandonment— was possible, but "it would be unlikely that a succeeding people should select the exact [previously occupied] habitation spot for their use. If the old locality had been intentionally reoccupied, the odds are that the dumps of the succeeding group would be located near but not precisely on those of the original inhabitants" (Ford 1936a:255). Thus mixing of complexes was more likely the result of continuous occupation: "It seems more reasonable to suppose that sites on which apparently subsequent complexes are mixed were either settled in the time of the older and were occupied on into the time of the following complex; or that the villages were inhabited during a period of transition from one complex to the other" (Ford 1936a:255–256).

Ford identified two transitional periods, or complexes—Coles Creek– with–Marksville and Deasonville-with-Marksville. To demonstrate that there were such transitional periods, Ford (1936a:262–263) discussed "certain decoration types which suggest that they are the results of an evolutionary trend which runs through two or more of the subsequent complexes," but he was careful to point out that such continuation "does not imply that this evolutionary process occurred in the local geographical area. In most cases it is more likely that the evidence is a reflection of the process taking place in some nearby territory." Ford was suggesting that particular attribute states of decoration types originated in and diffused from one "territory" to another, where they subsequently were incorporated into the local decoration complex. He noted, for example, how one type was found throughout the sequence of complexes, but it "also took on, in each complex, the features [read "attributes"] peculiar to that complex" (Ford 1936a:263). Such "lines of development" (Ford 1936a:263) provided historical linkage between complexes, but only in a chronological sense. The linkage created a sequence—in the sense that A came before B, which came before C—but it was not a phylogenetic sequence—in the sense that A contributed to the rise of B, which contributed to the rise of C.

Ford's conception was that design change rested almost entirely on the effects of outside influences. This was the view that was popular in American archaeology at the time (Lyman et al. 1997b). Metaphorically, a culture is a flowing (evolving) stream of ideas, but because cultures are not autonomous—they interact—the appropriate model for culture change is a braided stream, with each intersection of two trickles representing "cultural influences" (Stirling 1932:22). These influences are the result of ethnographically visible processes such as diffusion, trade, or even immigration, all of which provide a new source of variation for the local pottery tradition. New decoration complexes, or aggregates of types, thus represent the replacement of one culture by another. Breaks in the flow between complexes signify cultural (and temporal and heritable) discontinuity. By 1936 the braided-stream model was how Ford viewed culture change (O'Brien and Lyman 1998). Thus he ended his monograph on the surface collections by noting that "even with this modest beginning there is quite a temptation to see a story of ancient movements of people and cultural forces in the local region with ramifications spread over much of the eastern United States" (Ford 1936a:270).

Types and Measuring Time

It is not surprising that Ford chose the method to measure the passage of time that he did. By the early 1930s the use of historical types or "styles" (e.g., Rouse

1939) was commonplace in American archaeology (Lyman et al. 1997b), and even as rudimentary as Ford's formal knowledge of archaeological method was (O'Brien and Lyman 1998), he would have been exposed to it. For example, many of the presentations at the Conference on Southern Pre-History in 1932 (e.g., Collins 1932a; Stirling 1932) contained references to the direct historical approach. This method rests on traits that are shared among multiple trait complexes, or what were thought to be sets of culturally associated traits (Chapter 7). Overlapping traits are a form of "linkage" between assemblages of traits (or artifact types) and serve as the basis for placing those assemblages adjacent to one another in an ordering thought to comprise a sequence (Ford 1938a:262; Strong 1935:68). As we explained in Chapter 4, overlapping helps ensure that time's passage is being measured, and it does so because it implies heritable continuity.

Nelson, Kroeber, and others used variants or "styles" of the cultural trait "pottery" to measure time continuously, but Ford used them to measure it discontinuously. His concern with decoration complexes forced his hand—he had to use marker types, similar to the manner in which a biostratigrapher uses index fossils to correlate strata and assign them to periods. There was no way to determine whether there were phylogenetic connections across the boundaries of the complexes because there was no or minimal overlapping of types across complexes. Ford did not believe heritable continuity existed between his decoration complexes to any great degree, which is why those complexes and marker types could be identified in the first place. In Ford's view, complexes represented ethnic groups, and it was the cultural processes associated with those groups, especially group movement, that caused a new suite of pottery decorations to appear in a region.

Even in the few instances where Ford (e.g., 1936a:262) saw "an evolutionary trend which runs through two or more of the subsequent complexes," he chalked it up to outside influence that caused design motifs to "evolve." In only a single instance did he explore the ontological underpinnings of design continuity, but it was not in one of his many publications. Rather, it was in his master's thesis (Ford 1938b), completed two years after the surface-collection monograph was published. In it Ford attempted to demonstrate that if artifact types were defined properly, it should be possible to show, on the basis of homologous similarity, that certain types could be grouped into what he referred to as "significant idea groups." If so, then one could conclude that the types within the group were derived from a common ancestor (Ford 1938b:30). Groups of types could be linked together at successively higher levels of inclusivity, such as series and wares—groups that had but a single purpose: "the translation of ceramic history into the history of cultural spread and development" (Ford 1938b:86). An uncritical reading of what Ford was saying makes it sound as if by 1938 he had changed his mind on design evolution being influenced solely by outside forces, but this is not true. He simply was mimicking what Harold Colton and Lyndon Hargrave (1937), among others, had proposed with their hierarchical system of nomenclature for pottery classification (Ford 1940). For Ford, pottery decoration evolved, but it did so only with the help of outside influence. If a "common ancestor" for a series of pottery types could be identified, it would be in a locality far removed geographically from where its descendants were found.

Ford (1938b:5) believed it was possible to discover "general principles which may be expected to underlie" the creation of idea groups, but he did not pursue the matter. Kroeber (1931b), in fact, had outlined the basis for such a principle a few years earlier, and ironically that basis was homology, which Ford (1938b:30) stated was the basis for creating "significant idea groups." But whereas Ford was thinking of homology only in vague ancestor-descendant terms, Kroeber was thinking of it in deeper terms. For Kroeber, homology denoted true "genetic unity" (Kroeber 1931b:151)—what we referred to above as a direct phylogenetic connection—and it was this principle that in 1915 yielded a shift both in how time was measured and in the archaeological units used to measure it (Chapters 5 and 8). That was the year Kroeber used variants of a trait—pottery—to order surface collections of sherds from sites in the countryside around Zuni Pueblo, New Mexico, by means of frequency seriation. Kroeber could do this because his samples came from a very small region; Ford could not mimic this analysis because his assemblages of sherds came from a 6,000-square-mile region. A requirement of seriation is that the seriated collections come from a small area in order that variation in time outweighs variation across space (Dunnell 1970; O'Brien and Lyman 1999c; Chapter 5).

Kinds of Historical Types

To be useful for tracking time as a continuous variable, measurement units rendered as historical types must occupy a single span of time. But such units can have varied geographical distributions and occupy spans of time of varied duration. Recall from Chapter 4 that it is possible to model artifact form as varying continuously over time and across space (Figure 4.6). A different version of that model is presented in Figure 6.2, where a rendition of marker types used by Ford is included. Each rectangle represents an ideational unit that includes a particular amount of formal variation; shaded areas represent formal variation not measured by those units. Each column of rectangles (A–C) denotes a set of analytical units termed historical types. Those types vary within and between sets with respect to how much time and/or space they include. In column A analytical units include relatively large geographical areas but brief time spans. Further, there is no temporal overlap between types. As we noted above, these kinds of historical types later became known as horizon styles (Kroeber 1944; Willey 1945). In column B analytical units overlap in time but also include significant spatial variation. In column C analytical units overlap in time but do not include much spatial variation; thus, relative to the two other kinds of types, only time is measured. Cultural traits (Chapter 3) often had distributions such as those modeled in columns B and C; when they were like those in column B, debate ensued over what the historical significance of the units might comprise (e.g., Steward 1929).

The types constructed by Kroeber, Nelson, Spier, and Kidder approximated the rectangles shown in column C. For the most part, they monitored the passage of time rather than difference in geographic location. This kind of analytical unit had to be built by trial and error. Given such a mode of construction, the utility of a type for measuring the passage of time had to be tested—a point made explicit by Krieger (1944) when he indicated that archaeologically useful types must pass the historical-significance test. Did a type work at keeping track of time and only time?

We suspect a few of Ford's marker types had distributions like those in column C, and a few more had distributions like those in column B. This was in part because Ford was inconsistent in applying his three dimensions when he defined his types. Recall that many of the types were created using only two dimensions—motif and element—a strategy that resulted in more formal variation being included in some types than in others. The former types would tend to be found over larger geographic areas than the latter. Most of Ford's "marker types" had distributions that resembled those in column A. This was because Ford lumped various types together (Marksville type 31:23//101/102:1/2, for

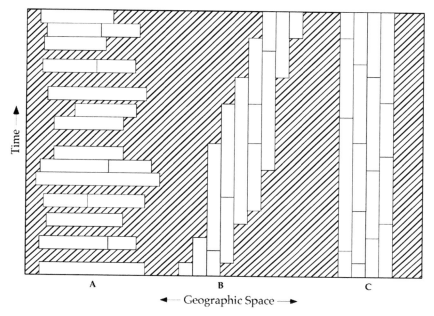

Figure 6.2. *Models of units used by archaeologists to measure time. Artifact form varies continuously along both axes, but there is no absolute scale on either axis. Each rectangle represents a unit used during analysis to measure variation; shaded areas represent formal variation not measured by those units. Each column of rectangles (A–C) denotes a set of units comprising a typology: A, analytical units include relatively large geographic areas but brief time spans, and they do not overlap in time; B, analytical units overlap through time but include spatial variation as well, and thus both change over time and variation over space are included; and C, analytical units overlap through time but do not include a change in spatial variation, and thus only time is measured. Units in A are equivalent to Ford's marker types and many horizon styles. See Figure 4.6 for an additional model.*

example), in essence creating types that included considerable variation; all of them measured time, but they also had large spatial distributions. The net result of that action, brought about in large part because Ford did not have access to the actual sherds when he switched from his earlier classification system to the one used in the 1936 monograph, was a conflation of time and space.

As we noted in Chapter 5, to seriate a group of archaeological assemblages successfully, those assemblages must meet three conditions: they must be of similar temporal duration; they must be from the same local area; and they must be from the same cultural tradition. The first two requirements are difficult to fulfill, but if they are fulfilled, then the third criterion is also likely to be satisfied. Although Ford did not specifically set out to satisfy the first two requirements, he explicitly stated that he chose his pottery samples from village sites because they were more likely to have been occupied for a similar duration (Ford 1936a:8). He also was attuned to the necessity of controlling for space and thus defined two areas—a northern and western area and a southern and eastern area—but this was insufficient control of geographic space to permit successful frequency seriations (O'Brien et al. 2000). It was, however, sufficient for the correlation of a site's ceramic assemblage with a particular decoration complex based on the frequencies of the marker types included in the assemblage.

As Ford's model of regional prehistory depicted in Figure 6.1 indicates, he believed he was dealing with a cultural tradition that branched at least three times prehistorically. This is perhaps why he had to structure his marker types so as to include considerable spatial variation and relatively little time. Such types allowed him to correlate roughly in time what were spatially remote sites. For example, sites assigned to the Deasonville complex were approximately the same age as sites assigned to the Coles Creek complex. Thus Ford's marker types worked much like horizon styles. Two years after his 1936 monograph appeared, Ford (1938a:262) anticipated this archaeological concept when he stated that a decoration complex comprising marker types represented a "distinct time horizon." Ford's marker types were, we believe, built by him to represent relatively brief spans of time and rather large geographic areas—precisely the distributions they should have if they are to serve the same function as a biostratigrapher's index fossils.

Ford's types were similar to Kroeber's, Nelson's, Spier's, and Kidder's types—they all comprised historical types—but Ford built his types in a different way and for a different purpose. These other individuals were interested in constructing geographically limited local chronologies based on a single site or several sites that were spatially close to one another. They were also interested in measuring time as a continuous variable. Thus their types entailed relatively limited geographic space and relatively long time spans, and the types overlapped across multiple assemblages. Ford, however, wanted to construct a regional history and to explain that history in the anthropological terms of diffusion, migration, and the like. To do so, his units had to encompass rather extensive spatial areas but limited time spans. Ford (e.g., 1949) would later construct historical types that had relatively smaller geographical and larger temporal distributions and then use their relative frequencies to order them via percentage stratigraphy. Those working in the Southwest eventually constructed units that encompassed larger geographic areas and smaller time spans (e.g., Colton 1939; Kidder 1924).

Warp and Weft, Traditions and Horizons

Elsewhere we report how we were able to build two fairly good (but far from perfect) seriation orders with Ford's data (O'Brien et al. 2000). Those results suggest that at least some of Ford's marker types seem to have spatio-temporal distributions like those modeled in Figure 6.2, columns B and C. Ford's marker types served well as index fossils for grouping assemblages into decoration complexes, but the assemblages can be arranged so as to only approximate the deterministic model of frequency seriation (types display perfect unimodal frequency distributions). Why do Ford's marker types serve well to place a site's pottery assemblage into a decoration complex but serve less well as units for a frequency seriation? To answer this question, we turn to Irving Rouse's consideration of some of the basics of the culture history approach to archaeology. Rouse (1954:222) used what he termed a "simile" of a rectangular piece of cloth, the "side edges of which represent the geographical limits . . . and the bottom and top edges, the limits . . . in time" to discuss those basics. Rouse (1954:222) wrote:

> The warp threads of the cloth consist of a series of regional traditions running from the bottom towards the top of the cloth, while the weft is composed of a number of horizon styles which extend from one side of the cloth towards the other. The cloth is decorated with a series of irregularly arranged rectangles, each representing a single culture, and these are so colored that they appear to form a series of horizontal bands.

Changing Rouse's wording a bit, we think it is easy to see what Ford might have been thinking when he performed the analysis that forms the heart of his 1936 monograph:

> The side edges of the cloth comprise the edges of the sample region. The bottom edge of the cloth is marked by the Marksville complex and the top edge by the ethnohistoric period and the Caddo, Tunica,

Natchez, and Choctaw complexes (Figure 6.1). The warp threads of the cloth consist of a series of decoration complexes running from the bottom toward the top of the cloth that should be marked by types with long time spans yet found over small areas, while the weft is composed of a number of marker types that extend from one side of the cloth toward the other and thus encompass large spatial areas but brief time spans. The cloth is decorated with a series of irregularly arranged rectangles, each representing a single decoration complex, and these are so colored that they appear to form a series of more or less horizontal bands (Figure 6.1).

In his 1936 monograph Ford did not pay any attention to the details of the warp threads—the types that would mark the slow flow of a cultural tradition and be seriable—but instead was concerned only with the weft threads—his own marker types, or what Rouse referred to as "horizon styles." Because of Ford's narrowly focused concern, we are not at all surprised that some of his marker types do not perform well in a frequency seriation and do not consistently signify heritable continuity (O'Brien et al. 2000). This does not mean that the temporal relations of the marker types indicated in Ford's master chronology are incorrect—at least some of them seem correct given excavations at Peck Village (Ford 1935a) and other sites. It does mean that there are historical aspects of Ford's chronology that require further testing.

Ford's 1936 monograph is often held up as the seminal "seriation" of archaeological materials from the Southeast. Only if the standard dictionary definition of "arrangement in a series" is referred to is this an accurate characterization. Although Ford's units were in one respect like those used by others 20 years earlier to order collections chronologically—they were historical types—Ford's units were constructed for a purpose different than frequency seriation or percentage stratigraphy. Units used in either of the latter must encompass relatively small areas of geographic space and large spans of time, whereas units used as marker types or index fossils must encompass relatively large areas of geographic space and brief spans of time. Many of his units have properties of marker types, properties that began to be made explicit only a decade later when the concepts of horizon style and tradition were explicitly defined and distinguished. Knowledge of the contrasts between the spatiotemporal properties measured by units that work well in frequency seriations and those that work well as marker types or index fossils was not critical to the trial-and-error process Ford used to build his types. Thus he never discussed those contrasts in his many publications. This would eventually get him into an argument with Albert Spaulding (O'Brien and Lyman 1998) over the nature of archaeological types, but that is a subject beyond our scope here.

Ford (1936a) clearly did not use frequency seriation to order his 103 collections of sherds. He, like many of his contemporaries, favored stratigraphic excavation and the principle of superposition as the best way to measure time as evidenced by artifacts (Ford 1936b, 1949). We argue in Chapter 8 that Ford was virtually the only archaeologist working between 1935 and 1965 who was aware of the treachery of excavating stratigraphically and treating stratigraphically bounded collections of artifacts as if they were manifestations of static entities others called cultures, phases, and the like. Ford also was aware of the utility of the direct historical approach as a chronometer, though he did not use it extensively. In the next three chapters, we discuss not only the direct historical approach (Chapter 7) and stratigraphic excavation (Chapter 8) as chronometers, we argue in Chapter 9 that Ford should be remembered best for his contributions to the method of graphing cultural change.

III. The Epistemology of Chronometers

After we had been studying the history of American archaeology for several years, we realized that we did not know how the direct historical approach worked, despite everyone we read implying that it was a straightforward technique and despite it predating virtually every other artifact-based chronometer we had studied. We found anthropologists and archaeologists had used the direct historical approach since at least the 1880s, when Edward B. Tylor mentioned its use. That the direct historical approach actually had three distinct analytical purposes was also somewhat surprising to us, though perhaps we were naive in our initial beliefs that it was merely a chronometer. In self-defense we note that when we were college students, what was even then (the late 1960s and 1970s) being referred to as "new" or "processual archaeology" was the bandwagon of the moment, and we along with our teachers climbed on (O'Brien et al. 2005). This meant that (so far as we remember) no one taught us what the direct historical approach actually is, probably because such ancient analytical methods that focused on simple descriptive culture history were anathema to the new archaeologists.

Later, when we researched the direct historical approach out of historical interest, we were again initially startled to discover that there was no clear statement in the literature regarding its analytical protocol. But as we explored further and came to learn how it was used, its underpinning ontological assumption (cultural transmission created heritable continuity) became clear. This was quite gratifying because that assumption—typically manifest as the overlapping of cultural traits across multiple aggregates of traits—reflected just what we had detected in the chronometers invented in the early 1900s. The implicit belief in cultural transmission and descent with modification that allowed one to track (cultural) change and thus to measure time based on change in artifact forms had a much deeper history than we had previously imagined. We suspect it was knowledge of the underpinning ontology of the direct historical approach that reinforced Kroeber's invention of frequency seriation as a chronometer.

In the context of exploring the nuances of the direct historical approach in Chapter 7, we also consider an approach to archaeological analysis that was in the eyes of some during the 1930s and 1940s a competitor with the direct historical approach. The competitor was the Midwestern Taxonomic Method, developed by Will C. McKern in an effort to bring analytical rigor to interpretations and terminology. The word "culture" had, by about 1930, come to denote archaeological manifestations that encompassed all manner of temporal durations and geographic spaces. McKern designed a cumulative aggregative hierarchy of cultural units modeled on the Linnaean biological taxonomy. He did not intend for his system to denote any sort of phylogenetic relationships between the included cultural units, though he quietly hoped that such might be revealed (Lyman and O'Brien 2003). Importantly, McKern's system was explicitly not chronometric, so it might seem strange that we include discussion of it in a book on archaeological chronometers. But however brief, some discussion of the Midwestern Taxonomic Method must be included because it played an important role in structuring archaeological inquiry; indeed, its overall rejection by many archaeologists highlights the fact that it was not chronometric.

Finally, Chapter 7 is a long chapter, nearly the same length as Chapter 2, which is symbolic of the other central topic examined in Chapter 7. That topic is the same as the one explored in Chapter 2—the ontologies of different versions of evolutionary theory. In Chapter 7 we return to the version of evolution known among biologists as orthogenesis that we merely introduced in Chapter 2. Such a return is mandatory to understanding the several ways in which the direct historical approach was used. Knowledge of the basics of orthogenesis clarifies the role of stages in models of evolutionary change; whether biological or cultural, stages are rungs on a ladder that inevitably progress toward perfection. Finally, the orthogenetic model of evolution helps illuminate why one form of ethnographic analogy was replaced by another coincident with the emergence of the new archaeology; simply put, the underpinning ontologies of the new analogy and the new archaeology were identical.

The direct historical approach was one of the (if not the) first artifact-based chronometer that archaeologists (and anthropologists) used, so it is appropriate that we begin the next section with a chapter on that approach. Artifact-based chronometers such as frequency seriation (Chapter 5) and the direct historical approach (Chapter 7) made time (or age) visible analytically and inferentially. If it was even possible, how could one confirm empirically that the orderings of artifacts that they produced were in fact chronological? In Chapter 8 we show that the principle of superposition of strata held the answer. Once *formal variation in artifacts was measured so as to seemingly reflect time, then strati-graphic excavation became a preferred field method for testing the chronological properties of artifact orderings. Archaeologists working in North America had long known about superposition as a chronometer, probably from paleontology and geology, but for any of several reasons they did not believe there was sufficient time depth or cultural change in the local archaeological record to warrant stratigraphic excavation. Part of the shift that was required for them to perceive such a warrant involved a change in the design of units used to measure formal variation in artifacts. Once artifacts were no longer viewed as cultural traits like pottery and arrowheads but rather as variants of cultural traits like shell-tempered, cord-marked jars and corner-notched points, shifts in their forms, their frequencies, or both were noted as marking the passage of time. Here again, units were critical to the successful implementation of a chronometer.*

Once artifact-based chronometry was established, the final step was to present the chronometric data in such a way that it was intuitively obvious or commonsensical to interpret what was being shown. The discussion in Chapter 9 documents how culture historians tested various techniques and eventually perfected a graphic means of showing that culture, manifest as artifact types and frequencies thereof, indeed changed over time. It is also shown in that chapter that not all graphs actually illustrate the data of change; some of those graphs are in fact interpretations of the data or simply beliefs about how change occurred. Once one knows the subtle differences between the two kinds of graphs—those that are empirical and those that are interpretive—they are easy to distinguish. So far as we know, no one has ever noticed these differences before.

We think it unfortunate that the graphic techniques described in Chapter 9 are seldom used anymore because in our view, they do a marvelous job of showing what they are intended to show. Fred Plog (1973:191) urged that what he called a "seriogram" could be used to provide a visual "record of the adoption of technological innovations over time" and that such graphs "explicate variability in the adoption process." He was advocating what Sarah Turnbaugh (Chapter 5) did when illustrating the history of women's bonnets. So far as we are aware, few archaeologists have followed Plog's suggestion in the more than 30 years since he made it.

7. The Direct Historical Approach

An analogy is a form of reasoning that produces an inference about an unknown and invisible property of a subject phenomenon. The unknown property is inferred based on the fact that it is observable among source phenomena that are visibly similar in at least some respects to the subject. The source is the known side of the analogy and comprises the analog; the subject is the side of the analogy that includes the unknown property. Analogical reasoning has been commonplace in American archaeology since at least the early nineteenth century (Baerreis 1961; Charlton 1981; Trigger 1989). Five decades ago Willey (1953c) identified two distinct kinds of archaeological analogy—what he termed "specific historical analogy" and "general comparative analogy." Although analogical reasoning has been extensively discussed in the archaeological literature, no one has explored the historical development of the two kinds, especially in terms of the theories that underpin them. That is one of our objectives in this chapter.

With respect to analogical reasoning and how it was used by archaeologists, we make two points. First, the two kinds of analogy identified by Willey rest on different theories of change, one being Darwinian evolution and the other orthogenesis. As we indicated in Chapter 2, these theories are decidedly different epistemologically and ontologically, and the former model was replaced with the latter model in the 1940s and 1950s. Second, a shift in the goals of American archaeology in the 1950s away from culture history and toward cultural reconstruction (Binford 1968a; Deetz 1970) occurred about the same time that Darwinian evolution was discarded. Accompanying the change in theory was a replacement of one kind of analogical reasoning, specific historical analogy, by its alternative, general comparative analogy. In the former, the ethnographic source analog is a direct evolutionary descendant of the ancestral archaeological subject; in the latter, the source analog is not a direct evolutionary descendant of the archaeological subject. Central to the history of these two kinds of analogy is the direct historical approach—a method that saw considerable use during the late nineteenth century and the first half of the twentieth century. The direct historical approach was one of the first artifact-based chronometers used by anthropologists and archaeologists, but it was used in two additional ways as well. In this chapter we distinguish the several ways in which archaeologists used the direct historical approach and the theories that underpin it.

Although our discussion suggests "direct historical analogy" would be more accurate historically and methodologically, we use the term "specific historical analogy" throughout because Willey (1953c) used this term. We begin with brief descriptions of Darwinian evolution and of orthogenesis. We next discuss each of the several distinct uses to which the direct historical approach was put. That discussion reveals why general comparative analogy came to be favored over specific historical analogy during the middle of the twentieth century. We then turn to a description of general comparative analogy and elaborate on why it rests on orthogenesis. How the change in goals of American archaeology during the 1950s articulates with general comparative analogy and orthogenesis is then discussed. We conclude with a consideration of the claim made in the 1890s and again in the 1960s and 1970s that specific historical analogs are more valid than general comparative analogs. This consideration is particularly critical within the larger focus of this book because it involves the basic notion of heritable continuity created by cultural transmission.

Theories of Change

We use the term "descent with modification" to refer to Darwin's (1859) version of evolutionary theory, which is based on the principle that heritable continuity exists between ancestor and descendant such that more or less perfect fidelity of replication of parental traits in offspring is ensured. Requisite mechanisms include transmission and natural selection, both of which involve sets of filters that influence fidelity and frequency of trait replication. Ontologically, sets or populations of things are more or less constantly in the process of becoming something else (changing) as a result of transmission and the action of the filters; this is materialism as described in Chapter 2. Direction of change within a lineage, or line of heritable continuity, is unpredictable because it is historically contingent in three ways: in terms of what is available for transmission, in terms of what is transmitted and thus might be replicated, and in terms of what actually is replicated (Ereshefsky 1992; Gould 1986). What is available for transmission depends on the random—with respect to what is or might be needed among descendants—generation of innovative variants; what actually is transmitted depends on the transmission mechanisms and their operation; what is replicated depends on the size of the transmitting population and the particular sorting filters in operation at the time of transmission. This is why the direction of change is largely unpredictable.

The result of Darwinian evolution has been characterized as "sorting" of available variants from one generation to the next (Vrba and Gould 1986) such that replication of variants over time is differential (Leonard and Jones 1987; Teltser 1995). When the sorting, or filtering, mechanism is natural selection, descent with modification is created by differential replication of available variants from one generation to the next. Descent with modification can also be created simply by the vagaries of transmission such that replication is differential from one generation to the next.

The second theory, orthogenesis, is multifaceted and complex. The origin of the term itself is controversial; it is variously said to have been coined by biologist G. H. T. Eimer in 1898 (Bowler 1979) and by biologist W. Haacke in 1893 (Grehan and Ainsworth 1985). Historically, various proponents had different views of orthogenesis, and our discussion is simplified. Orthogenesis rests on the notion that change within a lineage involves "nothing accidental or creative, for evolution 'proceeds in accordance with laws,' through a predetermined sequence of stages or phases" (Dobzhansky 1957:382). Heritability and transmission comprise part of this theory, but mechanisms resulting in sorting are unnecessary because only variations that fulfill an immediate, long-term, or eventual need are produced, transmitted, and replicated. Natural selection and other "external" forces play no role in causing a lineage to evolve along a particular line (Cronquist 1951). Natural selection's role in orthogenesis is termed channeling; mechanical constraints on the evolving entity's parts limit or direct the modifications that occur during descent (e.g., Gould 1982; Grehan and Ainsworth 1985).

Orthogenesis was thought by some biologists to account for the fact that organisms exhibited traits that appeared to have no obvious function (Bowler

1979). Some orthogenecists held that such traits could not be accounted for by natural selection because only those traits that fulfilled an obvious need were products of selection. Another mechanism was necessary to account for what in the late nineteenth and early twentieth centuries seemed to be nonadaptive trends evidenced by the fossil record. Many who subscribed to this version of orthogenesis held that there was a mysterious internal drive resulting in the appearance of new variants; others held that the force was external (environmental); still others held that new variants were produced by a combination of internal and external forces. Whatever the source of the cause, the result was the same—directed variation precluding the operation of natural selection. Orthogenesis suggests that the appearance of innovations follows "well-defined pathways of change. Such evolutionary trends [are] ascribed to [a] direction-giving force. . . . The evolution of phyletic lineages [occurs] along a predetermined linear pathway" (Mayr 1991:61, 183). The theory of orthogenetic evolution has been referred to as "the doctrine of 'straight-line' evolution" (Romer 1949:107).

Under either of the two theories of evolution, each lineage within a category of phenomena, despite its independence from every other lineage, can evolve parallel to or converge with all others. The modern concepts of parallel evolution and convergent evolution can be defined as follows: Parallelism results from the development of similar adaptive designs among closely related phenomena; convergence results from the development of similar adaptive designs among remotely related phenomena (Eldredge 1989:51). Evolutionists subscribing to descent with modification argue that the "very widespread occurrence of parallelism and convergence is the strongest sort of evidence for the efficacy of selection and for its adaptive orientation of evolution. . . . Yet . . . these processes do not produce *identity* even in the limited parts of structures most strongly affected by parallelism and convergence" (Simpson 1953:170–171). The last observation underscores the importance of classification to analytical efforts aimed at deciphering evolutionary history (Lyman and O'Brien 2002; O'Brien and Lyman 2000).

Orthogenetic evolution can entail convergence or parallelism because, for example, it begins with homogeneity and ends with heterogeneity, Herbert Spencer suggested (Carneiro 1972, 1973; Freeman 1974), or what could today be characterized as, say, every biological lineage beginning with generalists and ending with specialists (Gould 1970). Orthogenecists may quibble over the precise nature of the stages that organisms (or cultures) go through, how the stages are defined, and how particular empirical phenomena are classified, but they typically agree on the result—a descendant is somehow more complex (heterogeneous) or more fully developed and less primitive than its ancestor (Carneiro 1972; Jepsen 1949). Orthogenesis is in this sense progressive. The mechanism prompting change may be some "unknown and unknowable force" (Spencer, quoted in Freeman 1974:215), but the result is the same. This is not to say that orthogenetic evolution is inevitably teleological. Many evolutionists in the nineteenth century argued that it was not, preferring instead to call on elements of Lamarckism—believing that the environment in which a population of organisms was located somehow stimulated the internal drive and directed the appearance of new variants (Bowler 1979).

Boas (1920:312) referred to evolutionary theories of nineteenth-century anthropologists as comprising a notion of "orthogenetic development." Radin (1929:12) characterized those theories as involving "straight-line evolution," and Lowie (1937:27, 28) characterized them as involving evolution that was "predestined" because they held to "a fixed law of development." We agree with Radin's (1929:12) important observation that the nineteenth-century subscription to an orthogenetic theory of cultural evolution "deflected attention from the examination . . . of the mechanism of cultural transmission." Orthogenesis underpinned the work of Spencer, Tylor, Morgan, and numerous others in the nineteenth century, although Carneiro (1973:80n5) argues that Spencer found no value in Eimer's concept of orthogenesis. Alland (1974:273) points out, however, that Spencer's views changed over time and, more important, that one can find contradictory statements in Spencer's many writings, "which may be used to support diametrically opposed positions." Given the different views of what orthogenesis actually comprises, it is no surprise that some historians find elements of orthogenesis in Spencer's writings whereas others do not.

Many nineteenth-century anthropologists were orthogenecists who conceived of the development of cultural lineages as involving the more or less inevitable passage of cultures through a set series of stages (Simpson 1961a). This theory still underpins much American archaeology (Dunnell 1980, 1988; Lyman and O'Brien 1998; Chapter 2; see especially Spencer 1997 and selected references therein), paralleling the trend in modern anthropology (Rambo 1991). During the period 1875–1960, in American archaeology and anthropology elements of both descent with modification and orthogenesis were mixed together to produce evolutionary explanations of cultural phenomena (Chapter 2). The issue of whether cultural evolution is orthogenetic or comprises descent with modification sometimes took the form of a debate, such as that between White and Kroeber described in Chapter 2, but other times it was more implicit (see Lyman and O'Brien 2004b for detailed discussion). Because the two theories were indistinct to most American anthropologists and archaeologists working in the early and mid-twentieth century, elements of both underpinned various analytical procedures used at the time. Even in 1960 the two theories were not distinguished by anthropologists and archaeologists. Orthogenesis is mentioned and distinguished from descent with modification only by biologists who contributed chapters to Tax (1960); anthropologists and archaeologists who contributed chapters conflate the two theories and describe a form of cultural evolution that is a hybrid of the two theories. This mixing has deep roots, one clear example of which is found in the direct historical approach.

The Direct Historical Approach

The archaeological record of the Americas was viewed by many nineteenth-century archaeologists as a short extension into the past of the ethnographically documented record (Lyman et al. 1997b; Trigger 1989; Willey and Sabloff 1993). Cultures and human behaviors of the archaeological past were seen as basically identical to those observed and described ethnographically; thus they could be studied by those with minimal training in archaeology (Meltzer 1983). One result of this view was the regular use of what came to be formally known in the 1930s as the direct historical approach. Wedel (1938) apparently was the first person to use the term, although the method was decades old at that point. A curious historical footnote is that McKern (1934, 1937a) had earlier referred to the procedure as the "direct historical method," but Wedel's term is the one that stuck.

Formal recognition of the method is found in Dixon's (1913:565) presidential address to the American Anthropological Association, in which he stated, without elaboration, that "one would logically proceed to investigate a number of [sites of known ethnic affiliation], and work back from these," because it "is only through the known that we can comprehend the unknown, only from a study of the present that we can understand the past." Strong

(1933:275) states that Dixon "emphatically set forth" the procedure of the direct historical approach. Of Dixon's statements, de Laguna (1960:220) remarked that "although not the first, this is one of the earliest and clearest statements of what we now call the 'direct historical approach' in archaeology." We disagree with these evaluations because the exact protocol of the approach is not described by Dixon, nor is the underpinning ontology.

Strong (1935:55) was no more explicit than Dixon (1913) when he stated that "once the archeological criteria of [a historically documented] culture had been determined, it [is] then possible to begin the advance from the known and historic into the unknown and prehistoric." Strong (1953:393) later described the approach as "proceed[ing] from the known (documentary-ethnological) to the unknown (prehistoric-archaeological)," adding that such a procedure "is a clear application of [Edward B.] Tylor's advice." Tylor (1881:10), however, had simply remarked that "it is a good old rule to work from the known to the unknown." Perhaps Strong either was not intimately familiar with what Tylor said or was selective in what he quoted, because Tylor was not referring to specific historical analogy when he discussed his "rule." Rather, he was following his intellectual predecessors (Hodgen 1964; Stocking 1987) and referring to the use of ethnographic source cultures that were believed to be at the same stage of development as the archaeological subject cultures. Thus if one wanted to know something about an archaeological people who made stone tools but not pottery, the place to look for an analog was among modern or ethnographically known peoples who made stone tools but not pottery. Tylor was advocating the use of general comparative analogy, not specific historical analogy.

Fenton (1940:243, 165) noted that the direct historical approach involved proceeding "from the known groups to the unknown cultures and peoples that precede them" and indicated that "archeological studies should proceed from the [ethnically] known historic sites back through the protohistoric sites to the prehistoric period." Heizer (1941:101) used the term in the title of a work on California but not in his text, noting only that the method comprised "the correlated historical-ethnographical-archaeological approach." Similarly, Steward (1960) used the term in a paper title, but it is unclear from the article what the direct historical approach involves. De Laguna (1960:218) suggests that students use "the 'direct historical approach' [when reading a collection of turn-of-the-century articles on American archaeology] by working backwards from some such easily reached vantage point as [Martin et al. 1947]." She was referring to tracing an intellectual tradition or lineage back through time, but she did not elaborate on how students were to accomplish this.

In his synopsis of anthropological methods of chronometry, Sapir (1916:5) noted that there were two kinds of chronometric evidence, what he termed "direct and inferential." The former "meant such evidence as directly suggests temporal relations," and the latter comprised "such evidence as is inferred from data that do not in themselves present the form of a time sequence" (Sapir 1916:5). There were, in Sapir's view, three kinds of direct evidence: that which was "yielded by historical documents," statements of tribal history by tribal members, and "the stratified monuments studied by archaeology" (Sapir 1916:5, 9). Given that Sapir (1916) repeatedly referred to these as "direct historical evidence," we suspect his discussion was the inspirational source for the term "direct historical approach" coined by Wedel (1938). Sapir (1916), too, did not describe the analytical procedures of the direct historical approach.

The direct historical approach rarely appears, by its formal name or otherwise, in histories of American anthropology (Lowie 1937; Panchanan 1933). So far as we know, no one has pointed out that the direct historical approach was actually used for three distinct, although interrelated, purposes. In American archaeology these were: to identify the ethnic affiliation of an archaeological manifestation; to build relative chronologies of archaeological materials; and to gain insight into the human behaviors that were thought to have produced particular portions of the archaeological record. The last use was derived directly from the first two uses and was, simply, a kind of analogical reasoning built around both time or age and the notion of heritable continuity between ancestor and descendant. We think the reason no one ever pointed out that there were three distinct uses of the direct historical approach was because by about 1915 they were not distinct. Rather, the constituent parts were so intertwined that they were inseparable. In addition, by about 1930 the basic method was viewed as being so commonsensical that no one felt the need to explore its underpinnings in any great detail. This was not damning, but in considering the method to be commonsensical the underpinning theories were viewed in similar light, and that resulted both in mixing elements of the two theories and in ill-conceived statements about different kinds of ethnographic analogy in the middle of the twentieth century.

The Direct Historical Approach as an Ethnic Identifier

Writing after the heyday of the direct historical approach, Willey (1953a:372) produced one of the clearest statements concerning its use as a means of assigning ethnic identity to archaeological phenomena:

> Through a series of successive periods prehistoric cultures were linked to proto-historic, historic, and modern descendants. This type of study, sometimes called the "direct historical approach," has a theoretical basis in cultural continuity. Starting with known, documented habitation sites, certain cultural assemblages were identified and associated with particular tribal groups. Earlier archeological assemblages were then sought which were not too sharply divergent from the known historic ones, and the procedure was followed backward in time. . . .
>
> The establishment of prehistoric-to-historic continuity is of utmost importance as a springboard for further archeological interpretation, and, along with general chronological and distributional studies, it is one of the primary historical problems for the American archeologist.

Willey was correct: The theoretical basis of the direct historical approach lies in cultural continuity. Why is there continuity in the first place? The answer is because it was produced through the process of cultural transmission—a process explicitly named and discussed by Sapir (1916), who argued that cultural transmission ensured a high degree of fidelity in trait replication between ancestor and descendant. Willey's theory of "cultural continuity" rests squarely on the notion of cultural transmission, which finds empirical expression in the overlapping of cultural traits across the trait lists of the historically and ethnographically documented cultures and the archaeological manifestation(s) in question. Willey, like many other culture historians (e.g., Phillips et al. 1951), knew this, but as evidenced by the statements of Dixon, Strong, Fenton, and Heizer quoted above, they did not see the need to spell it out explicitly (Lyman 2001).

This is the line of reasoning used by Cyrus Thomas (1894) in his demonstration that the numerous earthworks scattered across the eastern and midwestern portions of North America were produced by the direct genetic and cultural ancestors of historically documented ethnic groups. In many respects

Thomas simply was verifying what many others, including Bureau of American Ethnology director John Wesley Powell, suspected. The vast amount of empirical evidence marshaled by Thomas, together with his analytical methods, marks his work as the formal genesis of the direct historical approach as an ethnic identifier—regardless of the scale at which distinct ethnicity was conceived (Dunnell 1991)—in American archaeology. Thomas referred continually to historical records of the sixteenth through eighteenth centuries, where it was documented that the post-Columbian Indians were sufficiently "culturally advanced" (being sedentary agriculturists) to have built the mounds and in some cases had actually been observed building mounds. Documenting typological similarity of artifacts from the historic and prehistoric periods established evolutionary linkages and demonstrated the utility of the direct historical approach as an ethnic identifier (O'Brien and Lyman 1999a).

Thomas claimed the evidence was there if anyone examined it critically, especially the fact that earthworks with European items in them were similar to those from presumed earlier periods. There was no logical reason to suspect that the mound builders were of Mexican origin or that Indian groups had pushed the mound builders out of the eastern United States. The archaeological record demonstrated to Thomas's satisfaction that a high degree of cultural continuity had existed for an untold age and that such threads of continuity showed no major disruptions. Change, of course, had occurred—this much was indicated in the myriad forms of earthworks recorded and the different kinds of artifacts found within them—but this type of change was an orderly, continuous progression as opposed to a punctuated, disruptive progression of cultural epochs such as was evident in the European Paleolithic–Neolithic sequence.

After Thomas's work, the ultimate goal of anthropology, especially as practiced by those connected with or trained through the Bureau of American Ethnology, was to write a full description of each ethnic group's culture before it disappeared under the onslaught of Euroamerican expansion. Such "salvage ethnography" was an attempt to determine the pristine, pre-Columbian nature of Native American cultures (Dunnell 1991). As the National Research Council's Committee on State Archaeological Surveys noted, the "reconstruction of the original culture of tribes at the time of their first meeting with the settlers is a most important problem" (Wissler et al. 1923:2). Archaeological data, because they were incomplete, played a secondary role to ethnographic data, being used primarily to help fill in gaps, which, given the then-prevalent notion that the American archaeological record had a shallow time depth, were not viewed as being particularly large. To ensure that the correct archaeological data were used to fill the gaps, one had to identify the ethnic affiliations of those data. Precisely how such an identification was made was not spelled out in great detail.

The literature of the late nineteenth and early twentieth centuries suggests the procedure could take one of two forms. Both forms find their roots in Sapir's (1916:6) suggestion that if a prehistoric artifact was recovered from the same geographic area as a formally identical ethnographic artifact, it could be concluded that the former was produced by the same ethnic group as the latter. These two criteria—identical geographic origins and typological identity— were separated and used independently in some applications. Mott (1938), for example, compared the geographic distributions of archaeologically defined culture units with the historically documented distributions of various ethnic groups. She concluded that archaeological units had been created by ethnic groups with the same geographic distributions as the archaeological units. Griffin (1937) used a similar procedure.

More commonly, however, the procedure followed involved assessing the similarity of sets of artifacts rendered as sets of cultural traits sometimes referred to as complexes. This procedure was spelled out in a pamphlet published by the National Research Council's Committee on State Archaeological Surveys:

> In all the states there are known sites of what were Indian villages during the period of colonization and in many of the States there still remain remnants of Indian tribes once living and flourishing there. It is thus possible to connect the immediate prehistoric with the historic. . . . When articles identical with those found on the historic sites occur on those of prehistoric origin, careful comparison with other sites in the locality will leave little doubt as to the identity of the people inhabiting the locality [Wissler et al. 1923:2–3].

The procedure entailed three basic steps. First, compile a list of cultural traits for the extant ethnic group under consideration. Second, convert that portion of the archaeological record under scrutiny into a list of cultural traits. Third, compare the two lists and when an ethnographic list corresponded (to some unspecified but relatively high degree) with an archaeological list in terms of the number of shared or overlapping traits, conclude that a match had been made. All that was demanded by that conclusion was heritable continuity between the two groups; the underlying theory could be either descent with modification or orthogenesis, as both entail cultural transmission. No discussion of theoretical nuances was necessary.

Wedel's (1938) work on the Pawnee exemplifies the comparison of trait lists. He compared three cultures in terms of traits they exhibited. Two cultures—the Lower Loup Focus and the Oneota Aspect—were archaeological, and one—Historic Pawnee—was ethnographic. The list contained 120 traits, of which the Historic Pawnee had 80, the Lower Loup Focus 82, and the Oneota Aspect 74. Wedel noted that all three cultural units shared 39 traits. The Historic Pawnee and Lower Loup Focus shared 55 traits, the Historic Pawnee and Oneota Aspect shared 42 traits, and the Lower Loup Focus and Oneota Aspect shared 48 traits. Based on these observations, Wedel (1938:11) stated that the "conclusion seems inescapable that the Lower Loup Focus stands in very much closer and more direct relationship genetically to the later historic Pawnee than to the contemporaneous Oneota peoples." Such connections were typical inferences (e.g., Boas 1904; Ford 1938b; Griffin 1943; Lowie 1912; Wissler 1916c), although "genetic" was used metaphorically to refer to relationships between cultural traits rather than to those between biological phenomena.

The Direct Historical Approach as a Chronometer

With minor methodological and theoretical extension, the same procedure used to demonstrate ancestor-descendant relationships was used to measure the passage of time. The methodological extension comprised building temporal sequences of artifacts by beginning with a list of cultural traits rendered as artifact types of various scales possessed by a historically documented culture and then working back ever deeper into the past by determining which traits (artifact types) were held by archaeologically represented cultures (Figure 7.1; see also Figure 4.3). The analyst could go beyond mere ethnic identification to temporal sequences by including the theoretical notion of sorting—that traits would come and go through the sequence but they would each appear only once or temporally continuously across multiple trait lists during the sequence. As Wissler (1917a:278) put it, "by working backward from the historic

Cultural Traits

	1	2	3	4	5	6	7	8	9	10	11	12
G*	+	+	+	+	+	+	+	+	+			
F	+	+	+	+	+	+	+		+			
E	+	+	+	+	+	+			+	+		
D		+	+	+	+	+			+	+	+	
C		+	+	+	+					+	+	+
B			+	+	+					+	+	+
A			+	+						+	+	+

Trait Lists

*Trait list known to date to the historical period.

Figure 7.1. A model of the direct historical approach used as a chronometer. Each column designated by a number represents a cultural trait (or artifact type); each row comprises a trait list (or artifact assemblage). Plus marks indicate a trait is present; blanks indicate a trait is absent. Row G consists of traits known to date to the historic period and thus chronologically anchors one end of the sequence; time passes from the bottom to the top (compare with Figure 4.3, which is the same graph without a chronological anchor). Each lower row designates an archaeological manifestation that is earlier in time than row G. The trait lists have been ordered using the principle of overlapping; each trait will occur during only one span of time and across multiple lists as a result of transmission and heritable continuity between contiguous lists.

period or . . . from a fixed date, it is possible by these methods to separate the older elements of culture from those of relatively recent origin. . . . In the main, [the method] first analyzes the cultural trait-complexes and then by comparative reasoning arranges them in time sequences." Perhaps not surprisingly, some archaeologists referred to this use of the direct historical approach as "historic archeology" (e.g., Strong 1935:55, 1940:353).

Assumptions underpinning use of the direct historical approach as a chronometer are that the traits shared by prehistoric cultures with their historically recent descendant culture(s) become progressively fewer in number as the traits in successively older cultures in a lineage are polled; the overlapping of traits across several temporally distinct yet contiguous cultures in a temporal sequence links them together in time; and the linkage represented by overlapping traits denotes a line of heritable continuity comprising an evolutionary lineage (Chapter 4). Archaeologists and anthropologists referred to the last as "historical continuity" (Ascher 1961) or "historical relatedness" (Parsons 1940); they seldom acknowledged explicitly that cultural transmission had resulted in heritable continuity between an ancestral and a descendant culture (Lyman 2001). This critical process was further obscured because the direct historical approach as a chronometer was not used as a means for determining cultural lineages or for writing the evolutionary history of an ethnographically documented culture. The theoretical reason why the direct historical approach worked as a chronometer—it monitored heritable continuity manifest in overlapping traits (Figure 7.1)—was unstated.

Sapir (1916) was virtually the only one to note that cultural transmission comprised the theoretical basis for use of the direct historical approach as a chronometer. This may have been of no great moment because overlapping could be affected by either orthogenesis or descent with modification, and although only the latter explicitly implicated sorting, no major mental gymnastics were required to conceive of sorting as a result of orthogenesis (Sapir 1916). The general failure to explicitly consider the theoretical reason why the approach worked as a chronometer, however, resulted in archaeologists viewing their chronologies as "largely a matter of inference from the data" (Wissler 1916b:487). Like his contemporaries (e.g., Gamio 1917; Kidder and Kidder 1917; Kroeber 1916a, 1916b; Nelson 1916; Sapir 1916; Spier 1917a, 1917b), Wissler believed that stratigraphic excavation provided more direct evidence of cultural chronology, but this belief was often based on a naïveté regarding the principle of superposition—that vertical position implied the relative age of artifacts as opposed to the relative order of their deposition (Lyman et al. 1997b; Chapter 8). Kidder (1924:45–46) did not describe any technique similar to the direct historical approach when discussing chronometers available in the 1920s, instead expressing preference for stratigraphic observation. Similarly, although Ford (1936b:103) wrote that "identifying the sites of villages mentioned in the chronicles of the first explorers [allows one to connect] these sites with a definite time period, and gives a starting point for the projection of the chronology back into the prehistoric," he went on to note that "vertical stratigraphy [constituted] the best basis for the relating of time changes." Finally, Lowie (1944:323) noted that in "the Plains Wm. D. Strong has demonstrated the value of combining a stratigraphic technique with a historical approach, applying the sound principle of working from the known backward to the unknown."

Perhaps lineages did not need to be constructed because, at least initially, it was believed that they would show minimal cultural development and change, given the perceived lack of time depth in the American archaeological record. Boas (1902:1), for example, had stated that it "seems probable that the remains found in most of the archaeological sites of America were left by a people similar in culture to the present Indians" (see additional discussion in Chapter 8). The perceived shallow time depth of the American archaeological record lessened the chances of convergence or parallelism resulting in shared traits; it appeared much more likely that such overlapping traits were the result of shared ancestry (Steward 1929; Swanton and Dixon 1914). But even after the time depth of the American archaeological record was extended significantly by the Folsom discovery in 1927, Swanton (1932:74) could state that "it is important beyond all else for you archaeologists to tie your discoveries into known tribes, after having done which you may trace them back into the mysterious past as far as you will, and your work will have more interest and more meaning for you and for us all." No one seemed too concerned about the theoretical warrant for using the direct historical approach as a chronometer.

Of equal yet largely unremarked theoretical importance was the fact that examination of temporal change in the list of cultural traits assumed no inevitable direction to the change (see Figure 4.3). It is precisely this lack of presumed direction that prompted various individuals to mention the necessity of a chronological anchor. Wissler (1916b:487) noted that "we must have a point of departure in the historic period, from which to work backward," but he did not say why. Others were explicit about why the chronological anchor of the present was mandatory. Kidder (1917:369) cautioned that the "only safe method for working out developments in decorative art is to build up one's sequences from chronologically sequent material, and so let one's theories form themselves from the sequences." Kroeber (1916a, 1916b) used the present as the historical anchor for his seminal frequency seriation so that he could determine in which direction change had occurred. Ford (1938a:263) was explicit about the necessity of using the present as a chronological anchor: "Without this tie-up it would be as logical for one end of the chronology to be recent as for the other." Cultural change was not orthogenetic because it had no inevitable direction.

Advocation of stratigraphy as the best way to build a chronology is further evidence that few archaeologists working in the early twentieth century believed cultural evolutionary change had an inevitable direction. Time had an inevitable direction, but cultural evolution did not. That there was no assumption of straight-line evolution involved in the use of the direct historical approach as a chronometer was made abundantly clear when it was used in the Great Plains to ascertain the history of local cultural lineages (Strong 1935, 1936, 1940; Wedel 1936, 1938, 1940). The sequence of cultural change evident there proceeded from sedentary horticulturalists to nomadic equestrian hunters; this is opposite to the sequence predicted on the basis of nineteenth-century orthogenetic cultural evolution (e.g., Morgan 1877; Tylor 1881). Indeed, Kidder (1931:4) noted that one must not assume "the crudest and most widely diffused remains [of ceramics were] the oldest" but instead test such hypotheses with independent chronological evidence such as stratigraphy. Had orthogenesis underpinned the chronometric properties of the direct historical approach, Kidder's caution would have been unnecessary because orthogenesis assumes that all stages and their order of expression within any given lineage are inevitable and sequential.

On the one hand, the fact that the theoretical underpinnings of the direct historical approach when used as an ethnic identifier were not explicitly recognized was not a fatal oversight by itself. Cultural transmission was all that was required, and everyone knew this. Hesitancy to accept the chronometric results of the direct historical approach, on the other hand, resided squarely in the failure to make explicit the theory (of cultural transmission and sorting) underpinning this use of the approach. Hesitancy of another form occurred for exactly the same reason when specific historical analogs were contrasted with general comparative analogs.

The Direct Historical Approach as Analogy

Once it had been established that the direct historical approach could be used both to place ethnographic or ethnic labels on archaeological cultures and as a means of measuring the passage of time, archaeologists took the logical next step and used the approach to create analogies. We say this was the logical next step, but perhaps it would be more precise to view the analogical use as a natural outgrowth of the first two steps, given that ethnicity and time are the two main ingredients of specific historical analogy. After placing a source and

subject in proper chronological order and establishing a line of descent between them, all that was left to do was mine the ethnographic source record for
information and then use it to reconstitute the archaeological subject phenomena into a dynamic cultural system. Fewkes (1896:158) was exceptionally clear
about this when he noted that a demonstration of evolutionary connection
between an ethnographic source culture and an archaeological subject culture
not only "implied that the former culture had been transmitted, [but that this]
renders it safe to apply the principle of interpreting archeology by ethnology."
Why it was "safe" apparently resided in the fact of cultural transmission and
heritable continuity; this notion that a phylogenetic connection strengthened
or made safe an ethnographic analogy would reappear in the 1960s.

To archaeologists working in the first half of the twentieth century, the
ethnographic record of the United States provided a rich source of information on dynamic, operating cultures. Information gleaned from that record
with respect to material culture allowed artifact function to be determined—
function not only in terms of how a tool was used but in terms of how it
was made, recycled, and so on—and it was only a short step from how a
tool was used to the behaviors of the people who manufactured and used
the tool. As Mott (1938:227–228) noted, "if an identification is established
between a historic tribe and an archaeological manifestation, then the whole
inter-related pattern of pre-recorded cultures receives a new orientation and
is linked to 'history.' . . . Once such a link is made, a mass of knowledge
concerning the economy, the techniques, the ceremonial life, and the location
of the people so identified merges with the written facts concerning them."
Thus "rounded conical stones . . . tipped over on their sides" on the floor of
an eleventh-century kiva provided "pretty good evidence for the existence of a
whole religious system" (Parsons 1940:215). It is not surprising that this line
of reasoning came to be known as the "direct ethnological approach" (Kehoe
1958).

As neat a package as specific historical analogy produces, there were at
least three problems with it. Eggan (1952:38) identified the first problem,
if only by implication: For "certain recent archaeological cultures the direct
historical method, once valid connections [of heritable continuity] are established, offers an avenue by which late [archaeological] manifestations may
be enlarged through inferences from ethnological horizons." The key word
in Eggan's remarks is "late," the implication being that the direct histori-

cal approach when used as analogy works progressively less well as the archaeological subject increases in age. This worrisome aspect of ethnographic analogy was noted by Slotkin (1952), and it continued to plague the use of ethnographic analogy into the 1960s, when it was pointed out that "although this approach may be an especially fruitful one when applied to recently extinct cultural systems, it is likely to yield misleading results when applied to the study of cultural materials produced by more ancient societies, especially societies more than 40,000 years extinct" (Freeman 1968:263). Here Freeman (1968:263) was speaking about specific historical analogy, as he noted that one should derive "from the study of a sample of modern societies, elements of sociocultural structure which are homologous with those of the prehistoric period."

A related issue was the fact that groups of people do not remain in one place on the landscape. They move around, and the greater the temporal distance between source and subject, the greater the possibility that one or the other moved. Willey (1953a:373) commonsensically pointed out that "in general, the most successful continuities . . . have been determined for those regions where there has been relatively little ethnic shifting in aboriginal or protohistoric times and where there still remain native populations with predominantly native cultures." He also noted that "a general, but not absolute, assumption which Americanists have followed in these reconstructions is that gradual and unbroken continuity of culture also implies continuity of population and that a sudden change or break in continuity is a reasonable indicator of population change" (Willey 1953a:373). This line of reasoning might have held for late-prehistoric cultures found in the same geographic area as the historically documented culture (Ford 1936b; Steward 1929; Stirling 1932), but what about older archaeological cultures? This question dogged culture historians well into the 1950s (Lyman et al. 1997b): How can one escape the problem of the increasing temporal distance between the source and the subject? The answer was, one cannot escape the problems imposed by the remote past on keeping an ancestor-descendant line intact; rather, one has to create a type of analogy independent of that relationship.

The second problem with specific historical analogy had to do with the kinds of traits being used. The use of specific historical analogs by culture historians grew from an interest in chronological sequences of cultural manifestations, in much the same way that post-Darwinian anatomists turned to homologous anatomical structures as indicators of evolutionary descent with modification (Lyman 2001). Users of the direct historical approach as a chronometer for studying the history of an ethnographically defined culture tried to focus specifically on homologous traits—those attributable to shared ancestry—because the underpinning, yet covert, theory was descent with modification (manifest as differential overlapping created by transmission and sorting). They knew, if only in rudimentary fashion, that nonhomologous traits could not be used to trace ancestry, and they were ever mindful of the difficulties in distinguishing between homologous traits and nonhomologous traits (e.g., Boas 1924; Kroeber 1931b; Lowie 1912; Sapir 1916; Steward 1929).

Identifying homologous traits and separating them from instances of convergence are as significant analytical hurdles in biology and paleobiology as they are in archaeology (Lyman 2001). The wings of eagles and those of crows are structurally as well as superficially similar; this is homologous similarity. The wings of eagles and those of bats are superficially, but not structurally, similar; this is nonhomologous similarity. There obviously are differences between the two kinds of traits, but how can they be distinguished? Sapir (1916:37) suggested cultural traits that display merely "superficial" similarity are probably not evolutionarily related and are likely the result of convergence, whereas those that display "fundamental" similarity are "historically related." Kroeber (1931b:151) was more explicit, although he used some of Sapir's words, and suggested that "where similarities are specific and structural and not merely superficial . . . has long been the accepted method in evolutionary and systematic biology." This was, and is, precisely how biologists distinguish between homologs and analogs. But despite Kroeber's insightful comment, few culture historians went the next step and explored the matter in theoretical or methodological fashion.

The third problem with the use of specific historical analogs was that evolutionary trends can be independent of one another as well as of no predictable direction. Although a direct historical link might exist between source and subject, it is unreasonable to think that the source side is an image identical to that of the subject side or that there has been no cultural change over the hundreds or thousands of years that passed in the interim. It also is unreasonable to assume that all traits of the subject culture evolved at equal and consistent rates. Instead, it is reasonable to assume that mosaic evolution took place. Mosaic evolution occurs when different characters (traits) within a lineage evolve independently of one another and each lineage evolves independently of every other lineage (Eldredge 1989). This concept can be extended to culture, where we can talk about the independence of lineages of automobiles from lineages of computers or the independence of lineages of lithic technologies from lineages of ceramic technologies. The QWERTY keyboard first developed in the 1870s has remained with us despite remarkable changes in how our finger strokes are mechanically and (increasingly) electronically transferred to paper.

Fewkes (1896:164) recognized the problem of mosaic evolution early on when he noted that the "vein of similarity of old and new can be used in an interpretation of ancient [myth and ritual], but we overstep natural limitations if by so doing we ascribe to prehistoric culture every conception which we find current among modern survivors." Parsons (1940) and others were obviously more optimistic, but many recognized Fewkes's central point (e.g., Kroeber 1919, 1923a; Sapir 1916).

Although the direct historical approach would be used throughout the 1920s and 1930s, particularly on the plains, it began to have competition from methods that did not depend on documenting ancestor-descendant relationships. One of the best known of those was a system of classification that became known as the Midwestern Taxonomic Method (McKern 1937a, 1937b, 1939). That so many culture historians working in the Midwest immediately embraced it tells us either that they were ready to abandon the direct historical approach or that they were looking for a method that was complementary. Our take (Lyman and O'Brien 2003; O'Brien and Lyman 1999a, 2001) is that the majority of culture historians viewed the Midwestern Taxonomic Method as a logical and complementary partner to the direct historical approach (see below).

The protocol for building the classification was worked out in the years immediately preceding the National Research Council's Indianapolis conference of 1935, primarily at the hands of W. C. McKern. A colleague of McKern's at the Milwaukee Public Museum later recalled why the method was needed:

> After the close of the 1929 field season our noon-time discussions began to concentrate on how a cultural classification system could be designed to serve the archaeological needs of the Wisconsin area. It was recognized at the outset that temporal considerations would

have to be ignored because no means was available for the relative dating of what had been found. Certain assumptions could have been made about how the prehistoric cultural traits had evolved and then one could have arranged the collected data to fit these assumptions. A hypothetical culture sequence could have been created by that approach but that was rejected by both of us as interestingly speculative but not worth the time that would have been required to develop it. What was wanted was a cultural classification system the criteria for which could be agreed to as valid by all who chose to become familiar with it and to use it. When it became unavoidably clear to both of us that temporal and developmental or evolutionary considerations could not be incorporated in the system, it was finally admitted that the system that was needed so urgently would have to be based on morphological or typological considerations alone [Fisher 1997:119].

That was exactly what the method was based on: "morphological or typological considerations alone." Time and space were to be ignored, at least initially (see below). In principle, the method was simple—a branching taxonomy with successively higher levels of inclusiveness. The building blocks of the method were called components, defined as assemblages of associated artifacts that represented the occupation of a place by a people. A component was not equivalent to a site unless a place had experienced only a single occupation (McKern 1939:308). Artifact trait lists were used to create higher-level groups. An archaeologist polled available components and identified those traits that linked—were shared by—various components; linked components then were placed together in a group termed a focus. Simultaneously, one used those same trait lists to identify traits that could be used to isolate one group of components from another group. Five levels of groups were specified. From least to most inclusive these were focus, aspect, phase, pattern, and base. Three kinds of traits were distinguished: linked traits were common to more than one unit; diagnostic traits were limited to a single unit; and determinants traits occurred in all members of a unit but in no other unit (Figure 7.2).

The Midwestern Taxonomic Method should not be equated with systems of biological classification that either are based on descent, such as cladistics, or from which inferences about descent can be drawn, such as the Linnaean taxonomic system, despite the fact that Fisher (1997) states that the basic ideas

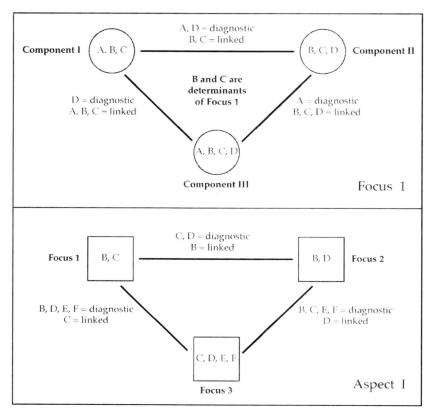

Figure 7.2. *The analytical relations among traits (capital letters), components (circles), and foci (squares) in the Midwestern Taxonomic Method.*

for the method were derived from that system. The Linnaean taxonomy was built in the eighteenth century purely on the basis of the morphometric similarity of organisms; it held no evolutionary implications until after the publication of Darwin's (1859) *Origin of Species* (Ereshefsky 1994). If the Midwestern Taxonomic Method shares anything in common with biological systematics, it is with phenetics, sometimes referred to as numerical taxonomy (Lyman and O'Brien 2003). Given that time was jettisoned from the Midwestern Taxonomic Method, it cannot be aligned with any system that uses history (ancestry) as a criterion for membership in a taxonomic unit. Geographic space was similarly omitted, no doubt at least in part because Wissler's (1917a) age-area theory (Kroeber 1931a) was no longer perceived as a valid chronometer (Hodgen 1942; Wallis 1925, 1945; Woods 1934).

In the Midwestern Taxonomic Method, form-related units were the building blocks of the classification. No longer did archaeologists have to argue about whether shell-tempered pottery was Siouan in origin or grit-tempered pottery Algonquian in origin. Fisher (1997:119) noted that McKern and others freely admitted that at some future point "patterns of arrangement" might emerge that would suggest not only "cultural relationships but perhaps evolutionary sequences as well"—a point underscored by Steward (1942:337) when he noted that the Midwestern Taxonomic Method was "not necessarily in conflict with the direct historical approach to archaeology." McKern (1937b, 1942) indicated that time and space would be considered only after archaeological complexes of traits had been established, at which time analytical efforts could turn to establishing historical linkages with ethnographically documented groups. Thus archaeologists who used the Midwestern Taxonomic Method regularly opted to include time and space in order to establish such linkages and to write evolutionary history (e.g., Cole and Deuel 1937; Griffin 1943; Ritchie 1937).

Several archaeologists attempted to integrate the results of classification with ethnographic results—Wedel's (1938) study of the Pawnees being a well-known example—and in some cases it appeared that there was no conflict between the direct historical approach and the Midwestern Taxonomic Method (e.g., Griffin 1937; Mott 1938). For example, Vickers (1948) compared traits in components, foci, and aspects—all units in the Midwestern Taxonomic Method—in Saskatchewan and Manitoba with traits found in local ethnographically documented cultures. On the basis of the comparison, Vickers (1948:36) concluded that "similarity of geographical distribution, close correlation in time, known continuation of burial and other traits from the [prehistoric] aspect to the historic tribe . . . all buttress the [inferred ethnic affinity of a particular archaeological manifestation]." Such studies showed that the direct historical approach and the Midwestern Taxonomic Method were compatible. Further, the results were predictable given the short time span between the source and subject sides of the analogy and the fact that they were linked through common ancestry.

The appearance of the Midwestern Taxonomic Method was a clear sign that by the 1930s archaeological emphasis was shifting away from specific historical analogy, with its roots in phylogeny, and toward general comparative analogy. This replacement, however, was only half the story, and it actually was of lesser importance than the other half—the abandonment of descent with modification in American archaeology in favor of orthogenesis that we documented in Chapter 2. The shift in the kind of preferred analogical reasoning in archaeology received much discussion in the literature (e.g., Anderson 1969; Ascher 1961; Binford 1967, 1968b; Chang 1967; Gould 1974; Lange 1980; Thompson 1958; Watson 1979; Willey 1953a, 1953c). The theories that underpinned each kind of analogy were, however, neither identified nor discussed, just as they had not been during the preceding 60 years. Surprisingly, of the three problems attending the use of specific historical analogs—temporal limitations, mosaic evolution, and identifying homologous traits—only the last was mentioned (Binford 1968a) after the shift from specific historical analogy to general comparative analogy had been made. Not surprisingly, that mention was in a conceptual context other than analogical reasoning. One result of the failure to explicitly consider the theoretical issues was repetition of Fewkes's (1896) earlier implication regarding the validity of specific historical analogs.

General Comparative Analogy and Orthogenesis

The 1940s and early 1950s constituted a period of considerable change in American archaeology, away from culture history and toward cultural reconstruction. Culture history was not abandoned in favor of reconstructionism. Rather, Americanists working prior to 1940 had always been aware of their alliance with anthropology. This is why Dixon (1913:558) could claim early on that "archeology is but prehistoric ethnology and ethnography." The use of specific historical analogy by culture historians was geared in large part toward making prehistoric behavior accessible—toward rewriting the archaeological record in ethnographic terms. After about 1945 archaeologists perceived themselves explicitly as "anthropologists who dig" (Deetz 1970:123). Similarly, it was said on more than one occasion by more than one individual that "New World archaeology is anthropology or it is nothing" (Phillips 1955:246–247).

Chronology and other nonanthropological issues addressed by culture historians were perceived as merely the first in a series of goals—not the final goal—of early twentieth-century American archaeology. As Steward (1942:339) noted, the ability "to describe archaeological materials in terms of time and space [was] the first elementary step toward understanding culture change"—a process he labeled "historical anthropology." Nevertheless, anthropologists (e.g., Bennett 1943; Kluckhohn 1949; Parsons 1940; Steward and Setzler 1938) on occasion felt compelled to remind archaeologists of what they took to be archaeology's larger anthropological goals and suggested ways that archaeologists might attain those goals, such as by determining the functions of particular artifacts, assessing their roles within a culture, and identifying behaviors signified by the artifacts. All such remarks simply underscored what archaeologists had long believed: Before they could begin to explain the archaeological record in anthropological terms and with anthropologically worded (ethnological) theory, that static record had to be reconstituted into one or more dynamic cultural systems complete with lists of human behaviors.

Analogy was the preferred tool for the job, but there were problems with using the traditional version—specific historical analogy. There was an alternative, however. In an early statement, Griffin (1943:336–337) referred to "the eventual reconstruction of the life and historic development of the peoples who inhabited the area." He also noted that the ethnographic record seldom provided the archaeologist with details of material culture. Most important, he suggested that when "definite historical connections cannot be made, correlations between ethnology and archaeology should not be formulated on a tribal-focus basis, but should be established on more general bases, such as the matching of an aspect or phase trait complex against the element list of some such ethnological division as the culture area" (Griffin 1943:341). (A "focus" is an archaeological culture unit in the Midwestern Taxonomic Method more or less equivalent to a tribe. An "aspect" and a "phase" are also within the Midwestern Taxonomic Method and are more general and inclusive archaeological culture units than a focus.) The basis for using a culture area as a criterion for selection of an appropriate source analog is unclear in Griffin's discussion, but we suspect it was the notion that similar cultures would be found in similar environments, and environment in part dictated the boundaries of culture areas.

Willey (1953c:229) referred to the alternative to specific historical analogy as " 'general comparative analogy,' in which we are interested in cultures for comparisons, in cultures of the same general level of technological development, perhaps existing under similar environmental situations." This was precisely the kind of analogy for which the Midwestern Taxonomic Method, with its emphasis on formal properties and deletion of time and space from consideration, was well suited. Thompson (1958:5) discussed the rationale for using that kind of analogy:

> The archaeologist who formulates an indicated conclusion is suggesting that there is a correlation between a certain set of archaeological material percepta and a particular range of sociocultural behavior. He must test this conclusion by demonstrating that an artifact-behavior correlation similar to the suggested one is a common occurrence in ethnographic reality. What actually happens is that he compares an artifact type which is derived from archaeological data with a similar artifact type in a known life situation. If the resemblance in the form of the 2 artifact types is reasonably close, he can infer that the archaeological type shares the technique, behavior, or other cultural activity which is usually associated with the ethnographic type.
>
> Thus the archaeologist proceeds from basic or descriptive data to a contextual or interpretive inference by demonstrating the existence and validity of various degrees of relation of likeness. This similarity or parallelism of relations is called analogy. Archaeological inference, and particularly that related to the reconstruction of cultural (and ecological) contexts, is impossible without recourse to analogy.

The difference between specific historical analogy and general comparative analogy was striking: In "the general comparative analogy, the artifact-behavior correlation derives from a pattern of repeated occurrences in a large number of cultures. In contrast, the specific historical type [of analogy] depends upon the existence of a direct continuity in a single culture or area" (Thompson 1958:5–6). In a more detailed discussion of the two kinds of ethnographic analogy, Ascher (1961:319) came down decidedly in favor of general comparative analogy because it required no demonstration of heritable continuity between source and subject. Instead, it specified "boundary conditions for the choice of suitable analogs" (Ascher 1961:319). As Ascher (1961:319) put it, "the canon is: seek analogies in cultures which manipulate similar environments in similar ways."

Heritable continuity was not required in general comparative analogy, as it had been in specific historical analogy. Yet several commentators repeated Fewkes's (1896) earlier statement and indicated that such a connection would strengthen the validity of an ethnographically based analogy (e.g., Anderson

1969; Ascher 1961; Binford 1967; Chang 1967; Lange 1980; Watson 1979). It was not unusual to read something like the following: The greater the degree of "cultural continuity" between the source and the subject, the greater "the likelihood of drawing a correct analogy" (Brumfiel 1976:398); or "the tightest analogies are direct historical" (Peterson 1971:240); or specific historical analogies "offer an inherently higher degree of probability of interpretation and should be sought [because such analogies offer a] greater probability that the [source analog] derived in the present is applicable to the past" in the geographic area containing the archaeological subject (Gould 1974:39). Specific historical analogies "were seen as having an inherently greater probability of being accurate approximations of behavioral realities than [general analogies]" (Gould 1980:35). No one, however, expressed in theoretical terms why a historical connection denoting heritable continuity made a specific historical analogy more valid than a general comparative analogy and its attendant "boundary conditions" (Ascher 1961). Instead, the reasons given were simplistic.

Green (1973:140) pointed out that one employs a general comparative analogy when "demonstration of prehistoric–historic cultural continuity is not possible." When this is the case, certain restrictions apply: "General analogy allows that a prehistoric culture may be compared with a contemporary one even though the two are not within the same cultural tradition [or line of heritable continuity]. However, the two groups should be at the same level of subsistence and live in comparable, although not necessarily identical, environments" (Green 1973:140). The warrant for the application of general comparative analogy is that cultures thought to be historical descendants of the prehistoric culture are unknown. The reasons for the restrictions placed on appropriate source analogs are implicit; together, they comprise the notion of convergence, or as Stahl (1993:244) aptly put it, "societies occupying comparable environments pursuing similar subsistence strategies [represent] comparable stages of evolutionary development." This statement requires that we briefly consider the concept of stage.

Prior to the late 1940s, stages were not explicitly defined as analytical units, and they were often equated with periods (Lyman and O'Brien 2001). So far as we are aware, Krieger (1953a:247–248) provided the first formal definition of a stage as an analytical unit when he contrasted it with a period as an analytical unit.

I will consider a [cultural evolutionary] "stage" a segment of a historical sequence in a given area, characterized by a dominating pattern of
economic existence. The general economic life and outlines of social
structure of past peoples can often be inferred from archaeological
remains and can be related to similar phenomena, whether the dates
are known or not. The term "period," on the other hand, might be
considered to depend upon chronology. Thus a stage may be recognized by content alone, and in the event that accurate dates can be
obtained for it in a given area, it could be said that the *stage* here existed
during such-and-such *period*. Further, the same stage may be said to
appear at different times or periods in different areas and also to end
at different times. A stage may also include several locally distinctive
culture complexes and minor time divisions.

Stages were, as Rowe (1962b:43) notes, a "legacy" of eighteenth- and
nineteenth-century cultural evolutionism. Stages provide the warrant for the
use of general comparative analogy, and that warrant resides squarely in orthogenesis. "Each stage is supposed to be characterized by a certain pattern of institutions, so that a certain kind of technology is associated with a certain kind
of social organization and certain economic, political, and religious ideas. It
is this last aspect of [orthogenetic] evolutionary theory which is particularly
attractive to archaeologists looking for a short-cut to cultural interpretation,
for it provides a method of reconstructing those aspects of culture for which
the archaeological record provides no direct evidence" (Rowe 1962b:43).

Within the theory of orthogenetic evolution, similar adaptive problems
faced by historically unrelated cultures in similar environments should result
in similar adaptive solutions termed stages as a result of convergence and/or
parallelism. Theoretical reasons as to why convergence should result were
not specified by archaeologists who adopted orthogenetic evolutionism after
the 1950s, even though Rowe (1962) noted the necessity of such. Appropriate
source analogs represent nonhomologous cultural traits that are in fact analogous in a Darwinian sense—they are similar as a sole result of functional
convergence. How to determine if similar traits were analogous (the result
of convergence) rather than homologous (the result of shared ancestry) was
also not considered, despite recognition of the problem (Binford 1968a). The
places to search for appropriate source analogs are among cultures found in

environments and with technologies similar to those of the archaeological sub-ject; ethnographic source cultures should be within the same adaptive stage as the archaeological subject culture. Adaptive—and by implication behavioral—similarity is the analytical focus of archaeologists who adopted orthogenetic evolutionism, not ethnic identity, history, or heritable continuity, all of which demand an analytical focus on homologous traits.

The requirements of the "new analogy," to use Ascher's (1961) term, not only replaced those of phylogenetic continuity but omitted the nondirectional (nonpredictable) theory of descent with modification. This is so because the evolutionary theory underpinning the use of general comparative analogy is orthogenesis. With implicit reference to the general comparative application of analogy, Binford (1962a:219) observed that "the study and establishment of correlations between types of social structure classified on the basis of behavioral attributes and structural types of material elements [are] one of the major areas of anthropological research yet to be developed. Once such corre-lations are established, archaeologists can attack the problems of evolutionary change in social systems." For such correlations to exist, cultural evolution had to involve cultural stages rendered as sets of functionally interdependent cultural traits.

Statements were made such as "the formal structure of artifact assem-blages together with the between element [or cultural trait] contextual rela-tionships should and do present a systematic and understandable picture of the total extinct cultural system" (Binford 1962a:219). Such presumed functional interdependence of cultural traits fit well with White's (1959c:8) conception of culture as a system and "an extrasomatic mechanism employed by a particular animal species in order to make its life secure and continuous." This concep-tion and its attendant definition were adopted by processual archaeologists of the 1960s and 1970s, along with the orthogenetic models of cultural evolution and their attendant stages as described by White (1959c), Steward (1955), Fried (1967), and others (Rambo 1991; Spencer 1997). Cultural evolution was orthogenetic—an inevitable (as a result of universal convergence, perhaps, and not necessarily affected by diffusion) linear passage through a set of adaptive stages. Largely because of this, Binford's statement and similar ones made by others resulted in archaeologists devoting their time not to developing ways to distinguish between homologous and nonhomologous forms but rather to searching for correlations between human behaviors and artifacts. Thus it was remarked in the 1970s that archaeologists of the 1960s "have probably spent more time in attempting to infer and describe lifeways associated with a given [cultural] stage than in accounting for changes from stage to stage" (Plog 1973:189; see also Binford 1977).

Correlations between archaeological phenomena and human behaviors were sought because of the emphasis beginning in the 1940s to make archaeology more anthropological (e.g., Binford 1962a; Caldwell 1959; Strong 1952; Woodbury 1963, 1972). Correlations were believed to exist because cultures conceived as systems representing evolutionary stages were rendered as sets of functionally integrated traits (Dunnell 1991). During the rise in popularity of processual archaeology, this belief was questioned by Rowe (1962b) and also by Trigger (1968:16), the latter suggesting that "identity or close similarity in material remains [may not indicate] identity in all aspects of culture, including language, social structure, and ideology." Nevertheless, it was later suggested by processualists that functional and adaptational similarities, rather than more purely phylogenetic connections, serve as the linkages between an archaeological subject and an ethnographic source (e.g., Greenberg and Spielbauer 1991). Functional and adaptational similarities were little more than general comparative analogies couched in terms of cultural systems conceived as adaptive stages.

By using general comparative analogy to reconstitute the archaeological record into something an ethnographer would recognize, archaeologists believed they could contribute to the construction of anthropological theory rather than act merely as technicians in the service of cultural reconstruction. Further, there was an "embarrassment of choices among [anthropological] theories" (Shelley 1999:603) from which to draw when trying to explain the archaeological record. Given this plethora of riches, one might expect that anthropological theory would have been a source of sufficient explanations for the archaeological record, but this was not the case. Otherwise, archaeologists who themselves study source-side analogs (e.g., Binford 1977; O'Connell 1995; Schiffer 1996; Simms 1992; Watson 1979) would not even today keep calling for the construction of general explanatory theory.

Although commentators in the 1960s did not mention many of the problems with specific historical analogs that their intellectual predecessors had identified, they did worry about one problem with general comparative analogy: Despite the restrictions of similar environment and similar technology placed on general comparative analogs, one could still find multiple-source analogs. The problem was perceived to be so great that Howell (1968:287) suggested that "reconstruction efforts [based on general analogies] be discouraged or very severely curtailed except for very recent time periods." Part of the reason for the repeated calls for general theory applicable to the archaeological record may well have resided in the fact that the use of multiple-source analogs can, and often does, result in a loss of resolution because of conflicting suggestions of the sources (Shelley 1999), a fact underscored by the use of multiple general-comparative-source analogs (e.g., Binford 1967, 1972:52–58; Munson 1969). The single-source analog demanded by specific historical analogy avoided this problem, but as was noted more than once, use of the single-source analog suggested by the direct historical approach "lessens the number of possible interpretations of an artifact, although it cannot guarantee completely valid interpretation" (Anderson 1969:134; see also Watson 1979). This problem has never been solved, as evidenced by the diversity of suggestions regarding how the number of possible interpretations might be reduced (e.g., Wolverton and Lyman 2000; Wylie 1989).

Evolution, Analogs, and Chronology

A change in the analytical goal of American archaeology—from one focused on historical questions to one focused on ahistorical (orthogenetic) anthropological questions—resulted generally in expanded use of ethnographic analogy and particularly in an increased use of general comparative analogs. Not only were specific historical analogs not always available, the direct historical approach was used less and less as a chronometer because first stratigraphy and then radiocarbon dating usurped that role (Nash 2000; O'Brien and Lyman 1999c). By the late 1940s the archaeological record was sufficiently well known to allow syntheses of local and regional cultural chronologies (Martin et al. 1947; Willey and Phillips 1955, 1958), and the time was ripe to move on to new problems (Caldwell 1959). One result was Ascher's (1961) belated birth announcement of the "new [general comparative] analogy," although there was nothing particularly new about it. It had always been there, eclipsed for a while by specific historical analogy but still present in the archaeological tool kit.

In an early programmatic statement characterizing general comparative analogy, Hewett (1908:591) stated that the "subject matter [of American archeology] lies mainly in the prehistoric period, but this must be studied in the light of auxiliary sciences which have for their field of investigation the living people." Interestingly, Hewett (1908:593) went on to remark that study of "cultural process" was accomplished "in the light of facts which ethnology lends to the interpretation of [prehistoric] phenomena." While he noted that the study of language history and evolution required direct historical connections, he implied that the study of the history and evolution of "cultural phenomena" did not (Hewett 1908:592). The implication is that, in the latter case, what would later become known as general comparative analogy was sufficient. An early example of using general comparative analogs was Harlan Smith's (1910) study entitled "The Prehistoric Ethnology of a Kentucky Site." Smith called on various ethnographically documented cultures in North America to sort prehistoric artifacts into those used by men and those used by women; to infer that a deer bone displaying a particular kind of artificial modification had been used as a hide scraper; to infer that deer toe bones with particular artificial modifications had served variously as gaming pieces or ornaments; and to derive other, similar analogy-based inferences of human behavior and artifact function. Heritable continuity played no role in Smith's study; it was purely general comparative analogy.

Because archaeologists had pride of place in having access to the full extent of humankind's past, they believed they could contribute to anthropological theory, particularly with respect to the processes of cultural evolution. They did not recognize that when they used general comparative analogs, they implicitly adopted a different version of evolutionary theory than that underpinning specific historical analogy. White (1947b:175) did not help matters when he remarked that as a cultural evolutionist, an archaeologist "would begin, naturally, with the present, with what we have before us. Then we would arrange other forms in the series in accordance with their likeness or dissimilarity to the present form." The suggestion that specific historical analogs could be applied under orthogenesis was unqualified—a point made all the more curious by the fact that research on the plains (e.g., Strong 1933, 1935, 1936; Wedel 1936) had made it abundantly clear that such an application was ill-advised.

As we noted in Chapter 2, Kroeber (1923a) did not confuse the two theories of evolution. But Nelson (1932:103) conflated the two when he "propose[d] to consider implements or mechanical inventions, i.e., material culture phenomena, as parts of a unique unfolding *process* which has much in common with that other process observed in the world of nature and generally called organic evolution." The conflation was further compounded by Nelson's (1932:111) remark that the mechanism of change was not natural selection working on undirected variation but rather "the old adage that necessity is the mother of invention"—variation directed by human intentions. This had a later parallel with White's (1943:339) claim that the human "urge" to improve was the "motive force as well as the means of cultural evolution." Such conflations of the two theories contributed to American archaeologists not recognizing the difference in the underpinning theory that accompanied the differences between specific historical analogs and general comparative analogs. Even if they had recognized the difference (and it is clear they did not), by the mid-1940s they had no choice but to change (Chapter 2).

Discard of the theory of descent with modification by American archaeologists had begun early in the twentieth century for various reasons. As we saw in Chapter 2, the few archaeologists who attempted to use biological methods and models in the 1930s were brought up short in their endeavors by overwhelming criticism. By the mid-1940s the disposal of Darwinian evolution was virtually complete, leaving orthogenesis as the only game in town. Use of that theory of evolution was, we suspect, reinforced by the observation of evolutionary trends in the archaeological record (e.g., Willey and Phillips 1955, 1958). Our suspicion is founded on the fact that paleontology was one of the last strongholds of orthogenesis within biology, in part because long spans of evolutionary trends were visible (Bowler 1979; Gould 1982, 1988). Straight lines of evolution were apparent among various sets of fossils to some paleontologists, and some but not all of them explained those lines in terms of orthogenesis, although by the mid-twentieth century most paleontologists had discarded orthogenesis in favor of descent with modification (Jepsen 1949; Romer 1949; Simpson 1953; Watson 1949).

Paleontologists who preferred descent with modification to orthogenesis noted that evolution was not a line of one form replacing another or a ladder of stages but rather a bush of multiple and overlapping forms (Simpson 1953); that any appearance of a line or ladder was the result of the way in which paleontologists had classified and arranged fossils against time (Jepsen 1949); and that an evolutionary line could only be said to be "directional when the direction is known" (Jepsen 1949:493). Today apparent evolutionary lines rendered as character gradients or chronoclines (Koch 1986) within a clade are labeled "trends" (Alroy 2000) and are explained as resulting from various constraints and mechanisms "channeling" evolution in particular directions (e.g., Gould 1982, 1988) rather than from some mysterious force directing the appearance of new variants. Once a trend is identified, the challenge is to explain it within the bounds of the theory of descent with modification (Alroy 2000; McShea 2000).

The appearance of trends in the cultural record was in large part a result of the classification of archaeological manifestations into stages (e.g., Willey and Phillips 1955, 1958). As Rowe (1962b:51) indicated, "because of the close association of stages with the theory of cultural evolution, virtually every archaeologist who uses stages to organize his data thereby builds into them certain assumptions about cultural development without being aware that he is doing so. Later, in making his cultural interpretations, he discovers the pattern of cultural development which was assumed in his system of organization [the stages] and thinks that he is deriving it empirically from the data." Dunnell (1988:178–180) later expanded on this point, underscoring the fact that the cultural traits chosen as definitive of particular cultural evolutionary stages are typically derived from a sample of societies thought to differ in terms of the evolutionary stage each represents. Those definitive traits vary with the societies polled and comprise empirical generalizations. As a result, trends in orthogenetically conceived cultural evolution were, and are, difficult to explain.

Because the stages comprise poorly defined analytical units that are really little more than empirical generalizations (Leonard and Jones 1987; Rambo 1991), the orthogenetic theory of cultural evolution necessitates concepts such as "devolution" (Carneiro 1972)—a concept that ignores the fact that evolution can be in either direction along the straight line of orthogenesis (Alland 1974). Paleobiologists (e.g., Gregory 1936; Simpson 1960) grappled with this problem of apparent reversals, often referring to Dollo's law (Gould 1970), which states that temporally remote character states do not recur in exactly the same form at a later time. Rather, the manner in which phenomena are classified makes it appear as if a reversal occurred. As Gould (1970:208) makes clear, Dollo was careful in phrasing his law precisely because of his interest in "the historical nature of evolutionary events." Dollo's law of irreversibility "functions as a guarantee that convergences can be recognized by preservation of some ancestral structure (incomplete reversion). Convergence is the major impediment to phylogenetic interpretations" (Gould 1970:206–207). In modern terms, Dollo's law allows evolutionists operating under the theory of descent with modification to distinguish between analogous (convergent) character states and homologous character states. One subset of the latter— shared derived character states—are used to reconstruct phylogenetic histories (O'Brien and Lyman 2003; O'Brien et al. 2001).

An implicit notion of Dollo's law attended use of the direct historical approach as a chronometer; otherwise, it could not have been used as such. The focus on homologous traits, necessitated when the direct historical approach was used as a chronometer, reflects that notion. Some cultural traits displayed cycles and recurred at various times (Kroeber 1919; Richardson and Kroeber 1940), a fact recognized by some archaeologists (e.g., Rands 1961). This no doubt contributed to the insistence that chronologies of artifacts erected on the basis of the direct historical approach and frequency seriation be tested with stratigraphic data. The insistence evaporated with the invention of radiometric chronometers in the 1950s. Simultaneously, there was a bit more explicit consideration of parallelism and convergence and of why these processes should occur in independent cultural lineages (e.g., Rands and Riley 1958). Orthogenesis held the answer; convergent and parallel evolution were to be expected because the process of orthogenetic evolution not only "meets basic needs" but creates similar cultural patterns by its "normalizing powers" (Steward and Shimkin 1961:484, 486). Spencer's "unknown force" was revealed to be human needs and urges.

Because orthogenetic cultural evolution dictated that similar evolutionary results be produced, convergence was to be expected. Convergence was not used as evidence of the power of natural selection; it was instead used as evidence of orthogenesis. Without demonstrating that convergence had in fact occurred, however, conclusions were tautological, just as Rowe (1962b) had indicated.

The Direct Historical Approach and Chronometry

Although many professed to know what the direct historical approach was and how to use it prior to 1950, no one described its analytical protocol in detail during the height of its use in the first half of the twentieth century. This was not only a result but a cause of its being used for three distinct analytical purposes—as an ethnic identifier, as a chronometer, and as a warrant for specific historical analogy. The theory underpinning the approach has not previously been considered in detail, perhaps because two of the three uses to which it could be put are readily accommodated by either descent with modification or orthogenesis. That the use of the direct historical approach as a chronometer was underpinned by the theory of descent with modification has not been previously recognized for two reasons. First, that theory had been discarded by 1950, and second, the role of the approach as a chronometer was usurped by other chronometers at about the same time.

The ultimate goal of American archaeologists to be contributors to anthropology rather than mere users of its products was thought to be attainable by the 1950s. It was also thought that that goal could be reached only by rendering the archaeological record in ethnographic terms (Lyman and O'Brien 2001). Such renderings could then be subsumed under the emerging orthogenetic evolutionism of White and Steward (Chapter 2). The century-long failure to explicitly distinguish between the particular theory of evolution that informed the use of specific historical analogy and the theory that informed the use of general comparative analogy resulted in the 1960s and 1970s in claims that the former was more valid than the latter. Given the distinctive theories that support each kind of analogy, we suspect that the reasoning underpinning this belief was as follows: Cultural traits of a direct historical analog are similar because they share ancestry and are also functionally and behaviorally similar precisely because they have (metaphorically) genetic affinity. The similarity of an ethnographic source and an archaeological subject of a direct historical analogy has two causes—a historical affinity or genetic connection and also a functional-behavioral connection. For a general comparative analogy, the cause of similarity is singular; the ethnographic source and the archaeological subject are similar as a result of a functional-behavioral connection rendered as convergence. The historical connection of a specific historical analogy is, it seems, the root of the belief that this sort of analogy is better than a general comparative analog. Either that, or those expressing the belief doubted that convergence was universal.

The cause of similarity between cultural traits in general comparative analogy (implicitly) comprises not only orthogenesis but also convergence, the warrant for which is provided by the boundary conditions of similar technologies and environments. Evolutionary convergence is, however, more often assumed than demonstrated. This notion harks back to anthropology of the seventeenth through nineteenth centuries and denies that existing primitive cultures used as analog sources have evolutionary histories (Hodgen 1964; Stocking 1987; Van Riper 1993). Thus existing primitive cultures are treated conceptually and analytically as evolutionarily stable states that first appeared in the remote past. Living fossils such as the coelacanth (Gorr and Kleinschmidt 1993) do exist, but paleontological evidence shows just how fallacious using such phenomena as behavioral-functional analogs can be (e.g., Crompton and Parker 1978). Descent with modification and orthogenesis have regularly been confused by American archaeologists. The history of the direct historical approach and its role in ethnographic analogy reveals some of the roots of this confusion.

On the one hand, use of the direct historical approach as a chronometer is hardly mentioned in recent historical overviews (Lyman et al. 1997b; Nash 2000), perhaps because it seems to be seldom used in this way these days. Its uses as an ethnic identifier and as a source of analogs, on the other hand, seem assured for at least the immediate future. The mandate of the Native American Graves Protection and Repatriation Act call for the ethnic identification of human remains, and the direct historical approach as an ethnic identifier can be used to serve that mandate. As the many recently published articles cited in this chapter demonstrate, modern American archaeologists continue to seek source analogs that are evolutionarily linked with archaeological manifestations in the belief that such specific historical analogs are better (more probable) than general comparative ones. All three uses are underpinned by the assumption that there is evolutionary continuity of some scale between the present and the past, an assumption that warrants more detailed study (see Dunnell 1991 for an initial effort). Understanding how and why the direct historical approach works in each of the three uses to which it has been, and is being, applied is mandatory to its continued application.

The direct historical approach was one of the first (if not the first) artifact-based chronometers used by anthropologists and archaeologists. So long as one believed, even if implicitly, that cultural transmission was the process that created linkages between aggregates of cultural traits or artifact types in the form of overlapping, the passage of time was a theoretically informed explanation of overlapping and the ability to arrange trait complexes in a series or sequence. The same implicit belief in the cause of overlapping underpinned (and as we suggested in Chapter 5, probably guided Kroeber's invention of) frequency seriation. Without explicit consideration of the theoretical processes that underpinned them, both of those chronometric methods were perceived only to make assessments of the age of artifacts inferential. Time was made analytically and inferentially visible, but questions remained. Were the orders of traits and artifacts really chronological orders? Was there an empirical way to confirm that those items were arranged with old objects at one end, young objects at the other end, and middle-aged objects in the middle? Indeed there was, or so archaeologists thought, and this was to pay attention to the superposed positions of artifacts in depositional strata. That chronometer is the subject of the next chapter.

8. American Stratigraphic Excavation

Gordon Willey (1968:40) was the first historian of American archaeology to use the term "stratigraphic revolution"—in quotation marks—to characterize the fieldwork of, particularly, Manuel Gamio, A. V. Kidder, and Nels C. Nelson during the second decade of the twentieth century. Taylor (1954:563) had previously characterized that work as involving a "time-space revolution" and still earlier had noted that these researchers' use of the "time-and-space approach" comprised a "revolution" (Taylor 1948:65, 73). Subsequently, others who have discussed the history of American archaeology have continued to use the term "stratigraphic revolution" (e.g., Givens 1992; Lyon 1996; Schuyler 1971; Willey and Sabloff 1974, 1993). Some histories do not use the terms "revolution" or "stratigraphic revolution" but instead make it sound as if whatever happened in the second decade of the twentieth century was critically important. Whether the term is used or not, many discussions of this era make it sound as if the event generally signified by the words "stratigraphic revolution" involved stratified (or at least vertically distinct) deposits and a change in excavation technique (e.g., Adams 1960; Browman and Givens 1996; Woodbury 1960a, 1960b).

Various statements attribute either the first stratigraphic excavations in North America to Nelson, Gamio, and Kidder (Adams 1960; Browman and Givens 1996; Heizer 1959; Schroeder 1979; Taylor 1954; Woodbury 1960a, 1960b), or at least the first significant stratigraphic excavations (Givens 1996; Willey 1953a; Willey and Sabloff 1974). Taylor (1954:564) indicated that Nelson's work in 1914 "was the first stratigraphic test in Americanist archaeology." Heizer (1959:216) stated that "N. C. Nelson's [1916] summary of his Tano excavations marks the beginning of a new era in American archaeology, since it called attention effectively to the results which stratigraphic excavation could produce." Lothrop (1961:10), too, remarked that the "introduction of stratigraphic field studies marks the beginning of a new era in Americanist archaeology." And Woodbury (1973:44) wrote that "by the time Kidder ended his work at Pecos [New Mexico] in 1929 the application of stratigraphy to archeological excavation . . . had ceased to be the untried experiment that it had seemed to many in 1915 and was standard procedure not only in the Southwest but in other parts of the Americas as well."

Such statements place undue emphasis on excavation method and ignore the more important issue of how artifacts were classified. Stratigraphic excavation was widely practiced in American archaeology before 1912. The literature of the 1920s and 1930s indicates that the probable source of the inaccuracies in modern histories is the so-called revolutionaries themselves. The literature of 1900–1920 indicates that stratigraphic excavation was initially used to confirm rather than create cultural chronologies. The real "revolution" in American archaeology lay not in a change in excavation technique such as is implied by the term "stratigraphic revolution" and various statements about that event. Rather, the change is found in how archaeologists began using observed shifts in the frequencies of artifact types to measure time. Despite the revolutionary nature of new methods for measuring culture change, these methods were all but abandoned by the mid-1930s, as archaeologists turned to using stratigraphic excavation to create chronologies of cultures. In this chapter we discuss late nineteenth- and early twentieth-century archaeological excavation and artifact classification methods. To begin, we define key terms.

Definitions of Key Terms

Cremeens and Hart (1995:17) are correct that "indiscriminate use of the terms such as level, stratum, horizon, and cultural layer has created ambiguities in the archaeological literature." Three other factors have also contributed to terminological ambiguity. First, definitions of a term are inconsistent from author to author, especially among introductory archaeology textbooks published over the past three decades. Second, whereas we suspect many archaeologists would claim to know "stratigraphic excavation" when they see it, this term is one of the least frequently defined terms we examined in the literature, second only to "stratum" in the paucity of published definitions. Third, definitions of some terms include critical terms that themselves are not defined, such as a definition of stratigraphic excavation that includes, but does not define, the term "stratum" (Givens 1996). Various terms have multiple definitions, each specific to a particular discipline or analytical context (e.g., Holliday 1990, 1992; Stein 1990). The terms we employ here are not intended to become universally standard but rather are specific to the questions of interest: What is stratigraphic excavation? When did stratigraphic excavation occur in the history of American archaeology? When did the measurement of cultural change over time first occur in American archaeology, and was it the result of adopting stratigraphic excavation? We begin with several basic terms before defining the terms of greatest concern in the context of the history of stratigraphic excavation in American archaeology.

Sediment is "particulate matter that has been transported by some process from one location to another" (Stein 1987:339; 1992:195). Soil "is the result of the complex interaction of a variety of physical, chemical, and biological processes acting on rock or sediment over time. . . . [It] is a natural entity that is a type of weathering phenomena" (Holliday 1992:102; see also Holliday 1990). Pedogenic (soil-forming) processes "are responsible for transforming sediments into soils" (Schiffer 1987:200). The distinction between sediments and soils is important because a soil has "visibly recognizable or distinguishable characteristics," which are used to divide them into horizons, but "stratigraphic relations, in particular the law of superposition, do not apply to the vertical relationships of individual soil horizons" (Cremeens and Hart 1995:26). Only the relative vertical positions of sediments are significant in terms of superposition.

Archaeologists have, over the past two decades, come to focus on formation processes (Schiffer 1987). There also has been increasing terminological discrimination within the North American Stratigraphic Code (North American Commission on Stratigraphic Nomenclature 1983) as well as attempts to modify that code for archaeological purposes (Gasche and Tunca 1983; Stein 1990). These factors have prompted some archaeologists to favor the term "deposit" over "stratum" (e.g., Schiffer 1987; Stein 1987). For purposes of this chapter, the two terms are considered synonymous; as Stein (1987:346) notes, "most archaeologists refer to any archaeological deposit that was identified according to its physical properties rather than its chronological properties as a stratum." A stratum or deposit is a three-dimensional unit of sediment that represents a depositional event and is distinguishable from other such units. Inclusion of the words "depositional event" denotes that all of the sediment particles—including artifacts—comprising a stratum were deposited at approximately the same time. We follow our predecessors and define stratification as the presence of (generally) vertically discrete layers of deposition or excavation and stratigraphy as an interpretation of the chronological meaning of layers.

Different individuals will identify different deposits, strata, or "natural layers" because they use different criteria to distinguish among them (Stein 1987:346–347). This means that the temporal boundaries and durations of the depositional event represented by such a unit will vary from investigator to investigator. Most archaeologists would nonetheless argue that keeping the artifacts found in one natural depositional unit separate from those in another for purposes of analysis is the preferred artifact-collection strategy (e.g., Deetz 1967; Praetzellis 1993; Rathje and Schiffer 1982). There are two basic reasons for this. First, artifacts within a stratum are stratigraphically associated (were deposited at the same time) and thus are, potentially, of approximately the same age (were created and used at the same time). This is the principle of association that originated with J. J. A. Worsaae in archaeology (Rowe 1962c). "*Association* refers to two or more archaeological items occurring together, usually within the same matrix" (Sharer and Ashmore 1993:126). The importance of this principle is that it allows one to infer that stratigraphically associated artifacts are contemporary or temporally associated in terms of when they were made and used; we refer to this as an inference of synchronic time. That it is an inference is clear from studies of site formation (Schiffer 1987). The second reason artifacts from different strata should be kept separate is that, given the principle of superposition, one can infer temporal differences between sets of artifacts from different vertically discrete units. We refer to this as an inference of diachronic time. That it is in fact an inference is clear when the definitions of superposition and stratigraphy are considered.

An artifact-collection strategy resulting in sets of artifacts being recovered from vertically distinct units—strata or deposits—comprises at least part of most definitions of stratigraphic excavation (e.g., Bower 1986:51, 190, 487; Browman and Givens 1996:80; Deetz 1967:16; Hester et al. 1975:82, 84; Hole and Heizer 1973:124; Sharer and Ashmore 1993:261; Stein 1987:346). Some individuals refer to arbitrary or metric excavation levels as "strata" (e.g., Nesbitt 1938), and others state or imply that the use of arbitrary levels as artifact-collection units comprises stratigraphic excavation (e.g., Browman and Givens

1996; Deetz 1967; Givens 1996; Heizer 1959; Taylor 1954; Thomas 1989; Willey and Sabloff 1993). Willey (1953a:365, 367) labels such excavation "continuous stratigraphy" and "vertical continuous stratigraphy." Certainly the boundaries of arbitrary units that are vertically distinct from one another define a period of deposition just as the boundaries of "natural" units do, although the former may represent only a fraction of the "natural" depositional event represented by the stratum or deposit from which they are derived. In this discussion, we ignore the sticky issue of an arbitrary unit that includes multiple natural depositional units.

Not only how the term "stratigraphic excavation" has been defined but also how it has been used by American archaeologists leads us to define it as follows: Stratigraphic excavation comprises removing artifacts and sediments from vertically discrete three-dimensional units of deposition and keeping those artifacts in sets based on their distinct vertical recovery proveniences for the purpose of measuring time either synchronically or diachronically. The vertical boundaries of the spatial units from which artifacts are collected may be based on geological criteria such as sediment color or texture or on metric (arbitrary) criteria such as elevation. The relative vertical recovery provenience of the artifacts is what is critical, and it stems from the basic notion of superposition. Vertical provenience may be relative to an arbitrarily located horizontal datum plane, and thus the archaeologist knows that one artifact was found at a higher elevation than another or that two artifacts were found at the same elevation. But the archaeologist may not know how those vertical locations relate to geological depositional events; this is the problem with inferring diachronic time typically associated conceptually with excavation using arbitrary levels (Praetzellis 1993). Knowing that vertical recovery proveniences correspond to some "natural" depositional units or strata is preferred. Knowing the correspondence, synchronic and diachronic time can be inferred based on the relative vertical positions of the artifacts. If synchronic time is of interest, artifacts recovered from one (or several contiguous) vertical location(s)—as denoted by arbitrary levels or strata—are inferred to be approximately contemporaneous. If diachronic time is of interest, artifacts recovered from superposed strata or arbitrary levels are inferred to be of different ages. Again, for sake of discussion, we ignore the analytical manipulations that must be accomplished and the interpretive hurdles that must be cleared in order to make sound inferences of either synchronic or diachronic time (e.g., Rowe 1961; Schiffer 1987).

Most discussions of the history of the "stratigraphic revolution" (e.g., Browman and Givens 1996; Willey and Sabloff 1974, 1993; Woodbury 1960a) imply that when American archaeologists became interested in diachronic time, excavation techniques were changed as a result. The beginnings of stratigraphic excavation are thought to mark the "stratigraphic revolution." The distinction between synchronic and diachronic time is, however, critical to disentangling the measurement of time from how sites are excavated, gaining insight to and understanding the history of stratigraphic excavation in American archaeology, and determining if there was a stratigraphic revolution in what seems to be the generally understood sense of the term.

In this chapter we demonstrate that prior to the so-called stratigraphic revolution, synchronic time was of great interest and resulted, on the one hand, in much excavation that, by our definition, was stratigraphic; questions concerning diachronic time were, on the other hand, often not asked prior to about 1910. American archaeologists prior to the second decade of the twentieth century were well aware not only of the principles of superposition and association but also of how to use them to infer time (Rowe 1961). Their awareness stemmed from the fact that, whether they were interested in synchronic or diachronic time (or both), and most often it was the former, they knew that to measure either sort of time artifacts had to be collected from vertically discrete units.

Synchronic and Diachronic Time at the End of the Nineteenth Century

Between about 1875 and 1925 many American archaeologists subscribed to the notion that the prehistoric past of North America had a shallow time depth (Meltzer 1983, 1985). Subscription to this notion typically meant that an archaeologist did not measure diachronic time because there was no such time to measure. But this does not mean that archaeologists failed to excavate stratigraphically, because only by excavating stratigraphically could they answer the questions of synchronic time in which they were interested. To illustrate this, we briefly review the work of two individuals; one was a staunch defender of the view that there was a shallow time depth to the American archaeological record, and the other was a firm believer that there was deep antiquity to human presence in North America.

William Henry Holmes (1890a:3) had worked for the U.S. Geological Survey before coming to the Bureau of (American) Ethnology. He was, not surprisingly, quite familiar with the principles of stratigraphic analysis and used them to strengthen his arguments that there was no evidence for paleolithic, or glacial-age, humans in North America. While better remembered for his interpretations of technologically crude stone artifacts as quarry refuse and representative of early stages of manufacture rather than as necessarily ancient tools made and used by paleolithic peoples, Holmes's discussions of the relevance of geological context are equally important. Holmes's reasoning is readily apparent in a pair of papers he published in 1892 and 1893. The paleolithic was, on the one hand, a technological stage that might occur at different times in different regions; paleolithic tools might have been made, used, and deposited subsequent to the glacial period, or relatively recently. On the other hand, the glacial period was typically thought to be represented by gravel beds, but not all gravel beds had been deposited during the glacial period (Holmes 1893). He warranted this point using the principle of association: Artifacts that were "of a high grade technically and functionally"—"neolithic"—had been found within gravel beds (Holmes 1892:296). To ensure that one had evidence of ancient people, one had therefore to recover artifacts of paleolithic grade that had been deposited simultaneously with sediments that had been laid down during the glacial period (Holmes 1892). Holmes (1892:297) was well aware of the problems involved in inferring time—either of the synchronic or diachronic sort—from what would today be called mixed deposits. He (e.g., Holmes 1890b:222) excavated sites and searched for evidence of stratified deposits because, to him, different strata represented "separate periods of occupation" or diachronic time.

Those who believed that people had been in North America since remote times also were well aware of the principles of stratigraphic analysis. Ernest Volk (1911:ix) explored deposits comprising and overlying those known as the Trenton Gravels of the Delaware River valley for "twenty-two years" around the end of the nineteenth century. He began his major monograph on that research by noting that the "special significance of the geological conditions" in which artifacts were found demanded that he begin with discussion of the deposits (Volk 1911:ix). The first 13 pages outline the general geological history of the area and describe the deposits in general terms. The remaining 114 pages describe the artifacts recovered from each of three major strata. Included are numerous photographs of artifacts "in place" in particular depositional units. The first page of the monograph makes it clear that Volk understood the principles of superposition and association. The Trenton Gravels had been laid down during the glacial age (in Volk's view); the artifacts found within that deposit had been laid down at the same time (in his view) and must therefore be of glacial age (Volk 1911:1, 126). His discussion makes it clear that he well knew the interpretive perils presented by mixed deposits. Volk carried out numerous excavations, noting such things as in which depositional unit artifacts were found and intrusive pits originated. His chronology of human occupation of the Delaware Valley comprised three periods, each denoted by a particular depositional unit: The remains of Glacial Man were found in the Trenton Gravels; the remains of Argillite Man dated to the "Intermediate Period" and were found in the "Yellow Soil" that was superposed over the Trenton Gravels; and remains of modern Indians were found in the "Black Soil" found at the top of the stratified column (Volk 1911:126).

Many individuals—including Holmes and Volk—excavated stratigraphically, by our definition, prior to the turn of the century (see Browman 2002b, 2003 for discussions of others). What, then, is so special about the second decade of the twentieth century that it is sometimes said that a "stratigraphic revolution" took place at that time? The special quality of that event is not found in a change in excavation techniques but rather in a two-part shift. First, archaeologists began to see that questions concerning diachronic time were answerable. Second, the questions were found to be answerable not by stratigraphic excavation but because artifacts were classified and analytically manipulated in new ways. To demonstrate these points, we need to consider techniques of stratigraphic excavation used at the time.

Techniques of Stratigraphic Excavation

Vertically superposed natural units generally are invisible from the modern ground surface. Such units must be visible or made visible by nature or by people to ensure that artifacts can be collected from them and kept separate based on their vertical provenience. Otherwise, one might use arbitrary or metric levels, in which case natural vertical units do not have to be exposed. Excavation strategies are as numerous and varied as the archaeologists who do the digging. Thus one must be cautious in identifying instances of stratigraphic excavation. As Browman and Givens (1996:80) point out, the measurement of time might be attained merely by "post facto stratigraphic observation," defined by them as the identification of "archaeological strata . . . in the walls of trenches excavated as single [vertical] units." This clearly seems to be what Holmes (e.g., 1890a) did in several cases. Our definition of stratigraphic excavation—removing artifacts and sediments from vertically discrete three-dimensional units of deposition and keeping those artifacts in sets based on their distinct vertical recovery proveniences for the purpose of measuring synchronic or diachronic time—allows the separation of such excavation from post facto stratigraphic observation.

Onion Peel or Bread Loaf?

Willey (1936:61–62) distinguishes between two excavation techniques that allow the archaeologist to record the stratum from which an artifact is derived. He describes one as "slicing like a bread loaf" and notes that only under some conditions is this technique "particularly favorable" (Willey 1936:58). It involves a thickness of sediment that "is vertically sliced off" (Willey 1936:58). Elsewhere (Lyman et al. 1997b:25) we refer to this as the Harrington-Peabody technique after two individuals who used it; here we refer to it as the bread loaf technique and note that it is probably best known as the Chicago method popularized by Fay-Cooper Cole and his students at the University of Chicago but introduced to North American archaeologists by Frederic Ward Putnam and his students (Browman 2002b, 2003). The other excavation technique Willey labels "pure 'onion peel,'" stating that it is "in most cases, the best means of excavation" and describing it as "peeling down, layer by layer, from the top of a mound" (Willey 1936:56).

The bread loaf technique appears to have been the preferred method early in the twentieth century. The purpose of the 1932 Conference on Southern Pre-history was to bring southeastern archaeologists up to speed intellectually and methodologically with what was happening in the Southwest and the East (O'Brien and Lyman 1999a, 2001). At the conference, Cole recommended the bread loaf technique:

> If [the site] is a mound it is staked out in squares (five foot squares are usually most convenient). A trench is started at right angles to the axis of the mound and is carried down at least two feet below the base. The face of the trench is now carried forward into the mound itself by cutting thin strips from top to bottom. At the same time the top is cut

back horizontally for the distance of a foot or more. If this procedure is followed it is possible to see successive humus layers as well as to note all evidences of intrusions. . . .

A village site is best uncovered by a series of trenches much like those used in mound work. A cut is made down to undisturbed soil and the earth is thrown backward as the excavation proceeds. Horizontal and vertical cutting should be employed in hopes of revealing successive periods of occupancy. The worker should never come in from the top. He should never be on top of his trench, otherwise lines of stratification will almost certainly be lost [Cole 1932:76, 78].

Cole did not mention the onion peel technique. About 20 years later Griffin (1956:27) indicated that the "ideal [excavation] technique would be to remove the natural and human deposits in the same order in which they were accumulated." This apparently is the ideal because he indicates that "excavation of stratified sites, where one cultural level is found overlying an earlier one, provides one type of relative chronology" (Griffin 1956:38). We say "apparently" because Griffin does not explicitly state that artifacts should be grouped based on their stratigraphic provenience. He mentions the "skinning or peeling" technique and notes that "if natural stratigraphy is present, the excavator should adjust his digging to recognize and take advantage of the resultant cultural groupings" (Griffin 1956:28), implying that the set of artifacts in each stratum comprises a culture. He then notes that if the stratification is complex or displays evidence of disturbance, one should use what he terms the "trench technique," the description of which identifies it as the bread loaf technique: "This proceeds, like the vertical slicing of a cake, by removing successive slices of the mound, usually by starting at the top of the slice and working toward the bottom. In this way a vertical profile is kept, and it is rather easy to see disturbances or special features in the mound earth" (Griffin 1956:28).

Modern discussions favor the onion peel technique (Bower 1986; Deetz 1967; Hole and Heizer 1973; Praetzellis 1993; Rathje and Schiffer 1982), and we doubt anyone would deny that it comprises stratigraphic excavation. But as Willey (1936) and Griffin (1956) note, the bread loaf technique also comprises stratigraphic excavation. That technique is mentioned in a few relatively recent texts (e.g., Hester et al. 1975:79), where it is noted that it "works well if isolating specific strata is your task and space-time systematics is your problem" (Knudson 1978:144). We have distinguished between onion peel and bread loaf techniques because these seem to have been the methods used around the turn of the twentieth century. The latter was more popular than the former until some time after the so-called stratigraphic revolution.

How Were Sites Excavated at the End of the Nineteenth Century?

Willey (1936:56) stated that onion peel excavation was a new technique. Cole (1932) indicates that it had not been universally adopted in the early 1930s, just as Griffin (1956) indicates it had not been universally adopted by the middle of the century. Interestingly, the authors of the classic studies typically heralded as comprising the stratigraphic revolution did not all use the onion peel technique. Nelson (1916) and Gamio (1913) both exposed one vertical face of a column of sediments and collected artifacts from arbitrary levels. It is not clear, however, if they peeled the top layer off completely before proceeding to the next layer. In his 1916 excavations at Zuni Pueblo, Spier (1917a) used arbitrary levels, apparently removing them from the top down. A year earlier he had used two techniques at Abbott Farm in New Jersey: "[T]he bulk of the material was removed in levels four inches in depth and sifted, while sections of particular interest were carefully sliced away with a trowel" (Spier 1916a:182). The former is a version of the onion peel technique, whereas the latter is the bread loaf technique. Kidder (1931:9–10) exposed two or more faces of a sediment column before collecting artifacts from natural depositional units. He peeled each vertically discrete unit completely off the top of the column before excavating lower units. Other individuals also used the onion peel method (e.g., Schmidt 1928), but some appear to have used the bread loaf technique (e.g., Vaillant 1930, 1931). How were people excavating prior to 1910?

Volk's (1911) photographs of in situ artifacts appear to depict the bread loaf technique, but he does not describe how he excavated. There are no published descriptions of how Raymond E. Merwin excavated, but George Vaillant proclaimed that Merwin's work of 1910–1911 comprised "the first stratigraphic excavation of a Maya ruin" (in Merwin and Vaillant 1932); Vaillant was able to propose a five-period sequence based on Merwin's notes. Jeffries Wyman (1868, 1875) knew superposed remains denoted temporal differences, perhaps learning the principle of superposition from Charles Lyell, with whom

Wyman excavated reptilian fossils in Nova Scotia and "explored the geology and various other aspects of the natural history around Richmond [Virginia]" (Murowchick 1990:58). Whatever the case, Wyman constructed a chronology of pottery types for the St. Johns River area of Florida (Wyman 1875), but he was not explicit about his excavation strategy. The fact that he could place many of the artifacts, faunal remains, and human remains he recovered into a temporal sequence leads us to suspect that at least some of his research comprised stratigraphic excavation and not just post facto stratigraphic observation.

The bread loaf technique was used by many individuals prior to early in the second decade of the twentieth century. Charles Peabody (e.g., 1904, 1908, 1910, 1913; Peabody and Moorehead 1904) used it in conjunction with a horizontal grid to guide his excavations and provide horizontal control (Browman 2002b, 2003). He consistently recorded the vertical and horizontal provenience of artifacts, burials, and features. Peabody was well aware that more deeply buried materials were older than materials located near the surface, and, given how he excavated, he generally knew which strata produced which artifacts. Writing about Bushey Cavern in Maryland, which he excavated in 1905, Peabody (1908:12) noted that "from the middle or white stratum of the stalagmite floor no bones or flint were taken and the presence of charcoal is doubtful. Below this the explorations found no traces of human or animal occupation contemporary with or previous to the laying down of the [stalagmite] floor." Peabody (1904) excavated Edwards Mound in Mississippi in 1901–1902 and noted which strata produced how many of each of two kinds of burials and which strata produced the most pottery (Peabody 1904:31, 38, 51). He concluded that "the mound has been built in two periods" (Peabody 1904:52). Peabody was interested in both diachronic and synchronic time.

Working at the turn of the century, Mark Harrington (1909a) sometimes did not make even post facto stratigraphic observations. At other times he used the bread loaf technique. In 1900–1901 Harrington (1909b) excavated several trenches in a New York rockshelter, noting there were three strata, the middle one containing no artifacts. He indicated which artifacts came from which stratum and presented two drawings of "vertical sections" of the stratification (Harrington 1909b:126–129). He reported that

> when the [excavations had] been completed, it was thought that everything of value had been found and removed from the cave; but on

further deliberation, taking into consideration the darkness of the cave and the blackness and stickiness of the cave dirt, it was thought best to sift the entire contents. The results were surprising. The earth had all been carefully troweled over, then thrown with a shovel so that it could be watched—but a great number of things had been overlooked, as the subsequent sifting showed. Of course all data as to depth and position have been lost, yet the specimens are valuable as having come from the cave [Harrington 1909b:128].

Harrington was aware of the significance of superposed strata and how to measure diachronic and synchronic time, and he employed discrete vertical units—in this case, strata—as artifact-collection units. His only comment regarding diachronic time, however, was to note that the uppermost stratum contained pottery but the lowermost did not.

Harrington (1924a:235) also used the bread loaf technique to excavate an open site in New York in 1902. After digging "test holes [to determine] the depth and richness of the deposit [Harrington chose the parts of the site that] warranted more thorough excavation." Then he exposed a vertical face "at the edge of the [site] deposit." This vertical face was extended down through the "village layer," or "the accumulated refuse of the Indian Village," which included various depositional units such as layers of shells, ash, and black sediment. The face extended into the sterile stratum beneath the village layer. "A trench of this kind was carried forward by carefully digging down the front with a trowel, searching the soil for relics, then, with a shovel, throwing the loose earth thus accumulated back out of the way into the part already dug over, so as to expose a new front"; once a trench was completed, "another trench was run parallel and adjacent to the first on its richest side, and so on, until the investigator was satisfied that he had covered the entire deposit, or at least as much as his purpose required" (Harrington 1924a:235). In the deepest stratum, Harrington found "stemmed arrow points and crude crumbling pottery of a somewhat more archaic character than most of the specimens" recovered from higher strata (Harrington 1924a:245). He also noted that the archaic artifacts were stratigraphically "below the village layer" (Harrington 1924a:283).

William H. Dall used the bread loaf technique to excavate Alaskan shell middens late in the nineteenth century. Dall (1877:47) cleared the surface of "vegetable mold" and dug down to obtain "a good 'face' to work on." He would often start excavations

> near the edge of the shell-heap, if possible taking a steep bank bordering the sea or on some adjacent rivulet, and run a ditch [trench] into the deposit, going down until the primeval clay or stony soil was reached, and this was steadily pushed, even when quite barren of results in the shape of implements, until the day's work was done. This latter gave us a clear idea of the formation and constitution of the shell-heaps; enabled me to distinguish between the different strata and their contents; to make the observations repeatedly; to fully confirm them by experience in many localities; and thus to lay the foundation for the generalizations suggested in this paper [Dall 1877:47].

Dall (1877) discussed cultural change—diachronic time—and outlined a sequence of Littoral, Fishing, and Hunting periods, each of which was represented by a particular kind of deposit or stratum and which he documented in consistently superposed positions at various sites. He also was aware of synchronic time; he described the artifacts, faunal remains, and human remains that were found in each of the three superposed depositional units. His artifact-collection strategy was sufficiently refined that he could note differences between the frequencies and kinds of artifacts within individual strata as well as between them.

Willey (1994:122) indicates that Holmes "carried out stratigraphic digging in the Valley of Mexico . . . as early as 1884." Holmes's (1885) report resulting from that work does not, however, indicate that he excavated. Rather, it suggests that he merely inspected several vertical exposures created by various construction-related activities and noted that the exposed deposits comprised "strata." His discussion of what thus seem to be post facto stratigraphic observations nonetheless is extremely important because it underscores the potential ambiguity of such observations for identifying a stratigraphic revolution. Holmes clearly perceived the importance of knowing the stratigraphic provenience of artifacts. The exposures he studied provided

> a most welcome opportunity of beginning the study of the ceramic art of Mexico from the standpoint of actual observation of relics in place. Superb as are the collections within the Mexican Museum, their

study is rendered extremely unsatisfactory by the absence of detailed information in regard to their origin and chronology. Fortunately the section of deposits here presented reads with the readiness of an open book, giving not only the proper sequence to its own treasures, but, I doubt not, making clear the relative position of many other relics that would, otherwise, go unclaimed and unclassified [Holmes 1885:68].

Among the exposures Holmes examined was one "in a continuous vertical wall nearly a hundred feet long and more than eight feet deep" (Holmes 1885:69). Such exposures allowed Holmes (1885:70, 72) to determine that the superposed positions of pottery he observed "accumulated with the soil and are not subsequent intrusions"; to distinguish which depositional units were strictly the result of geological processes and which were the result of human behavior; and to note that the pottery was often "distributed in horizontal layers throughout a vertical series more than six feet in thickness." Holmes described the pottery as consisting largely of "three varieties of ware" and noted not only the relative vertical positions of each but suggested as well that the frequencies of each varied through the vertical sequence, though he did not mention what the precise frequencies were. He assigned each of the three wares variously to a particular period, people, or tribe.

Holmes apparently did not excavate at all, let alone stratigraphically, as he made no mention of digging. Nonetheless, he documented culture change using shifts in the kind and frequencies of pottery across a vertical section of deposits, which he inferred denoted the passage of time. Willey (1994:122) notes that Gamio (1913) and Boas (1913) fail to mention Holmes's work and suggests their oversight was intentional—a result of the animosity between Holmes and Boas. Whatever the case, the fact remains that Holmes did not excavate—it seems he merely pulled sherds from the vertical exposures at his disposal—though his work certainly resulted in the documentation of culture change and the measurement of both synchronic and diachronic time. One might argue that Holmes's efforts of 1884 fail to qualify as stratigraphic excavation because he did not excavate. Such an argument would, however, imply that the difference between using vertically discrete units as artifact-recovery units and as excavation units is the most significant aspect of a definition of stratigraphic excavation (e.g., Browman and Givens 1996:80). Focusing on this aspect forces one to accept as stratigraphic excavation only those cases in which dirt was moved (and meet all other criteria of the definition) and precludes acceptance of efforts such as Holmes's that used discrete vertical units only as artifact-recovery units and resulted in the measurement of synchronic and diachronic time.

Of course, we also have defined stratigraphic excavation as entailing the removal of sediment, but we emphasize that we do not find that criterion to be the most important one comprising the definition. The utility of the definitive criterion of sediment removal seems to reside only in aiding the recognition of Browman and Givens's post facto stratigraphic observation and in the distinction of such observation from stratigraphic excavation. Givens (1996:295) implies that Max Uhle's 1902 excavation of the Emeryville Shellmound in California was stratigraphic because it was "stratum by stratum" (Uhle 1907:8), or onion peel; Browman and Givens (1996:82) state that "there is no evidence that Holmes [1885] employed stratigraphic excavation," though his interpretation was "informed by the strati[fication] that he observed." The method of artifact collection thus seems to be the most important definitive criterion of stratigraphic excavation to historians concerned with what happened in American archaeology during the second decade of the twentieth century. Given Taylor's (1948, 1954) characterization of that period as involving a time-space revolution and the remarks of others who have not used the term "stratigraphic revolution," we believe a focus on the method of artifact collection—particularly the excavation strategy—is misplaced. Rather than asking if there was a "stratigraphic revolution," historians should ask, When did Americanists excavate stratigraphically—remove sediments in discrete vertical units—for the purpose of measuring the passage of time? The measurement of time comprises the significant change in archaeological epistemology.

Many archaeologists employed discrete vertical units as artifact-collection units during the pre-1912 period, and many noted that superposed artifacts and/or deposits could be inferred to measure diachronic time. Almost everyone made the latter assumption, though, as we will see, it was not until after 1915 that methods of measurement were devised. Skinner (1917) mentioned individuals who had worked in the Northeast and made post facto stratigraphic observations and inferred chronology in 1893 and 1900. Will and Spinden (1906) used the bread loaf technique in 1905 and also made post facto chronological observations on the basis of superposition; Pepper (1916), working in

1904, made post facto chronological observations on the basis of superposition, as did Schrabisch (1909); and Pepper (1920) excavated stratigraphically at Pueblo Bonito in 1896–1899 (Reyman 1989). Many individuals were making chronological inferences on the basis of stratigraphic observations between 1910 and 1915 (e.g., Aitken 1917, 1918; De Booy 1913; Fewkes 1914; Haeberlin 1917, 1919; Hawkes and Linton 1916, 1917; Hewett 1916; Heye 1916; Mills 1916). But few of these archaeologists were concerned with measuring the passage of time, even though the artifacts they collected, given their proveniences in different strata, were known to fall into different time periods. Why were they not concerned?

Why Not Diachronic Time?

Working in 1914, Fred Sterns (1915:121) observed that "the proof of [cultural] sequences must be grounded on stratigraphic evidence, and stratified sites have been very rare [in North America]. Hence such a site has a high scarcity value and warrants special study even though it be otherwise of minor importance." Observations that stratified sites were rare were frequent in the middle of the second decade of the twentieth century, when the results of Nelson's, Kidder's, and Gamio's work were just becoming known (e.g., Sapir 1916; Spinden 1915). Sterns and most of his contemporaries did not devote much effort to studying diachronic time because many of them, like Sterns (1915:125), observed that "an important fact arguing against any great difference in time between the upper and lower ash-beds is that the pottery and the flint and bone implements found in these two sets of fireplaces show absolutely no difference in type."

That most everyone knew superposed artifacts marked the passage of time, yet few asked questions involving diachronic time, is exemplified by the seldom-mentioned work of Frederic Loomis and D. B. Young (1912), who excavated a shell mound in Maine in 1909. They chose that particular mound because it "has never been disturbed by previous excavation" (Loomis and Young 1912:18)—a statement that leads us to suspect they were well aware of the importance of vertical provenience. They used the bread loaf excavation technique: "[T]he heap was [plotted] in sections five feet wide, and as each section was worked, every find (of a tooth, tool, bit of pottery, etc.) was recorded, both as to its horizontal position and vertical depth. . . . [Vertical s]ections of the heap were plotted from time to time" (Loomis and Young

1912:19). They noted that in some strata, "the shells were very much broken up, apparently due to tramping and building fires on them. Where the shells were but little broken, and free from ashes, they would seem to indicate rapid accumulation, and offered but little in the line of finds. . . . Where the layers were made of ashes and finely broken shells, the period of accumulation was longer and agreeing with that, the numbers of articles found in these layers was also greater" (Loomis and Young 1912:19–20).

Loomis and Young (1912:20–21) illustrated the general stratigraphy of the mound in one figure, and in another they presented a diagram of a vertical section that showed "the depth at which each find was made in [two five-foot-wide trenches] and the relative abundance and relationship of the different articles." As Spier (1915:346) later observed, the second figure "would be improved by the addition of lines indicating the position of the several [stratigraphic] layers, that [the artifacts'] relation to the strata . . . might be made clear." This is a predictable comment from someone interested in diachronic time and site-formation processes (see below), but Loomis and Young had no such interests. Rather, they compared the total of all materials recovered from the stratigraphically excavated site with all materials from other sites in other loci. They knew time was measured by superposition, but they were not asking questions about diachronic time and thus did not use the data produced by their stratigraphic excavation to address such questions.

Between 1900 and 1915 virtually everyone agreed that superposition of strata had chronological significance. Even Wissler (1909:xiii), referring to Harrington's (1909b) excavations that showed pottery was present in shallow strata but absent from deep strata, indicated that interest in rockshelters in the northeastern United States was "partly due to the obvious analogies to European caves, but chiefly to their apparent presentation of chronological cultural differences respecting the use of pottery." Such "chronological cultural differences" were founded on superposed artifacts. But the work of Holmes, Dall, Wyman, and others who inferred diachronic time was not frequently emulated for three reasons. First, as we noted earlier, the prehistoric past of the Americas was conceived to be shallow by many (Meltzer 1983, 1985); there was minimal time for culture change to have taken place, so it was thought that it had not taken place. Second, when stratified deposits contained artifacts, those in the deeper layers were perceived to be no different or at most insignificantly different than those in the shallow layers because they were categorized in ways that were not conducive to detecting temporal differences. And third, the conception of culture change held by many archaeologists around the end of the nineteenth century granted that only major events of change were significant and worthy of study.

Regarding the first point, at precisely the time the so-called stratigraphic revolution took place, Sapir (1916:9) suggested that "America is so vast a stretch of land in proportion to the relatively meagre aboriginal population and, as compared with the old world, of such recent occupancy that the chances of superimposition of cultures and races at a single spot are fairly slim." The third point—conceptions of culture change—is documented by Rowe (1975), but the second—artifact categorization—has not been discussed. These last two points are intimately interrelated, and we discuss them below.

Notions of Culture Change

American archaeologists working between 1900 and 1915 "generally defined the culture and archaeological areas in ways that would typify the savagery-barbarism-civilization social evolution model" of Morgan (Browman and Givens 1996:83). The discovery of pottery in relatively recently deposited strata, such as had been reported by Harrington (1909b), signified a cultural change of the epochal, or qualitative, sort that not only mimicked the cultural changes then perceived in Europe but that could also be subsumed within Morgan's model of cultural change. Minor temporal changes in culture—such as shifts in the kind of pottery—were perceived to be unimportant. Willey and Sabloff (1974:87, 1993:91), on the one hand, suggest that prior to 1900, the lack of evidence of major change and the lack of a concept of microchange contributed to the failure in the Americas to measure diachronic time via stratigraphic excavation. Archaeologists lacked evidence of time depth and so could not counter the early twentieth-century antievolutionism mentality of anthropology in general (Willey and Sabloff 1993:94).

We disagree with the last point. Rowe (1975:158) notes that Kroeber (1909), who accepted stratified deposits as valid chronometric tools, rejected Uhle's (1907) cultural sequence because it "did not conform to a European model of change by evolutionary stages." Morgan's model prompted Kroeber to reject Uhle's stratigraphic findings. After the so-called stratigraphic revolution, individuals who had been trained by Boasians explained the record in terms reminiscent of the European model. Nelson, who was trained by Kroeber, used "ethnographic terminology" to characterize American cultural development as comprising "lower hunters, higher hunters, pastoral nomads, sedentary agriculturists, and industrialists" (Nelson 1919b:137) and wrote about "the technological evolution of the industrial stages within given culture areas" (Nelson 1937:85). That Kroeber (1909) rejected Uhle's sequence within the context of an evolutionary model and without evidence of a temporally deep archaeological record suggests Willey and Sabloff's perspective is misguided. We prefer their suggestion that what so affected archaeology's failure to pursue inferences of diachronic time as evidenced by stratified deposits was the coarse scale of measuring cultural change; the measurement units were very general technological or economic stages evidenced by very general categories of artifacts. Fine-scale temporal resolution demanded fine-scale variation in artifacts to be measured.

Peabody (1904:38), like many of his contemporaries, categorized all "articles of clay" as "vases" and recognized only "bowls," "pot-shaped vessels," and "bottles." There is no trace in his writings of an attempt to denote "styles" of ceramic vessels that would shortly be found to measure the passage of time. The "Report of the Committee on Archeological Nomenclature" prepared for the American Anthropological Association stated that there was no assumed "theory of development, interrelation, or conventionalization of forms or types in any manner whatsoever" included in the set of terms (Wright et al. 1909:114). The authors wanted to standardize classification terminology simply to enhance communication among investigators. While they shifted scales from Peabody's "vases" to attributes of pottery, there was no chronological purpose behind that shift. Not everyone was so shortsighted.

In his introduction to the volume containing papers by Harrington (1909a, 1909b) and others, Wissler made three important observations. First, he noted that all of the contributing researchers had "followed the same general method of reconstructing the prehistoric culture by welding together the available ethno-historical and archaeological data, a method justified by the failure to find neither local evidences of great antiquity nor indications of successive or contemporaneous culture types" (Wissler 1909:xiii). The direct historical approach was in use, and there was, as yet, no clear evidence of epochal change in cultures similar to that evident in Europe; both imply a more Darwinian, less stagelike history of change in North America (Chapters 2 and

7). However, the second thing Wissler noted was that the absence of pottery from deep strata in some caves did not indicate "its contemporaneous absence throughout the whole area, [but] no adequate explanation for these differences presents itself, a condition raising a problem of something more than local significance" (Wissler 1909:xiii–xiv). Some, but certainly not all, deep strata contained pottery; perhaps the difference was chronological and comprised a change in cultural epoch. Finally, Wissler (1909:xiv) indicated that in putting the volume together, his plan was to "omit the long detailed descriptions of the minute individualities of specimens so often encountered in our literature on the ground that such microscopic work reveals, in the main, what are relatively unimportant variations, rarely of value in the solution of cultural problems." The volume focused on cultural traits (Chapter 3). Wissler wanted to use such phenomena to map the geographic distribution of cultures. Thus, when commenting on Holmes's (1914) prehistoric culture areas, Wissler (1916b:486) remarked that "if we had the data, centers of archeological distribution could be located analogous to the trait centers noted in the historic period. . . . [T]he culture area map is a classification of traits found among the living tribes and belongs therefore to one definite chronological period."

But documenting spatial variation in cultural distributions was not all that Wissler and others were after. Holmes's (1914) areas represented a "cultural stratum" chronologically earlier than those of the historic period that Wissler (1916b:487) had mapped. Wissler was focusing on geographic space and diachronic time simultaneously from the perspective of the age-area concept (Kroeber 1931a; Lyman et al. 1997b:63–65). He acknowledged that "the determination of chronology by stratigraphic strategy" was the appropriate method in archaeology (Wissler 1916b:487), but the important point is that he was focusing on cultural traits. "We must discover the nature and characteristics of this unit," stated Wissler (1923:51). He recognized that the analytical problem of sorting out temporal and spatial variation in artifact form reduced to "understanding the principles of classification" (Wissler 1916b:486). One needed to discover "new types of artifacts" (Wissler 1916b:487)—new ways to classify cultural traits such as pottery—to help measure diachronic time and write culture history. By 1915 or 1916 Wissler knew exactly what those types should consist of; we discuss how he came to know this below.

Uhle (1907), Dall (1877), and others had perceived what they believed to be cultural change in superposed aggregates of artifacts. Given the then generally perceived shallow time depth of human occupation in the Americas, these and other instances of stratigraphic excavation seem to have been merely applications of good archaeological technique. Harrington (1909b), for example, recognized that good technique allowed determination of what was temporally associated with what in our sense of synchronic time. What happened that is of utmost importance is that superposed evidence of cultural change of a different sort swung the tide from viewing stratigraphic excavation merely as sound technique to viewing it as requisite to archaeology as a science. It was not some sudden insight that superposition measured time that resulted in the adoption of a new excavation method. Rather, once culture change of a different kind than, say, a Paleolithic to Mesolithic to Neolithic transition was shown to be analytically visible, superposition became the initial means to test conclusions regarding that new kind of change.

Detecting and Measuring Nonepochal Culture Change

Kroeber (e.g., 1909), like his contemporaries after the turn of the century, subscribed to the notion that superposed artifacts were of different ages. He rejected, however, again like his contemporaries, the significance of the kind of change represented by artifacts in a vertical column of sediments:

> The civilization revealed by [archaeology] is in its essentials the same as that found in the same region by the more recent explorer and settler. . . . [N]either archaeology nor ethnology has yet been able to discover either the presence or absence of any important cultural features in one period that are not respectively present or absent in the other.
>
> . . . [A]rchaeology at no point gives any evidence of significant changes in culture. . . . [D]ifferences between the past and present are only differences in detail, involving nothing more than a *passing change of fashion* in manufacture or in manipulation of the same process [Kroeber 1909:3–5, emphasis added].

Thus, relative to Uhle's (1907) work in California, Kroeber (1909:15–16) spoke of the "upper and more recent strata of the Emeryville mound," but he also argued that the "distinct progression and development of civilization having taken place during the growth of the deposit" represented "a change of degree only, and one in no way to be compared even for a moment with a transition as fundamental as that from palaeolithic to neolithic." Hence the archaeological record of California contained evidence of culture change but not on the order of the European record. This is not a rejection of Morgan's European model but only a rejection of its applicability to the American archaeological record. As Rowe (1962a:399–400) put it, "Kroeber at this time visualized cultural change in terms of major shifts in technology and subsistence; any changes of less moment were insignificant." Kroeber (1920:187) once remarked that "nowhere in southern California have [sic] there been any accredited reports of potsherds being found at deep levels. This is one of the few matters in which close observation of stratification promises to be a fruitful method of attack in California archaeology." As in the Northeast, the early absence and later presence of pottery would be a cultural change of some moment.

A decade after the so-called stratigraphic revolution, Kroeber had not changed his mind regarding the culture history of California. In his *Handbook of the Indians of California*, he wrote that "the upshot of the correlation of findings of archaeology and ethnology is that not only the general Californian culture area, but even its subdivisions or provinces, were determined a long time ago and have ever since maintained themselves with relatively little change" (Kroeber 1925b:926). After acknowledging that superposed artifacts denoted the passage of time and seriating various collections, Kroeber (1925b:930) noted that "the basis of culture remained identical during the whole of the shell-mound period" and that throughout the period of human occupancy of California, "civilization, such as it was, remained immutable in all fundamentals." Elsewhere he remarked that in California, there was "little evidence of stratification"; there was "practically no indication of different cultural types being represented within the same area"; and when stratified sequences of artifacts were available, there was "no question that the finer and better made pieces came from the later strata. But it is the quality and finish that are involved, rather than new types," and "the principal types . . . occur in all strata" (Kroeber 1923b:140–141). In these cases Kroeber was examining the functional composition of superposed assemblages rather than their stylistic composition. When Kroeber was able to detect and thus to measure culture change, it was not by using functional types nor was it by noting the early absence of pottery and the latter presence of it in a stratified column of sediment. Rather, Kroeber did something else.

Fluctuating Frequencies of Styles

In 1915 Kroeber (1916a, 1916b) made surface collections of sherds from more than a dozen sites near Zuni, New Mexico. He then seriated those collections based on the relative frequencies of one pottery type and suggested that the resulting arrangement measured the passage of time (Chapter 5). He also made two statements regarding the seriated collections. First, the assemblages represented "sub-periods," or "short epochs" (Kroeber 1916a:44); the changes were not of the magnitude of those evident in the European prehistoric record, but they were epochal nonetheless. Second, the cultural "subdivisions [denoted by the assemblages] shade into one another . . . [and] there is no gap or marked break between periods" (Kroeber 1916a:44); the cultural change he had documented represented a continuum precisely because of the overlap of types across multiple assemblages. That these two statements were ontologically contradictory—essentialist epochs are not continuous with one another—escaped notice for decades. The important point here is that Kroeber measured cultural change not by studying the qualitative characters of cultures such as was thought to be manifest in trait lists (Chapter 3) but rather by studying the fluctuations of frequencies of types, or what were even then becoming known as "styles."

Kroeber (1916b:14) was clear about the archaeological significance of what he was proposing: "[T]he outlines of a thousand years' civilizational changes which the surface reveals are so clear, that there is no question of the wealth of knowledge that the ground holds for the critical but not over timid excavator." However, he also was cautious, noting that for chronological inference, the "final proof is in the spade" (Kroeber 1916b:20). This is a clear endorsement of stratigraphic excavation for purposes of measuring diachronic time; in fact, it recommends that inferences of diachronic time based on other lines of evidence be tested with collections from stratigraphic excavations.

Kroeber's (1916a, 1916b) innovative work at Zuni Pueblo demonstrated that change in cultures through time could be detected as changes in the frequencies of artifact types (his 1909 "passing change in fashion") rather than as the wholesale replacement of one type or cultural trait by another. This raises the question of why a few short years earlier Kroeber (1909) had viewed Uhle's (1907) conclusions about culture change as insignificant but at Zuni the evidence of culture change was somehow significant. It is not a question of the significance of the cultural change, though this has been suggested as playing a role in Kroeber's invention of frequency seriation (Rowe 1962a). It was the accidental discovery that temporal difference was analytically visible that drove Kroeber, who later remarked that it was his work with the Zuni potsherds that gave the "first stirrings [of his] confidence that time differences could be ascertained" (Kroeber 1952:230). Kroeber "volunteered to spend the summer [of 1915] at Zuni Pueblo" and study local social organization (Wissler 1915:397). In the evenings he wandered across the surrounding country collecting sherds. As we noted in Chapter 5, Kroeber (1916b) reasoned that one particular type of pottery was oldest based on its association with and relatively high frequency around deteriorated ruins, which were thought to represent ancient sites, and its absence from or low frequency on sites known to have been occupied during the historic period: "It therefore seemed as if a progressive decrease of the proportion of [the apparently old type] were a characteristic of the lapse of time in the Zuni Valley irrespective of 'period' " (Kroeber 1916b:15). Fortuitous and accidental, pure and simple.

In 1916 Spier (1917a, 1917b) sought to test Kroeber's conclusions. He made further surface collections at Zuni and seriated the assemblages based on the relative frequencies of pottery types. Spier also excavated in arbitrary levels to test the chronology suggested by his and Kroeber's seriations. In so doing, he, too, demonstrated that relative frequencies of pottery types could be used to monitor change in cultures—the unimodal frequency distributions of types indicated by frequency seriation were mimicked by frequencies of pottery types within superposed assemblages. The diachronic temporal implications of Spier's and Kroeber's frequency seriations could be tested and vindicated empirically via stratigraphic excavation, in particular by what later became known as "percentage stratigraphy" (Willey 1939:142; see Chapter 9).

Nelson, working in the Galisteo Basin of New Mexico in 1912–1915, had his own suspicions regarding matters of chronology. His contributions reside in several areas. First, he demonstrated that pottery types altered in absolute frequency through time, just as Kroeber and Spier did; second, he characterized the pattern of fluctuating frequencies as "very nearly normal frequency curves" (what he in fact meant was a unimodal curve); third, he reasoned that such a frequency distribution over time reflected the fact that "a style of pottery . . . came slowly into vogue, attained a maximum and began a gradual decline" (Nelson 1916:167). He, like Kroeber and Spier, was able to measure culture change using not the then-typical qualitative differences in artifact assemblages, such as the presence or absence of pottery, but rather by documenting—in revolutionary fashion—the changing frequencies of types of pottery within a vertical column of sediment.

Nelson had found a couple of types of pottery in superposed positions by the end of the first field season. That was why he was there; he and Wissler (who sent Nelson to the Southwest) hoped "in time to gain not only an idea of prehistoric conditions but perhaps also an adequate explanation of the origin, the antiquity and the course of development leading up to a better understanding of the present status of aboriginal life in the region" (Nelson 1913:63). Why would Wissler send him off on such a wild goose chase given the general consensus within the discipline that humankind's tenure in the Americas had minimal time depth? In a critical passage, Nelson indicates it was not a wild goose chase.

> The greater portion of the country in question seems unfit for almost any sort of aboriginal existence, being either mountainous or desert-like plateau, lacking water. . . . [Yet] there are on record for the region about three hundred [prehistoric] ruins, some of them very large. [A complete survey would probably] reveal twice the listed number of abandoned pueblos. . . . [Thus] the implied population mounts to figures out of proportion on the one hand, to the productivity of the country and on the other, to the historically known facts. We may, therefore, reasonably suspect a lengthy occupation by either a shifting or a changing population; in other words, that the ruins in question are not of the same age [Nelson 1916:161].

Nelson figured there had to be some temporal difference in order to account for all those people who had occupied all those sites. All he had to do was demonstrate that such a difference was present. He did so in revolutionary fashion by arranging the frequencies of pottery types, or styles, against their vertical provenience and inferring that the shifting frequencies marked the passage of time. Nelson's (1916) work was less accidental than Kroeber's, but the results of both were the same—diachronic time could be made analytically visible if one classified artifacts in particular ways rather than sorting them as cultural traits and if their frequencies were noted rather than merely their presence or absence.

Kidder and Kidder (1917), using stratigraphic columns that were undisturbed by intrusive burials (Kidder 1924, 1931, 1932; Kidder and Shepard 1936), mimicked Nelson's technique of arranging frequencies of pottery types against their vertical proveniences. Kidder (1919:301) stated that he found Spier's (1917b) technique to be "fundamental" to archaeology. Unlike Nelson and Spier, however, Kidder and Kidder used stratigraphic (depositional) units rather than arbitrary ones. Whereas Nelson had listed the absolute frequencies of types per arbitrary level, Kidder and Kidder (1917:340)—like Spier (1917a, 1917b)—plotted the relative frequencies of pottery types per stratum, thereby circumventing the effects of different excavation volumes. The graphs Kidder and Kidder produced comprised percentage stratigraphy and again showed that diachronic time and thus culture change could be measured analytically (see Chapter 9 for an example). That the ordering of pottery-type frequencies was chronological was thought to be indisputable—undisturbed strata provided the chronologically superposed series of frequencies of pottery styles.

This means of assessing pottery chronology based on type frequencies was not replicated by Kidder (1924, 1931, 1932; Kidder and Shepard 1936) in his later reports on the Pecos excavations, despite his clear recognition of the importance of frequency data (e.g., Kidder 1921). Willey and Sabloff (1974:95) and Givens (1992:67–68) imply that Kidder (1931) used percentage stratigraphy in later work, but in fact the application they refer to was done by Charles Amsden (1931). In most of his later work, Kidder used particular pottery types as index fossils much like James Ford did some years later (Chapter 6), thus abandoning percentage stratigraphy and following a precedent he had set initially (e.g., Kidder 1915, 1917). What was that precedent?

Kinds of Seriation

Kidder (1931:7) said he had "attempted a seriation, on comparative grounds, of the material available" in 1914–1915, and he cited his own work (Kidder 1915) as demonstration. Givens (1992:44) and Browman and Givens (1996:86) state that Kidder seriated pottery. There is no evidence in Kidder (1915) that he seriated sherds in the same manner that Kroeber (1916a, 1916b) and Spier (1917a, 1917b) had. Kidder (1915) performed what Rowe (1961:327) later characterized as "ordering by continuity of features and variation in themes." This is precisely what Evans (1850, 1875) had done 65 years earlier with British gold coins, and it differed markedly from Kroeber's and Spier's technique of frequency seriation (Lyman et al. 1997b; O'Brien and Lyman 1999c)—a patently American invention. Kidder probably learned the technique from George A. Reisner, who had worked in Egypt (Browman and Givens 1996:86), where Rowe's "ordering by continuity of features and variation in themes" was used by Petrie (e.g., 1899). We term this particular technique "phyletic seriation" (Lyman et al. 1997b:54).

The misconception that "seriation" was introduced to Americans by European-trained archaeologists resides in the failure to distinguish among different seriation techniques. Browman and Givens (1996:83), for example, attribute the "statistical method" of examining the fluctuations of type frequencies—Kroeber's frequency seriations and Nelson's, Spier's, and Kidder's percentage stratigraphy—to the influence of Petrie. However, Petrie (1899) first performed a phyletic seriation of his pottery, and only after establishing an order on this basis did he examine the frequencies of pottery types. Petrie (1899:297) listed five "methods" for ordering sets of grave goods: (1) superposition, but this was rarely possible; (2) "series of development or degradation of form; very valuable if unimpeachable"; (3) "statistical grouping by proportionate resemblance"; (4) "grouping of similar types, and judgement by style; giving a more detailed arrangement of the result of the 3rd method"; and (5) temporal dispersion of each type. Petrie (1899:297) remarked that the second method—phyletic seriation—was "of the highest value. It enables a long period to be ranged in approximate order, and serves as a scale for noting the rise or disappearance of other types." Phyletic seriation is the basis for ordering and precedes the examination of type frequencies, which are merely added on to the arrangement. Step four of Petrie's procedure implies that he placed little if any faith in frequency seriation.

Among American archaeologists, Uhle (1902, 1903) and Kidder (1915, 1917) mimicked Petrie's phyletic-seriation technique, but only Uhle (1902) referenced Petrie's work. Uhle (1902), like Petrie, used phyletic seriation but trusted the chronological results of superposed artifacts more than the results of such a seriation. So far as we have been able to determine, Uhle did not use percentage stratigraphy, but Kroeber did in conjunction with phyletic seriation (e.g., Kroeber and Strong 1924).

In a lecture delivered on May 9, 1923, Uhle remarked that "all forms of life, and inorganic substances as well, are subject to the laws of evolution. . . . According to these laws, all forms are derived from one another in a regular evolutionary order, appearing successively in time and spreading out in space, changing and perfecting themselves continually to adapt themselves better and better to their environments" (Uhle, in Rowe 1954:63). Uhle argued that change manifest as organic and cultural evolution is continuous yet gradual. "We can thus speak of types [species], but the types are not lasting" (Uhle, in Rowe 1954:63). Things, including artifacts, are always in the process of becoming something else, and this is a "fundamental law of change in ethnological and archaeological types" (Uhle, in Rowe 1954:64). For Petrie, Kidder, Uhle, and even Wissler (1916c), typological similarity denoted a similar position in a developmental lineage. This is phyletic seriation. Kroeber (e.g., Kroeber and Strong 1924) did use this particular seriation technique, but when he seriated the potsherds from Zuni in the second decade of the twentieth century, it was on the basis of the frequencies of types. What he did in 1916 was revolutionary.

Something quite new and innovative was afoot in American archaeology during the second decade of the twentieth century, but it was not stratigraphic excavation in the sense that most historians use the term, nor was it Petrie's technique of phyletic seriation for sorting artifacts into a chronological series. Rather, it was a shift in focus from cultural traits to types or styles of individual traits and from arranging artifacts on the basis of phyletic seriation to arranging them on the basis of type frequencies. The analytical procedure was to determine the frequencies of styles in each of several collections and then to seriate those frequencies and/or plot them in the order indicated by their superposed positions. Archaeologists could do a frequency seriation and then test the diachronic temporal significance of that arrangement using percentage stratigraphy, or they could omit the first step and simply excavate stratigraphically and use the data to perform a percentage-stratigraphy analysis. This innovative analytical method of studying frequencies of artifact styles swept through the discipline in part because, as Dunnell (1986a:29) put it, "for the first time it was possible to do archaeology and be wrong! This jerked archaeology out of the business of speculative natural history and placed it firmly in the realm of science." The revolution occurred because, for the first time, diachronic time was indisputably (it was thought) rendered visible analytically; it was demonstrable that past cultures were to some degree different from those documented by ethnographers. Archaeology could now claim to provide information on humankind's tenure in the Americas obtainable in no other way. Prior to that, archaeology "enjoyed little esteem and [was] the intellectual 'poor boy' in the field of anthropology" (Willey and Sabloff 1974:86).

The Real Revolution

Nelson and Kroeber in 1916, followed quickly by Spier and Kidder in 1917, demonstrated that diachronic time in the form of culture change could be monitored as a gradual continuum of shifting frequencies of artifact types. Fluctuating frequencies of types provided a new and different way to measure diachronic time and culture change than that implied by Morgan's model of progressive evolution from one cultural stage to the next. This chronometer also differed from Gamio's (1913) demonstration that distinct pottery types occupied more or less distinct vertical positions with minimal overlap. What Gamio did analytically seems to have differed little from what Holmes (1885) had done 28 years earlier, except that Gamio excavated whereas Holmes apparently did not. Adams (1960:99) indicates that Gamio drew "percentage charts and graphs," but these were not published and thus did not have any impact on methods.

Browman and Givens (1996:85) suggest that Wissler (1916a) initially was unimpressed with Nelson's work because Wissler viewed the waxing and waning of a cultural trait's popularity merely as "noise in the system." Wissler (1916a:194–195), however, was specifically comparing the frequency distributions of specimens—regardless of type or style—over vertical space between two horizontal loci in order to argue that one of those loci consisted of a natural deposit of artifacts. He never said or implied that frequency distributions of types were unimportant for measuring diachronic time. In fact, he noted that the unimodal frequency distributions documented by Nelson were displayed by "specific styles in ceramic art" and represented "stylistic pulsations" (Wissler 1916a:195–196). These were not noise; they comprised the signature of diachronic time.

Wissler (1916a:190) stated that "Mr. Nelson's [1916] decisive chronological determinations in the Galisteo Pueblo group" was an excellent example of how a scientific result "depends upon the method of handling data." The next year Wissler (1917a:275) remarked that the "uninterrupted occupation of an area would not result in good examples of stratification [of cultures], but would give us deposits in which culture changes could be detected only in the qualities and frequencies of the most typical artifacts; for example, Nelson's pottery series from New Mexico." That sentence, along with his comments published in 1916 (Wissler 1916a), indicates that Wissler immediately recognized the significance of what Nelson had done rather than coming to this conclusion later. Nelson, of course, was doing the work at Wissler's direction (Nelson 1948; Wissler 1915).

What was the catalyst for what came to be mislabeled the stratigraphic revolution? Where is the source of the revolution found? Everyone working prior to 1900 knew that the artifacts recovered from superposed vertically discrete depositional units could be inferred to represent diachronic time and culture change, so the source of the revolution did not reside in a new awareness of the principle of superposition. For Kroeber, the source resided in purely fortuitous events, but we suspect the revolution would have happened even without those events. Spier mimicked Kroeber's work, and the literature of the second decade of the twentieth century indicates that Kroeber was the source of the revolution for Spier. Where did the source reside for Kidder? Apparently it resided with Nelson; as we noted earlier, Kidder (1917) initially seriated artifacts phyletically, then acknowledged and mimicked Nelson's percentage-stratigraphy analysis at Pecos (Kidder and Kidder 1917), and finally used marker or index types (Kidder 1924). The source for Nelson, apparently, was Max Uhle (Woodbury 1960a, 1960b). To understand these observations, we turn next to a consideration of Spier's and Nelson's work prior to the middle of the second decade of the twentieth century.

Leslie Spier

In April 1912 the state legislature of New Jersey "authorized the commencement of archeological investigations under the direction of the Geological Survey of New Jersey. The Department of Anthropology of the American Museum of Natural History inaugurated systematic archeological research in the summer of 1912" (Spier 1913:676). The personnel involved were Leslie Spier, Alanason Skinner, and Max Schrabisch. Spier (1913:677) reported that by the end of the 1912 field season, numerous prehistoric sites had been found; those sites displayed a lack of "homogeneity" in their surface manifestations. By the end of the 1913 field season, Spier (1913:679) observed that "the number of sites within [the] limited area [examined] is too large for all to have belonged to [the historic or colonial] period." Evidence elsewhere (e.g., Harrington 1909b) suggested time differences in archaeological remains to "independent observers" and constituted "proof that this [heterogeneity of cultural remains] is indeed a problem for serious study" (Spier 1913:679).

As Spier later noted, his efforts those first couple of years had "succeeded in bringing to light several stratified sites" (Spier 1918b:221). With such sites he could address the problem of heterogeneous archaeological sites. Spier began to examine the problem in 1913 when he excavated several sites in such a manner as to be able to note not only which stratum an artifact came from but also the vertical provenience—to the nearest inch—of each artifact (e.g., Spier 1918b:218–219). We suspect that he did so for several reasons. He was well aware of Mercer's (1897) earlier work in the area (see Browman 2002a for extended discussion of Mercer's contributions to American archaeology). Mercer (1897:72) had dug a trench through a mound adjacent to the Delaware River and concluded that the mound was stratified and contained the remains of "two village sites, set one upon the other,—an upper and a lower." Mercer knew the superposed "village sites" were different in age, but he lamented that

> the upper site might have been inhabited one or five hundred years after the lower was overwhelmed. If, therefore, we sought for inference as to the relative age of the two sites, we could only hope to find it in a comparison of the relics discovered. Realizing this, the depth, position, and association of all the specimens found, and particularly their occurrence above or below the lines of stratification, was carefully noted [Mercer 1897:74]

Although Mercer recognized the temporal significance of superposition, he was not alone in conflating relative and absolute time scales (O'Brien and Lyman 1998). While Mercer (1897:82) did not provide details about how he excavated this particular mound (he excavated other sites stratigraphically), he did provide details regarding the different kinds of artifacts he found in the "two stages of occupancy. The layers prove a difference in time, short or long."

Mercer (1897) used superposition to argue that temporal differences accounted for the variation in artifact kinds comprising the stratum-specific assemblages. Spier (1913) picked up on that observation, but he was working near the famous deposits around Trenton, New Jersey, that had played a role in the debate over the possible presence of glacial-age humans in North America (e.g., Volk 1911). No doubt because of where he was working, Spier (1916b) was asked to review some of the literature that suggested there was evidence for a distinctive ancient culture in the general area. In his review, Spier (1916b) argued that Hawkes and Linton (1916) had equated two "dissimilar" cultures (see also Linton 1917). Spier was thinking about how to identify and explain distinct cultures in the archaeological record; in his view, similar stratigraphic position might not be a valid indicator for "the identification of cultures" (Spier 1916b:566). Did the artifacts from the middle, yellow-sand layer found in the Trenton area represent a culture distinct from that of the historic peoples who had occupied the lower Delaware River and whose artifacts were said to be found in the black soil overlying the yellow sand? Had perhaps the artifacts in the yellow sand originally been deposited in the black soil and, as a result of some turbation process, ended up in the yellow sand?

Continuing the American Museum's work in New Jersey, Spier (1916a, 1918b) excavated near Trenton in 1914; he excavated again in 1915, this time more extensively "as the stratigraphic relations dictated" (Spier 1918b:169). Spier used the bread loaf excavation technique in 1914: "[T]renching proceeded by scraping the breast or face of the trench with a trowel. The depth below the plane of contact of [the uppermost] black and [middle] yellow soils . . . and the lateral position of each [artifact] specimen was noted before it was removed" (Spier 1918b:180; see also Spier 1916a:182). In 1915 Spier excavated several trenches using the bread loaf technique and excavated others with arbitrary four-inch levels (Spier 1916a:182). Although he was not specifically asking chronological questions about superposed remains, what he was asking—had the artifacts in the yellow sand unit been deposited with that unit?—ultimately was critical. Spier showed that the materials not only consistently occupied a particular vertical position within the yellow stratum but also that those materials consistently displayed a particular frequency distribution when plotted throughout that stratum vertically. He termed it a "typical frequency distribution" that reflected a "normally variable series" (Spier 1916a:186, 1918b:185, 192).

Spier attempted to figure out the reasons for the vertically arranged frequency distribution that the artifacts displayed. The artifacts, he concluded, were not "intrusive from the [overlying] black soil"; had they been, "we would find the maximum frequency [of artifacts] at the plane of contact [stratigraphic boundary between the black soil and yellow sand units] with frequencies diminishing with depth" (Spier 1918b:186–187). Instead, the maximum frequency was near the middle of the yellow-sand unit. Wissler (1916a:197) and

Spier (1918b) interpreted this frequency distribution as evidence of redeposition, an interpretation supported by a similar distribution of nonartifactual pebbles. Might this distribution "characterize the occupation of the site" (Spier 1918b:201)? Wissler (1916a) and Spier (1918b) showed that, when summed, the artifacts reported by Loomis and Young (1912) displayed no such unimodal frequency distribution across vertical space, nor did Nelson's (1916) pottery when not distinguished by type. Spier (1918b) also argued that Kidder's pottery from Pecos (Kidder and Kidder 1917) did not display such a distribution. The unimodal frequency distributions exhibited by Nelson's sherds occurred only for "specific styles in ceramic art and not the typical distribution for the ceramic art of San Cristobal as a whole" (Wissler 1916a:195). Only sherds of particular "styles" displayed a unimodal frequency distribution, not sherds as a whole or cultural trait. The Trenton artifacts, all made of stone, were a "trait" as a whole, as was Nelson's pottery (Wissler 1916a:196).

Spier (1918b) was clear on the significance of frequency distributions. Nelson's (1916) pottery represented a "single trait" that, "because of its variability," allowed one to trace the history of associated "traits" such as architecture (Nelson 1919b:134); Kidder and Kidder's (1917) pottery, when considered as a "trait" as a whole, did not display unimodal frequency distributions. "In both pueblos [San Cristobal and Pecos] certain types of pottery give distributions of the normal type. . . . But these are not comparable to the Trenton series since they represent fluctuations in single cultural traits—stylistic pulsations—which attain their maxima at the expense of other similar traits" (Spier 1918b:201). Do not be confused by Spier's equation of each type of pottery with a unique cultural trait; any such equation would quickly disappear in the next few years as types became known as styles.

Spier (1918b:218–219) began plotting the absolute frequencies of artifacts late in 1913, about the time that Nelson (1916) was first observing the stratigraphic positions of different kinds of pottery in the Southwest. Wissler wanted to show that the Trenton materials were naturally deposited in order to perpetuate the museum's long-standing position that the artifacts were not Pleistocene in age (Meltzer 1983). Recall that Spier, Nelson, and Wissler were working at the American Museum, that the Trenton and San Cristobal analyses were temporally coincident, and that absolute frequencies of artifacts were used in both analyses. In later analyses, Spier (1917a, 1917b, 1918a, 1919) used percentages of artifact types, as did Nelson (1920). Nelson (1916:166) adjusted the absolute frequencies of his San Cristobal pottery to account for different excavation volumes. This brought his sherd tallies in line with Spier's (1918b) Trenton data and allowed Wissler (1916a:195) and Spier to use that pottery data as evidence to argue that the Trenton materials had not been deposited by people. To have converted his tallies to relative frequencies would have negated the necessity of adjusting for different excavated volumes, but it would also have made Nelson's data incomparable with the Trenton data. What was Nelson thinking? Did Spier and Wissler influence his choice of analytical technique? We think not and instead believe Nelson was mimicking the technique of one of his predecessors.

Nels C. Nelson

Nels C. Nelson had found superposed remains before the 1914 field season when he excavated a sedimentary column at San Cristobal in 10 arbitrary one-foot-thick levels, but he noted that in those earlier cases, "there is often no appreciable [chronological] differentiation of remains" (Nelson 1916:163). When he found evidence of chronological differentiation, it was between the types at the ends of a continuum of several pottery types, and thus he lamented that such instances were "merely clean-cut superpositions showing nothing but time relations" (Nelson 1916:163). But when two types in the continuum were found stratigraphically mixed together, "one gradually replacing the other[, this] was the evidence wanted, because it accounted for the otherwise unknown time that separated the merely superposed occurrences of types and from the point of view of the merely physical relationships of contiguity, connected them" (Nelson 1916:163). Thus in one sense Nelson replaced the then-prevalent notion that culture change could be modeled as a flight of stairs with a model that viewed culture change as a gradually ascending ramp (e.g., Nelson 1919b, 1919c, 1932), albeit a ramp that moved through progressively more advanced stages (Figure 2.6). Plotting frequencies of types against time (rendered as geologically vertical space) would illustrate the gradual and continuous cultural evolution Nelson sought and eventually allow one to document the relative ages of the cultural stages (e.g., Nelson 1937). Unremarked was the process that "connected" superposed types; the connection was manifest as overlapping artifact types, and the process was cultural transmission.

How could one be sure that the fluctuating artifact frequencies reflected cultural change within a continuum rendered as a column of sediment and not something else, such as, say, sample size? Nelson had the answer well before he ever went to the Southwest. Uhle (1907) had excavated at the Emeryville Shellmound in 1902. Nelson, at the time a graduate student at Berkeley, undertook a stratigraphic excavation at Emeryville in 1906 (Nelson 1996) and mimicked one of Uhle's seldom-remarked analytical innovations. Uhle (1907:39) adjusted the frequencies of artifacts recovered per stratum to account for the different volumes excavated per stratum. Nelson (1996:5) did exactly the same thing. Such an adjustment allowed Uhle to track and interpret the shifting frequencies of various kinds of artifacts across the 10 strata he distinguished and to speak of possible phylogenetic connections—based on "common traits"— between the "two people[s]" he identified as having occupied the mound (Uhle 1907:40). It was just such connections, as noted above, that Nelson sought at San Cristobal. Continuous frequency distributions of artifacts allowed Nelson (1996:13) to observe that various artifact categories increased or decreased in abundance from one stratum to the next—over diachronic time—not as a result of variation in excavated volume but as a result of culture change. It is not surprising, however, that Nelson did not make much of these sorts of observations at the time. His academic adviser, Kroeber (1909), was, after all, not impressed with Uhle's inferences of culture change. Working for Wissler and the American Museum a few years later, Nelson did not hesitate to make inferences.

Clark Wissler

Recall Clark Wissler's (1916a) remark regarding the rise and fall of the popularity of a cultural trait. That same year, Nelson (1916) identified this as what was to become a central tenet of the culture history paradigm—the popularity principle (Lyman et al. 1997b:43). Here was a way, even in the absence of superposed artifact-collection units, to measure cultural change through time—one that already had a commonsense warrant (e.g., Kroeber 1909; Wissler 1916a). The seriation and percentage-stratigraphy work of Nelson, Kroeber, Spier, and Kidder showed that cultural change could be detected analytically using fluctuating frequencies of artifact styles. Wissler (1919) edited the volume in which Kroeber's (1916b) and Spier's (1917a) work appeared, and he acknowledged Kidder's work. Wissler sent Spier to New Mexico in 1916 (Nelson 1948) specifically to test Kroeber's (1916a, 1916b) suspected chronology. An extensive time depth to the archaeological record of the New World was unnecessary to detect temporal change in culture; based initially on Nelson's and Kroeber's and later on Kidder's and Spier's work, such change was readily apparent in the changing frequencies of pottery types over chronological spans of less than a thousand years if the pottery types were of particular kinds. Those kinds would shortly become known as "styles" and would later be referred to as "historical" or "temporal types" (Steward 1954).

Why was Wissler (e.g., 1917b) so enamored with the "stratigraphic revolution"? His enthusiasm was not because archaeologists had suddenly recognized that superposed artifacts documented the passage of time; that had been recognized for decades. To answer the question, it is necessary to appreciate Wissler. To him, the ideas behind cultural traits diffuse across space to form culture areas. The older traits are on the peripheries of the area, having diffused there from the center, while the younger traits are near the center of the area (see Kroeber 1931a for a review). Thus a set of superposed collections from a site in the center of a culture area "presents a conclusion as to the chronology . . . that is fully consistent with the workings of culture in general [it is a time-space continuum], but is also based upon correlated and verifiable empirical observations" (Wissler 1919:vii). Nelson's (1919a, 1919b) superposed unimodal frequency distributions measured cultural change in a way that was fully consistent with Wissler's age-area concept (e.g., Wissler 1919) and in fact confirmed the chronological implications of Wissler's spatial analysis (Nelson 1919b:139). Here was archaeological proof of one of the major anthropological paradigms of the early twentieth century that attempted to contend with change over time. There is little wonder that Wissler was excited.

The analytical results produced by Nelson, Kroeber, Kidder, and Spier comprise the real revolution in American archaeology: Culture change could be measured by the waxing and waning of the popularity—manifest as frequencies—of artifact types. Americanists did not require an archaeological record that had the extensive time depth or the major epochs of change evident in Europe. American archaeology could be its own kind of science, complete with unique data, methods, and questions. Moreover, the answers produced could be tested empirically by paying attention to the relative vertical positions of artifacts.

The End of the Revolution

Shortly after the so-called stratigraphic revolution, Wissler (1921:15) remarked that pottery is "so plastic in origin as to give almost free rein to styles of artistic expression and the use of decorative technique. . . . The [chronological] record, therefore, is in the simple pot-sherds, and our problem was to find a method for reading it." He went on to state that "the best indexes to time differences are the changing styles of pottery" and that "pottery characters are the most accessible and lend themselves most readily to the method of superposition" (Wissler 1921:23). A shift in scale from noting the presence or absence of pottery to studying variants of pottery had taken place. Wissler (1919:vii), like virtually everyone else at the time, perceived superposed positions of artifact styles as requisite "to verify the chronological relations the [frequency seriations of Kroeber and Spier] suggested." That the stratigraphic positions of different styles of artifacts might have little relationship to the age of those styles does not seem to have received consideration for some time, and when it did, it was misguided (Hawley 1937). Two analytical traditions grew out of the middle of the second decade of the twentieth century—one focusing on change measured by fluctuations in the frequencies of types, another focusing on the identification of superposed cultures by using marker types. Regardless of the tradition in which one participated, the role of stratigraphic excavation no longer was to confirm the diachronic meaning of kinds of artifacts; rather, it was used to create chronologies. Superposition was the chronometer.

The focus on culture change measured by type frequencies is epitomized by the work of those associated with the American Museum of Natural History. This analytical tradition is exemplified in the work of Erich Schmidt (1928), who excavated under the auspices of the museum and used an excavation technique similar to Kidder's—trench around a column so that three or four sides are exposed, then excavate each of the exposed strata. This was an onion peel–like technique. Schmidt then followed Nelson's and Spier's lead and used percentage stratigraphy to work out the history of pottery change. George Vaillant (1930, 1931), who had worked with Kidder at Pecos, worked for the American Museum in the Valley of Mexico in the late 1920s. He used a bread loaf–like excavation technique and focused on index fossils, but he also considered fluctuations in type frequencies. Nelson (1920) excavated two stratigraphic columns in six-inch levels and used percentage stratigraphy at

Pueblo Bonito in 1916 (see also Wissler 1921). Spier (1918a, 1919) continued his work in the Southwest in 1917 and 1918 and ordered surface collections from sites using frequency seriation. Kroeber (1925a), although not directly affiliated with the American Museum, did a percentage-stratigraphic analysis, but because it failed to produce clear results, he ordered surface-collected Archaic materials from the Valley of Mexico using frequency seriation.

Some archaeologists of the period 1917–1930 used frequency seriation or percentage stratigraphy to measure time and monitor culture change, but the majority simply looked at superposed artifacts and then labeled aggregates of artifacts "cultures" or the like (e.g., Harrington 1924b; Hawkes and Linton 1917; Loud and Harrington 1929; Roberts 1929). This majority included prehistorians connected with the International School of American Archaeology and Ethnology (e.g., Gamio 1924; Hewett 1916). As Wissler (1917a) had noted, when there was little stratification, one might be forced to examine the frequency of artifact styles to measure time. The presence of stratification was typically thought to denote a discontinuous occupation by multiple successive cultures. As Fowke (1922:37) observed, "The intermittent character of occupancy is . . . shown by the distinct segregation of numerous successive layers of kitchen refuse." Stratified sites were eagerly sought, but when they were not found, arbitrary vertical levels were used to obtain superposed collections (Praetzellis 1993).

Predictably, given archaeologists' preoccupation with diffusion, migration, and other ethnographically documented processes that create visible disjunctions in the cultural record, percentage stratigraphy and frequency seriation—two of the most innovative methods ever devised by Americanists and the heart of the so-called stratigraphic revolution—were used less and less after 1930. Rising to assume their original place of primacy were vertically bounded assemblages of artifacts that became known as components (see below). Frequency seriation in particular, and percentage stratigraphy to a lesser degree, never again enjoyed a role equivalent to that of superposition as a way to measure time because superposition was perceived, as it had been from the beginning, to be more trustworthy than the other two methods (Rowe 1961). The use of vertical units, whether of the depositional or arbitrary sort, to measure diachronic and synchronic time reinforced the perception that artifacts within vertically bounded recovery units comprised real, discrete entities rather than accidental (results of deposition) chunks of a cultural continuum.

Strata no longer were geological depositional units; they were archaeological units.

Received wisdom in the history of American archaeology has been that the revolution in 1915–1917 was over stratigraphic excavation. It was not; rather, it concerned a shift from tracking the presence or absence of cultural traits as a whole to monitoring frequencies of trait variants or artifact types through time. Just as clearly, the revolution was short-lived. Its effect was to prompt archaeologists to more consistently ask questions about diachronic time and culture change and to focus on vertically discrete units because, as Nelson, Kidder, Kroeber, and Spier had demonstrated, time and culture change were analytically visible if the analyst used the appropriate artifact types.

Why Begin to Measure Time with Superposition?

Willey and Sabloff (1974:94) correctly note that neither Gamio nor Nelson "claimed any credit for originality or revolutionary discovery." Spier and Kidder could be added to this statement. The reason they did not claim such credit is clear: They were not doing anything particularly new or revolutionary in terms of excavation strategies. Only historians of archaeology have claimed or implied there was a revolution in excavation technique. This leaves unanswered the question of why several archaeologists at about the same time decided that they needed to measure diachronic time.

The need generally pertained to particular and very local chronological problems. Nelson (1916:162) stated that when he went back to San Cristobal in 1914, he sought to test a suspected local sequence of four pottery types: "By the opening of the [1914] season, it was reasonably certain, both from internal evidence and from various general considerations, what was the chronological order of the four apparent pottery types, but tangible proof was still wanting." He suspected the relative chronological positions of pottery types, but only by excavating at San Cristobal was he able to establish empirically their relative chronological positions (Nelson 1916:163–166); all previous superpositional indications of chronology were "incomplete and fragmentary, each showing merely the time relations of two successive pottery types at some place or other in the total series of four or five types" (Nelson 1916:163). Nelson's use of the word "merely" demonstrates that he viewed the temporal implications of superposed pottery types as nothing out of the ordinary. A few years later

Nelson (1919c:133) remarked that "there was always a set problem to be solved, but it was a purely local one."

Kidder, too, had a particular and local problem in mind when he turned his attention to Pecos Pueblo. The historically documented occupation of Pecos was impressive: "So long an occupation does not seem to have occurred at any other place in New Mexico available for excavation and it was hoped that remains would there be found so stratified as to make clear the development of the various Pueblo arts and to enable students to place in their proper chronological order numerous New Mexican ruins" (Kidder 1916:120). Establishing this chronology was the "chief reason for the choice of Pecos" (Kidder 1916:120). Kidder (e.g., 1916, 1917) was, like Nelson, only trying to solve a regional chronological problem. The same can be said for Spier's efforts in the Northeast, though he was sidetracked; his intent in the Southwest, of course, was to test Kroeber's conjectured chronology.

In his particular influence on Gamio, Boas merely sought the solution of a several-years-old local problem. Late in the first decade of the twentieth century, Zelia Nuttall (1926) was sufficiently familiar with the archaeological record of the Valley of Mexico to suspect that different kinds of clay figurines and pottery represented temporally distinct cultures. Subsequently, she asked workers to collect artifacts from under the Pedregal lava—artifacts that clearly "antedated any Aztec remains" (Nuttall 1926:246), which had been found above the lava flow. At about the same time, Gamio (1909) "recognized [what he believed was] a succession of various styles of figurines and pottery" (Vaillant 1935:289). How could the suspected chronological relations of these various materials be validated empirically? "To ascertain the relative age of these archaeological deposits [actually, the cultural remains referred to as Aztec, Teotihuacán, and Archaic, or de los Cerros], I [Boas] entrusted an excavation in one of the brickyards to Sr. M. Gamio, a Fellow of the [International] School [of American Ethnology and Archaeology in Mexico City]" (Boas 1913:176). Gamio (1913) ultimately identified the superposed relations of the three types of remains.

Nowhere in the writings of Gamio, Kidder, Nelson, or Spier—nor in Boas's (1912, 1913) discussions—do we find any hint of rhetoric or polemic lauding the virtues of stratigraphic excavation. The reasons why there was no rhetoric are clear: Virtually all archaeologists, both before and after 1912–1915, either were excavating stratigraphically or already knew the chronological value of doing so. Thus there could hardly have been a "stratigraphic revolution" in the usual sense in which this term is used.

Why Does the Discipline Think There Was a "Stratigraphic Revolution"?

Two decades after the so-called stratigraphic revolution, Nelson (1937:86) remarked that in the Americas, "stratigraphic investigations" had only "begun in earnest about thirty years ago." Nelson unfortunately focused on the importance of the stratigraphic provenience of artifacts and failed to mention the role that typology played (e.g., Nelson 1919c, 1938). Similarly, in his discussion of that time, Kidder (1924:45–46) indicated that the "ideal form of chronological evidence is provided by stratigraphy, i.e., when remains of one type are found lying below those of another." Kidder devoted three full paragraphs to the importance of stratigraphy, but only two sentences referred to the role of typology, and those—as does the one quoted here—failed to underscore its critical significance. Wissler (1917b:100), too, in what might be thought of as the birth announcement of the first "new archaeology" (Browman and Givens 1996), indicated that when asking questions of chronology, an archaeologist "must actually dissect section after section of our old Mother Earth for the empirical data upon which to base [our] answers." He failed to note the role of typology in artifact-based chronometers such as percentage stratigraphy and frequency seriation.

The myth of an American stratigraphic revolution was begun post facto by the very individuals responsible for the "revolution." We doubt that their intent was devious or to mislead the discipline. Instead, they simply misrepresented the history of American archaeology between about 1895 and 1915. People had been noting the vertical proveniences of artifacts in vertical exposures of deposits and had been using the bread loaf excavation technique to record such proveniences for decades. What they were not doing was classifying potsherds and other artifacts in such a manner as to permit the measurement of time. That is where the revolution resided in 1915; Nelson and Kidder, as did Boas and Gamio, suspected what the chronological sequence of pottery types was in their respective areas. Stratigraphic excavation merely confirmed those suspicions by showing that those types and/or their frequencies occupied different vertical positions in a column of sediment. Similarly, the ordering of Kroeber's surface assemblages had been accomplished by frequency seriation; Spier confirmed the temporal significance of that ordering by percentage stratigraphy—noting the frequency distribution of types collected from geologically superposed positions.

Stratigraphic excavation's role at the time of the so-called stratigraphic revolution was confirmatory rather than creational. Taylor (1954:564) indicated that the confirmatory role emerged because archaeologists first did a surface survey, collecting sherds that they would then arrange in what they thought was a temporal sequence "to outline the problem and the potential; then stratigraphic testing in chosen sites [was done] to resolve seriational uncertainties and check results." Griffin (1959:386) stated that "Spier combined Kroeber's seriation with Nelson's stratigraphy, applied these techniques to Zuni sites, and strengthened the sequence of ceramic styles outlined by Kroeber"; he should have said "tested and confirmed." Schroeder (1979:8) indicated that stratigraphic excavation was initially a confirmational strategy: The chronologies of Kidder and Kroeber that were based on surface collections were "checked by the first stratigraphic tests undertaken in the Southwest and double-checked by excavation in various Pueblos." The paucity of such statements on the initially confirmational role of stratigraphic excavation no doubt contributed to the misconception that there was a stratigraphic revolution.

Negative Impacts of the "Stratigraphic Revolution"

Historians consistently fail to consider whether stratigraphic excavation had any negative impacts on American archaeology. One such negative effect was that each stratum or deposit conceptually came to comprise a chunk of the cultural continuum that was somehow real in an ethnographic sense; a set of associated artifacts recovered from a vertically discrete unit represented a steady state in a cultural lineage. This notion had its origins as early as the recognition that a stratum comprised a depositional event and that the materials within such a unit could be inferred to be approximately contemporaneous.

Archaeologists working between 1860 and 1900 used the terms "bed" (Dall 1877; Holmes 1890a), "deposit" (Dall 1877; Holmes 1890a; Wyman 1875), "layer" (Dall 1877; Holmes 1885, 1890a; Mercer 1897; Wyman 1875), and "stratum" (Dall 1877; Mercer 1897; Wyman 1875) to denote vertically distinct, natural depositional units. Sometimes, though, they spoke of a "deposit" as a horizontally distinct unit (Holmes 1890a; Wyman 1875). After the turn of the century Harrington (1909a:175), Schrabisch (1909:146), and Wissler

(1909:xiii) used the term "levels"; Hawkes and Linton (1916:49, 1917:487–488), Peabody (1908:12), and Schrabisch (1909:153) used "stratum"; and Loomis and Young (1912:19) used "layer." All were referring to natural depositional units. Some used the term "deposit" to refer to a horizontally distinct unit (e.g., Harrington 1909a). Terminological confusion was exacerbated by use of the terms "layer" (Kroeber 1925b:928), "level" (Kroeber 1925a:376), and "stratum" (Spier 1917a:266) to denote vertically discrete, arbitrary vertical units of excavation.

The use of numerous terms to denote the same thing and the use of one term to denote different things were bad enough. The situation grew worse. The terms in use generally were merely labels for portions of a sedimentary column. But people had a hand in the formation of at least some of those portions. How was this to be denoted? Holmes (1890a) used the term "artificial deposits" to label those depositional units that owed their horizontal and vertical position and internal structure to human activities. Parker (1916) excavated in 1906 in such a manner as to be able to note the associations between grave goods and human skeletons—to measure synchronic time— and he made detailed stratigraphic observations of the burial pits he exposed. Parker (1916:477) used the terms "occupied soil" and "Indian dirt," and Boas (1913:176) used the term "archaeological deposits" to refer to depositional units that contained artifacts and burials. There seems to have been an effort to distinguish terminologically those depositional units that contained artifacts from those that did not. This no doubt contributed to the conception that individual strata or deposits that contained artifacts signified something in particular.

Dall (1877:49) thought that the strata he distinguished "correspond approximately to actual stages in the development of the population which formed them." The depositional units he identified corresponded to stages of cultural development such as those identified by Morgan (1877). Archaeological remains in particular strata were equated with particular cultures by Dixon (1913:559), who wrote of "numerous and far-reaching ethnic movements, resulting in a stratification of cultures, such that later [cultures] have dispossessed and overlain earlier." Wissler (1916b:487) used the term "cultural strata" to denote temporally distinct units of culture or an ethnographic unit typically called a culture.

As we noted earlier, close on the heels of the so-called stratigraphic revolution came the concept of component (Colton 1939; Gladwin and Gladwin 1934; McKern 1937a, 1939). Components were sets of artifacts, the "setness" of which was determined by stratification; a component comprised those artifacts determined to be associated in synchronic time on the basis of the boundaries of strata. A component was conceived to be a manifestation of a culture, which reinforced the notion that depositional units had cultural (ethnographic-like) reality. Belief in the cultural reality of stratigraphically defined components was also reinforced by construing such units as occupations. Willey's (1938:18) statement is typical: "Occupation zones [strata] are of varying thickness [and are comprised of] bands of decayed refuse [each comprising] another occupation." By the 1950s these notions were axioms. They were accepted by the participants in the Society for American Archaeology's 1955 Seminar on Cultural Stability (Thompson 1956) and were reiterated by others (e.g., Spaulding 1955). Following Phillips and Willey (1953), Rouse (1955:713) stated that a component is an occupation and "corresponds [to] a layer of refuse, analysis unit, or whatever other division is made." Following Willey and Phillips (1958), Trigger (1968:15) stated that a component is "a single period of occupation in the history of a given site"; it should be brief enough in temporal duration "that one can assume that no significant culture change took place during it"; and it "can usually be distinguished from [other components] by means of natural or artificial stratigraphy." Such conceptions ultimately reinforced the apparent utility and validity of modeling cultural evolution as a flight of stairs (Figure 2.6).

As far as we know, James Ford was the only culture historian to note explicitly that allowing breaks in the temporal continuum of culture change to be dictated by depositional events—stratigraphic boundaries—was potentially fallacious (O'Brien and Lyman 1998). Ford (1962:45) argued that in so doing, "we have allowed [human] history to be separated into periods by chance historical events." Ford was correct. Adoption of a conception of archaeological strata as somehow culturally real created serious problems. The tempo of culture change could no longer be measured along a continuum if one used the limits of depositional units to dictate the boundaries of cultural periods. Those boundaries had no necessary causal relation to culture change, and they created the appearance of cultural stasis rendered as difference between superposed sets of artifacts (Plog 1973, 1974). The adoption of stratigraphic excavation as the strategy for creating chronologies in the 1930s was the root of the problem.

There Was No Stratigraphic Revolution

Most histories of American archaeology that cover the first two decades of the twentieth century have stopped short of identifying why a stratigraphic revolution might have taken place. When Gamio, Nelson, Kidder, and Spier excavated stratigraphically, each addressed a specific and local chronological problem that grew from the relatively extensive knowledge they had of the areas in which they were working. They perceived what they believed were chronological differences in the materials they were studying and wanted to confirm those perceptions empirically. There was no change in their conception of the depositional record—it reflected the passage of time and could therefore serve to confirm their chronological beliefs—or in their conception of significant cultural change as involving the transformation from one cultural epoch to another.

Principles of stratigraphic interpretation—particularly superposition and association—contributed to the establishment of what became known as culture history. During the second decade of the twentieth century, temporal change in culture was found to be visible despite the shallow time depth then thought to be reflected in the American archaeological record. Time was visible if artifacts were classified in particular ways. Kroeber, Nelson, Kidder, and Spier used the depositional record to confirm that the apparent change in culture construed as the waxing and waning of the popularity of variants of particular cultural traits—rendered as the frequencies of artifact types—in fact measured diachronic time. Previously, American archaeologists had paid close attention to superposition when excavating, but they had not devoted much effort to developing a way to answer questions of diachronic time because they were not often asking such questions. What comprised the revolution was the discovery that one had to construct particular types of artifacts, not just note the presence or absence of cultural traits, to detect the passage of time analytically. The discipline chose largely to adopt only the superpositional component of this work, and that resulted in turn in the adoption of concepts such as components and phases and a discontinuous (essentialist and orthogenetic) model of culture change.

The potential of the measurement of continuous cultural change rendered as fluctuations in the frequencies of artifact types has yet to be fully exploited in archaeology, despite the several-decades-old recommendation that the potential should be exploited (Plog 1973). Shortly after the so-called stratigraphic revolution, culture historians invented various techniques to depict continuous cultural change graphically. It is to those techniques that we turn our attention in the next chapter.

9. Graphic Depictions of Culture Change

One innovative artifact-based chronometric method developed early in the history of archaeology was seriation. In later years it has been confused with other chronological methods, so we find it defined as "the determination of the chronological sequence of styles, types, or assemblages of types (cultures) by any method or combination of methods. Stratigraphy may be employed, or the materials may be from surface sites" (Hester et al. 1975:272). We also read that the "principle of seriation was allied to stratigraphy" (Willey and Sabloff 1993:96), or that Ford used seriation in his work in the Southeast during the 1930s (Chapter 6), or that Kidder used seriation to construct a cultural chronology in the Southwest (Chapter 8), or that Nelson "for the first time made a strict use of statistical methods developed in Europe, and reported this method in 1916" (McGregor 1965:42).

Such statements result from the conflation of the particulars of analytical techniques developed and used by those who founded the culture-historical approach and their failure to explicitly define and distinguish among distinct techniques. As might be anticipated from Chapter 8, sloppy use of terms has resulted in misunderstanding the history of seriation, the various techniques by which it may be implemented, and its relation to the use of artifacts contained in superposed sediments for chronological purposes. Such misunderstanding should, after reading the preceding chapters, no longer exist. In this chapter we first clear up any remaining misunderstanding by providing explicit definitions of key terms based on how various analytical techniques were first used and by reviewing the history of various techniques employed to present data concerning artifact collections ordered into what are inferred to be chronological sequences.

Today there are a number of statistically and computer-assisted techniques for seriating collections of artifacts, though these date from the mid-1960s. Prior to 1960 two techniques founded on the frequencies of types were used to sort assemblages into what was inferred to be chronological order. One involved tables of numbers, and the other involved graphs. Both were also used to display the passage of time as reflected by cultural change, but confusion arose because sometimes the stratigraphically superposed positions of collections were used to create the order and other times they were not. Also confusing matters was the fact that graphs sometimes summarized empirical data, and at other times they reflected a researcher's interpretations and only dimly reflected a data set. Our second focus in this chapter is to distinguish graphs having similar appearances but constructed on different bases. Ultimately, we show how the use of numbers to sort collections evolved into the use of graphs, and we trace much of the modern terminological confusion to the similarities of graphs constructed using distinctly different protocols.

Terms
Seriation

As far as we have been able to discover, Sapir (1916:13) was the first American anthropologist to use the term "seriation" when he indicated that "cultural seriation" was a method "often used to reconstruct historical sequences from the purely descriptive material of cultural anthropology." He noted that the "tacit assumption involved in this method is that human development has normally proceeded from the simple or unelaborated to the complex"; "evidence derived from seriation . . . fits far better with the evolutionary than with the strictly historical method of interpreting culture"; and this method "is probably at its best in the construction of culture sequences of simple-to-complex type in the domain of the history of artifacts and industrial processes, particularly where the constructions are confined to a single tribe or to a geographically restricted area" (Sapir 1916:13–15). Thus cultural seriation was based on the presumption of progressive cultural evolution (Chapter 2). Seriation as an analytical technique can be based on this presumed course of cultural change and in some instances was, such as Kidder's (1915) suspicion that, because of its greater technological sophistication, glazed pottery was more recent than unglazed pottery. But, as we will see, seriation need not be based on such an assumption.

Spier (1917a:281, 1917b:281) was the first American archaeologist to use the term "seriation," and he did not reference Sapir's paper. Spier used the term to refer to Kidder's (1915) work, characterizing it as "the hypothetical seriation of several pottery techniques" (Spier 1917a:252). Spier (1917a:252, 281) also used the term to refer to the work of Kroeber (1916a, 1916b), his mentor, though he characterized Kroeber's work as "the hypothetical ranking of surface finds and the observation of concurrent variations." That the characterizations differed suggests the analyses performed by Kidder and Kroeber differed. As we indicated in earlier chapters, Kidder's (1915, 1917) seriations were indeed of a different sort than Kroeber's. Spier's (1917a:252) crediting of "Kidder for the concept of seriation [and] Kroeber for ranking and concurrent variation" should have precluded any confusion of two distinct analytical techniques, but this was not the case. Repetition 50 years later (Taylor 1963:379) of Spier's notations, for example, failed to distinguish between the two techniques and thus exacerbated the confusion. Other discussions of seriation (e.g., Rowe 1961; Rouse 1967), while distinguishing between evolutionary, or developmental, seriation—Kidder's version—and other seriation techniques, have also failed to clarify matters.

Although recognized for his use of what later became known as frequency seriation when awarded the Viking Fund Medal, Spier, like his contemporaries, did not explicitly define seriation in his seminal papers (Spier 1917a, 1917b). He later characterized seriation as a method in which the "remains of a stylistic variable (such as pottery) occurring in varying proportions in a series of sites are ranged [ordered], by some auxiliary suggestion, according to the seriation [ordering] of one element (one pottery type)" (Spier 1931b:283). Although this was what Kroeber (1916a, 1916b) had done (Chapters 4 and 5), others who later used frequency seriation seem to have ordered their collections on the basis of multiple types. The "auxiliary suggestion" to which Spier (1931b) referred—earlier characterized by him as a "principle for the seriation of the data" (Spier 1917a:281)—was the expectation that the relative frequencies of pottery types through time would exhibit smooth changes that approximated a unimodal curve. This principle has subsequently served as the underlying guide to performing a frequency seriation—ordering collections of artifacts using relative frequencies of artifact types (Dunnell 1970, 2000; Rouse 1967; Teltser 1995).

The creation of terminological confusion cannot be laid solely at Spier's feet. Kidder (1919:298) characterized Spier's (1917a, 1918, 1919) work as involving the "seriation" of artifact collections on the basis of a single type of artifact and the subsequent testing of the validity of the final arrangement on the basis of "concurrent variations in the accompanying wares." Kidder referred to Spier's "hypothetical ranking of surface finds and the observation of concurrent variations" as "seriation." Analytically, Spier (1917a, 1917b) was simply mimicking what Kroeber (1916a, 1916b) had done—ordering collections based on frequencies of types—plus the additional step of testing the chronological significance of those orders with stratigraphically superposed collections. Kroeber did not originally refer to his particular analytical technique as seriation. He later referred to some of his own efforts as "non-stratigraphical comparison of the frequency of several types of ceramic decoration" (Kroeber 1925a:406); these are correctly categorized as frequency seriations. Definitions of seriation offered over the past half century, however, tend not to echo Spier's and Kroeber's usage of the term to indicate ordering collections of artifacts based solely on the concurrent variations in the frequencies of types.

Kroeber (1927:626) also spoke of Uhle's (1902, 1903) "stylistic seriation" of Peruvian material. Uhle (1902:754) asserted that the "method applied by Flinders Petrie in Egypt to prove the succession of styles by gradually changing character of the contents of graves differing in age has given remarkable results," though as we noted in Chapter 8, both Uhle and Petrie placed more trust in the chronological implications of stratigraphically superposed artifacts. Petrie (e.g., 1899, 1901) called his seriation "sequence dating," a term repeated by few American archaeologists (e.g., Heizer 1959:375). Praetzellis (1993:76) states that "seriation was developed by Flinders Petrie for the analysis of excavated Egyptian ceramics, and apparently brought to North America by Max Uhle who introduced it to Alfred Kroeber." We agree with Trigger (1989:202) that "although Kroeber may have learned the basic principles of typology and seriation from Boas and known of Petrie's work, his technique of seriation was not based on the same principles as Petrie's." We described Petrie's analytical protocol in detail in Chapter 8, where we also argued that he seems to have placed little trust in the chronological significance of fluctuating frequencies of artifact types. We referred to Petrie's ordering technique as phyletic seriation; Rowe (1961) referred to it as "similiary seriation"; and Rouse (1967) termed it "developmental seriation."

Willey and Sabloff (1993:113) suggest that Kroeber popularized and "made explicit" the notion of phyletic seriation: "This was done in a series of papers in the 1920s, in which Kroeber shifted from the potsherd frequency seriation he had pioneered in the Southwest to a grave-lot and stylistic approach that could be adapted to the Uhle [Peruvian] collections." While it is true that Kroeber and his students did use phyletic seriation (e.g., Kroeber and Strong 1924; Strong 1925), there already was significant precedence for such a principle of ordering in Kidder's (1915, 1917) work as well as in anthropology generally (e.g., Sapir 1916; Wissler 1916c). Within American archaeology, the basic notion of phyletic seriation was later manifest in the concept of a (ceramic) "series," a term first used by Kidder (1917:370) and later adopted by Colton and Hargrave (1937:2–3) and Wheat et al. (1958). Recall from earlier chapters that it was Kroeber's use of frequencies of types of Zuni potsherds that made his work unique.

Between about 1915 and 1935, several different terms were being applied to the same analytical technique; simultaneously, the same or a similar term was being applied to distinct techniques (Figure 9.1). As we noted in Chapter 4, we prefer Rowe's (1961:326) definition of seriation as "the arrangement of archaeological materials in a presumed chronological order on the basis of some logical principle other than superposition. . . . The logical order on which the seriation is based is found in the combinations of features of style or inventory which characterize the units, rather than in the external relationships of the units themselves." We like this definition precisely because it underscores that the ordering is based on formal attributes of the seriated materials; it is based on intrinsic characteristics of the artifacts and not on superposition or any other chronometer; if it was based on known chronological data, then it would be a time-series analysis (Chapter 5). Rouse (1967:156) appears to agree but fails to emphasize this point sufficiently. Dunnell (1970:310), too, seems to agree that the ordering produced during seriation is based solely on formal properties of the seriated materials without reference to their stratigraphic positions or other independent chronometric data, noting that arrangements resulting from seriation "are strictly formal orders. . . . They must be inferred to be chronologies." Similarly, Braun (1985:509) states that "archaeological seriation asks the question, 'Can we order this set of objects or places according to their relative ages, based on their physical characteristics?' " Frequency seriation involves ordering collections of presumably historical types such that

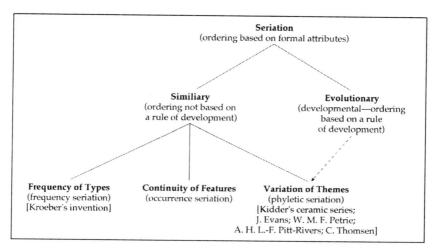

Figure 9.1. A taxonomy of seriation techniques. Seriation comprises techniques of ordering based on formal similarities. Evolutionary seriation—ordering based on an assumed rule of development—can inform any of the similiary techniques, but it most often informs phyletic seriation (see the example in Figure 2.3).

each type has a continuous distribution and a unimodal frequency distribution. The ordering is based solely on type frequencies.

Whether an order in fact measures the passage of time is an entirely different matter—a point recognized by both Spier (1917a, 1917b) and Kroeber (1916b:20), the latter of whom stated that the proof that his frequency seriation monitored the passage of time was "in the spade." This was one reason why Kidder (1916) went to Pecos Pueblo—to test the sequence he had derived using phyletic seriation (Kidder 1915) and to confirm and add to Nelson's sequence. As we concluded in Chapter 8, the stratigraphic revolution so often mentioned in the literature actually comprised use of the principle of superposition as a chronological tool to confirm rather than, as is typically claimed, to discover the passage of time. There are several aspects of that principle that require elaboration here.

Superposition

Prior to the end of the nineteenth century, American archaeologists in general believed that artifacts in lower or deeper strata were older than those in higher or shallower strata. This belief derived from the notion of superposition, defined by Rowe (1961:324) as follows: "In any pile of deposition units in which the top and bottom of the pile can be identified, the order of succession from bottom to top gives the order of deposition." What most American archaeologists failed to realize was that "the principle of superposition offers absolute certainty only of the sequence of deposition units at a particular site" (Rowe 1961:326). There was no assurance that the relative ages of artifacts contained in strata were accurately reflected by the order in which the containing strata were deposited. Because of the artifact-centric view of archaeologists, they eventually developed notions such as "reversed stratigraphy" and "mixed strata" to account for cases where suspected relative ages of artifacts were out of order stratigraphically (Lyman et al. 1997b:74–78; Stein 1990). Early in the twentieth century, however, such notions were not well developed, and as we indicated in Chapter 8, the principle of superposition was used virtually without question to confirm suspected or to determine unknown chronologies of artifacts.

In the work that led to his first use of the term "seriation," Spier (1917a, 1917b) not only used frequency seriation to order collections, but he also used an analytical technique later termed "percentage stratigraphy" (Willey 1939) to confirm that the results of his and Kroeber's (1916a, 1916b) frequency seriations monitored the passage of time. He tested the notion that the unimodal frequency distribution of types—the popularity principle—was a valid rule for ordering assemblages. If artifact-type frequencies fluctuated unimodally through superposed strata—which, it was thought, measured time, given the principle of superposition—then the popularity principle was valid (Spier 1916a; Wissler 1916a). Because of Spier's simultaneous use of two unique techniques for ordering artifacts without clear terminological distinction, they were confused with one another in later literature, and this contributed to the misconception that there was a stratigraphic revolution (Chapter 8).

Frequency seriation does not employ superposition to arrange collections; rather, it focuses on the frequencies of types and employs only the popularity principle—Kroeber's and Spier's concurrent variations in frequencies—to order collections. Percentage stratigraphy uses the superposed positions of artifact assemblages to establish their order and arrays the relative frequencies of types against their stratigraphic positions. Thus Spier (1917a, 1917b) was able to test the results of his frequency seriations not only in terms of the correctness of the ordering but also in terms of whether the ordering actually measured time, as indicated by the vertically superposed spatial positions of assemblages. Kidder and Kidder (1917) used percentage stratigraphy for virtually the same purpose. In doing so, Spier and Kidder and Kidder independently also tested the validity of the popularity principle as a valid chronometric principle. Deetz and Dethlefsen (1965; Dethlefsen and Deetz 1966) would some 50 years later perform additional tests of that principle.

We prefer the term "percentage stratigraphy" to describe what Spier (and Kidder and Kidder) did, though the term was first used by Gordon Willey (1939) two decades after Spier's work. Spier (1931b:281) indicates that the method he used in 1916 (Spier 1917a, 1917b) was a "combination of Kroeber's method [frequency seriation of surface samples] with Nelson's," the latter comprising, according to Spier (1917b:281), the "stratigraphic observation of refuse deposits." McGregor (1941:54) later described the percentage-stratigraphy technique—what he called a "combined statistical-stratigraphic method"—as involving classifying sherds, tallying each type's frequency from each area of excavation "and tabulat[ing the] relative abundance of occurrence [of each type] on a large chart," and comparing different areas of excavation to determine where a "specific type was most abundant in relation to all the others, and in this manner it is possible to reconstruct the order of building of the [site]." Although Spier (1917a:253) noted that Nelson demonstrated the "practicability of obtaining samples of sherds at random from the successive levels of the [refuse] heap, and . . . [that] the proportions of the constituent wares at each level indicate the course of the pottery art," Nelson (1916) did not calculate the relative or proportional abundances of the pottery types he discussed. Rather, he presented the absolute abundances of each type per uniform volume of excavated sediment; why he did so was discussed in Chapter 8.

Percentage stratigraphy involves placing the proportional abundances of artifact types per vertically defined assemblage against each assemblage's vertical provenience within a single site. Unlike frequency seriation, which orders assemblages only on the basis of the popularity principle, percentage stratigraphy uses the vertical provenience of collections as the basis of ordering, with the expectation that the ordered frequencies will display a unimodal distribution (the popularity principle). As documented in Chapter 8, after Spier's (1917a, 1917b, 1918, 1919) work, numerous individuals used percentage stratigraphy both to measure time and to determine if their types in fact measured time. This technique for ordering collections was variously referred to as the "stratigraphic observation of refuse heaps" (Spier 1917a:252), "pottery stratification" (Hawley 1934:62), "refuse stratigraphy" (Reiter 1938a:100), "vertical stratigraphy" (Ford 1936a:103), "stratigraphic tests" (Martin 1936:104), and "stratigraphic investigation" (Schmidt 1928:256).

Given the set of terms used to refer to what we are calling percentage stratigraphy, the term "ceramic stratigraphy" may seem redundant. This term was first used—without definition—by Nelson (1919b:133) to characterize his work at Pueblo San Cristobal (Nelson 1916)—work that we categorize as the predecessor of percentage stratigraphy because Nelson examined fluctuations in the absolute frequencies of types. Drucker (1943b), too, used the term "ceramic stratigraphy" without definition; he examined shifts in absolute and relative frequencies of ceramic types through a vertical column of sediment, and thus his work is better characterized as percentage stratigraphy. Nelson (1919b) did not define "ceramic stratigraphy," but Willey's (1939) later use of this term—again without explicit definition—indicates that the passage of time can be detected by monitoring the relative vertical positions of different pottery types within a site. Gamio (1913) used this technique to confirm the suspected sequence of pottery in the Valley of Mexico.

Ceramic stratigraphy (somewhat of a misnomer, since any kind of artifact ostensibly could be used) is similar to occurrence seriation (Dempsey and Baumhoff 1963; Dunnell 1970; Rouse 1967) because it focuses, unlike percentage stratigraphy or frequency seriation, on the presence or absence of temporally sensitive types rather than on their fluctuating frequencies. But as with percentage stratigraphy, ceramic stratigraphy derives its ordering of types from the relative vertical (superposed) positions of types in a column of sediment. Unlike occurrence seriation, ceramic stratigraphy does not sort collections such that types display a continuous occurrence across multiple collections, though this is, implicitly, the expected result. The discontinuous occurrence of a type through a vertical sequence of depositional units might indicate that the type is not temporally sensitive, the samples are inadequate, or the strata are "mixed" or "reversed."

Interdigitation

As first used by Willey (1949), interdigitation denotes the integration of percentage-stratigraphy data from several distinct excavation units and/or sites into a summary graph of bars, the widths of which denote the proportional frequency of a type (Figure 9.2). Bars are each given a unique shading or stippling to denote horizontal recovery provenience—usually the site—and

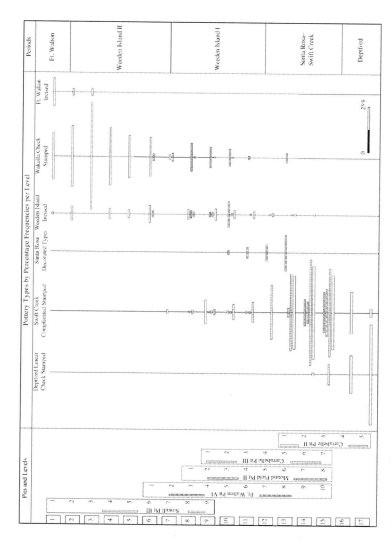

Figure 9.2. *Willey's interdigitated percentage-stratigraphy data. Each bar's shading is unique to its horizontal recovery provenience, as indicated in the left column, and the width of each bar reflects the relative abundance of a type (after Willey 1949:Figure 14).*

are centered in columns such that each column represents a distinct type. Although in operation interdigitation is similar to frequency seriation, the one thing that cannot be violated is the vertical order of the site-specific bars. Otherwise, the principle of ordering is the same as that which guides frequency seriation: Arrange the bars such that the final ordering within each column approximates as closely as possible a unimodal frequency distribution.

Not everyone was clear on actually how to interdigitate percentage-stratigraphy data, but they seem to have understood the basic notion. Martin (1936:108), for example, employed percentage-stratigraphy data from various southwestern areas, and although he attempted to interdigitate these data in order "to work out a correlation between building periods and pottery collected from floors," he had little success. Ford and Willey (1940:136) appear to have published one of the earliest approximations of an interdigitation. They sorted two Louisiana sites, each representing what we would today call a single component, and merely stacked one on top of the other. They did not refer to their effort as interdigitation, but their graph foretold of things to come (O'Brien and Lyman 1998). Drucker (1943a:Figure 44) integrated ceramic-frequency data from four "stratigraphic trenches" excavated in Tres Zapotes in Veracruz, Mexico, but his summary graph shows only the relative positions of the arbitrary levels excavated in each trench rather than type frequencies. Given that he presented the percentage-stratigraphy data for each trench in tabular form (Drucker 1943a:91–99), one could construct a bar graph of interdigitated data if such were desired.

Probably the best-known instance of interdigitation is found in Ford's (1949) study of ceramics from Virú Valley, Peru, though Willey (1953b:10) referred to Ford's efforts as comprising "horizontal stratigraphy or seriation." This was unfortunate, as it no doubt fed the myth that Ford used frequency seriation throughout his career when in fact he rarely used it (Chapter 6). It also was unfortunate that Phillips (1951:109) referred to what we are calling interdigitation as "the method of combining two or more stratigraphic cuts on the same site in a single interpolated seriation." By this wording, "interpolated seriation" is synonymous with interdigitation, and this added to the confusion.

Terminological Confusion

The earliest arrangements of artifact types meant to denote the passage of time were varied in appearance and in the analytical technique used to generate them. Gamio (1913) used what we have termed ceramic stratigraphy, Nelson (1916) used a precursor of percentage stratigraphy, Kidder variously used percentage stratigraphy (Kidder and Kidder 1917) and phyletic seriation (Kidder 1915, 1917), Kroeber (1916a, 1916b) used frequency seriation, and Spier (1917a, 1917b) used both frequency seriation and percentage stratigraphy. As documented in Chapter 6, Ford's 1936 analysis of more than 100 collections of ceramic sherds is often referred to as seriation, but it in fact is not seriation nor is it interdigitation. A good characterization of his work is cross-dating or typological correlation.

We suspect the sorts of terminological ambiguities documented above characterize the innovative periods of any discipline. Attempts by several individuals working somewhat independently to solve an analytical problem result in multiple innovative techniques that are in some ways similar and in other ways distinct. People try to emulate one or more of the innovations without completely understanding them, which in turn produces further innovation. To enhance communication, names are assigned to various innovative techniques, but no one really knows intimately what comprises a particular technique or which term goes with which technique. Confusion results and is perpetuated if no one stops to take stock and tidy up a bit. We hope to have cleaned up some of the terminological ambiguities, but other sorts of ambiguities remain. The remainder of this chapter examines the analytical use of type frequencies to measure time and how those measurements are presented.

Techniques for Studying Changes in Artifact Frequency
Beginning with Numbers

Nelson (1916) presented a table of numbers representing the absolute abundances of pottery types within individual vertical excavation units. Kroeber (1916a, 1916b) and Spier (1917a) presented their data in the form of tables of numbers representing both the absolute and the relative, or proportional, frequencies of their various pottery types within each assemblage. This was a reasonable strategy, but when numerous types and many different collections were involved, seeing the unimodal frequency distributions that were supposed to reflect the popularity principle became difficult. Spier (1917a) calculated a correlation coefficient to show that the frequencies of his types shifted as they should relative to one another, and while this helped, the gen-

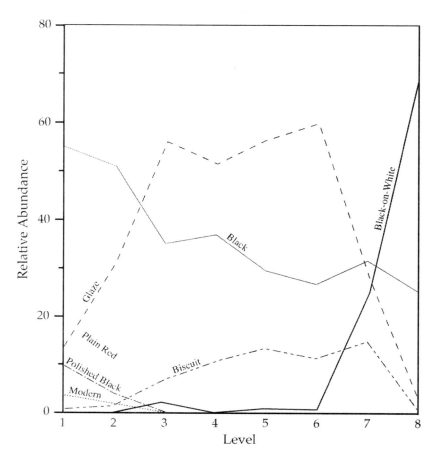

Figure 9.3. A broken-stick graph showing the fluctuating frequencies of ceramic types over "level," or vertical, space (inferred to represent time) (after Kidder and Kidder 1917:Figure 54, cut X).

eral lack of statistical sophistication of the discipline significantly reduced the utility of the strategy.

Kidder (1919:301) found Spier's (1917a) work to comprise "good method" and to be "fundamental." Perhaps not surprisingly, then, Kidder and Kidder (1917) published tables of numbers in which they presented both the absolute and the relative frequency of pottery types arranged against vertical recovery provenience. They then plotted the relative frequencies of these seven types against vertical provenience in what we will call a broken-stick graph but might be better known as a frequency polygon (Figure 9.3). The distributions of some of the types in this and other graphs presented by Kidder and Kidder

(1917) seemed to approximate the popularity principle, but other types did not clearly show unimodal frequency distributions, either because the individual types did not display such distributions or the graph was too busy to allow ready perception of such a distribution. Kidder (1924, 1936b) later abandoned the study of fluctuating frequencies of artifact types.

Tables of numbers provided the raw data, but they were difficult to interpret: One had to track each column of numbers, which represented a style, to determine if that artifact type displayed a unimodal frequency distribution. If the table summarized data for a dozen types and a similar number of collections, reading it was difficult. Take, for example, the first true frequency seriation to be published after 1920 of which we are aware—Kniffen's (1938) seriation of 12 sites in Iberville Parish, Louisiana. Kniffen (1938:200) presented his data in tabular form, replicated here as Table 9.1. This is a particularly complex example because it represents not only a frequency seriation but also Ford's method of arranging collections based on marker types (Chapter 6); the "analysis is based on Ford's criteria" (Kniffen 1938:199). The table contains frequency data for what Ford (1936a) called "marker types"; "other than marker" types, which were characteristic of a "pottery complex" (Chapter 6); and "unrelated," or noncharacteristic, types. Inspection of Table 9.1 suggests the arrangement was based on ordering the Caddo marker type such that it displayed a unimodal frequency distribution, with the exception that the temporally earlier Marksville marker type took precedence when it was present. Other type frequencies merely tagged along and thus typically do not display unimodal frequency distributions. Whatever the particulars of procedure followed to produce the arrangement in Table 9.1, it is difficult to see unimodal frequency distributions of individual types simultaneously.

The Use of Broken-Stick and Diamond Graphs

Kidder and Kidder's (1917) broken-stick graphs were mimicked by some (e.g., Amsden 1931; Collier and Murra 1943; Martin 1936; Reiter 1938a; Schmidt 1928), while others continued to present tables of numbers to demonstrate the popularity principle at work (e.g., Kroeber and Strong 1924; Strong 1925). Other researchers tried different graphic techniques in the 1930s to illustrate percentage-stratigraphy data; some of these, such as Dutton's (1938:90) confusing bar graphs and Nesbitt's (1938:Figure 6) pie diagrams (one per vertically superposed unit), are extremely difficult to read. Many of the graphs generated

Table 9.1. Kniffen's (1938) frequency seriation of sites in Iberville Parish, Louisiana

Site	Natchez M	Natchez OT	Tunica M	Tunica OT	Caddo OT	Bayou Cutler M	Bayou Cutler OT	Coles Creek M	Deasonville M	Deasonville OT	Marksville M	Unrelated
1	5	29	9	6	7		1				1	46
2	19	14	4	13	10		8	1	2	4		28
3	6	11			3	20						61
4			2	9	10	34	36	4		2		4
5	11				3	72	10					9
6	1		1		1	82	5					12
7						84	11	3				
8						86	8	2	1			3
9						86	8	2				5
10						66	15	1	2		2	13
11					4	33	10	15	2	2	17	17
12						27	40				20	14

Note: Natchez, Tunica, and Caddo sherd complexes date to the historic period; the prehistoric complexes are arranged in order from Bayou Cutler (most recent) to Marksville (oldest). Note that relative frequences of sherds represented at each site do not necessarily total 100 percent. M designates marker type(s); OT designates other types; "Unrelated" designates noncharacteristic types.

by frequency seriation and percentage stratigraphy were, however, so similar in appearance that confusion could have been predicted. Such confusion was exacerbated when Ford (1952a:323) remarked that one of the styles of graph he used was formally identical to a "developmental chart which E. B. Sayles [1937] used to show the history of utilitarian stone artifacts in Hohokam. Sayles, in turn, may have adapted this graph style from paleontology." In a footnote associated with this statement, Ford (1952a:323n5) characterized his own development of the graphic technique as a personally "slow and painful process of crystallization" beginning in 1935. Ford began with percentage stratigraphy (Chapter 6) and stuck with it whenever possible, using frequency seriation only when geologically superposed collections were unavailable (e.g., Ford 1949, 1951, 1952a, 1952b). But Ford was not always explicitly clear about which analytical technique he was using (O'Brien and Lyman 1998). Further, there was already some precedence in the use of graphs to illustrate fluctuating frequencies of types through time, and these probably added to the confusion. There initially were two independent developments in the use of graphs—diamond graphs and bar graphs—but neither was founded in frequency seriation.

E. B. Sayles's (1937:118) developmental chart (Figure 9.4)—a diamond graph—illustrates the history of types of stone tools recovered from the Hohokam site of Snaketown in Arizona. It is not a frequency seriation, though it has the general appearance of one; neither is it a graph depicting percentage stratigraphy. Rather, it comprises Sayles's inference of the history of the graphed artifact categories. Five facts make this clear. First, the graph was constructed after the chronology of periods had been established on the basis of Haury's (1937) studies of superposed ceramics. Second, the graphed categories are not stylistic or temporal types but instead are functional, technological, or morphological (descriptive) types. This does not mean they will not monitor the passage of time, but it does reduce the probability that they will display unimodal frequency distributions (Dunnell 1970; Kroeber 1919; Hole and Shaw 1967). Third, the width of the diamonds at any particular horizontal position is meant to denote the popularity of particular artifact categories, but the sum of those widths is never consistently the same from one horizontal position to the next. If actual relative frequencies were graphed, the widths would always sum to the same total width (100 percent). It is unlikely that Sayles was graphing absolute frequencies of raw tallies of each kind of artifact given the fourth fact about his graph: Sayles (1937:113) had no data

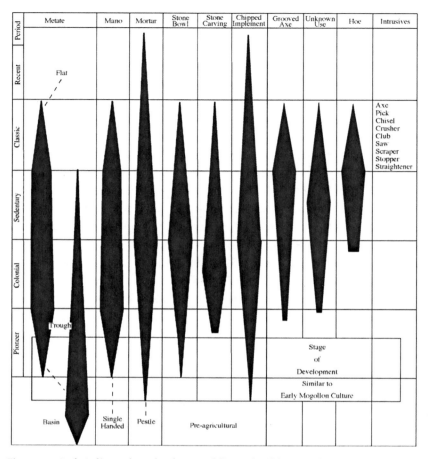

Figure 9.4. Sayles's diamond graph. The sum of diamond widths varies between horizontal positions. This graph comprises Sayles's interpretation of the history of the popularity of the various artifact categories (after Sayles 1937:Figure 48).

from Snaketown for the time period prior to his "Pioneer" period, nor did he have data for his "Recent" time period, yet both are included in the graph. Finally, Sayles presented in tabular form the frequencies of items in the artifact categories he graphed, though the categories in his table (Sayles 1937:Figure 42) do not match precisely those he graphed.

Sayles (1937) cited no references that might have served as an inspiration for his graphic technique. Perhaps he derived the notion from a similar graph published earlier by Ronald Olson (1930), who earned his bachelor's and master's degrees under the advisership of Leslie Spier at the University of Washing-

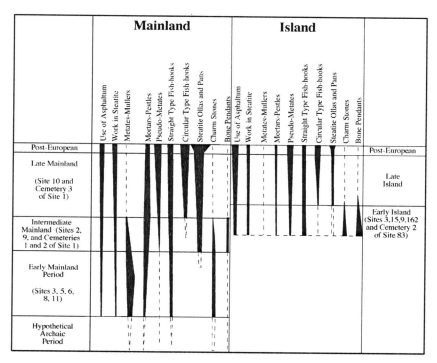

Figure 9.5. Olson's diamond graph, which he labeled "Reconstruction of prehistoric cultural changes." The diamond widths do not sum consistently to the same width between horizontal positions; the graph comprises Olson's interpretation of the popularity of the various types (after Olson 1930:Figure 3).

ton in 1925 and 1926 and then attended the University of California–Berkeley from 1926 to 1929, working under Kroeber's tutelage (Drucker 1981; Stewart 1980). Olson was, therefore, trained in archaeological method by two of the innovators of frequency seriation and percentage stratigraphy. The graph he published in 1930 (Figure 9.5) is the earliest graph of this form of which we are aware. Prior to that time, only broken-stick graphs had been published to illustrate the history of artifact types. Olson, however, cited no references as sources of inspiration for the form of graph he presented, but it is not difficult to surmise that his advisers had a hand in this innovation. Plog (1973:191) referred to a graph of this form as a "seriogram," and we suspect he meant for this term to apply to any form of graph that shows the (empirical or inferential) increase and decrease of a type's frequency.

Olson's graph carries the caption "Reconstruction of prehistoric cultural changes, Chumash area." It is not a frequency seriation for the same reasons that Sayles's is not. First, in both cases the basic chronology was known before the graph was produced. Second, the artifact categories are general functional or descriptive types rather than styles. Third, the widths of the diamond-like figures at any particular horizontal position in the graph do not consistently sum to the same width from one horizontal position to the next. Olson presented only absolute abundances in his data tables, albeit corrected for differences in excavated volumes, and apparently did not calculate relative abundances.

Olson's graph, like Sayles's, is an interpretation of what Olson believed the popularity history of the graphed types to be. The graph indicates, Olson (1930:20–21) said, that some artifact categories "passed out of vogue" and others were "developed"; there "are no indications of sudden or major shifts in pattern of culture"; and there "is long adherence to primitive uniformity in the few objects needed to secure a livelihood." Such interpretations clearly were founded on the popularity principle, but, strangely, here they were applied to functional types, whereas the principle initially had been developed to account for stylistic types. However, even Kroeber (e.g., 1925b) himself regularly confused the two.

Rouse (1939:85–87) graphed the "temporal distributions" of types and the fluctuating frequencies of pottery modes or attributes through time using diamond graphs. He stated that he used "the method called 'seriation' by Spier" to construct a "hypothetical sequence of sites" that was then "tested by means of a . . . combination of both 'seriation' and 'stratigraphy,' to use Spier's terms" (Rouse 1939:28), but in fact seriation was only a small part of what Rouse did. Rouse first sorted sites into two periods on the assumption that those with pottery were later than those without pottery. Then he used the direct historical approach to sort the sites with pottery into a sequence of two periods, placing sites with pottery most like that described historically in the most recent group and sites with pottery less like that historically documented in a middle-period group. He then had three periods. Third, he used the relative abundance of a single presumably late type of pottery to order sites within the middle period, based on the assumption that progressively older sites would have proportionately less and less of that type. This use of a Lyellian curve–like procedure (Chapter 4) gave him four periods. Finally, on the basis of the relative frequency of particular modes, he ordered two sites in the middle period (of the three with pottery) that otherwise seemed contemporaneous. The result was a six-period sequence, and Rouse (1939:75) was explicit that these were "arbitrarily defined," noting that the periods were "numbered instead of named [to emphasize] the arbitrary nature of the [resulting time] scale."

Rouse then calculated the relative frequencies of eight modes per period across the periods. Because the selected modes tended to display unimodal frequency distributions, this, in Rouse's eyes, provided a "statistical validation" of the hypothetical sequence. Finally, he compiled percentage-stratigraphy data for the eight modes with the expectation that "if the postulated sequence were valid . . . the frequencies of each of the eight modes should vary from the bottom to the top levels of single middens in the same directions that they vary [through periods in] the [hypothetical] sequence" (Rouse 1939:69–72). The results, Rouse (1939:71) indicated, "seem to substantiate the validity of the postulated sequence."

Thus Rouse used a combination of analytical techniques to construct, and then another technique to test, a chronological sequence. His diamond graph was meant to show the changing frequencies of modes through the six periods. Rouse (1939:84) stated that he constructed the graph from his data tables. That this graph is an interpretation is clear from several of its features. First, the data tables have no pottery listed in Period I, yet Rouse's graph indicates pottery is present. Second, the diamonds variously expand and contract within periods, when in fact the data in the tables are presented by period, so any graphed change in frequencies should occur at the boundaries between periods.

None of the three graphs discussed above is a direct reflection of empirical data; rather, the graphs represent what the researchers believed the frequency distribution of types or modes to be through time. Others who produced such graphs (e.g., Beardsley 1948:Figure 2; Carter 1941:Figure 24; Heizer and Fenenga 1939:Chart 2) also tended to use them to present their interpretations rather than as devices by which empirical data might be summarized. For example, Ford (1949, 1952a) used diamond graphs, but he did so exactly as his predecessors had done. Ford's graphs had a basis in empirical data, but they were interpretations that diverged to varying degrees from the reality of those data, as Spaulding (1953) did not hesitate to point out.

The Use of Centered-Bar Graphs

The use of diamond graphs by culture historians was eclipsed by the use of bar graphs, which often were employed in conjunction with both frequency seriation and percentage stratigraphy. This contributed to the confusion of these two distinct analytical techniques. The history of the use of what we are calling bar graphs is complex. Bar graphs appear to have originated with Ford, but they were used by Martin and others at virtually the same time. We begin with Ford's work and that of some of his colleagues and then turn to Martin's efforts.

Working at a small site in Louisiana in 1934, Ford (1935a:6) excavated in arbitrary levels, the thicknesses of which varied as he attempted to collect from each "an appreciable amount of material." He knew which ceramic types comprised various "decoration complexes"—knowledge based in part on the corresponding geographic distributions of those types and the historical distributions of distinct ethnic groups; these were his "complex markers," or "marker types." He plotted the relative frequencies of these marker types, plus other, nondiagnostic types, against their vertical provenience (Figure 9.6). This was an early version of a bar graph used in the service of percentage stratigraphy. Note that the width of the bars is a graphic representation of data, not an interpretation. Thus the bars shift widths only at the horizontal boundaries that separate them into vertically discrete units, and their widths always sum to 100 percent within a period and between periods. Ford's use of bar graphs expanded a few years later when he presented nearly all of the percentage-stratigraphy data from an extensively excavated site with such graphs (Ford and Quimby 1945). He did not interdigitate the various excavation units to derive an overall chronology for the site, probably because it appeared to represent what later became known as a single-component site. It probably was Ford's graphic method, however, that inspired one of his collaborators to produce the first bar graph that might be thought of as representing a frequency seriation.

In 1942 George Quimby, who had been working with Ford for several years (O'Brien and Lyman 1998), presented a paper that was published the following year. Quimby (1943:543) noted that his purpose was "to construct a synthetic chronology as a temporal frame within which to view the ceramic content of a prehistoric Indian culture complex called the Goodall focus."

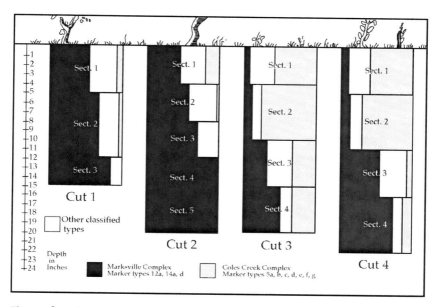

Figure 9.6. Ford's graph of percentage-stratigraphy data. Each column represents a unique horizontal location; different shading represents different types; and the widths of each set of bars in a row within a column sum to 100 percent (after Ford 1935a:Figure 9).

The geographic distribution of the 10 "components" in the general area of southwestern Michigan known to belong to this focus suggested a north-south trend in the "distribution, frequency, and cultural similarity [of] traits" (Quimby 1943:545). Quimby reasoned that perhaps this geographic trend was also chronological if diffusion were involved. He then ordered the relative frequencies of pottery types using each latitudinally designated area as a "period" and lumping components within each. The basis of the ordering was geographic location. He presented not only the absolute abundances of each pottery type in tabular form but also a bar graph, each bar segment representing "the percentages of the pottery types by periods" (Quimby 1943:546) and, we might add, by latitude.

Quimby's (1943:Figure 2) graph is reproduced, with the addition of an indication of latitude, here as Figure 9.7. Quimby (1943:546) interpreted the graph as indicative of the passage of time when he spoke of the "persistent [occurrence of one type] throughout all four periods" and the "waning" or "declining popularity" of another type. Quimby was interpreting the units as if they were like those modeled in column A of Figure 4.6 and column B in Figure

6.2. Is his graph a frequency seriation, given that the basis of the ordering was geographic location and a presumed direction of diffusion rather than frequencies of the artifacts? In the strict wording of the definition we provide above, it is not. However, it is close to being such a seriation if one realizes that the graph illustrates a case of what Deetz and Dethlefsen (1965) two decades later termed the Doppler Effect, at least insofar as Quimby was correct to suggest that diffusion was playing a role. Quimby's graph not only must be considered in the history of graphic techniques for summarizing the changing frequencies of artifact types through time, but it also must be considered in the history of frequency seriation. He knew he was monitoring spatial difference, and he presumed he also was measuring temporal difference, given his thoughts about the role of diffusion. Explicit recognition that one had to control for geographic space in order to help ensure that only time was being measured was, at the time Quimby wrote, only then emerging. As Willey (1940:675), for example, noted, "age-area implications are a potential factor" influencing the fluctuating frequencies of types.

Quimby's graph was a summary rendition of empirical data. In this respect, it aligns with Ford's bar graphs of percentage-stratigraphy data. Ford (1951, 1952a; Ford et al. 1955; Phillips et al. 1951) continued to produce such graphs in the 1950s, all of them founded on and illustrating in summary fashion percentage-stratigraphy data, much of it interdigitated to produce a master chronology. These graphs were the source of Ford's interpretations of culture history; rarely did he produce a diamond graph as an interpretation (e.g., Ford 1949:Figure 8, 1952a). Only a very small portion of one graph produced by Ford is, strictly speaking, a frequency seriation, and this was meant to fill a gap in the master chronology produced by interdigitation of percentage-stratigraphy data from the VirúValley (Ford 1949:Figure 4). The only major frequency seriation involving Ford's data was done by Bennyhoff (1952), who, much to Ford's (1952b) consternation, ignored the fact that much of Ford's data that Bennyhoff seriated came from superposed contexts. Frequency seriation produced graphs of "more handsome appearance" than Ford's (1952b:250)—and the popularity principle is much more obvious in Bennyhoff's graph than in Ford's—but Bennyhoff's graph violated the temporal implications of superposition and the rule of interdigitation that the known superposed relationships of collections should not be ignored or reversed.

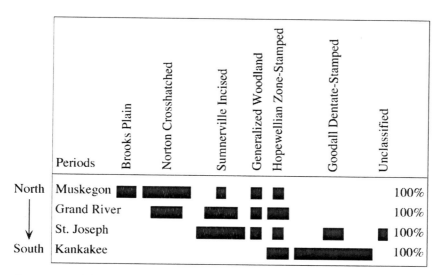

Figure 9.7. Quimby's seriation based on geographic space. Compare with the model of units in column A of Figure 4.6. Bar widths in each row sum to 100 percent (after Quimby 1943:Figure 2).

Martin (1936) initially used broken-stick graphs to report percentage-stratigraphy data, and why he shifted to a form of bar graph within a few years (Martin 1938, 1939) is not clear. Whatever the reason, he did not interdigitate his data because he could detect "no consistent variations or periodic fluctuations" (Martin 1938:276; see also Martin 1939:454). A few years later he again used a bar graph to illustrate the relative frequency of various artifact types from different proveniences of a single site (Martin 1943:Figure 91; Martin and Rinaldo 1947:Figure 125). Interestingly, the caption of one of these graphs includes the statement, "Chart devised by Don Lehmer" (Martin 1943:245). The word "devised" implies the graph was Lehmer's innovation, yet Martin had earlier published identical graphs.

After additional years of work and a better understanding of the cultural chronology where he was working, Martin still did not know some of the particular details. He wrote, "In seeking, then, trends within [frequencies of] pottery types and any other significant observations that might accrue from a comprehensive visual presentation of data, we decided to employ a graphic method similar to that used by James A. Ford and others in their studies of archaeology of the southeastern United States (Ford and Willey 1940; Ford and Quimby 1945)" (Martin et al. 1949:196). Prior to that time, the bars denoting relative frequencies in Martin's graphs had been right aligned; now, they were centered in a column, just as Ford's graphs of the early 1940s were. Not only was Martin et al.'s (1949:Figure 71) resultant graph a frequency seriation of assemblages of pottery, each from a different house floor, they called it a seriation: "What we have attempted . . . is a seriation of house units based on pottery percentages. . . . In making the graph no consideration was given to sites, phases, tree-ring dates or other knowledge" (Martin et al. 1949:196–197). After the seriation had been performed, whether the resulting order reflected the passage of time was tested and confirmed by tree-ring dates and stratigraphy.

The frequency seriation rendered as a bar graph by Martin et al. (1949) was modified slightly a year later when Martin and Rinaldo (1950b:Figure 141) added some new data. A portion of the graph, reproduced here as Figure 9.8, was published in a subsequent paper, again with modifications in light of newly acquired data (Martin and Rinaldo 1950a:Figure 216). Just prior to the publication of these later two frequency seriations, Rinaldo (1950) published a frequency seriation for materials in a nearby area. His discussion echoes that of Martin et al. (1949) and adds details. Rinaldo (1950:94) reported that the technique used "was a variation on a graphic method used by James Ford and others in their studies of archaeology of the southeastern United States (Ford and Willey 1940; Ford and Quimby 1945)." But he also followed this sentence with the statement, "Such a method is not foreign to the Southwest as it is essentially the classical type of seriation that Spier used in his '[An] Outline for [a] Chronology of Zuñi Ruins.' However, in our graph it is represented in a column-wedge type graph similar to that used by Haury and Sayles in illustrating relative frequencies of artifact types through time at Snaketown (Gladwin et al. 1937)." Rinaldo was correct; his seriation (and those of Martin) was founded on the same—popularity—principle as Spier's, a principle that began with Kroeber and Nelson. He also correctly noted that the graphic technique had been borrowed. But Rinaldo was incorrect in another respect; as we noted earlier, what Sayles did was not at all similar to what Kroeber, Spier, or Rinaldo and Martin did, either analytically or conceptually.

Graphing Culture Change

There were, to be sure, variations in the graphic techniques used to display what had been observed. Webb and DeJarnette (1942) plotted absolute frequencies of various artifact categories against arbitrary levels (depth) in a histogram, the bars being right aligned. Beals et al. (1945) used percentage

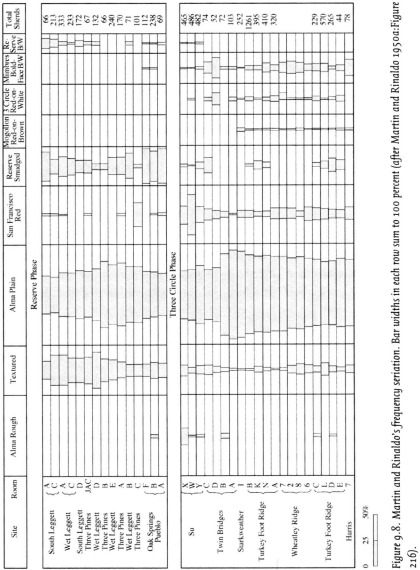

Figure 9.8. Martin and Rinaldo's frequency seriation. Bar widths in each row sum to 100 percent (after Martin and Rinaldo 1950a:Figure 216).

stratigraphy to develop a chronology, and they drew a new form of broken-stick graph with the lines denoting frequency drawn so as not to cross one another and the cumulative areas under them summing to 100 percent; they drew bar graphs; and they phyletically seriated design elements of their pottery. Some archaeologists continued to use tables of numbers to present percentage-stratigraphy data (e.g., Bird 1943; Drucker 1943a, 1943b; Ekholm 1944; Rowe 1944). As mentioned earlier, Martin and Rinaldo did true seriations without the aid of superposition and without interdigitation to help order collections. They and their associates continued to do so through the 1950s, producing numerous bar graphs like those in Figure 9.8 (Bluhm 1957:Figure 13; Martin et al. 1956:Figure 71; Martin et al. 1957:Figure 52; Rinaldo 1959:Figure 119). But some who published in the series where these papers appeared used similar graphs to illustrate percentage-stratigraphy data and to create a chronology, referring to the data presented in those graphs as "seriation data" (Spoehr 1957:124) and the analytical technique used as "seriation of sherd units from refuse deposits" (Collier 1955:101).

Ritchie and MacNeish (1949:99) knew the basic sequence of pre-Iroquoian "cultures" in New York based on "previous stratigraphic evidence." They used frequency seriation—what they referred to as "the actual process of seriation"—to arrange various assemblages within each of those cultures, noting that the basic assumption of the procedure was that "closely comparable [relative frequency] values [of types] indicated a corresponding proximity in time and space" (Ritchie and MacNeish 1949:99). They also noted that "the materials are arranged in overlapping or interdigitating sequence" (Ritchie and MacNeish 1949:98), but they did not use superposition to help with the integration of the various assemblages. Their graphs consist of right-aligned bars, the widths of which denote the relative frequencies of types. That same year, Willey (1949) published his interdigitated percentage-stratigraphy data (Figure 9.2). The simultaneous publication of these two reports in which the term "interdigitation" was used probably contributed to its abandonment, because in Ritchie and MacNeish's case it was part of the analytical process of frequency seriation, whereas in Willey's case it was part of the process of integrating percentage-stratigraphy data from different sites.

Strong and Evans (1952) produced a ceramic chronology for the Virú Valley based on interdigitated percentage-stratigraphy data. The caption associated with their figure reads, in part, "Correlation chart of the ceramic stratigraphy of . . . sherds" (Strong and Evans 1952:Figure 34). This graph is very similar in appearance and identical in the way it was constructed to Ford's (1949) earlier ones for the VirúValley. Collier's (1955:Figures 46 and 47) bar graphs of interdigitated percentage-stratigraphy data appeared a few years later, at the same time that Evans's (1955:Figure 11) bar graphs of interdigitated percentage-stratigraphy data did. Both authors smoothed the bar graphs with dotted lines, just as Ford (1949, 1951, 1952a) had done earlier, but only Ford's graphs for the Southeast were the subject of Spaulding's (1953) wrath. Brainerd (1951) and Robinson (1951) had just published their discussions of a statistical technique for sorting collections, and Spaulding thought such a technique was much more objective and would produce more accurate results than Ford's procedure of visually sorting bars of various widths.

Terminological confusion was rampant in the 1950s. Evans (1955:Figure 11), for example, used interdigitated percentage-stratigraphy data from various sites to derive an overall sequence, but he then used that sequence to help determine the direction of time's flow by employing frequency seriation to sort and arrange collections from other sites. As he noted, "Good and meaningful seriation cannot be attained without some method that will indicate absolutely which is the top and which is the bottom of the seriated sequence" (Evans 1955:77). He used percentage-stratigraphy data, just as Spier (1917a, 1917b) had done 40 years earlier, to determine which end of his seriation was up. His bar graphs of seriated and percentage-stratigraphy data were, however, so similar in appearance that confusion over which was which was a predictable result. A few years later Ford (1962:Figure 1) himself categorized Evans's work as frequency seriation only. Meggers and Evans (1957) and Evans and Meggers (1960) published numerous bar graphs, some representing frequency seriations, some interdigitated percentage-stratigraphy data; virtually all were termed seriations.

Sloppy use of terms in conjunction with similarities of graphs depicting changing frequencies of artifact types contributed to the confusion of frequency seriation and interdigitated percentage-stratigraphy data and to the myth that Ford regularly seriated artifact collections. We believe Ford himself contributed to both. In his retrospective overview, Ford stated:

> In the second decade of this century the idea became current that quantities of [types] of material found should be listed, and "Percentage

Stratigraphy" almost became a fad. Proportions were graphed as well as tabulated, but there was as yet no idea that these frequencies might be a reflection of cultural phenomena. "Percentage Stratigraphy" was looked upon as somewhat inferior to clear-cut superposition [which consisted of] finding one culture or cultural phase superimposed over another with clear differentiation between the two.

The use of popularity curves of types, and the construction of chronologies by discovering the frequency patterns formed by types, developed in the 1930's and has become increasingly popular, particularly in the work of American archaeologists [Ford 1962:5.]

What Ford meant by the term "percentage stratigraphy" is similar to the way in which we have defined it. Ford (1962:4) also correctly attributed the introduction of frequency seriation in American archaeology to Kroeber, but he incorrectly attributed the invention of the technique by Kroeber to the influence of Petrie and Uhle (Chapters 4 and 8). Ford (1962) failed to keep the distinction between percentage stratigraphy and frequency seriation straight in his history of the techniques. He incorrectly linked his own early work (Ford 1936a) with Spier's (1917b); as we argued in Chapter 6, what Ford did was to sort surface collections into periods based on index fossils—periods founded on percentage-stratigraphy data—and he did not order those assemblages within the periods. Spier (1917a, 1917b) used percentage-stratigraphy data to confirm the temporal significance of his frequency seriations of surface collections. Ford (1962) also incorrectly categorized Vaillant's (e.g., 1930, 1931) work as involving percentage stratigraphy. In our view (Lyman et al. 1997b), Vaillant's work was founded on index fossils and ceramic stratigraphy; he presented frequencies of types after the basic sequence had been worked out, but merely to show the abundances of various types within particular periods.

Ford relied heavily on percentage-stratigraphy data and never on frequency seriation alone to construct a chronology. To attribute the use of frequency seriation to him is incorrect; to attribute popularizing it as an analytical technique to him is more correct. That popularity was the result of his clearly readable percentage-stratigraphy graphs, not his use of frequency seriation. The waxing and waning popularity of a type was clearly visible in the bar graphs Ford pioneered. Those graphs were empirical, unlike the diamond graphs of Olson (1930), Sayles (1937), Rouse (1939), and others. As

Bennyhoff (1952:231) indicated regarding the chronology for the VirúValley, Ford's "ingenious graphic presentations of data are of general interest to archaeologists and can be expected to influence students of prehistory working in fields other than Peru." The references cited in this chapter indicate that Bennyhoff's prediction came true, but not without the cost of an extremely confusing terminology.

Studying Culture Change

In a recently published encyclopedia of archaeology, seriation is described as follows:

> Seriation includes a number of relative dating techniques . . . . based on a reconstruction of typological or stylistic changes in material culture through time. . . .
>
> To construct the seriation for an area, stratified sites usually are examined. By examining typological or stylistic shifts from the different strata, these changes can be placed in a relative chronological order. Once the seriation of an area is unraveled at a single or several stratified sites, it can be used to place other sites into a regional temporal ordering through [artifact] cross-dating [Stone 1996:634].

As should be clear from our discussion in this chapter, we find such a characterization of seriation to be not only ambiguous but also incorrect. It conflates several distinct analytical techniques, thereby leading to confusion regarding the history of the discipline and how particular chronological problems might be solved.

Martin and Rinaldo should be recognized for their innovative frequency seriations, whereas Ford should be credited for his innovative graphic technique, with the qualification that Ford was graphing percentage-stratigraphy data. That the graphs of Ford and of Martin and Rinaldo had very similar appearances and displayed the popularity principle in concise and clearly perceptible fashion no doubt contributed to the confusion among the techniques of frequency seriation, percentage stratigraphy, and interdigitation. Focusing only on the overall appearance of such graphs misses the critical distinction of the artifact-frequency data and procedures used to order them.

Frequency seriation, percentage stratigraphy, and interdigitation are interrelated through their common adherence to the popularity principle—each historical type will have a continuous distribution through time and display a single waxing and waning. Otherwise, they are distinct. Frequency seriation, on the one hand, is not phyletic seriation. It arranges collections on the basis of attributes internal to the collections—specifically, the frequencies of types—which phyletic seriation ignores. Some attribute external to the collections, such as superposition or another source of chronological data, must be called upon to determine the direction of time's flow. On the other hand, percentage stratigraphy in conjunction with interdigitation arranges collections largely on the basis of attributes external to the collections—their superposed positions. It precludes the necessity of determining the direction of time's flow after the arrangement is completed because that is already known on the basis that superposition not only monitors order of deposition but also (inferentially) the age of deposited particles, including artifacts. The inferred age of artifacts is of course potentially incorrect, but the net result seems to have been that ordering collections according to the popularity principle and thus on the basis of the frequencies of artifact types minimally demanded appropriately defined types (something Kroeber struggled with mightily in his seminal frequency seriations, as shown in Chapter 5), calculation of relative frequencies of types, and (prior to the computer age) some manual sorting of frequencies. It was a lot easier simply to note where artifacts fell in a stratified column of sediment because that procedure really did not require appropriately defined types that displayed unimodal frequency distributions because stratification had already sorted the frequencies of types. It came to matter little that the type frequencies ordered by stratification might not be unimodal distributions (e.g., Binford 1968; Collins 1965; Mellars 1965).

That the results of both frequency seriation and interdigitated percentage-stratigraphy data can be presented in similar form graphically should no longer cause us to think that the analytical steps in both are identical or that creating an ordering based on frequency seriation involves the use of superposition as a principle of arrangement. Perhaps unfortunately, in adopting stratified deposits as the chronometer of choice, archaeologists not only discarded the more strictly artifact-based chronometers such as the various seriation techniques, but they also forgot the critical nature of that most significant step in the entire procedure—artifact classification, the topic we conclude with in the next chapter.

10. Artifact Classification and Artifact-Based Chronometry

Several years ago we wrote a book in which we discussed how to apply several of the chronometers discussed in the preceding chapters (O'Brien and Lyman 1999c). As in *Measuring Time with Artifacts*, in that earlier book we focused on what are known as relative-dating methods. These methods measure time on an ordinal—greater than, less than—scale. The difference in age of two events is unknown when such methods are used; rather, we know only whether one event is older (or younger) than another. A plethora of books on archaeological dating methods has been produced over the past several decades. Virtually without fail these books concern what are typically referred to as absolute-dating methods, which measure time on an interval scale such that we know that the difference in age of two events is, say, 1,000 years, as well as that one event occurred about 3500 BC and the other occurred about 2500 BC. Given that absolute, or fine-scale, chronometric resolution and precision are not always available, and in light of the few pages in books on archaeological dating methods devoted to ordinal-scale chronometry, we thought that it was necessary to produce a textbook on the methods of relative dating. Similar thinking was behind the production of this book on the histories of various methods of relative dating.

To be sure, there are histories of various absolute and relative chronometers (see chapters and references in Nash 2000 and Truncer 2003). In our view those histories focus on documenting what happened when and where and who was involved, and they devote less time to exploring the why of archaeological chronometers. We hasten to add that by the "why" of archaeological chronometers we do not mean that the authors of those histories have ignored the reason(s) for the invention of a particular chronometer. Rather, we mean that they have not explored the epistemology and ontology of a chronometer from a historical perspective. We have in mind such things as the requirement of a chronometer identified by Gould (1987) and described in Chapter 5. A "chronometer of history has one, and only one, rigid requirement—something must be found that changes in a recognizable and irreversible way through time, so that each historical moment bears a distinctive signature" (Gould 1987:157). Fulfilling that requirement involves epistemology and largely involves designing units—in most cases cultural traits or artifact types—that serve as temporal signatures. Another property of the why of archaeological chronometry is the underpinning ontology; in the case of the chronometers discussed here, that property resides in the process of cultural transmission. As in biological evolution, the mere process of cultural transmission typically is less than perfect, and thus fidelity of replication is imperfect. This results in "genetically related" phenomena that occur at different times having different, often (but not always) unique, characteristics. If those characteristics are indeed unique, they constitute temporally "distinctive signatures."

Because cultural transmission is not identical to genetic transmission, chronometric results based on artifacts are not as straightforward to interpret as one might hope. As we observed in Chapter 7, biologists in general and paleobiologists in particular have Dollo's law, which states that characters and character states that occur at one time do not recur in exactly the same form at another time. Biological evolution is, under this law, irreversible. Anthropologists and archaeologists do not seem to be aware of this law; at least they have not applied it or a version of it to cultural phenomena. Instead, as we documented in Chapter 2, they have worried about the possibility of horizontal (within a generation) transmission at least muting and at worst (the typical presumption) totally obscuring any phylogenetic signal that might be apparent in arrays of cultural traits. Hindsight is, of course, 20-20, and so it is easy to suggest that if archaeologists had but paid closer attention to the related discipline of paleontology, they might have picked up on the subtle point of Dollo's law that we noted in Chapter 7. That point is that Dollo was concerned with inferring phylogeny and thus distinguished between convergence (analogous similarity) and shared ancestry (homologous similarity) within a specific model of descent with modification. Recurrence and, by simple extension of reasoning, convergence might be analytically discernible if phenomena were classified appropriately.

Kroeber (1931b, 1943) attempted to introduce the distinction between analogous and homologous traits to anthropology but with little effect. How much his failure to clarify the role of ancestral traits in reckoning phylogeny played in that lack of effect is unclear, though again with hindsight we suspect it may have contributed at least somewhat. Another reason his caution went largely unheeded is that when he first made his suggestion (Kroeber 1931b), anything remotely explicit with respect to evolution in general was already anathema in anthropology. When he reiterated his caution a decade later (Kroeber 1943), any hint of Darwinian ontology was being replaced by Spencerian thinking at the hands of White (Chapters 2 and 7). These events are important to understanding our discipline's history.

There are other interrelated and multifaceted reasons for producing a book on the history of archaeological chronometers that measure time on an ordinal scale. We turn to them in the next section. This leads in turn to a consideration of what we have learned from our historical studies of archaeology's relative chronometers. A final brief consideration of the important role of classification in artifact-based chronometers is then presented. Returning to a theme we introduced in Chapter 1, we conclude with a very brief statement on the relationship of this volume to our own agenda for archaeology.

Why Should We Care about the History of Archaeological Chronometry?

Virtually ever since the term "archaeologists" could be applied to a group of individuals who studied the remote past, archaeologists have considered the archaeological record—the stuff (usually "artifacts" of various scales) out there to be studied and the structure (contexts, associations, spatial arrangements) in which the stuff occurs—to constitute three dimensions of variation (Spaulding 1960; Willey 1953a): form, space, and time. Which artifact forms exist? Where do particular forms occur geographically? When were particular forms made and used? The first two dimensions are readily and directly visible; the last is invisible because the archaeological record is a modern phenomenon. Archaeologists are interested in when items were made and used; therefore the time dimension must be made visible analytically. Prior to the development of dendrochronological methods in the 1920s and radiocarbon dating in the late 1940s, the only methods of determining an artifact's age involved consideration of the form of that artifact, the artifact's position in a stratified column of sediment, and whether it occurred historically or only pre-historically. These, then, were the methods that were pursued and developed by archaeologists. Even though time could be measured only on an ordinal scale—often perceived as a disadvantage—this was better than not being able to measure time at all. In addition, there was an attendant advantage to these methods over some of the absolute-dating methods developed later.

The advantage just mentioned constitutes the second reason for producing this book. The artifact-based chronometers we have discussed here comprise what are known as direct-dating techniques. By this is meant the fact that the target event—the event whose age we seek—is also the dated event (Dean 1978). Most absolute chronometers are indirect-dating techniques; such techniques date an event (the dated event) that is somehow (usually stratigraphically, hopefully temporally) associated with the target event. The target event is only "indirectly" dated because one must assume that the associated "dated" event is of at least approximately if not exactly the same age as the target event. On the one hand, radiocarbon dating can be a direct-dating technique if the dated material is tissue from an organism and we wish to know when that organism was alive. If, on the other hand, we want to know the age of a projectile point or pottery sherd (target item) that is stratigraphically associated with the organic tissue that is dated (dated item), then radiocarbon dating is an indirect-dating technique. It should be clear from our discussions in preceding chapters that, by and large, the artifact-based chronometers we have discussed are direct-dating techniques because the manufacture of an artifact (and its subsequent, more or less immediate use) is dated by the coalescence of the attributes making up the artifact or by the aggregation and deposition of the set of artifacts making up the collection that is dated (hence our use of the term "artifact-based" chronometers). The creation of the dated event is what is dated, and that event is the creation of the artifact or assemblage. The dated event is the target event; hence many of the chronometers discussed in preceding chapters involve direct dating.

The first reason to write this book was to explore the ontology and epistemology of artifact-based chronometry within a historical perspective. The second reason was to highlight the perhaps seldom appreciated fact that artifact-based chronometers are typically only ordinal scale, but they are also direct-dating techniques and therefore are unlike more familiar absolute-dating techniques that typically are indirect methods of dating. The third reason for this book, then, was to underscore the fact that several of the chronometers we have discussed measure time fairly continuously. The direct historical approach (Chapter 7), frequency seriation (Chapters 4 and 5), and various forms of time-series analysis (Chapter 5), such as percentage stratigraphy, fall into this group. Marker types, as we showed in Chapter 6, tend to measure time less continuously because they often include periods of time of relatively short duration, although there is no reason they could not be designed to measure periods of longer duration. Stratigraphic excavation (Chapter 8) tends to fall more toward the pole of measuring time discontinuously because each of what are often termed "assemblages" of artifacts derives from a distinct stratum or unit of deposition, such as an arbitrary metric level, and is treated as a synchronic unit with a mean or average age. The same can happen with each assemblage of artifacts that plays a role in frequency seriation or each aggregate of cultural traits specified in an analysis using the direct historical approach as a chronometer. Stability is artificially input to each assemblage by the grouping process, which perforce makes each artifact or trait synchronous with every other one in the assemblage. Change is forced to occur at the boundaries between assemblages (Plog 1974).

Time averaging produces what are today variously referred to as coarse-grained or palimpsest assemblages. The former concerns an aggregate of artifacts, features, and so on that is the product of multiple events such that the relationship between an event and a set of artifacts is obscure; the latter is a coarse-grained assemblage that also owes some of its properties to nonhuman agents of assemblages formation (after Binford 1980). Of course, whether an assemblage of artifacts is accurately characterized by either of these labels depends on the temporal scale of the research question(s) being asked, a fact recognized some time ago (Brooks 1982) but seldom explicitly acknowledged subsequently. To assist in making the point about grain, consider that typing this sentence took several seconds, that it involved multiple events known as key strokes, and that it is but one small part of this entire volume. What is the temporal scale of the assemblage of letters making up the preceding aggregate of letters we call a sentence? From the perspective of the time it took to perform the individual keystrokes and create the individual letters, the assemblage is coarse-grained. From the perspective of the sentence, the temporal scale of the assemblage of letters is equivalent to that of the sentence. From the perspective of the book in which the sentence occurs, the temporal scale of the assemblage of letters (the sentence) is perhaps too fine to be of analytical use because the sentence represents but an instant in time relative to the time it took to write the entire book. In sum, whether something is coarse-grained with respect to temporal resolution is a function of the perspective one takes; in research endeavors that perspective will be dictated by the question(s) being asked.

Lessons Learned

The preceding point regarding temporal scale or grain is one of several important lessons that we have learned from studying the history of archaeological chronometers. The scale or resolution of our chronometers depends at least in part on the units that attend them and in part on the scale of event under consideration and its larger temporal context. More generally, detailed historical analysis focusing on the why of chronometry shows us not only how but why various chronometers work the way they do. This should ensure against the misuse and abuse of those chronometers in the future or the confusion of one with another, such as when seriation and percentage stratigraphy are confused because of similar graphing conventions (Chapter 9). It may also eventually result in innovative improvements to one or more of these chronometers or perhaps even the invention of a new chronometer. It seems to us, for example, that Kroeber's development of frequency seriation was informed by an implicit notion of how the direct historical approach works. Simply put, frequency seriation and the direct historical approach both work on the basis of the principle of overlapping, the principle that also underpinned Nelson's search for linkages between stratigraphically superposed assemblages.

Another thing we have learned is that Kroeber's work with hem lengths and other features of women's clothing represents an early time-series analysis of character states of artifacts. This means of temporal analysis has seldom been replicated in the archaeological literature (see Braun 1985 for a notable exception), yet it, along with the various graphing methods discussed in Chapter 9, remains a straightforward tool for analysis as well as for presenting research results. As Fred Plog (1973:191) noted more than three decades ago, archaeologists typically use what we term centered-bar graphs in a synchronic fashion—"We seriate in order to date the archeological units from which the artifacts were taken"—even though such a graph "is a record of the adoption of technological innovations over time." Plog was arguing that what he termed a "seriogram" (the example he shows is what we referred to in Chapter 9 as a diamond graph) could serve the analytical and interpretive function of a time-series analysis, with the advantage that the rate of adoption of forms relative to the discontinuance (or stability) of use of other forms could be simultaneously monitored. We agree with his conclusion that "we have failed to realize [frequency seriation's] diachronic potential and have emphasized [its] synchronic applications" (Plog 1973:192).

We are aware of very few seriograms in the literature (e.g., Binford 1968; Collins 1965; Mellars 1965) but note that they are valuable because it does not take much thought to figure out what they show. If you are comfortable with the vertical dimension representing time passing from bottom to top (a throwback to the principle of superposition and diachronic time), with phenomena plotted in the same row being from the same assemblage (a throwback to the principle of association and synchronic time), and with a column representing the same type or class of phenomena regardless of vertical location of plotted phenomena, then a seriogram shows at a glance what was going on in terms of the history of the plotted phenomena.

One lesson we learned is that "ancient," seemingly outmoded (low-tech) analytical techniques might be of value in today's high-tech world. Another is that the data contained in some of the seminal discussions of those an-cient methods are still useful. Kroeber's hem-length data could be useful for teaching time-series analysis to students; it might also be useful for exploring various aspects of culture change and process when modern analytical tech-niques are applied to it (e.g., Lowe and Lowe 1982). These data might assist in exploring nuances of various analytical techniques, such as we argued in Chapter 5 with respect to the effect of the temporal duration of artifact assem-blages on the result of a frequency seriation. Indeed, it is this last point—the influence of analytical units that attend artifact-based chronometers—that we have attempted to focus on in this book. First, the resolution and precision of measurement of time with artifacts depend on how those items are classi-fied; second, different chronometers demand different units, as the models in Figures 4.6 and 6.3 make clear. We return to this point below.

We know that overlapping is critical to the successful application of the direct historical approach and frequency seriation. It is not really required of time-series analysis or stratigraphic excavation, though in some cases it is in the latter, depending on the purpose of the excavation—is it to confirm the chronological implications of a frequency seriation, or is it merely to establish which artifact type came first, which came second, and so on? Nor is overlapping critically important to the use of marker types, though here one might make the case that overlapping is manifest as the sharing of one or a few marker types between assemblages placed in the same period. This sort of sharing underpins cross-dating (Patterson 1963) and also biostratigraphy (Eldredge and Gould 1977). In neither is a form of vertical transmission necessary (Eldredge and Gould 1977), and as implied by Lyellian curves (Chapter 4), the possibility of evolutionary transitions from one form to another is in some ways virtually antithetical to cross dating and the use of index fossils or marker types.

One significant lesson we learned from the history of archaeological chronometry is the important role of theory. Any success enjoyed by the chronometers we discuss clearly is the result of their foundation on the basic notion of descent with modification, regardless of the source of the variation or the mechanism(s) that sorts variants and leads to their differential replication over time. Without a thorough and explicit exploration of that theory during the peak period of use of the chronometers under consideration, it is no wonder that, at the time, some individuals expressed skepticism regarding their applicability, their utility, or their validity (e.g., Phillips et al. 1951; Spaulding 1953). Nor are we particularly surprised by such skepticism even today. Lack of understanding or knowledge of the basics of how these analytical tools work—and that is surely all that they are—is no legitimate grounds for dismissal or distrust.

Units, Again

In several places in the book we have underscored the importance of chronometric units. The epistemological difficulty with artifact-based chronometers is determination of which units—artifact types—serve as chronological signatures among any given set of artifacts, whether from one site or from multiple sites, from excavations or from surface collections. The means of determining those signatures depends, whether we realize it or not, on our ontology. Is change conceived of as continuous (materialism) or discontinuous (essentialism)? Without conscious awareness of your own ontology, you will probably struggle with building chronometric units. Excellent examples of the epistemological difficulty and the lack of an explicit ontological basis reside in Kroeber's (Chapter 5) grappling with pottery types at Zuni, Nelson's (Chapter

8) efforts to find linkages between stratigraphically superposed collections of artifacts, and Ford's (Chapter 6) design of marker types. We modeled what various of these units look like in preceding chapters (Figures 2.1, 4.6, and 6.2). Because building units is, in our view, one of the most critical issues facing any research endeavor—we often tell our students that various analytical and conceptual problems and disagreements reduce to a classification problem—we take the opportunity in the next few pages to touch on it one final time.

To begin, let us presume we adopt the materialist ontology. A population of phenomena that are somehow related "evolves" through time by processes of transmission, some (usually minor) degree of lack of fidelity of replication, and sorting processes (differential replication of variants over time). Ford (1962) presented a great archaeological model of part of this combination of processes, and we show that model in Figure 10.1. Each of the three illustrated lineages comprises a phyletic seriation or time-series analysis (depending on whether the age of each illustrated specimen was known a priori). Heritable continuity between each pottery type is implied but difficult to perceive directly. This model can be redrawn more conceptually, as in Figure 10.2. The shaded area represents a lineage as manifested by empirical specimens; its overall change in horizontal position over vertical space represents temporal change in form. If this were a biological lineage, each vertically discrete piece—bounded by dashed lines—or several contiguous pieces of the lineage would be termed a "chronospecies" (Pearson 1998). Specimens representing the lineage are sorted on the basis of their temporal (usually stratigraphic) propinquity, and each set of specimens so designated is described in terms of one or more attributes. Descriptions of each unit are derived from the set of specimens polled and often are written as statements of central tendency. Summaries of data generated are rendered as averages of each set of specimens (biological population, archaeological component or assemblage) and can be used to illustrate evolutionary change or stasis within the lineage. Identification of larger-scale or more inclusive units (biological family, cultural phase) typically uses significant changes in the averages, such as might be detected by comparison of specimens below stratum C in Figure 10.2 with those above it and by comparison of specimens below stratum G in Figure 10.2 with those above it. A sense of temporal discontinuity and lack of heritable continuity are

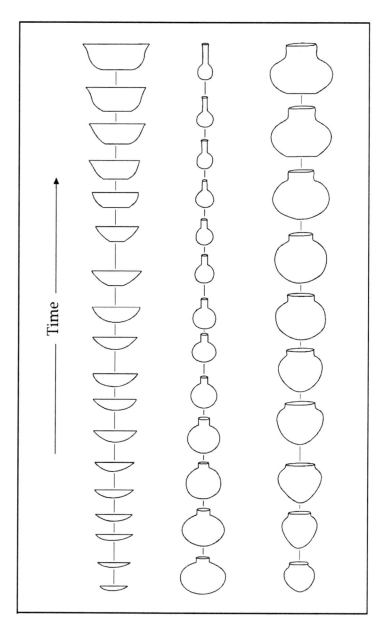

Figure 10.1. Ford's model of culture change manifest in artifacts (after Ford 1962). The consistent and gradual change in each of the three forms through time implies heritable continuity and cultural transmission; each line constitutes an evolutionary lineage.

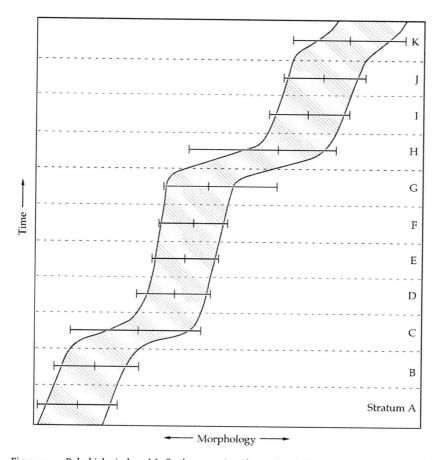

Figure 10.2. Paleobiological model of a chronospecies. The crosshatched area represents the range of morphology represented by specimens within a lineage over time. This model displays the average (center vertical line crossing a horizontal line) and range (horizontal line bounded by a vertical line at each end) of a form plotted against time (vertical axis); each solid horizontal line is a chronospecies. Specimens between dashed horizontal lines are measured as a set, and a measure of central tendency characterizes the set. Assemblages of specimens are designated by ages, perhaps stratigraphic boundaries.

built in to how the units (chronospecies or chronotypes) have been carved out of the continuum.

The direct historical approach, frequency seriation, and percentage stratigraphy (when it seeks evidence of the popularity principle) require units of a different sort than those illustrated in Figures 10.1 and 10.2. They require specimens that are sorted solely on the basis of their formal similarity. How this is done is illustrated by the model in Figure 10.3; each type is (in this model) a horizontally delimited chunk of the lineage. Specimens are identified as members of a particular type or ideational unit (Chapter 2) if and only if they display the definitive attributes of that type. Identification is irrespective of a specimen's stratigraphic provenience, and thus each type's temporal duration may vary as indicated by the solid vertical line attending each type in Figure 10.3. In a sense, descriptive units are imposed on specimens by the identification process. The model implies that each form—referred to in biology as a "morphospecies" (Pearson 1998)—occurs continuously and only once during a lineage's history. If relative frequencies of each unit in each of several strata were added, the illustration in Figure 10.3 would be a centered-bar graph like those in Figures 5.1 and 5.2. In Figure 10.3 each type is approximately equally different morphologically from every other unit (assuming the horizontal axis is interval scale). This model shows the advantage of units built in this manner: It recognizes the definition of evolution as change in the frequencies of analytically discrete variants over time that are related. It also illustrates the overlap of units from one time period to the next (if the lineage in Figure 10.3 was also carved into pieces like those in Figure 10.2). Thus it models heritable continuity as shifting frequencies of types over time, just as Darwin did and as modern evolutionists do today.

With respect to chronometry, either model in Figure 10.2 or 10.3 would work. It should be clear, for example, that Ford's marker types (Chapter 6) align well with the model in Figure 10.2. Kroeber's pottery types (Chapter 5) align closely with the model in Figure 10.3. Cultural traits (Chapter 2) and Lyell's species (Chapter 4) could be of either sort, depending on their scale of inclusiveness. Recognizing these types of nuances in the chronometric units reveals much about how and why various chronometers work the way they do, and that is an important lesson also.

Final Thoughts

Our demonstration that cultural transmission and descent with modification underpin early archaeological chronometry should not be taken as presentism for our own agenda within the discipline (e.g., O'Brien and Lyman 2000, 2003). Such demonstration in fact hardly legitimates our preferred epistemology or ontology. Rather, what is interesting from a historical perspective is that many of the same arguments are made today as were made in the 1930s

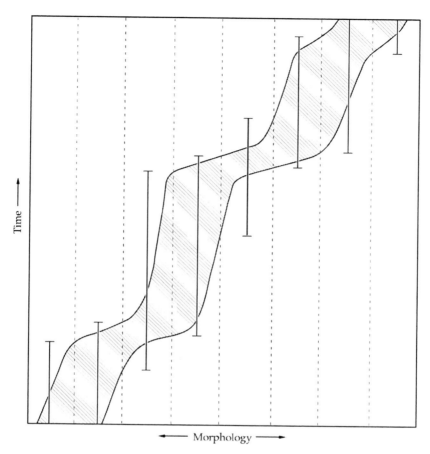

Figure 10.3. *Paleobiological model of morphospecies. The dashed vertical lines denote the extent of morphological variation included within each form, and the solid vertical lines with horizontal bars at their ends denote the temporal range of each form. Each form is a morphospecies. Each horizontal section bounded by vertical dashed lines represents an ideational unit, and each solid vertical line represents the temporal duration of an ideational unit. Assemblages of specimens are designated by limits of formal variation, so overlap from one time period to another of several forms is expected.*

and 1940s—that any attempt to adapt (not just adopt) Darwinian evolutionary theory to the archaeological record is at best misguided and at worst simply wrongheaded (e.g., Bamforth 2002; Spencer 1997). We of course find such criticisms equally misguided (Lyman and O'Brien 1998; O'Brien et al. 2003). As we have argued at length elsewhere, the best (most fit?) ideas in science may eventually win out, but whether or not they do, the diversity and variety of ideas in any field of inquiry drive that field toward whatever its goals might be

(O'Brien et al. 2005). Our point here is to contribute to the diversity of ideas regarding the history of chronometry in archaeology in the hopes that our contribution will add to the progress of that field, whether in the form of additional archival research, disputes over historical details, or further discussion of who did what where and why they did it.

Let us emphasize, then, that we find it fascinating that archaeologists working during the first half of the twentieth century employed, if implicitly, at least an incipient notion of cultural transmission and evolution that shares many characteristics with modern Darwinian theory. To be sure, because the underpinnings of their work were based in large part on common sense, and because even the use of the word "evolution" was reason to doubt someone's anthropological acumen at the time (Harris 1968), archaeologists missed or misunderstood many of the nuances of the theory. Thus it is not surprising that they also failed to keep pace with developments in Darwinian and evolutionary theory and modifications to the theory as it developed into the modern version. Nor are we surprised that archaeologists paid scant attention to what today often is referred to as paleobiology rather than the allegedly more descriptive and historical and less theoretical (and less nomothetic?) paleontology, despite the fact that they could have potentially learned a lot about the evolutionary process, whether biological or cultural. What we have learned with respect to our own agenda is the deep history of certain anti(Darwinian) evolution notions in archaeology. This gives us some groundwork on which to build a counterargument; it reveals the kind of arguments we need to present if we hope to succeed in convincing the discipline that Darwinism indeed has something to offer archaeology. Based on our understanding of the history of artifact-based chronometry in archaeology, we think that it most definitely does have something to offer.

Source Acknowledgments

Permissions to reprint the chapters were granted as follows:

Chapter 2: Courtesy of the American Anthropological Association. Originally published in 1997 ((c) 1997) as "The Concept of Evolution in Early Twentieth-Century Americanist Archaeology" in *Rediscovering Darwin: Evolutionary Theory in Archeological Explanation*, edited by C. M. Barton and G. A. Clark, pp. 21–48, Archeological Papers of the American Anthropological Association, No. 7. Reprinted by permission of the University of California Press.

Chapter 3: Courtesy of the *Journal of Anthropological Research* and the University of New Mexico. Originally published in 2003 ((c) 2003) as "Cultural Traits: Units of Analysis in Early Twentieth-Century Anthropology" in *Journal of Anthropological Research* 59:225–250. Reprinted with permission.

Chapter 4: Courtesy of the Society for American Archaeology. Originally published in 2000 ((c) 2000 by the Society for American Archaeology) as "Chronometers and Units in Early Archaeology and Paleontology" in *American Antiquity* 65:691–707. Reprinted by permission from *American Antiquity*.

Chapter 5: Courtesy of the *Journal of Anthropological Research* and the University of New Mexico. Originally published in 2002 ((c) 2002) as "A. L. Kroeber and the Measurement of Time's Arrow and Time's Cycle" in *Journal of Anthropological Research* 58:313–338. Reprinted with permission.

Chapter 6: Courtesy of the Southeastern Archaeological Conference. Originally published in 2000 as "Time, Space, and Marker Types: Ford's 1936 Chronology for the Lower Mississippi Valley" in *Southeastern Archaeology* 19:46–62. Reprinted by permission from the Southeastern Archaeological Conference.

Chapter 7: Courtesy of Kluwer Academic/Plenum Publishers. Originally published in

2001 as "The Direct Historical Approach and Analogical Reasoning in Archaeology" in *Journal of Archaeological Method and Theory* 8:303–342. Reprinted with permission.

Chapter 8: Courtesy of Kluwer Academic/Plenum Publishers. Originally published in 1999 as "Americanist Stratigraphic Excavation and the Measurement of Culture Change" in *Journal of Archaeological Method and Theory* 6:55–108. Reprinted with permission.

Chapter 9: Courtesy of the Society for American Archaeology. Originally published in 1998 ((c) 1998 by the Society for American Archaeology) as "Seriation, Superposition, and Interdigitation: A History of Americanist Graphic Depictions of Culture Change" in *American Antiquity* 63:239–261. Reprinted by permission from *American Antiquity*.

References Cited

Adams, R. E.
   1960 Manuel Gamio and Stratigraphic Excavation. *American Antiquity* 26:99.
Aitken, R. T.
   1917 Porto Rican Burial Caves. *Nineteenth International Congress of Americanists, Proceedings*, pp. 224–228.
   1918 A Porto Rican Burial Cave. *American Anthropologist* 20:296–309.
Alland, A., Jr.
   1972 Cultural Evolution: The Darwinian Model. *Social Biology* 19:227–239.
   1974 Why Not Spencer? *Journal of Anthropological Research* 30:271–280.
Allen, M. S.
   1996 Style and Function in East Polynesian Fish-Hooks. *Antiquity* 70:97–116.
Alroy, J.
   2000 Understanding the Dynamics of Trends within Evolving Lineages. *Paleobiology* 26:319–329.
Amsden, C. A.
   1931 Black-on-White Ware. In *The Pottery of Pecos*, Vol. 1, by A. V. Kidder, pp. 17–72. Papers of the Southwestern Expedition, Phillips Academy No. 5. Yale University Press, New Haven, Connecticut.
Anderson, K. M.
   1969 Ethnographic Analogy and Archeological Interpretation. *Science* 163:133–138.
Art, H. W. (editor)
   1993 *The Dictionary of Ecology and Environmental Science*. Henry Holt, New York.
Ascher, R.
   1961 Analogy in Archaeological Interpretation. *Southwestern Journal of Anthropology* 17:317–325.
Aunger, R.
   1999 Culture Vultures. *The Sciences* 39(5):36–42.
   2000 (editor) *Darwinizing Culture: The Status of Memetics as a Science*. Oxford University Press, Oxford.

2002 *The Electric Meme: A New Theory of How We Think.* Free Press, New York.

Baerreis, D. A.

1961 The Ethnohistoric Approach and Archaeology. *Ethnohistory* 8:49–77.

Bamforth, D. B.

2002 Evidence and Metaphor in Evolutionary Archaeology. *American Antiquity* 67:435–452.

Barnett, H. G.

1940 Culture Processes. *American Anthropologist* 42:21–48.

1942 Invention and Culture Change. *American Anthropologist* 44:14–30.

1953 *Innovation: The Basis of Cultural Change.* McGraw-Hill, New York.

Beals, R. L., G. W. Brainerd, and W. Smith.

1945 *Archaeological Studies in Northeast Arizona.* University of California, Publications in American Archaeology and Ethnology 44, Pt. 1.

Beardsley, R. K.

1948 Culture Sequences in Central California Archaeology. *American Antiquity* 14:1–28.

Benedict, R.

1932 Configurations of Culture in North America. *American Anthropologist* 34:1–27.

Bennett, J. W.

1943 Recent Developments in the Functional Interpretation of Archaeological Data. *American Antiquity* 9:208–219.

1944 The Development of Ethnological Theory as Illustrated by Studies of the Plains Sun Dance. *American Anthropologist* 46:162–181.

1954 Interdisciplinary Research and the Concept of Culture. *American Anthropologist* 56:169–179.

Bennyhoff, J. A.

1952 The Virú Valley Sequence: A Critical Review. *American Antiquity* 17:231–249.

Benzon, W. L.

2002 Colorless Green Homunculi. *Human Nature Review* 2:454–462.

Bidney, D.

1944 On the Concept of Culture and Some Cultural Fallacies. *American Anthropologist* 46:30–44.

1946 On the So-called Anti-Evolutionary Fallacy: A Reply to Leslie A. White. *American Anthropologist* 48:293–297.

Binford, L. R.

1962a Archaeology as Anthropology. *American Antiquity* 28:217–225.

1962b A New Method of Calculating Dates from Kaolin Pipe Stem Samples. *Southeastern Archaeological Conference Newsletter* 9(1):19–21.

1965 Archaeological Systematics and the Study of Culture Process. *American Antiquity* 31:203–210.

1967 Smudge Pits and Hide Smoking: The Use of Analogy in Archaeological Reasoning. *American Antiquity* 32:1–12.

1968a Archeological Perspectives. In *New Perspectives in Archeology*, edited by S. R. Binford and L. R. Binford, pp. 5–32. Aldine, Chicago.

1968b Methodological Considerations of the Archaeological Use of Ethnographic Data. In *Man the Hunter*, edited by R. B. Lee and I. DeVore, pp. 268–273. Aldine, Chicago.

1968c Some Comments on Historical versus Processual Archaeology. *Southwestern Journal of Anthropology* 24:267–275.

1972 *An Archaeological Perspective*. Seminar Press, New York.

1977 General Introduction. In *For Theory Building in Archaeology*, edited by L. R. Binford, pp. 1–10. Academic Press, New York.

1980 Willow Smoke and Dogs' Tails: Hunter-Gatherer Settlement Systems and Archaeological Site Formation. *American Antiquity* 45:4–20.

Binford, S. R.

1968 Variability and Change in the Near Eastern Mousterian of Levallois Facies. In *New Perspectives in Archeology*, edited by S. R. Binford and L. R. Binford, pp. 49–60. Aldine, Chicago.

Bird, J. B.

1943 *Excavations in Northern Chile*. American Museum of Natural History, Anthropological Papers 38, Pt. 4.

Birdsell, J. B.

1957 On Methods of Evolutionary Biology and Anthropology. Part II. Anthropology. *American Scientist* 45:393–400.

Blackmore, S.

1999 *The Meme Machine*. Oxford University Press, Oxford.

2000 The Power of Memes. *Scientific American* 283(4):64–73.

Bluhm, E. A.

1957 *The Sawmill Site: A Reserve Phase Village, Pine Lawn Valley, Western New Mexico*. Fieldiana: Anthropology 47, Pt. 1.

Boas, F.

1891 Dissemination of Tales among the Natives of North America. *Journal of American Folk-Lore* 4:13–20.

1896a The Growth of Indian Mythologies. *Journal of American Folk-Lore* 9:1–11.

1896b The Limitations of the Comparative Method of Anthropology. *Science* 4:901–908.

1902 Some Problems in North American Archaeology. *American Journal of Archaeology* 6:1–6.

1903 The Decorative Art of the North American Indians. *Popular Science Monthly* 63:481–498.

1904 The History of Anthropology. *Science* 20:513–524.

1908 Decorative Designs of Alaskan Needle-Cases: A Study in the History of Conventional Designs, Based on Materials in the U.S. National Museum. *U.S. National Museum, Proceedings* 34:321–344.

1909 The Relationships of the Eskimos of East Greenland. *Science* 30:535–536.

1911 Review of *Methode der Ethnologie*, by F. Graebner. *Science* 34:804–810.

1912 International School of American Archaeology and Ethnology in Mexico. *American Anthropologist* 14:192–194.

1913 Archaeological Investigations in the Valley of Mexico by the International School, 1911–12. *Eighteenth International Congress of Americanists, Proceedings*, pp. 176–179.

1920 The Methods of Ethnology. *American Anthropologist* 22:311–321.

1924 Evolution or Diffusion? *American Anthropologist* 26:340–344.

1930 Anthropology. *Encyclopaedia of the Social Sciences* 2:73–110.

1932 The Aims of Anthropological Research. *Science* 76:605–613.

Bohannan, P., and M. Glazer

1988 *High Points in Anthropology*. 2nd ed. McGraw-Hill, New York.

Bower, J.

1986 *In Search of the Past: An Introduction to Archaeology*. Dorsey, Chicago.

Bowler, P. J.

1979 Theodor Eimer and Orthogenesis: Evolution by "Definitely Directed Variation." *Journal of the History of Medicine and Allied Sciences* 34:40–73.

Boyd, R., and P. J. Richerson

1985 *Culture and the Evolutionary Process*. University of Chicago Press, Chicago.

Brainerd, G. W.

1951 The Place of Chronological Ordering in Archaeological Analysis. *American Antiquity* 16:301–313.

Braun, D. P.

1985 Absolute Seriation: A Time-Series Approach. In *For Concordance in Archaeological Analysis*, edited by C. Carr, 509–536. Westport, Boulder, Colorado.

Brew, J. O.

1946 *Archaeology of Alkali Ridge, Southeastern Utah*. Peabody Museum of American Archaeology and Ethnology, Papers 21.

Brooks, R. L.

1982 Events in the Archaeological Context and Archaeological Explanation. *Current Anthropology* 23:67–75.

Brower, J. C., and W. A. Burroughs

1982 A Simple Method for Quantitative Biostratigraphy. In *Quantitative Stratigraphic Correlation*, edited by J. M. Cubitt and R. A. Reyment, pp. 61–83. Wiley, Chichester, England.

Browman, D. L.

2002a Henry Chapman Mercer: Archaeologist and Culture Historian. In *New*

Perspectives on the Origins of Americanist Archaeology, edited by D. L. Browman and S. Williams, pp. 185–208. University of Alabama Press, Tuscaloosa.

2002b Origins of Americanist Stratigraphic Excavation in North America: The Peabody Museum Method and the Chicago Method. In *New Perspectives on the Origins of Americanist Archaeology*, edited by D. L. Browman and S. Williams, pp. 242–264. University of Alabama Press, Tuscaloosa.

2003 Origins of Americanist Stratigraphic Excavation Methods. In *Picking the Lock of Time: Developing Chronology in American Archaeology*, edited by J. Truncer, pp. 22–39. University of Florida Press, Gainesville.

Browman, D. L., and D. R. Givens

1996 Stratigraphic Excavation: The First "New Archaeology." *American Anthropologist* 98:80–95.

Browman, D. L., and S. Williams (editors)

2002 *New Perspectives on the Origins of Americanist Archaeology*. University of Alabama Press, Tuscaloosa.

Brumfiel, E. M.

1976 Review of *Guide to Ethnohistorical Sources: Handbook of Middle American Indians*, Vols. 12–15, edited by H. F. Cline. *American Antiquity* 41:398–403.

Bruner, E. M.

1956 Cultural Transmission and Cultural Change. *Southwestern Journal of Anthropology* 12:191–199.

Caldwell, J. R.

1959 The New American Archeology. *Science* 129:303–307.

Camardi, G.

1999 Charles Lyell and the Uniformity Principle. *Biology and Philosophy* 14:537–560.

Carneiro, R. L.

1972 The Devolution of Evolution. *Social Biology* 19:248–258.

1973 Structure, Function, and Equilibrium in the Evolutionism of Herbert Spencer. *Journal of Anthropological Research* 29:77–95.

2003 *Evolutionism in Cultural Anthropology: A Critical History*. Westview Press, Boulder, Colorado.

Carter, G. F.

1941 Archaeological Notes on a Midden at Point Sal. *American Antiquity* 6:214–226.

Caughley, G.

1977 *Analysis of Vertebrate Populations*. Wiley, London.

Cavalli-Sforza, L. L., and M. W. Feldman

1981 *Cultural Transmission and Evolution: A Quantitative Approach*. Princeton Monographs in Population Biology 16.

Chang, K. C.

   1967 Major Aspects of the Interrelationship of Archaeology and Ethnology. *Current Anthropology* 8:227–243.

Charlton, T. H.

   1981 Archaeology, Ethnohistory, and Ethnology: Interpretive Interfaces. *Advances in Archaeological Method and Theory* 4:129–176.

Chatfield, C.

   1975 *The Analysis of Time Series: Theory and Practice.* Chapman and Hall, London.

Christenson, A. L. (editor)

   1989 *Tracing Archaeology's Past: The Historiography of Archaeology.* Southern Illinois University Press, Carbondale.

Clements, F. E.

   1928 Quantitative Method in Ethnography. *American Anthropologist* 30:295–310.

Clements, F. E., S. M. Schenck, and T. K. Brown

   1926 A New Objective Method for Showing Special Relationships. *American Anthropologist* 28:585–604.

Cole, F.-C.

   1932 Exploration and Excavation. In *Conference on Southern Pre-History*, pp. 74–78. National Research Council, Washington DC.

Cole, F.-C., and T. Deuel

   1937 *Rediscovering Illinois.* University of Chicago Press, Chicago.

Collier, D.

   1955 *Cultural Chronology and Change as Reflected in the Ceramics of the Virú Valley, Peru.* Fieldiana: Anthropology 43.

Collier, D., and J. V. Murra.

   1943 *Survey and Excavations in Southern Ecuador.* Fieldiana: Anthropology 35.

Collins, D. M.

   1965 Seriation of Quantitative Features in Late Pleistocene Stone Technology. *Nature* 205:931–932.

Collins, H. B., Jr.

   1932a Archaeology of Mississippi. In *Conference on Southern Pre-History*, pp. 37–42. National Research Council, Washington DC.

   1932b Excavations at a Prehistoric Indian Village Site in Mississippi. *United States National Museum, Proceedings* 79(32):1–22.

Colton, H. S.

   1939 *Prehistoric Culture Units and Their Relationships in Northern Arizona.* Museum of Northern Arizona, Bulletin 17.

Colton, H. S., and L. L. Hargrave.

   1937 *Handbook of Northern Arizona Pottery Wares.* Museum of Northern Arizona, Bulletin 11.

Cowgill, G. L.

    1968 Review of *Computer Analysis of Chronological Seriation*, by F. Hole and M. Shaw. *American Antiquity* 33:517–519.

    1972 Models, Methods and Techniques for Seriation. In *Models in Archaeology*, edited by D. L. Clarke, pp. 381–424. Methuen, London.

Cremeens, D. L., and J. P. Hart

    1995 On Chronostratigraphy, Pedostratigraphy, and Archaeological Context. In *Pedological Perspectives in Archaeological Research*, edited by M. E. Collins, B. J. Carter, B. G. Gladfelter, and R. J. Southard, pp. 15–33. Soil Science Society of America, Special Publication No. 44. Madison, Wisconsin.

Crompton, A. W., and P. Parker

    1978 Evolution of the Mammalian Masticatory Apparatus. *American Scientist* 66:192–201.

Cronquist, A.

    1951 Orthogenesis in Evolution. *Research Studies of the State College of Washington* 19:3–18.

Custer, J. F.

    2001 Culture History and Its Histories. *North American Archaeologist* 22:403–425.

Dall, W. H.

    1877 On Succession in the Shell-Heaps of the Aleutian Islands. *Contributions to North American Ethnology* 1:41–91.

Dancey, W. S.

    1998 Review of *The Rise and Fall of Culture History*, by R. L. Lyman, M. J. O'Brien, and R. C. Dunnell. *Southeastern Archaeology* 17:103–104.

Darwin, C.

    1859 *On the Origin of Species by Means of Natural Selection, or the Preservation of Favored Races in the Struggle for Life*. Murray, London.

Davis, D. D.

    1983 Investigating the Diffusion of Stylistic Innovations. *Advances in Archaeological Method and Theory* 6:53–89.

Dawkins, R.

    1976 *The Selfish Gene*. Oxford University Press, New York.

Dean, J. S.

    1978 Independent Dating in Archaeological Analysis. *Advances in Archaeological Method and Theory* 1:223–255.

De Booy, T.

    1913 Certain Kitchen-Middens in Jamaica. *American Anthropologist* 15:425–434.

Deetz, J.

    1967 *Invitation to Archaeology*. Natural History Press, Garden City, New York.

    1970 Archeology as Social Science. *American Anthropological Association, Bulletin* 3(3):115–125.

Deetz, J., and E. Dethlefsen

1965 The Doppler Effect and Archaeology: A Consideration of the Spatial Aspects of Seriation. *Southwestern Journal of Anthropology* 21:196–206.

1967 Death's Head, Cherub, Urn and Willow. *Natural History* 76(3):29–37.

1971 Some Social Aspects of New England Colonial Mortuary Art. In *Approaches to Social Dimensions of Mortuary Practices*, edited by J. A. Brown, pp. 30–38. Society for American Archaeology Memoir No. 25.

de Laguna, F.

1960 American Archeology. In *Selected Papers from the American Anthropologist, 1888– 1920*, edited by F. de Laguna, pp. 218–222. American Anthropological Association, Washington DC.

Dempsey, P., and M. Baumhoff

1963 The Statistical Use of Artifact Distributions to Establish Chronological Sequence. *American Antiquity* 28:496–509.

Dethlefsen, E., and J. Deetz

1966 Death's Heads, Cherubs, and Willow Trees: Experimental Archaeology in Colonial Cemeteries. *American Antiquity* 31:502–510.

Dixon, R. B.

1913 Some Aspects of North American Archeology. *American Anthropologist* 15:549–577.

Dobzhansky, T.

1957 On Methods of Evolutionary Biology and Anthropology. Part I. Biology. *American Scientist* 45:381–392.

Driver, H. E.

1938 Culture Element Distributions: VIII, The Reliability of Culture Element Data. *Anthropological Records* 1:205–220.

1962 *The Contribution of A. L. Kroeber to Culture Area Theory and Practice.* Indiana University Publications in Anthropology and Linguistics, Memoir 18.

1965 Survey of Numerical Classification in Anthropology. In *The Use of Computers in Anthropology*, edited by D. Hymes, pp. 302–344. Mouton, The Hague.

1973 Cultural Diffusion. In *Main Currents in Cultural Anthropology*, edited by R. Naroll and F. Naroll, pp. 157–183. Appleton-Century-Crofts, New York.

Driver, H. E., and A. L. Kroeber

1932 *Quantitative Expression of Cultural Relationships.* University of California, Publications in American Archaeology and Ethnology 31, Pt. 4.

Drucker, P.

1943a *Ceramic Sequences at Tres Zapotes, Veracruz, Mexico.* Bureau of American Ethnology, Bulletin 140.

1943b *Ceramic Stratigraphy at Cerro de las Mesas, Veracruz, Mexico.* Bureau of American Ethnology, Bulletin 141.

1981 Obituary: Ronald Leroy Olson. *American Anthropologist* 83:605–607.

Dunnell, R. C.

1970 Seriation Method and Its Evaluation. *American Antiquity* 35:305–319.

1971 *Systematics in Prehistory*. Free Press, New York.

1978 Style and Function: A Fundamental Dichotomy. *American Antiquity* 43:192–202.

1980 Evolutionary Theory and Archaeology. *Advances in Archaeological Method and Theory* 3:35–99.

1981 Seriation, Groups, and Measurements. In *Manejo de Datos y Metodos Matematicos de Arqueologia*, edited by G. L. Cowgill, R. Whallon, and B. S. Ottaway, pp. 67–90. Union Internacional de Ciendias Prehistoricas y Protohistoricas, Mexico D.F.

1982 Science, Social Science, and Common Sense: The Agonizing Dilemma of Modern Archaeology. *Journal of Anthropological Research* 38:1–25.

1986a Five Decades of American Archaeology. In *American Archaeology: Past and Future*, edited by D. J. Meltzer, D. D. Fowler, and J. A. Sabloff, pp. 23–49. Smithsonian Institution Press, Washington DC.

1986b Methodological Issues in Americanist Artifact Classification. *Advances in Archaeological Method and Theory* 9:149–207.

1988 The Concept of Progress in Cultural Evolution. In *Evolutionary Progress*, edited by M. H. Nitecki, pp. 169–194. University of Chicago Press, Chicago.

1991 Methodological Impacts of Catastrophic Depopulation on American Archaeology and Ethnology. In *Columbian Consequences* Vol. 3: *The Spanish Borderlands in Pan-American Perspective*, edited by D. H. Thomas, pp. 561–580. Smithsonian Institution Press, Washington DC.

1995 What Is It That Actually Evolves? In *Evolutionary Archaeology: Methodological Issues*, edited by P. A. Teltser, pp. 33–50. University of Arizona Press, Tucson.

2000 Seriation. In *Archaeological Method and Theory: An Encyclopedia*, edited by L. Ellis, pp. 548–551. Garland, New York.

Dutton, B. P.

1938 *Leyit Kin, a Small House Ruin, Chaco Canyon, New Mexico*. University of New Mexico Bulletin, Monograph Series 1, Pt. 6.

Eggan, F. R.

1952 The Ethnological Cultures and Their Archeological Backgrounds. In *Archeology of Eastern United States*, edited by J. B. Griffin, pp. 35–45. University of Chicago Press, Chicago.

Ekholm, G. F.

1944 *Excavations at Tampico and Panuco in the Huasteca, Mexico*. American Museum of Natural History, Anthropological Papers 38, Pt. 5.

Eldredge, N.

    1989 *Macroevolutionary Dynamics.* McGraw-Hill, New York.

Eldredge, N., and S. J. Gould

    1972 Punctuated Equilibria: An Alternative to Phyletic Gradualism. In *Models in Paleobiology,* edited by T. J. M. Schopf, pp. 82–115. Freeman, Cooper, San Francisco.

    1977 Evolutionary Models and Biostratigraphic Strategies. In *Concepts and Methods of Biostratigraphy,* edited by E. G. Kauffman and J. E. Hazel, pp. 25–40. Dowden, Hutchinson and Ross, Stroudsburg, Pennsylvania.

Eldredge, N., and M. J. Novacek

    1985 Systematics and Paleobiology. *Paleobiology* 11:65–74.

Emerson, T. E.

    1998 Review of *The Rise and Fall of Culture History,* by R. L. Lyman, M. J. O'Brien, and R. C. Dunnell. *Illinois Archaeology* 10:356–358.

Ereshefsky, M.

    1992 The Historical Nature of Evolutionary Theory. In *History and Evolution,* edited by M. H. Nitecki and D. V. Nitecki, pp. 81–99. State University of New York Press, Albany.

    1994 Some Problems with the Linnaean Hierarchy. *Philosophy of Science* 61:186–205.

Evans, C.

    1955 *A Ceramic Study of Virginia Archeology.* Bureau of American Ethnology, Bulletin 160.

Evans, C., and B. J. Meggers

    1960 *Archeological Investigations in British Guiana.* Bureau of American Ethnology, Bulletin 177.

Evans, J.

    1850 On the Date of British Coins. *Numismatic Chronicle and Journal of the Numismatic Society* 12(4):127–137.

    1875 On the Coinage of the Ancient Britons and Natural Selection. *Royal Institution of Great Britain, Proceedings* 7:24–32.

Fenton, W. N.

    1940 Problems Arising from the Historic Northeastern Position of the Iroquois. In *Essays in Historical Anthropology of North America in Honor of John R. Swanton,* pp. 159–251. Smithsonian Miscellaneous Collections 100.

Fewkes, J. W.

    1896 The Prehistoric Culture of Tusayan. *American Anthropologist* 9:151–173.

    1914 Prehistoric Objects from a Shell-Heap at Erin Bay, Trinidad. *American Anthropologist* 16:200–220.

Finley, R.

    1931 *The Lady of Godey's: Sarah Josepha Hale.* J. B. Lippincott, Philadelphia.

Fisher, A. K.

 1997 Origins of the Midwestern Taxonomic Method. *Midcontinental Journal of Archaeology* 22:117–122.

Fisher, D. C.

 1994 Stratocladistics: Morphological and Temporal Patterns and Their Relation to Phylogenetic Process. In *Interpreting the Hierarchy of Nature*, edited by L. Grande and O. Rieppel, pp. 133–171. Academic Press, San Diego.

Fitting, J. E. (editor)

 1973 *The Development of North American Archaeology: Essays in the History of Regional Traditions*. Anchor Press, Garden City, New York.

Flannery, K. V.

 1967 Culture History v. Culture Process: A Debate in American Archaeology. *Scientific American* 217(2):119–122.

Ford, J. A.

 1935a *Ceramic Decoration Sequence at an Old Indian Village Site near Sicily Island, Louisiana*. Louisiana Department of Conservation, Anthropological Study No. 1.

 1935b An Introduction to Louisiana Archaeology. *Louisiana Conservation Review* 4(5):8–11.

 1935c Outline of Louisiana and Mississippi Pottery Horizons. *Louisiana Conservation Review* 4(6):33–38.

 1936a *Analysis of Indian Village Site Collections from Louisiana and Mississippi*. Louisiana Department of Conservation, Anthropological Study No. 2.

 1936b Archaeological Methods Applicable to Louisiana. *Louisiana Academy of Sciences, Proceedings* 3:102–105.

 1938a A Chronological Method Applicable to the Southeast. *American Antiquity* 3:260–264.

 1938b An Examination of Some Theories and Methods of Ceramic Analysis. Unpublished Master's thesis, Department of Anthropology, University of Michigan, Ann Arbor.

 1940 Review of *Handbook of Northern Arizona Pottery Wares*, by H. S. Colton and L. L. Hargrave. *American Antiquity* 5:263–266.

 1949 *Cultural Dating of Prehistoric Sites in Virú Valley, Peru*. American Museum of Natural History, Anthropological Papers 43, Pt. 1.

 1951 *Greenhouse: A Troyville Coles Creek Period Site in Avoyelles Parish, Louisiana*. American Museum of Natural History, Anthropological Papers 44, Pt. 1.

 1952a *Measurements of Some Prehistoric Design Developments in the Southeastern States*. American Museum of Natural History, Anthropological Papers 44, Pt. 4.

 1952b Reply to "The Virú Valley Sequence: A Critical Review." *American Antiquity* 17:250.

1962 A Quantitative Method for Deriving Cultural Chronology. Pan American Union, Technical Manual No. 1.

Ford, J. A., P. Phillips, and W. G. Haag

1955 The Jaketown Site in West-Central Mississippi. American Museum of Natural History, Anthropological Papers 45, Pt. 1.

Ford, J. A., and G. I. Quimby Jr.

1945 The Tchefuncte Culture, an Early Occupation of the Lower Mississippi Valley. Society for American Archaeology Memoir No. 2.

Ford, J. A., and G. R. Willey.

1940 Crooks Site, a Marksville Period Burial Mound in La Salle Parish, Louisiana. Louisiana Department of Conservation, Anthropological Study No. 3.

Forey, P. L.

1990 Cladistics. In Palaeobiology: A Synthesis, edited by D. E. G. Briggs and R. Crowther, pp. 430–434. Blackwell, Oxford.

Fowke, G.

1922 Archeological Investigations. Bureau of American Ethnology, Bulletin 76.

Fowler, D. D., and D. R. Wilcox (editors)

2003 Philadelphia and the Development of Americanist Archaeology. University of Alabama Press, Tuscaloosa.

Fox, R. C.

1986 Species in Paleontology. Geoscience Canada 13:73–84.

Freeman, D.

1974 The Evolutionary Theories of Charles Darwin and Herbert Spencer. Current Anthropology 15:211–237.

Freeman, L. G., Jr.

1968 A Theoretical Framework for Interpreting Archaeological Materials. In Man the Hunter, edited by R. B. Lee and I. DeVore, pp. 262–267. Aldine, Chicago.

Fried, M. H.

1967 The Evolution of Political Society. Random House, New York.

Gamio, M.

1909 Restos de la cultura Tepaneca. Anales del Museo Nacional de Arqueologia, Historia y Etnología 1(6):241–253.

1913 Arqueologia de Atzcapotzalco, D.F., Mexico. Eighteenth International Congress of Americanists, Proceedings, pp. 180–187.

1917 Investigaciones arqueológicas en México. Nineteenth International Congress of Americanists, Proceedings, pp. 125–133.

1924 The Sequence of Cultures in Mexico. American Anthropologist 26:307–322.

Gasche, H., and Ö. Tunca

1983 Guide to Archaeostratigraphic Classification and Terminology: Definitions and Principles. Journal of Field Archaeology 10:325–335.

Gingerich, P. D.

    1985 Species in the Fossil Record: Concepts, Trends, and Transitions. *Paleobiology* 11:27–41.

Givens, D. R.

    1992 *Alfred Vincent Kidder and the Development of Americanist Archaeology.* University of New Mexico Press, Albuquerque.

    1996 History of Archaeology from 1900 to 1950: Archaeology of the Americas. In *The Oxford Companion to Archaeology,* edited by B. M. Fagan, pp. 295–296. Oxford University Press, New York.

Gladwin, H. S.

    1936 Editorials: Methodology in the Southwest. *American Antiquity* 1:256–259.

Gladwin, H. S., E. W. Haury, E. B. Sayles, and N. Gladwin

    1937 *Excavations at Snaketown.* Medallion Papers No. 25.

Gladwin, W., and H. S. Gladwin

    1930 *A Method for the Designation of Southwestern Pottery Types.* Medallion Papers No. 7.

    1934 *A Method for the Designation of Cultures and Their Variations.* Medallion Papers No. 15.

Golbeck, A. L.

    1980 Quantification in Ethnology and Its Appearance in Regional Culture Trait Distribution Studies (1888 to 1939). *Journal of the History of the Behavioral Sciences* 16:228–240.

Goldenweiser, A.

    1925 Diffusion and the American School of Historical Ethnology. *American Journal of Sociology* 31:19–38.

Gordon, A. D., and R. A. Reyment

    1979 Slotting of Borehole Sequences. *Journal of the International Association of Mathematical Geology* 11:309–327.

Gorenstein, S.

    1977 History of American Archaeology. In *Perspectives on Anthropology 1976,* edited by A. F. C. Wallace, J. L. Angel, R. Fox, S. McLendon, R. Sady, and R. Sharer, pp. 86–100. American Anthropological Association, Special Publication No. 10.

Gorr, T., and T. Kleinschmidt

    1993 Evolutionary Relationships of the Coelacanth. *American Scientist* 81:72–82.

Gould, R. A.

    1974 Some Current Problems in Ethnoarchaeology. In *Ethnoarchaeology,* edited by C. B. Donnan and C. W. Clewlow Jr., pp. 27–48. University of California, Institute of Archaeology, Archaeological Survey Monograph No. 4.

    1980 *Living Archaeology.* Cambridge University Press, Cambridge.

Gould, S. J.

> 1970 Dollo on Dollo's Law: Irreversibility and the Status of Evolutionary Laws. *Journal of the History of Biology* 3:189–212.
>
> 1982 Darwinism and the Expansion of Evolutionary Theory. *Science* 216:380–387.
>
> 1986 Evolution and the Triumph of Homology, or Why History Matters. *American Scientist* 74:60–69.
>
> 1987 *Time's Arrow, Time's Cycle: Myth and Metaphor in the Discovery of Geological Time.* Harvard University Press, Cambridge, Massachusetts.
>
> 1988 Trends as Changes in Variance: A New Slant on Progress and Directionality in Evolution. *Journal of Paleontology* 62:319–329.

Gould, S. J., and N. Eldredge

> 1993 Punctuated Equilibrium Comes of Age. *Nature* 366:223–227.

Gould, S. J., N. L. Gilinsky, and R. Z. German

> 1987 Asymmetry of Lineages and the Direction of Evolutionary Time. *Science* 236:1437–1441.

Graebner, F.

> 1905 Kulturkreise und Kulturschichten in Ozeanien. *Zeitschrift für Ethnologie* 37:28–53.
>
> 1911 *Methode der Ethnologie*, Vol. 1. Ethnologische Bibliothek, Heidelberg.

Grayson, D. K.

> 1983 *The Establishment of Human Antiquity.* Academic Press, New York.

Green, E.

> 1973 The Use of Analogy for Interpretation of Maya Prehistory. *Journal of the Steward Anthropological Society* 4:139–159.

Greenberg, A. M., and R. H. Spielbauer

> 1991 Prehistoric and Historic Linkages: Problems and Prospects. In *New Dimensions in Ethnohistory*, edited by B. Gough and L. Christie, pp. 25–41. Canadian Museum of Civilization, Canadian Ethnology Service, Mercury Series, Paper 120.

Gregory, W. K.

> 1936 On the Meaning and Limits of Irreversibility of Evolution. *American Naturalist* 70:517–528.

Grehan, J. R., and R. Ainsworth

> 1985 Orthogenesis and Evolution. *Systematic Zoology* 34:174–192.

Griffin, J. B.

> 1937 The Archaeological Remains of the Chiwere Sioux. *American Antiquity* 2:180–181.
>
> 1943 *The Fort Ancient Aspect: Its Cultural and Chronological Position in Mississippi Valley Archaeology.* University of Michigan, Museum of Anthropology, Anthropological Papers No. 28.

1956 The Study of Early Cultures. In *Man, Culture, and Society*, edited by H. L. Shapiro, pp. 22–48. Oxford University Press, New York.

1959 The Pursuit of Archeology in the United States. *American Anthropologist* 61:379–389.

Haag, W. G.

1959 The Status of Evolutionary Theory in American History. In *Evolution and Anthropology: A Centennial Appraisal*, edited by B. J. Meggers, pp. 90–105. Anthropological Society of Washington, Washington DC.

Haeberlin, H. K.

1917 Some Archaeological Work in Porto Rico. *American Anthropologist* 19:214–238.

1919 Types of Ceramic Art in the Valley of Mexico. *American Anthropologist* 21:61–70.

Hallowell, A. I.

1965 The History of Anthropology as an Anthropological Problem. *Journal of the History of the Behavioral Sciences* 1:24–38.

Hancock, J. M.

1977 The Historic Development of Concepts of Biostratigraphic Correlation. In *Concepts and Methods of Biostratigraphy*, edited by E. G. Kauffman and J. E. Hazel, pp. 3–22. Dowden, Hutchinson and Ross, Stroudsburg, Pennsylvania.

Hargrave, L. L.

1932 *Guide to Forty Pottery Types from the Hopi Country and the San Francisco Mountains, Arizona*. Museum of Northern Arizona, Bulletin 1.

Harper, C. W., Jr.

1980 Relative Age Inference in Paleontology. *Lethaia* 13:239–248.

Harrington, J. C.

1954 Dating Stem Fragments of Seventeenth and Eighteenth Century Clay Tobacco Pipes. *Quarterly Bulletin of the Archaeological Society of Virginia* 9(1):9–13.

Harrington, M. R.

1909a Ancient Shell Heaps near New York City. In *The Indians of Greater New York and the Lower Hudson*, edited by C. Wissler, pp. 167–179. American Museum of Natural History, Anthropological Papers 3.

1909b The Rock-Shelters of Armonk, New York. In *The Indians of Greater New York and the Lower Hudson*, edited by C. Wissler, pp. 123–138. American Museum of Natural History, Anthropological Papers 3.

1924a *An Ancient Village Site of the Shinnecock Indians*. American Museum of Natural History, Anthropological Papers 22, Pt. 5.

1924b The Ozark Bluff-Dwellers. *American Anthropologist* 26:1–21.

Harris, M.

1968 *The Rise of Anthropological Theory*. Crowell, New York.

Haury, E. W.

1937 Stratigraphy. In *Excavations at Snaketown*, by H. S. Gladwin, E. W. Haury, E. B. Sayles, and N. Gladwin, pp. 19–35. Medallion Papers No. 25.

Hawkes, E. W., and R. Linton

1916 A *Pre-Lenape Site in New Jersey*. University of Pennsylvania Museum, Anthropological Publications 6, Pt. 3.

1917 A Pre-Lenape Culture in New Jersey. *American Anthropologist* 19:487–494.

Hawley, F. M.

1934 *The Significance of the Dated Prehistory of Chetro Ketl*. University of New Mexico Bulletin, Monograph Series 1, Pt. 1.

1937 Reversed Stratigraphy. *American Antiquity* 2:297–299.

Heizer, R. F.

1941 The Direct-Historical Approach in California Archaeology. *American Antiquity* 7:98–122.

1959 (editor) *The Archaeologist at Work: A Source Book in Archaeological Method and Interpretation*. Harper, New York.

Heizer, R. F., and F. Fenenga

1939 Archaeological Horizons in Central California. *American Anthropologist* 41:378–399.

Herskovits, M. J.

1926 The Cattle Complex in East Africa. *American Anthropologist* 28:230–272, 361–388, 494–528, 633–664.

1945 The Processes of Cultural Change. In *The Science of Man in the World Crisis*, edited by R. Linton, pp. 143–170. Columbia University Press, New York.

Hester, T. R., R. F. Heizer, and J. A. Graham

1975 *Field Methods in Archaeology*. 6th ed. Mayfield, Palo Alto, California.

Hewett, E. L.

1908 The Groundwork of American Archeology. *American Anthropologist* 10:591–595.

1916 Latest Work of the School of American Archaeology at Quirigua. In *Holmes Anniversary Volume: Anthropological Essays*, edited by F. W. Hodge, pp. 157–162. N.p., Washington DC.

Heye, G. C.

1916 Certain Mounds in Haywood County, North Carolina. In *Holmes Anniversary Volume: Anthropological Essays*, edited by F. W. Hodge, pp. 180–186. N.p., Washington DC.

Hodgen, M. T.

1942 Geographical Diffusion as a Criterion of Age. *American Anthropologist* 44:345–368.

1964 *Early Anthropology in the Sixteenth and Seventeenth Centuries*. University of Pennsylvania Press, Philadelphia.

Hole, F., and R. F. Heizer

 1973 *Prehistoric Archeology: A Brief Introduction*. Holt, Rinehart and Winston, New York.

Hole, F., and M. Shaw

 1967 *Computer Analysis of Chronological Seriation*. Rice University Studies 53, Pt. 3.

Holliday, V. T.

 1990 Pedology in Archaeology. In *Archaeological Geology of North America*, edited by N. Lasca and H. Donahue, pp. 525–540. Geological Society of North America, Centennial Special Volume 4.

 1992 Soil Formation, Time, and Archaeology. In *Soils in Archaeology: Landscape Evolution and Human Occupation*, edited by V. T. Holliday, pp. 101–117. Smithsonian Institution Press, Washington DC.

Holmes, W. H.

 1885 Evidences of the Antiquity of Man on the Site of the City of Mexico. *Anthropological Society of Washington, Transactions* 3:68–81.

 1890a A Quarry Workshop of the Flaked-Stone Implement Makers in the District of Columbia. *American Anthropologist* 3:1–26.

 1890b A West Virginia Rock-Shelter. *American Anthropologist* 3:217–225.

 1892 Modern Quarry Refuse and the Paleolithic Theory. *Science* 20:295–297.

 1893 Gravel Man and Palaeolithic Culture: A Preliminary Word. *Science* 21:29–30.

 1903 *Aboriginal Pottery of the Eastern United States*. Bureau of American Ethnology, Annual Report (1898–1899) 20.

 1914 Areas of American Culture Characterization Tentatively Outlined as an Aid in the Study of Antiquities. *American Anthropologist* 16:413–446.

Howell, F. C.

 1968 The Use of Ethnography in Reconstructing the Past. In *Man the Hunter*, edited by R. B. Lee and I. DeVore, pp. 287–288. Aldine, Chicago.

Hull, D. L.

 1965 The Effect of Essentialism on Taxonomy—Two Thousand Years of Stasis. *British Journal for the Philosophy of Science* 15:314–326, 16:1–18.

 1979 In Defense of Presentism. *History and Theory* 18:1–15.

Huxley, J. S.

 1956 Evolution, Cultural and Biological. In *Current Anthropology*, edited by W. L. Thomas Jr., pp. 3–25. University of Chicago Press, Chicago.

Jepsen, G. L.

 1949 Selection, "Orthogenesis," and the Fossil Record. *American Philosophical Society, Proceedings* 93:479–500.

Johnson, K. W., and B. C. Nelson

 1990 The Utina: Seriations and Chronology. *Florida Anthropologist* 43:48–62.

Kehoe, A. B.

 1998 *The Land of Prehistory: A Critical History of American Archaeology*. Routledge, New York.

2000 Evolutionary Archaeology Challenges the Future of Archaeology: Response to O'Brien and Lyman. *Review of Archaeology* 21(2):33–38.

Kehoe, A. B., and M. B. Emmerichs (editors)

1999 *Assembling the Past: Studies in the Professionalization of Archaeology.* University of New Mexico Press, Albuquerque.

Kehoe, T. F.

1958 Tipi Rings: The "Direct Ethnological" Approach Applied to an Archeological Problem. *American Anthropologist* 60:861–873.

Kidder, A. V.

1915 *Pottery of the Pajarito Plateau and of Some Adjacent Regions in New Mexico.* American Anthropological Association, Memoir 2, Pt. 6.

1916 Archeological Explorations at Pecos, New Mexico. *National Academy of Sciences, Proceedings* 2:119–123.

1917 A Design-Sequence from New Mexico. *National Academy of Sciences, Proceedings* 3:369–370.

1919 Review of *An Outline for a Chronology of Zuñi Ruins; Notes on Some Little Colorado Ruins; Ruins in the White Mountains, Arizona,* by L. Spier. *American Anthropologist* 21:296–301.

1921 Review of *Hawikuh Bonework,* by F. W. Hodge. *American Anthropologist* 23:363–365.

1924 *An Introduction to the Study of Southwestern Archaeology, with a Preliminary Account of the Excavations at Pecos.* Papers of the Southwestern Expedition, Phillips Academy No. 1. Yale University Press, New Haven, Connecticut.

1927 Southwestern Archaeological Conference. *Science* 66:489–491.

1931 *The Pottery of Pecos,* Vol. 1. Papers of the Southwestern Expedition, Phillips Academy No. 5. Yale University Press, New Haven, Connecticut.

1932 *The Artifacts of Pecos.* Papers of the Southwestern Expedition, Phillips Academy No. 6. Yale University Press, New Haven, Connecticut.

1936a Discussion. In *The Pottery of Pecos,* Vol. II, by A. V. Kidder and A. O. Shepard, pp. 589–628. Papers of the Southwestern Expedition, Phillips Academy No. 7. Yale University Press, New Haven, Connecticut.

1936b Introduction. In *The Pottery of Pecos,* Vol. II, by A. V. Kidder and A. O. Shepard, pp. xvii xxxi. Papers of the Southwestern Expedition, Phillips Academy No. 7. Yale University Press, New Haven Connecticut.

Kidder, A. V., and A. O. Shepard

1936 *The Pottery of Pecos,* Vol. II. Papers of the Southwestern Expedition, Phillips Academy No. 7. Yale University Press, New Haven, Connecticut.

Kidder, M. A., and A. V. Kidder

1917 Notes on the Pottery of Pecos. *American Anthropologist* 19:325–360.

Klimek, S.

1935 *Culture Element Distributions: I, The Structure of California Indian Culture.* University of California, Publications in American Archaeology and Ethnology 37, Pt. 1.

Kluckhohn, C.

1936 Some Reflections on the Method and Theory of the Kulturkreislehre. *American Anthropologist* 38:157–196.

1939 On Certain Recent Applications of Association Coefficients to Ethnological Data. *American Anthropologist* 41:345–377.

1949 *Mirror for Man*. McGraw-Hill, New York.

1960 The Use of Typology in Anthropological Theory. In *Selected Papers of the Fifth International Congress of Anthropological and Ethnological Sciences*, edited by A. F. C. Wallace, pp. 134–140. University of Pennsylvania Press, Philadelphia.

Kluckhohn, C., and W. H. Kelly

1945 The Concept of Culture. In *The Science of Man in the World Crisis*, edited by R. Linton, pp. 78–106. Columbia University Press, New York.

Kniffen, F. B.

1938 The Indian Mounds of Iberville Parish. In *Reports on the Geology of Iberville and Ascension Parishes*, edited by H. V. Howe, pp. 189–207. Louisiana Geological Survey, Geological Bulletin No. 13.

Knudson, S. J.

1978 *Culture in Retrospect: An Introduction to Archaeology*. Houghton Mifflin, Boston.

Köbben, A. J. F.

1967 Why Exceptions? The Logic of Cross-Cultural Analysis. *Current Anthropology* 8:3–34.

Koch, P. L.

1986 Clinal Geographic Variation in Mammals: Implications for the Study of Chronoclines. *Paleobiology* 12:269–281.

Krieger, A. D.

1944 The Typological Concept. *American Antiquity* 9:271–288.

1953a Basic Stages of Cultural Evolution. In *An Appraisal of Anthropology Today*, edited by S. Tax, L. C. Eisley, I. Rouse, and C. F. Voegelin, pp. 247–250. University of Chicago Press, Chicago.

1953b New World Culture History: Anglo-America. In *Anthropology Today*, edited by A. L. Kroeber, pp. 238–264. University of Chicago Press, Chicago.

Kroeber, A. L.

1904 *Types of Indian Culture in California*. University of California, Publications in American Archaeology and Ethnology 2, Pt. 3.

1908 Anthropology in California. *Science* 27:281–290.

1909 The Archaeology of California. In *Putnam Anniversary Volume*, edited by F. Boas, R. B. Dixon, A. L. Kroeber, F. W. Hodge, and H. I. Smith, pp. 1–42. Stechert, New York.

1916a Zuni Culture Sequences. *National Academy of Sciences, Proceedings* 2:42–45.

1916b *Zuni Potsherds*. American Museum of Natural History, Anthropological Papers 18, Pt. 1.

1917a The Superorganic. *American Anthropologist* 19:163–213.

1917b The Tribes of the Pacific Coast of North America. *Nineteenth International Congress of Americanists, Proceedings*, pp. 385–401.

1919 On the Principle of Order in Civilization as Exemplified by Changes of Fashion. *American Anthropologist* 21:235–263.

1920 Review of *Certain Aboriginal Pottery from Southern California*, by G. G. Heye. *American Anthropologist* 22:186–188.

1923a *Anthropology*. Harcourt, Brace, New York.

1923b *The History of Native Culture in California*, 123–142. University of California, Publications in American Archaeology and Ethnology 20.

1925a *Archaic Culture Horizons in the Valley of Mexico*. University of California, Publications in American Archaeology and Ethnology 17, Pt. 7.

1925b *Handbook of the Indians of California*. Bureau of American Ethnology, Bulletin 78.

1927 Coast and Highland in Prehistoric Peru. *American Anthropologist* 29:625–653.

1931a The Culture-Area and Age-Area Concepts of Clark Wissler. In *Methods in Social Science*, edited by S. A. Rice, pp. 248–265. University of Chicago Press, Chicago.

1931b Historical Reconstruction of Culture Growths and Organic Evolution. *American Anthropologist* 33:149–156.

1935a History and Science in Anthropology. *American Anthropologist* 37:539–569.

1935b *Preface*. University of California, Publications in American Archaeology and Ethnology 37, Pt. 1.

1936 *Culture Element Distributions: III, Area and Climax*. University of California, Publications in American Archaeology and Ethnology 37, Pt. 3.

1937 Preface. *Anthropological Records* 1:1–4.

1940 Stimulus Diffusion. *American Anthropologist* 42:1–20.

1943 Structure, Function and Pattern in Biology and Anthropology. *Scientific Monthly* 56:105–113.

1944 *Peruvian Archaeology in 1942*. Viking Fund Publications in Anthropology No. 4.

1946 History and Evolution. *Southwestern Journal of Anthropology* 2:1–15.

1948 *Anthropology: Culture Patterns and Processes*. Rev. ed. Harcourt, Brace, New York.

1952 *The Nature of Culture*. University of Chicago Press, Chicago.

1957 *Style and Civilization*. Cornell University Press, Ithaca, New York.

1960 Evolution, History, and Culture. In *Evolution After Darwin*, Vol. 2: *The Evolution of Man*, edited by S. Tax, pp. 1–16. University of Chicago Press, Chicago.

Kroeber, A. L., and W. D. Strong

    1924 *The Uhle Pottery Collections from Chincha*. University of California, Publications in American Archaeology and Ethnology 21, Pt. 1.

Lange, F. W.

    1980 Prehistory and Hunter/Gatherers: The Role of Analogs. *Mid-Continental Journal of Archaeology* 5:133–147.

Leonard, R. D., and G. T. Jones

    1987 Elements of an Inclusive Evolutionary Model for Archaeology. *Journal of Anthropological Archaeology* 6:199–219.

Lesser, A.

    1952 Evolution in Social Anthropology. *Southwestern Journal of Anthropology* 8:134–146.

Lewontin, R. C.

    1974 *The Genetic Basis of Evolutionary Change*. Columbia University Press, New York.

Linton, R.

    1917 Review of *A Pre-Lenape Site in New Jersey*: A Reply. *American Anthropologist* 19:144–146.

    1936 *The Study of Man*. Appleton—Century, New York.

Lipo, C. P.

    2001a Community Structures among Late Mississippian Populations of the Central Mississippi River Valley. In *Posing Questions for a Scientific Archaeology*, edited by T. L. Hunt, C. P. Lipo, and S. L. Sterling, pp. 175–216. Bergin and Garvey, Westport, Connecticut.

    2001b *Science, Style and the Study of Community Structure: An Example from the Central Mississippi River Valley*. British Archaeological Reports, International Series 918.

Lipo, C. P., M. E. Madsen, R. C. Dunnell, and T. Hunt

    1997 Population Structure, Cultural Transmission, and Frequency Seriation. *Journal of Anthropological Archaeology* 16:301–334.

Longacre, W. A.

    1998 Review of *The Rise and Fall of Culture History*, by R. L. Lyman, M. J. O'Brien, and R. C. Dunnell. *American Anthropologist* 100:794–795.

Loomis, F. B., and D. B. Young

    1912 On the Shell Heaps of Maine. *American Journal of Science* 34:17–42.

Lothrop, S. K.

    1961 *Essays in Pre-Columbian Art and Archaeology*. Harvard University Press, Cambridge, Massachusetts.

Loud, L. L., and M. R. Harrington

    1929 *Lovelock Cave*. University of California, Publications in American Archaeology and Ethnology 25.

Love, M. W.

1993 Ceramic Chronology and Chronometric Dating: Stratigraphy and Seriation at La Blanca Guatemala. *Ancient Mesoamerica* 4:17–29.

Lowe, J. W. G., and E. D. Lowe

1982 Cultural Pattern and Process: A Study of Stylistic Change in Women's Dress. *American Anthropologist* 84:521–544.

Lowie, R. H.

1912 On the Principle of Convergence in Ethnology. *Journal of American Folk-Lore* 25:24–42.

1917 *Culture and Ethnology.* McMurtrie, New York.

1918 Survivals and the Historical Method. *American Journal of Sociology* 23:529–535.

1920 *Primitive Society.* Liveright, New York.

1937 *The History of Ethnological Theory.* Rinehart, New York.

1944 American Contributions to Anthropology. *Science* 100:321–327.

1956 Reminiscences of Anthropological Currents in America Half a Century Ago. *American Anthropologist* 58:995–1016.

Lumsden, C. J., and E. O. Wilson

1981 *Genes, Mind, and Culture: The Coevolutionary Process.* Harvard University Press, Cambridge, Massachusetts.

Lyell, C.

1833 *Principles of Geology,* Vol. III. Murray, London.

Lyell, K. M.

1881 *The Life, Letters and Journals of Sir Charles Lyell,* Vol. I. Murray, London.

Lyman, R. L.

1994 *Vertebrate Taphonomy.* Cambridge University Press, Cambridge.

2000 Building Cultural Chronology in Eastern Washington: The Influence of Geochronology, Index Fossils, and Radiocarbon Dating. *Geoarchaeology* 15:609–648.

2001 Culture Historical and Biological Approaches to Identifying Homologous Traits. In *Style and Function in Archaeology,* edited by T. D. Hurt and G. F. M. Rakita, pp. 69–89. Bergin and Garvey, Westport, Connecticut.

Lyman, R. L., and J. L. Harpole

2002 A. L. Kroeber and the Measurement of Time's Arrow and Time's Cycle. *Journal of Anthropological Research* 58:313–338.

Lyman, R. L., and M. J. O'Brien

1998 The Goals of Evolutionary Archaeology: History and Explanation. *Current Anthropology* 39:615–652.

2001 Introduction. In *Method and Theory in American Archaeology* by G. R. Willey and Phillips, pp. I.1 I.78. University of Alabama Press, Tuscaloosa.

2002 Classification. In *Darwin and Archaeology: A Handbook of Key Concepts,* edited by J. Hart and J. E. Terrell, pp. 69–88. Bergin and Garvey, Westport, Connecticut.

2003 *W. C. McKern and the Midwestern Taxonomic Method*. University of Alabama Press, Tuscaloosa.

2004a A History of Normative Theory in Americanist Archaeology. *Journal of Archaeological Method and Theory* 11:369–396.

2004b Nomothetic Science and Idiographic History in Twentieth-Century Americanist Anthropology. *Journal of the History of the Behavioral Sciences* 40:77–96.

Lyman, R. L., M. J. O'Brien, and R. C. Dunnell

1997a (editors) *Americanist Culture History: Fundamentals of Time, Space, and Form*. Plenum Press, New York.

1997b *The Rise and Fall of Culture History*. Plenum Press, New York.

Lyon, E. A.

1996 *A New Deal for Southeastern Archaeology*. University of Alabama Press, Tuscaloosa.

Malinowski, B.

1931 Culture. *Encyclopaedia of the Social Sciences* 4:621–646.

1960 *A Scientific Theory of Culture and Other Essays*. Reprinted. Oxford University Press, New York. Originally published, 1944.

Mallory, V. S.

1970 Biostratigraphy—A Major Basis for Paleontologic Correlation. In *Proceedings of the North American Paleontological Convention*, edited by E. L. Yochelson, pp. 553–566. Allen Press, Lawrence, Kansas.

Marquardt, W. H.

1978 Advances in Archaeological Seriation. *Advances in Archaeological Method and Theory* 1:257–314.

Martin, P. S.

1936 *Lowry Ruin in Southwestern Colorado*. Fieldiana: Anthropology 23, Pt. 1.

1938 *Archaeological Work in the Ackmen-Lowry Area, Southwestern Colorado, 1937*. Fieldiana: Anthropology 23, Pt. 2.

1939 *Modified Basket Maker Sites, Ackmen-Lowry Area, Southwestern Colorado, 1938*. Fieldiana: Anthropology 23, Pt. 3.

1943 *The SU Site: Excavations at a Mogollon Village, Western New Mexico, Second Season, 1941*. Fieldiana: Anthropology 32, Pt. 2.

Martin, P. S., G. I. Quimby, and D. Collier

1947 *Indians before Columbus: Twenty Thousand Years of North American History Revealed by Archeology*. University of Chicago Press, Chicago.

Martin, P. S., and J. B. Rinaldo

1947 *The SU Site: Excavations at a Mogollon Village, Western New Mexico, Third Season, 1946*. Fieldiana: Anthropology 32, Pt. 3.

1950a Sites of the Reserve Phase, Pine Lawn Valley, Western New Mexico. Fieldiana: Anthropology 38, Pt. 3.

1950b Turkey Foot Ridge Site: A Mogollon Village, Pine Lawn Valley, Western New Mexico. Fieldiana: Anthropology 38, Pt. 2.

Martin, P. S., J. B. Rinaldo, and E. Antevs

1949 Cochise and Mogollon Sites, Pine Lawn Valley, Western New Mexico. Fieldiana: Anthropology 38, Pt. 1.

Martin, P. S., J. B. Rinaldo, and E. R. Barter

1957 Late Mogollon Communities: Four Sites of the Tularosa Phase, Western New Mexico. Fieldiana: Anthropology 49, Pt. 1.

Martin, P. S., J. B. Rinaldo, E. A. Bluhm, and H. C. Cutler

1956 Higgins Flat Pueblo, Western New Mexico. Fieldiana: Anthropology 45, Pt. 1.

Maschner, H. D. G. (editor)

1996 Darwinian Archaeologies. Plenum, New York.

Mason, O. T.

1886 Resemblances in Arts Widely Separated. American Naturalist 20:246–251.

1890 The Educational Aspect of the United States National Museum. Johns Hopkins University Studies in Historical and Political Science 8:504–519.

1895 Similarities in Culture. American Anthropologist 8:101–117.

1896 Influence of Environment upon Human Industries or Arts. Smithsonian Institution, Annual Report (1894), 639–665.

Mayr, E.

1959 Darwin and the Evolutionary Theory in Biology. In Evolution and Anthropology: A Centennial Appraisal, edited by B. J. Meggers, pp. 1–10. Anthropological Society of Washington, Washington DC.

1961 Cause and Effect in Biology. Science 134:1501–1506.

1969 Principles of Systematic Zoology. McGraw—Hill, New York.

1972 The Nature of the Darwinian Revolution. Science 176:981–989.

1982 The Growth of Biological Thought: Diversity, Evolution, and Inheritance. Harvard University Press, Cambridge, Massachusetts.

1987 The Ontological Status of Species: Scientific Progress and Philosophical Terminology. Biology and Philosophy 2:145–166.

1991 One Long Argument. Harvard University Press, Cambridge, Massachusetts.

McCormick, T. C.

1939 Quantitative Analysis and Comparison of Living Cultures. American Sociological Review 4:463–474.

McGee, R. J., and R. L. Warms

2000 Anthropological Theory: An Introductory History. Mayfield, Mountain View, California.

McGregor, J. C.

1941 Southwestern Archaeology. Wiley, New York.

1965 Southwestern Archaeology. 2nd ed. University of Illinois Press, Urbana.

McKee, J. K., J. F. Thackeray, and L. R. Berger
1995 Faunal Assemblage Seriation of Southern African Pliocene and Pleistocene Fossil Deposits. *American Journal of Physical Anthropology* 96:235–250.

McKern, W. C.
1934 Certain Culture Classification Problems in Middle Western Archaeology. National Research Council, Committee on State Archaeological Surveys, Circular No. 17.
1937a Certain Culture Classification Problems in Middle Western Archaeology. In *The Indianapolis Archaeological Conference*, pp. 70–82. National Research Council, Washington DC.
1937b Comments. In *The Indianapolis Archaeological Conference*, p. 53. National Research Council, Washington DC.
1939 The Midwestern Taxonomic Method as an Aid to Archaeological Culture Study. *American Antiquity* 4:301–313.
1942 Taxonomy and the Direct Historical Approach. *American Antiquity* 8:170–172.

McKern, W. C., T. Deuel, and C. E. Guthe
1933 On the Problem of Culture Classification. NRC Circular Letter of April 4, 1933. National Research Council Archives, Washington DC. Reprinted in R. L. Lyman and M. J. O'Brien, *W. C. McKern and the Midwestern Taxonomic Method*. University of Alabama Press, Tuscaloosa, 2003.

McNett, C. W., Jr.
1979 The Cross-Cultural Method in Archaeology. *Advances in Archaeological Method and Theory* 2:39–76.

McNutt, C. L.
1973 On the Methodological Validity of Frequency Seriation. *American Antiquity* 38:45–60.
2001 Review of *Seriation, Stratigraphy, and Index Fossils: The Backbone of Archaeological Dating*, by M. J. O'Brien and R. L. Lyman. *American Anthropologist* 103:225–226.

McShea, D. W.
2000 Trends, Tools, and Terminology. *Paleobiology* 26:330–333.

Meggers, B. J., and C. Evans
1957 *Archeological Investigations at the Mouth of the Amazon*. Bureau of American Ethnology, Bulletin 167.

Mellars, P. A.
1965 Sequence and Development of Mousterian Traditions in South-Western France. *Nature* 205:626–627.

Meltzer, D. J.
1983 The Antiquity of Man and the Development of American Archaeology. *Advances in Archaeological Method and Theory* 6:1–51.

1985 North American Archaeology and Archaeologists 1879–1934. *American Antiquity* 50:249–260.

1989 A Question of Relevance. In *Tracing Archaeology's Past: The Historiography of Archaeology*, edited by A. L. Christenson, pp. 5–19. Southern Illinois University Press, Carbondale.

Mercer, H. C.

1897 *Researches upon the Antiquity of Man in the Delaware Valley and the Eastern United States*. University of Pennsylvania Series in Philology, Literature, and Archaeology 6.

Merwin, R. E., and G. C. Vaillant

1932 *The Ruins of Holmul, Guatemala*. Peabody Museum of American Archaeology and Ethnology, Memoirs 3, Pt. 2.

Mills, W. C.

1916 Exploration of the Tremper Mound in Scioto County, Ohio. In *Holmes Anniversary Volume: Anthropological Essays*, edited by F. W. Hodge, pp. 334–358. N.p.: Washington DC.

Morgan, L. H.

1877 *Ancient Society*. Holt, New York.

Mott, M.

1938 The Relation of Historic Indian Tribes to Archaeological Manifestations in Iowa. *Iowa Journal of History and Politics* 36:227–314.

Munson, P. J.

1969 Comments on Binford's "Smudge Pits and Hide Smoking: The Use of Analogy in Archaeological Reasoning." *American Antiquity* 34:83–85.

Murdock, G. P.

1932 The Science of Culture. *American Anthropologist* 34:200–215.

1940 The Cross-Cultural Survey. *American Sociological Review* 5:361–370.

1945 The Common Denominator of Cultures. In *The Science of Man in the World Crisis*, edited by R. Linton, pp. 123–142. Columbia University Press, New York.

1949 *Social Structure*. Macmillan, New York.

1957a Anthropology as a Comparative Science. *Behavioral Science* 2:249–254.

1957b World Ethnographic Sample. *American Anthropologist* 59:664–687.

Murowchick, R. E.

1990 A Curious Sort of Yankee: Personal and Professional Notes on Jeffries Wyman (1814–1874). *Southeastern Archaeology* 9:55–66.

Naroll, R.

1961 Review of *Evolution and Culture*, edited by M. D. Sahlins and E. R. Service. *American Anthropologist* 63:389–392.

1964 On Ethnic Unit Classification. *Current Anthropology* 5:283–312.

Nash, S. E. (editor)

    2000 *It's about Time: A History of Archaeological Dating in North America.* University of Utah Press, Salt Lake City.

Neiman, F. D.

    1995 Stylistic Variation in Evolutionary Perspective: Implications for Middle Woodland Ceramic Diversity. *American Antiquity* 60:7–36.

Nelson, N. C.

    1913 Ruins of Prehistoric New Mexico. *American Museum Journal* 13:62–81.

    1916 Chronology of the Tano Ruins, New Mexico. *American Anthropologist* 18:159–180.

    1919a The Archaeology of the Southwest: A Preliminary Report. *National Academy of Sciences, Proceedings* 5:114–120.

    1919b Human Culture. *Natural History* 19:131–140.

    1919c The Southwest Problem. *El Palacio* 6:132–135.

    1920 *Notes on Pueblo Bonito.* American Museum of Natural History, Anthropological Papers 27, Appendix.

    1932 The Origin and Development of Material Culture. *Sigma Xi Quarterly* 20:102–123.

    1937 Prehistoric Archeology, Past, Present and Future. *Science* 85:81–89.

    1938 Prehistoric Archaeology. In *General Anthropology*, edited by F. Boas, pp. 146–247. Heath, Boston.

    1948 Clark Wissler, 1870–1947. *American Antiquity* 13:244–247.

    1996 Excavation of the Emeryville Shellmound, Being a Partial Report of Exploration for the Dep't. of Anthro during the Year 1906. Originally written in 1906. First published in *Excavation of the Emeryville Shellmound, 1906: Nels C. Nelson's Final Report*, edited by J. M. Broughton, pp. 1–47. University of California, Archaeological Research Facility, Contributions No. 54.

Nesbitt, P. H.

    1938 *Starkweather Ruin: A Mogollon—Pueblo Site in the Upper Gila Area of New Mexico, and Affiliative Aspects of the Mogollon Culture.* Logan Museum Bulletin No. 6.

North American Commission on Stratigraphic Nomenclature

    1983 North American Stratigraphic Code. *American Association of Petroleum Geologists Bulletin* 67:841–875.

Nuttall, Z.

    1926 The Aztecs and Their Predecessors in the Valley of Mexico. *American Philosophical Society, Proceedings* 65:245–255.

O'Brien, M. J.

    1996 *Paradigms of the Past: The Story of Missouri Archaeology.* University of Missouri Press, Columbia.

O'Brien, M. J., J. Darwent, and R. L. Lyman

    2001 Cladistics Is Useful for Reconstructing Archaeological Phylogenies: Paleoindian Points from the Southeastern United States. *Journal of Archaeological Science* 28:1115–1136.

O'Brien, M. J., and R. L. Lyman

1998 *James A. Ford and the Growth of Americanist Archaeology.* University of Missouri Press, Columbia.

1999a The Bureau of American Archaeology and Its Legacy to Southeastern Archaeology. *Journal of the Southwest* 41:407–440.

1999b *Measuring the Flow of Time: The Works of James A. Ford, 1935–1941.* University of Alabama Press, Tuscaloosa.

1999c *Seriation, Stratigraphy, and Index Fossils: The Backbone of Archaeological Dating.* Kluwer Academic/Plenum, New York.

2000 *Applying Evolutionary Archaeology: A Systematic Approach.* Kluwer Academic/Plenum, New York.

2001 *Setting the Agenda: The National Research Council Archaeological Meetings of 1929, 1932, and 1935.* University of Alabama Press, Tuscaloosa.

2002 The Epistemological Nature of Archaeological Units. *Anthropological Theory* 2:37–56.

2003 *Cladistics and Archaeology.* University of Utah Press, Salt Lake City.

O'Brien, M. J., R. L. Lyman, and J. Darwent

2000 Time, Space, and Marker Types: Ford's 1936 Chronology for the Lower Mississippi Valley. *Southeastern Archaeology* 19:46–62.

O'Brien, M. J., R. L. Lyman, and R. D. Leonard

2003 What Is Evolution? A Response to Bamforth. *American Antiquity* 68:573–580.

O'Brien, M. J., R. L. Lyman, and M. B. Schiffer

2005 *Archaeology as a Process: Processualism and Its Progeny.* University of Utah Press, Salt Lake City.

O'Connell, J. F.

1995 Ethnoarchaeology Needs a General Theory of Behavior. *Journal of Archaeological Research* 3:205–255.

O'Hara, R. J.

1988 Homage to Clio, or, Toward an Historical Philosophy for Evolutionary Biology. *Systematic Zoology* 37:142–155.

Olson, R. L.

1930 *Chumash Prehistory.* University of California, Publications in American Archaeology and Ethnology 28, Pt. 1.

Opler, M. E.

1959 Component, Assemblage, and Theme in Cultural Integration and Differentiation. *American Anthropologist* 61:955–964.

Palmer, C. T., B. E. Fredrickson, and C. F. Tilley

1997 Categories and Gatherings: Group Selection and the Mythology of Cultural Anthropology. *Evolution and Human Behavior* 18:291–308.

Panchanan, M.

1933 A History of American Anthropology. University of Calcutta Press, Calcutta.

Parker, A. C.

1916 Excavations in an Erie Indian Village and Burial Site at Ripley, Chautauqua County, New York. New York State Museum, Bulletin 117.

Parsons, E. C.

1940 Relations between Ethnology and Archaeology in the Southwest. American Antiquity 5:214–220.

Patterson, T. C.

1963 Contemporaneity and Cross-Dating in Archaeological Interpretation. American Antiquity 28:389–392.

1995 Toward a Social History of Archaeology in the United States. Harcourt Brace, Fort Worth, Texas.

Peabody, C.

1904 Exploration of Mounds, Coahoma County, Mississippi. Peabody Museum of American Archaeology and Ethnology, Papers 3, Pt. 2.

1908 The Exploration of Bushey Cavern, near Cavetown, Maryland. Phillips Academy, Department of Archaeology, Bulletin No. 4, Pt. 1.

1910 The Exploration of Mounds in North Carolina. American Anthropologist 12:425–433.

1913 Excavation of a Prehistoric Site at Tarrin, Department of the Hautes Alpes, France. American Anthropologist 15:257–272.

Peabody, C., and W. K. Moorehead

1904 The Exploration of Jacobs Cavern, McDonald County, Missouri. Phillips Academy, Department of Archaeology, Bulletin No. 1.

Pearson, P. N.

1998 Evolutionary Concepts in Biostratigraphy. In Unlocking the Stratigraphical Record: Advances in Modern Stratigraphy, edited by P. Doyle and M. R. Bennett, pp. 123–144. Wiley, Chichester, England.

Pepper, G. H.

1916 Yacatas of the Tierra Caliente, Michoacan, Mexico. In Holmes Anniversary Volume: Anthropological Essays, edited by F. W. Hodge, pp. 415–420. N.p., Washington DC.

1920 Pueblo Bonito. American Museum of Natural History, Anthropological Papers 27.

Peterson, N.

1971 Open Sites and the Ethnographic Approach to the Archaeology of Hunter—Gatherers. In Aboriginal Man and Environment in Australia, edited by D. J. Mulvaney and J. Golson, pp. 239–248. Australian National University Press, Canberra.

Petrie, W. M. F.

    1899 Sequences in Prehistoric Remains. *Journal of the Royal Anthropological Institute of Great Britain and Ireland* 29:295–301.

    1901 Diospolis Parva. *Egyptian Exploration Fund Memoirs* 20.

Phillips, P.

    1951 Review of *Archeology of the Florida Gulf Coast*, by G. R. Willey, and of *The Florida Indian and His Neighbors*, edited by J. W. Griffin. *American Anthropologist* 53:108–112.

    1955 American Archaeology and General Anthropological Theory. *Southwestern Journal of Anthropology* 11:246–250.

Phillips, P., J. A. Ford, and J. B. Griffin

    1951 *Archaeological Survey in the Lower Mississippi Alluvial Valley, 1940–1947*. Peabody Museum of Archaeology and Ethnology, Papers 25.

Phillips, P., and G. R. Willey

    1953 Method and Theory in American Archaeology: An Operational Basis for Culture-Historical Integration. *American Anthropologist* 55:615–633.

Pitt-Rivers, A. H.

    1870 Primitive Warfare, Sec. III; On the Resemblance of the Weapons of Early Races, Their Variations, Continuity and Development of Form—Metal Period. *Royal United Service Institute, Journal* 13:509–539.

    1875a The Evolution of Culture. *Royal Institution of Great Britain, Proceedings* 7:496–520.

    1875b On the Principles of Classification Adopted in the Arrangement of His Anthropological Collection, Now Exhibited in the Bethnal Green Museum. *Journal of the Anthropological Institute of Great Britain and Ireland* 4:293–308.

Plog, F. T.

    1973 Diachronic Anthropology. In *Research and Theory in Current Archeology*, edited by C. L. Redman, pp. 181–198. Wiley, New York.

    1974 *The Study of Prehistoric Change*. Academic Press, New York.

Plog, S., and J. L. Hantman

    1986 Multiple Regression Analysis as a Dating Method in the American Southwest. In *Spatial Organization and Exchange*, edited by S. Plog, pp. 87–113. Southern Illinois University Press, Carbondale.

    1990 Chronology Construction and the Study of Prehistoric Culture Change. *Journal of Field Archaeology* 17:439–456.

Praetzellis, A.

    1993 The Limits of Arbitrary Excavation. In *Practices of Archaeological Stratigraphy*, edited by E. C. Harris, M. R. Brown III, and G. J. Brown, pp. 68–86. Academic Press, London.

Quimby, G. I.

    1943 The Ceramic Sequence within the Goodall Focus. *Michigan Academy of Science, Arts and Letters* 28:543–548.

Radin, P.

1929 History of Ethnological Theories. *American Anthropologist* 31:9–33.

1933 *The Method and Theory of Ethnology: An Essay in Criticism.* McGraw-Hill, New York.

Rafferty, J.

1994 Gradual or Step-Wise Change: The Development of Sedentary Settlement Patterns in Northeast Mississippi. *American Antiquity* 59:405–425.

Rambo, A. T.

1991 The Study of Cultural Evolution. In *Profiles in Cultural Evolution*, edited by A. T. Rambo and K. Gillogly, pp. 23–109. University of Michigan Museum of Anthropology, Anthropological Papers No. 85.

Rands, R. L.

1961 Elaboration and Invention in Ceramic Traditions. *American Antiquity* 26:331–340.

Rands, R. L., and C. L. Riley

1958 Diffusion and Discontinuous Distribution. *American Anthropologist* 60:274–297.

Rathje, W. L., and M. B. Schiffer

1982 *Archaeology.* Harcourt Brace Jovanovich, New York.

Raup, D. M., and S. J. Gould

1974 Stochastic Simulation and Evolution of Morphology—Towards a Nomothetic Paleontology. *Systematic Zoology* 23:305–322.

Raup, D. M., S. J. Gould, T. J. M. Schopf, and D. S. Simberloff

1973 Stochastic Models of Phylogeny and the Evolution of Diversity. *Journal of Geology* 81:525–542.

Redfield, R., R. Linton, and M. J. Herskovits

1936 Memorandum for the Study of Acculturation. *American Anthropologist* 38:149–152.

Reed, E. K.

1940 Review of *Prehistoric Culture Units and Their Relationships in Northern Arizona*, by Harold S. Colton. *American Antiquity* 6:189–192.

Reiter, P.

1938a *The Jemez Pueblo of Unshagi, New Mexico.* University of New Mexico Bulletin, Monograph Series 1, Pt. 5.

1938b Review of *Handbook of Northern Arizona Pottery Wares*, by Harold S. Colton and Lyndon L. Hargrave. *American Anthropologist* 40:489–491.

Reyman, J. E.

1989 The History of Archaeology and the Archaeological History of Chaco Canyon, New Mexico. In *Tracing Archaeology's Past: The Historiography of Archaeology*, edited by A. L. Christenson, pp. 41–53. Southern Illinois University Press, Carbondale.

Richardson, J., and A. L. Kroeber

1940 *Three Centuries of Women's Dress Fashions: A Quantitative Analysis.* Anthropological Records 5, Pt. 2.

Rinaldo, J. B.

1950 *An Analysis of Culture Change in the Ackmen-Lowry Area.* Fieldiana: Anthropology 36, Pt. 5.

1959 *Foote Canyon Pueblo, Eastern Arizona.* Fieldiana: Anthropology 49, Pt. 2.

Rindos, D.

1985 Darwinian Selection, Symbolic Variation, and the Evolution of Culture. *Current Anthropology* 26:65–88.

Ritchie, W. A.

1937 Culture Influences from Ohio in New York Archaeology. *American Antiquity* 2:182–194.

Ritchie, W. A., and R. S. MacNeish

1949 The Pre-Iroquoian Pottery of New York State. *American Antiquity* 15:97–124.

Roberts, F. H. H., Jr.

1929 *Shabik'eshchee Village: A Late Basket Maker Site in the Chaco Canyon, New Mexico.* Bureau of American Ethnology, Bulletin 92.

Robinson, D. E.

1975 Style Changes: Cyclical, Inexorable, and Foreseeable. *Harvard Business Review* 53(6):121–131.

1976 Fashions in Shaving and Trimming of the Beard: The Men of the Illustrated London News, 1842–1972. *American Journal of Sociology* 81:1133–1141.

Robinson, W. S.

1951 A Method for Chronologically Ordering Archaeological Deposits. *American Antiquity* 16:293–301.

Romer, A. S.

1949 Time Series and Trends in Animal Evolution. In *Genetics, Paleontology and Evolution,* edited by G. L. Jepsen, G. G. Simpson, and E. Mayr, pp. 103–120. Princeton University Press, Princeton, New Jersey.

Rose, K. D., and T. M. Bown

1986 Gradual Evolution and Species Discrimination in the Fossil Record. In *Vertebrates, Phylogeny, and Philosophy,* edited by K. M. Flanagan and J. A. Lillegraven, pp. 119–130. University of Wyoming, Contributions to Geology, Special Paper No. 3.

Rouse, I. B.

1939 *Prehistory in Haiti: A Study in Method.* Yale University, Publications in Anthropology No. 21.

1954 On the Use of the Concept of Area Co-tradition. *American Antiquity* 19:221–225.

1955 On the Correlation of Phases of Culture. *American Anthropologist* 57:713–722.

1967 Seriation in Archaeology. In *American Historical Anthropology: Essays in Honor of Leslie Spier*, edited by C. L. Riley and W. W. Taylor, pp. 153–195. Southern Illinois University Press, Carbondale.

1972 *Introduction to Prehistory: A Systematic Approach*. McGraw-Hill, New York.

Rowe, J. H.

1944 *An Introduction to the Archaeology of Cuzco*. Peabody Museum of American Archaeology and Ethnology, Papers 27, Pt. 2.

1954 *Max Uhle, 1856–1944: A Memoir of the Father of Peruvian Archaeology*. University of California, Publications in American Archaeology and Ethnology 46.

1961 Stratigraphy and Seriation. *American Antiquity* 26:324–330.

1962a Alfred Louis Kroeber, 1876–1960. *American Antiquity* 27:395–415.

1962b Stages and Periods in Archaeological Interpretation. *Southwestern Journal of Anthropology* 18:40–54.

1962c Worsaae's Law and the Use of Grave Lots for Archaeological Dating. *American Antiquity* 28:129–137.

1975 Review of *A History of American Archaeology*, by G. R. Willey and J. A. Sabloff. *Antiquity* 49:156–158.

Rudwick, M. J. S.

1978 Charles Lyell's Dream of a Statistical Paleontology. *Paleontology* 21:225–244.

1990 Introduction. In *Principles of Geology*, by C. Lyell, pp. vii lv. University of Chicago Press, Chicago.

1996 Cuvier and Brongniart, William Smith, and the Reconstruction of Geohistory. *Earth Sciences History* 15:25–36.

Sackett, J. R.

1981 From de Mortillet to Bordes: A Century of French Palaeolithic Research. In *Towards a History of Archaeology*, edited by G. Daniel, pp. 85–99. Thames and Hudson, London.

Sahlins, M. D.

1960 Evolution: Specific and General. In *Evolution and Culture*, edited by M. D. Sahlins and E. R. Service, pp. 12–44. University of Michigan Press, Ann Arbor.

Sahlins, M. D., and E. R. Service (editors)

1960 *Evolution and Culture*. University of Michigan Press, Ann Arbor.

Sanderson, S. K.

1990 *Social Evolutionism: A Critical History*. Blackwell, Cambridge, Massachusetts.

Sapir, E.

1916 *Time Perspective in Aboriginal American Culture, a Study in Method*. Canada Department of Mines, Geological Survey, Memoir 90.

Sayles, E. B.

1937 Stone: Implements and Bowls. In *Excavations at Snaketown*, by H. S. Gladwin,

E. W. Haury, E. B. Sayles, and N. Gladwin, pp. 101–120. Medallion Papers No. 25.

Schiffer, M. B.

1979 Some Impacts of Cultural Resource Management on American Archaeology. In *Archaeological Resource Management in Australia and Oceania*, edited by J. R. McKinlay and K. L. Jones, pp. 1–11. New Zealand Historic Places Trust, Wellington.

1987 *Formation Processes of the Archaeological Record*. University of New Mexico Press, Albuquerque.

1996 Some Relationships between Behavioral and Evolutionary Archaeologies. *American Antiquity* 61:643–662.

Schmidt, E. F.

1928 *Time-Relations of Prehistoric Pottery Types in Southern Arizona*. American Museum of Natural History, Anthropological Papers 30, Pt. 5.

Schrabisch, M.

1909 Indian Rock-Shelters in Northern New Jersey and Southern New York. In *The Indians of Greater New York and the Lower Hudson*, edited by C. Wissler, pp. 139–165. American Museum of Natural History, Anthropological Papers 3.

Schroeder, A. H.

1979 History of Archeological Research. In *Southwest*, edited by A. Ortiz, 5–13. *Handbook of North American Indians*, Vol. 9, William C. Sturtevant, general editor. Smithsonian Institution, Washington DC.

Schuyler, R. L.

1971 The History of American Archaeology: An Examination of Procedure. *American Antiquity* 36:383–409.

Setzler, F. M.

1933a Hopewell Type Pottery from Louisiana. *Washington Academy of Sciences, Journal* 23:149–153.

1933b Pottery of the Hopewell Type from Louisiana. *United States National Museum, Proceedings* 82(22):1–21.

Sharer, R. J., and W. Ashmore

1993 *Archaeology: Discovering Our Past*. 2nd ed. Mayfield, Mountain View, California.

Shelley, C.

1999 Multiple Analogies in Archaeology. *Philosophy of Science* 66:579–605.

Simms, S. R.

1992 Ethnoarchaeology: Obnoxious Spectator, Trivial Pursuit, or the Keys to a Time Machine? In *Quandaries and Quests: Visions of Archaeology's Future*, edited by L. Wandsnider, pp. 186–198. Southern Illinois University, Center for Archaeological Investigations, Occasional Paper No. 20.

Simpson, G. G.

1949 *The Meaning of Evolution*. Columbia University Press, New York.

1951 The Species Concept. *Evolution* 5:285–298.

1953 *The Major Features of Evolution*. Columbia University Press, New York.

1960 Evolutionary Determinism and the Fossil Record. *Scientific Monthly* 71:262–267.

1961a Comments on Cultural Evolution. *Daedalus* 90:514–518.

1961b *Principles of Animal Taxonomy*. Columbia University Press, New York.

1967 *The Meaning of Evolution*. Rev. ed. Yale University Press, New Haven, Connecticut.

Skinner, A.

1917 Chronological Relations of Coastal Algonquian Culture. *Nineteenth International Congress of Americanists, Proceedings*, pp. 52–58.

Slotkin, J. S.

1952 Some Basic Methodological Problems in Prehistory. *Southwestern Journal of Anthropology* 8:442–443.

Smith, A. B.

1994 *Systematics and the Fossil Record: Documenting Evolutionary Patterns*. Blackwell, London.

Smith, H. I.

1910 *The Prehistoric Ethnology of a Kentucky Site*. American Museum of Natural History, Anthropological Papers 6, Pt. 2.

Snead, J. E.

1996 *Ruins and Rivals: The Making of Southwest Archaeology*. University of Arizona Press, Tucson.

1998 Review of *The Rise and Fall of Culture History*, by R. L. Lyman, M. J. O'Brien, and R. C. Dunnell. *Journal of Anthropological Research* 54:265–266.

Sober, E.

1980 Evolution, Population Thinking, and Essentialism. *Philosophy of Science* 47:350–383.

South, S.

1955 Evolutionary Theory in Archaeology. *Southern Indian Studies* 7:10–32.

Spaulding, A. C.

1953 Review of *Measurements of Some Prehistoric Design Developments in the Southeastern States*, by James A. Ford. *American Anthropologist* 55:588–591.

1955 Prehistoric Cultural Development in the Eastern United States. In *New Interpretations of Aboriginal American Culture History*, edited by B. J. Meggers and C. Evans, pp. 12–27. Anthropological Society of Washington, Washington DC.

1960 The Dimensions of Archaeology. In *Essays in the Science of Culture in Honor of Leslie A. White*, edited by G. E. Dole and R. L. Carneiro, pp. 437–456. Crowell, New York.

Spencer, C. S.

1997 Evolutionary Approaches in Archaeology. *Journal of Archaeological Research* 5:209–264.

Spier, L.

1913 Results of an Archeological Survey of the State of New Jersey. *American Anthropologist* 15:675–679.

1915 Review of "On the Shell Heaps of Maine," by F. B. Loomis and D. B. Young. *American Anthropologist* 17:346–347.

1916a New Data on the Trenton Argillite Culture. *American Anthropologist* 18:181–189.

1916b Review of *A Pre-Lenape Site in New Jersey*, by E. W. Hawkes and R. Linton. *American Anthropologist* 18:564–566.

1917a An Outline for a Chronology of Zuñi Ruins. American Museum of Natural History, Anthropological Papers 18, Pt. 3.

1917b Zuñi Chronology. *National Academy of Sciences, Proceedings* 3:280–283.

1918a *Notes on Some Little Colorado Ruins*. American Museum of Natural History, Anthropological Papers 18, Pt. 4.

1918b *The Trenton Argillite Culture*. American Museum of Natural History, Anthropological Papers 22, Pt. 4.

1919 *Ruins in the White Mountains, Arizona*. American Museum of Natural History, Anthropological Papers 18, Pt. 5.

1931a Historical Interrelation of Culture Traits: Franz Boas' Study of Tsimshian Mythology. In *Methods in Social Science*, edited by S. A. Rice, pp. 449–457. University of Chicago Press, Chicago.

1931b N. C. Nelson's Stratigraphic Technique in the Reconstruction of Prehistoric Sequences in Southwestern America. In *Methods in Social Science*, edited by S. A. Rice, pp. 275–283. University of Chicago Press, Chicago.

Spinden, H. J.

1915 Notes on the Archeology of Salvador. *American Anthropologist* 17:446–487.

Spoehr, A.

1957 *Marianas Prehistory: Archaeological Survey and Excavations on Saipan, Tinian and Rota*. Fieldiana: Anthropology 48.

Stahl, A. B.

1993 Concepts of Time and Approaches to Archaeological Reasoning in Historical Perspective. *American Antiquity* 58:235–260.

Stanley, S. M.

1979 *Macroevolution: Pattern and Process*. Freeman, San Francisco.

Stanley, S. M., W. O. Addicott, and K. Chinzei

1980 Lyellian Curves in Paleontology: Possibilities and Limitations. *Geology* 8:422–426.

Stein, J. K.

　1987 Deposits for Archaeologists. *Advances in Archaeological Method and Theory* 11:337–393.

　1990 Archaeological Stratigraphy. In *Archaeological Geology of North America*, edited by N. Lasca and J. Donahue, pp. 513–523. Geological Society of North America, Centennial Special Volume 4.

　1992 Organic Matter in Archaeological Contexts. In *Soils in Archaeology: Landscape Evolution and Human Occupation*, edited by V. T. Holliday, pp. 193–216. Smithsonian Institution Press, Washington DC.

Sterns, F. H.

　1915 A Stratification of Cultures in Nebraska. *American Anthropologist* 17:121–127.

Stevens, S. S.

　1946 On the Theory of Scales of Measurement. *Science* 103:677–680.

Steward, J. H.

　1929 Diffusion and Independent Invention: A Critique of Logic. *American Anthropologist* 31:491–495.

　1941 Review of *Prehistoric Culture Units and Their Relationships in Northern Arizona*, by H. S. Colton. *American Antiquity* 6:366–367.

　1942 The Direct Historical Approach to Archaeology. *American Antiquity* 7:337–343.

　1944 Re: Archaeological Tools and Jobs. *American Antiquity* 10:99–100.

　1949 Cultural Causality and Law: A Trial Formulation of the Development of Early Civilizations. *American Anthropologist* 51:1–27.

　1951 Levels of Sociocultural Integration: An Operational Concept. *Southwestern Journal of Anthropology* 7:374–390.

　1953 Evolution and Process. In *Anthropology Today*, edited by A. L. Kroeber, pp. 313–326. University of Chicago Press, Chicago.

　1954 Types of Types. *American Anthropologist* 56:54–57.

　1955 *Theory of Culture Change: The Methodology of Multilinear Evolution.* University of Illinois Press, Urbana.

　1956 Cultural Evolution. *Scientific American* 194(5):69–80.

　1960 Carrier Acculturation: The Direct Historical Approach. In *Culture in History: Essays in Honor of Paul Radin*, edited by S. Diamond, pp. 732–744. Columbia University Press, New York.

　1962 Alfred Louis Kroeber, June 11, 1876 October 5, 1960. *National Academy of Sciences, Biographical Memoirs* 36:192–253.

Steward, J. H., and F. M. Setzler

　1938 Function and Configuration in Archaeology. *American Antiquity* 4:4–10.

Steward, J. H., and D. B. Shimkin

　1961 Some Mechanisms of Sociocultural Evolution. *Daedalus* 90:477–497.

Stewart, O. C.

    1980 Memorial to Ronald L. Olson (1895–1979). *Journal of California and Great Basin Anthropology* 2:162–164.

Stirling, M. W.

    1929 Discussion of Mr. Hodge's Paper. In *Report of the Conference on Midwestern Archaeology, Held in St. Louis, Missouri, May 18, 1929,* pp. 24–28. National Research Council, Bulletin No. 74.

    1932 The Pre-historic Southern Indians. In *Conference on Southern Pre-History,* pp. 20–31. National Research Council, Washington DC.

Stocking, G. W., Jr.

    1965 On the Limits of "Presentism" and "Historicism" in the Historiography of the Behavioral Sciences. *Journal of the History of the Behavioral Sciences* 1:211–218.

    1987 *Victorian Anthropology.* Free Press, New York.

Stone, T.

    1996 Seriation. In *The Oxford Companion to Archaeology,* edited by B. M. Fagan, pp. 634–635. Oxford University Press, New York.

Strong, W. D.

    1925 *The Uhle Pottery Collections from Ancon.* University of California, Publications in American Archaeology and Ethnology 21, Pt. 4.

    1933 The Plains Culture Area in the Light of Archaeology. *American Anthropologist* 35:271–287.

    1935 An Introduction to Nebraska Archeology. *Smithsonian Miscellaneous Collections* 93, Pt. 10.

    1936 Anthropological Theory and Archaeological Fact. In *Essays in Anthropology: Presented to A. L. Kroeber in Celebration of His Sixtieth Birthday, June 11, 1936,* edited by R. H. Lowie, pp. 359–368. University of California Press, Berkeley.

    1940 From History to Prehistory in the Northern Great Plains. In *Essays in Historical Anthropology of North America in Honor of John R. Swanton,* pp. 353–394. Smithsonian Miscellaneous Collections 100.

    1952 The Value of Archeology in the Training of Professional Anthropologists. *American Anthropologist* 54:318–321.

    1953 Historical Approach in Anthropology. In *Anthropology Today,* edited by A. L. Kroeber, pp. 386–397. University of Chicago Press, Chicago.

Strong, W. D., and C. Evans Jr.

    1952 *Cultural Stratigraphy in the Virú Valley, Northern Peru.* Columbia University Press, New York.

Swanson, E. H., Jr.

    1959 Theory and History in American Archaeology. *Southwestern Journal of Anthropology* 15:120–124.

Swanton, J. R.
    1932 The Relation of the Southwest to General Culture Problems of American Pre-History. In *Conference on Southern Pre-History*, pp. 60–74. National Research Council, Washington DC.

Swanton, J. R., and R. B. Dixon
    1914 Primitive American History. *American Anthropologist* 16:376–412.

Szalay, F. S., and W. J. Bock
    1991 Evolutionary Theory and Systematics: Relationships between Process and Pattern. *Zeitschrift für Zoologische Systematik und Evolutionsforschung* 29:1–39.

Taylor, W. W.
    1948 *A Study of Archeology*. American Anthropological Association Memoir 69.
    1954 Southwestern Archaeology, Its History and Theory. *American Anthropologist* 56:561–575.
    1963 Leslie Spier, 1893–1961. *American Antiquity* 28:379–381.

Tax, S. (editor)
    1960 *Evolution After Darwin*. 3 vols. University of Chicago Press, Chicago.

Teltser, P. A.
    1995 Culture History, Evolutionary Theory, and Frequency Seriation. In *Evolutionary Archaeology: Methodological Issues*, edited by P. A. Teltser, pp. 51–68. University of Arizona Press, Tucson.

Thomas, C.
    1894 *Report on the Mound Explorations of the Bureau of Ethnology*. Bureau of Ethnology Annual Report 12.

Thomas, D. H.
    1989 *Archaeology*. 2nd ed. Holt, Rinehart and Winston, Fort Worth, Texas.

Thompson, R. H.
    1956 (editor) An Archaeological Approach to the Study of Cultural Stability. In *Seminars in Archaeology: 1955*, edited by R. Wauchope, pp. 31–57. Society for American Archaeology Memoir No. 11.
    1958 *Modern Yucatecan Maya Pottery Making*. Society for American Archaeology Memoir No. 15.

Trigger, B. G.
    1968 *Beyond History: The Methods of Prehistory*. Holt, Rinehart and Winston, New York.
    1989 *A History of Archaeological Thought*. Cambridge University Press, Cambridge.
    1998 Review of *The Rise and Fall of Culture History*, by R. L. Lyman, M. J. O'Brien, and R. C. Dunnell. *Journal of Field Archaeology* 25:363–366.

Trueman, E. R.
    1979 Species Concept. In *The Encyclopedia of Paleontology*, edited by R. W. Fairbridge and D. Jablonski, pp. 764–767. Dowden, Hutchinson and Ross, Stroudsburg, Pennsylvania.

Truncer, J. (editor)

2003 Picking the Lock of Time: Developing Chronology in American Archaeology. University Press of Florida, Gainesville.

Turnbaugh, S. P.

1979 The Seriation of Fashion. Home Economics Research Journal 7:241–248.

Tylor, E. B.

1871 Primitive Culture, Vol. I. Murray, London.

1881 Anthropology. Watts, London.

1889 On a Method of Investigating the Development of Institutions; Applied to Laws of Marriage and Descent. Journal of the Royal Anthropological Institute of Great Britain and Ireland 8:245–272.

Uhle, M.

1902 Types of Culture in Peru. American Anthropologist 4:753–759.

1903 Pachacamac. University of Pennsylvania Press, Philadelphia.

1907 The Emeryville Shellmound. University of California, Publications in American Archaeology and Ethnology 7.

Vaillant, G. C.

1930 Excavations at Zacatenco. American Museum of Natural History, Anthropological Papers 32, Pt. 1.

1931 Excavations at Ticoman. American Museum of Natural History, Anthropological Papers 32, Pt. 2.

1935 Early Cultures of the Valley of Mexico: Results of the Stratigraphical Project of the American Museum of Natural History in the Valley of Mexico, 1928–1933. American Museum of Natural History, Anthropological Papers 35, Pt. 3.

Valentine, J. W., and C. L. May

1996 Hierarchies in Biology and Paleontology. Paleobiology 22:23–33.

Van Riper, A. B.

1993 Men among the Mammoths: Victorian Science and the Discovery of Human Prehistory. University of Chicago Press, Chicago.

Von Vaupel Klein, J. C.

1994 Punctuated Equilibria and Phyletic Gradualism: Even Partners Can Be Good Friends. Acta Biotheoretica 42:15–48.

Vickers, C.

1948 The Historic Approach and the Headwaters Lake Aspect. Plains Archaeological Conference News Letter 1:31–37.

Volk, E.

1911 The Archaeology of the Delaware Valley. Peabody Museum of American Archaeology and Ethnology, Papers 5.

Vrba, E. S.

1980 Evolution, Species and Fossils: How Does Life Evolve? South African Journal of Science 76:61–84.

Vrba, E. S., and S. J. Gould

1986 The Hierarchical Expansion of Sorting and Selection: Sorting and Selection Cannot Be Equated. *Paleobiology* 12:217–228.

Wallis, W. D.

1925 Diffusion as a Criterion of Age. *American Anthropologist* 27:91–99.

1928 Probability and the Diffusion of Culture Traits. *American Anthropologist* 30:94–106.

1945 Inference of Relative Age of Culture Traits from Magnitude of Distribution. *Southwestern Journal of Anthropology* 1:142–159.

Watson, D. M. S.

1949 The Evidence Afforded by Fossil Vertebrates on the Nature of Evolution. In *Genetics, Paleontology and Evolution*, edited by G. L. Jepsen, G. G. Simpson, and E. Mayr, pp. 45–63. Princeton University Press, Princeton, New Jersey.

Watson, P. J.

1979 The Idea of Ethnoarchaeology: Notes and Comments. In *Ethnoarchaeology: Implications of Ethnography for Archaeology*, edited by C. Kramer, pp. 277–287. Columbia University Press, New York.

1990 Trend and Tradition in Southeastern Archaeology. *Southeastern Archaeology* 9:43–54.

Webb, W. S., and D. DeJarnette

1942 *An Archaeological Survey of Pickwick Basin in the Adjacent Portion of the States of Alabama, Mississippi, and Tennessee*. Bureau of American Ethnology, Bulletin 129.

Wedel, W. R.

1936 *An Introduction to Pawnee Archeology*. Bureau of American Ethnology, Bulletin 112.

1938a *The Direct-Historical Approach in Pawnee Archaeology*. Smithsonian Miscellaneous Collections 97, Pt. 7.

1938b Hopewellian Remains near Kansas City, Missouri. *U.S. National Museum, Proceedings* 86:99–106.

1940 Culture Sequence in the Central Great Plains. In *Essays in Historical Anthropology of North America in Honor of John R. Swanton*, pp. 291–352. Smithsonian Miscellaneous Collections 100.

Weeden, P.

1977 Study Patterned on Kroeber's Investigation of Style. *Dress* 3:9–19.

Wheat, J. B., J. C. Gifford, and W. W. Wasley

1958 Ceramic Variety, Type Cluster, and Ceramic System in Southwestern Pottery Analysis. *American Antiquity* 24:34–47.

White, L. A.

1938 Science Is Sciencing. *Philosophy of Science* 5:369–389.

1943 Energy and the Evolution of Culture. *American Anthropologist* 45:335–356.

1945a Diffusion vs. Evolution: An Anti-evolutionist Fallacy. *American Anthropologist* 47:339–356.

1945b History, Evolutionism and Functionalism: Three Types of Interpretation of Culture. *Southwestern Journal of Anthropology* 1:221–248.

1947a Culturological vs. Psychological Interpretations of Human Behavior. *American Sociological Review* 12:686–698.

1947b Evolutionary Stages, Progress, and the Evolution of Cultures. *Southwestern Journal of Anthropology* 3:165–192.

1948 The Individual and the Culture Process. *Science* 108:585–586.

1949 *The Science of Culture: A Study of Man and Civilization.* Farrar, Straus and Giroux, New York.

1959a The Concept of Culture. *American Anthropologist* 61:227–251.

1959b The Concept of Evolution in Cultural Anthropology. In *Evolution and Anthropology: A Centennial Appraisal,* edited by B. J. Meggers, pp. 106–125. Anthropological Society of Washington, Washington DC.

1959c *The Evolution of Culture: The Development of Civilization to the Fall of Rome.* McGraw—Hill, New York.

Will, G. F., and H. J. Spinden

1906 *The Mandans: A Study of Their Culture, Archaeology and Language.* Peabody Museum of American Archaeology and Ethnology, Papers 3, Pt. 4.

Willey, G. R.

1936 A Survey of Methods and Problems in Archaeological Excavation, with Special Reference to the Southwest. Unpublished Master's thesis, Department of Archaeology, University of Arizona, Tucson.

1938 Time Studies: Pottery and Trees in Georgia. *Proceedings of the Society for Georgia Archaeology* 1:15–22.

1939 Ceramic Stratigraphy in a Georgia Village Site. *American Antiquity* 5:140–147.

1940 Review of *Prehistory in Haiti: A Study in Method,* by Irving Rouse. *American Anthropologist* 42:673–675.

1945 Horizon Styles and Pottery Traditions in Peruvian Archaeology. *American Antiquity* 10:49–56.

1949 *Archeology of the Florida Gulf Coast.* Smithsonian Miscellaneous Collections 113.

1953a Archaeological Theories and Interpretation: New World. In *Anthropology Today,* edited by A. L. Kroeber, pp. 361–385. University of Chicago Press, Chicago.

1953b *Prehistoric Settlement Patterns in the Virú Valley, Peru.* Bureau of American Ethnology, Bulletin 155.

1953c What Archaeologists Want. In *An Appraisal of Anthropology Today,* edited by S. Tax, L. C. Eisley, I. Rouse, and C. F. Voegelin, pp. 229–230. University of Chicago Press, Chicago.

1960 Historical Patterns and Evolution in Native New World Cultures. In *Evolution After Darwin*, Vol. 2: *The Evolution of Man*, edited by S. Tax, pp. 111–141. University of Chicago Press, Chicago.

1961 Review of *Evolution and Culture*, edited by M. D. Sahlins and E. R. Service. *American Antiquity* 26:441–443.

1968 One Hundred Years of American Archaeology. In *One Hundred Years of Anthropology*, edited by J. O. Brew, pp. 26–53. Harvard University Press, Cambridge, Massachusetts.

1994 Review of *The Archaeology of William Henry Holmes*, by D. J. Meltzer and R. C. Dunnell. *Journal of Field Archaeology* 21:119–123.

Willey, G. R., and P. Phillips

1955 Method and Theory in American Archaeology, II: Historical-Developmental Interpretation. *American Anthropologist* 57:723–819.

1958 *Method and Theory in American Archaeology.* University of Chicago Press, Chicago.

Willey, G. R., and J. A. Sabloff

1974 *A History of American Archaeology.* Freeman, San Francisco.

1980 *A History of American Archaeology.* 2nd ed. Freeman, New York.

1993 *A History of American Archaeology.* 3rd ed. Freeman, New York.

Willey, M. M.

1929 The Validity of the Culture Concept. *American Journal of Sociology* 35:204–219.

Williams, P. A.

2002 Of Replicators and Selectors. *Quarterly Review of Biology* 77:302–306.

Wissler, C.

1909 Introduction. In *The Indians of Greater New York and the Lower Hudson*, edited by C. Wissler, pp. xiii–xv. American Museum of Natural History, Anthropological Papers 3.

1915 Explorations in the Southwest by the American Museum. *American Museum Journal* 15:395–398.

1916a The Application of Statistical Methods to the Data on the Trenton Argillite Culture. *American Anthropologist* 18:190–197.

1916b Correlations between Archeological and Culture Areas in the American Continents. In *Holmes Anniversary Volume: Anthropological Essays*, edited by F. W. Hodge, pp. 481–490. N.p., Washington DC.

1916c The Genetic Relations of Certain Forms in American Aboriginal Art. *National Academy of Sciences, Proceedings* 2:224–226.

1916d Psychological and Historical Interpretations for Culture. *Science* 43:193–201.

1917a *The American Indian.* McMurtrie, New York.

1917b The New Archaeology. *American Museum Journal* 17:100–101.

1919 *General Introduction*, pp. iii ix. American Museum of Natural History, Anthropological Papers 18.

1921 Dating Our Prehistoric Ruins. *Natural History* 21:13–26.

1923 *Man and Culture*. Crowell, New York.

Wissler, C., A. W. Butler, R. B. Dixon, F. W. Hodge, and B. Laufer.

1923 *State Archaeological Surveys: Suggestions in Method and Technique*. National Research Council, Washington DC.

Wolverton, S., and R. L. Lyman

2000 Immanence and Configuration in Analogical Reasoning. *North American Archaeologist* 21:233–247.

Woodbury, R. B.

1960a Nels C. Nelson and Chronological Archaeology. *American Antiquity* 25:400–401.

1960b Nelson's Stratigraphy. *American Antiquity* 26:98–99.

1963 *The Teaching of Archaeological Anthropology: Purposes and Concepts*, pp. 223–232. American Anthropological Association, Memoir 94.

1972 Archaeology in Anthropology. *American Antiquity* 37:337–338.

1973 *Alfred V. Kidder*. Columbia University Press, New York.

Woods, C. A.

1934 A Criticism of Wissler's North American Culture Areas. *American Anthropologist* 36:517–523.

Wright, J. H., J. D. McGuire, F. W. Hodge, W. K. Moorehead, and C. Peabody.

1909 Report of the Committee on Archeological Nomenclature. *American Anthropologist* 11:114–119.

Wylie, A.

1989 Archaeological Cables and Tacking: The Implications of Practice for Bernstein's "Options Beyond Objectivism and Relativism." *Philosophy of Social Science* 19:1–18.

Wyman, J.

1868 An Account of Some Kjoekkenmoeddings, or Shell-heaps, in Maine and Massachusetts. *American Naturalist* 1:561–584.

1875 *Fresh-Water Shell Mounds of the St. John's River, Florida*. Peabody Academy of Science, Memoir 4.

Index

CPSIA information can be obtained at www.ICGtesting.com
Printed in the USA
LVOW132306301012

305165LV00011B/9/P

9 780803 280526